# THE
# SORCERER'S
# APPRENTICE

# Other titles

**Life and Games of Mikhail Tal**
Mikhail Tal

**Averbakh's Selected Games**
Yuri Averbakh

**Fire on Board: Shirov's Best Games**
Alexei Shirov

**Smyslov's 125 Selected Games**
Vasily Smyslov

**Taimanov's Selected Games**
Mark Taimanov

**Uncompromising Chess**
Alexander Belyavsky

**Attack with Mikhail Tal**
Mikhail Tal and Iakov Damsky

**Quickest Chess Victories of all Time**
Graham Burgess

**Opening Repertoire for the Positional Player**
Eduard Gufeld

**Opening Repertoire for the Attacking Player**
Eduard Gufeld

**The Scandanavian**
John Emms

**Accelerated Dragons**
John Donaldson and Jeremy Silman

# THE
# SORCERER'S
# APPRENTICE

## DAVID BRONSTEIN
### and
## TOM FÜRSTENBERG

**EVERYMAN** CHESS

Copyright © 1995 David Bronstein and Tom Fürstenberg

First published 1997 by Cadogan Books plc,
now Everyman Publishers plc, Gloucester Mansions,
140 Shaftesbury Avenue, London, WC2H 8HD
Reprinted 1998 (with corrections), 1999

Distributed in North America by The Globe Pequot Press, 6 Business Park Rd,
P.O. Box 833, Old Saybrook, Connecticut 06475-0833, USA

All other sales enquiries should be directed to Everyman Publishers plc,
Gloucester Mansions, 140 Shaftesbury Avenue, London, WC2H 8HD

British Library Cataloguing in Publication Data
A CIP catalogue record for this book is available from the British Library

ISBN 1 85744 151 6

Typeset by ChessSetter

Cover illustration by Sammy Rubinstein, son of Eugenie Lew and Akiba Rubinstein,
another grandmaster to share David's fate as one of the strongest players never to
become World Champion

Cover design by Brian Robins

Printed in Great Britain by Redwood Books, Trowbridge, Wiltshire.

To **Esther-Molka Duwid Aptaker**
and **Iohonon Boruch Bronstein**
who were born one hundred years ago.

**David Ionovich Bronstein**

To a man with a kind heart
and a brilliant mind,
always generous to others...

**Tom Fürstenberg**

# Contents

The Sorcerer's Apprentice 9

A Word to the Reader 15

Devik 19

40 25

40 Combinations 29

50 69

50 Games with Comments 71

60 201

60 Games with Diagrams 205

70 263

70 Picturesque Games 273

One Horse is faster than another 287

Index of Opponents 295

Index of Openings 297

List of Results 299

# The Sorcerer's Apprentice

When I was about 6 or 7 years old I often went for long walks by myself through the forest, and when I grew tired I would lie on my back watching the trees and listening to the wind. It was then that I wondered if the wind was caused by the swaying tree tops or if the wind made the tree tops sway.

This thought came back to me when I read somewhere of what Petrosian had said about David: 'The younger generation of players think that modern chess began with such things as the *Informator* but players of my generation know that it started with Bronstein!'

It was an extremely difficult task trying to make a selection for this book as there are literally hundreds and hundreds of David Bronstein's games in my home. Quite a few of them have never been published before. I guess they await other books, yet to be written.

David and I have worked many hours together. This was an extremely tiring but, in the end, a very rewarding experience for both of us. Many, many times I had to rewrite his comments as he was not satisfied. Games were replaced with others ... and replaced again. Comments were changed and ... changed again. Our grandmaster wanted to make games and comments easy to understand and to explain in simple terms the beauty of a real fight on the chessboard, the elements of strategy and the finesses of combinations. Have we succeeded? You, the reader, will be the judge of that.

Many times I have benefited from David's fantastic memory. He recalled dates, places, games, events and incidents as if they occurred yesterday. For instance, when he looked at his game with Donner (page 277), played more than 30 years ago, he immediately saw there was something wrong but could not pinpoint what it was. I checked and indeed there were two moves missing!

When we selected photographs for this book and looked at the one from the Candidates Tournament in Amsterdam 1956, where David was shown seated behind the board without his opponent, I asked him whom he was playing. He looked a couple of seconds at the position on the board and recognised his game with Herman Pilnik!

Often, when we looked at a game, instead of making the annotations he started reminiscing. I heard many fascinating stories which, I imagine, should all be part of David's autobiography. He has been working on it now for several years but, besides a basic outline and a couple of chapters, nothing has come of it. Because of his very complicated life, our chess hero just doesn't have the time! This is a pity because he has so many incredible stories to tell and he is the only person who can do it. He allowed me to use some of them in this book but don't worry, there are more than enough left for his autobiography.

Whilst touring through Switzerland in 1965 giving simultaneous exhibitions, Paul Keres, who always memorised all travel time-tables and knew precisely all the complicated rules of travel, decided to send luggage back home separately by boat quite cheaply instead of having to carry it himself. However, if it were at least 100 kgs, the cost per kilo would be greatly reduced. As it was not possible to take home any prize-money in hard currency it was usually converted into goods beforehand. Keres had already done some shopping but did not yet have enough to make up 100 kgs. So, on a free day Paul Keres knocked on David's door. 'I know that you have not yet done any shopping for yourself. Would you like to come along now and buy something heavy for yourself?'

he said. David was of course bewildered by this question until Keres explained his reasons. They went to a shop and David looked for many things he could use but Paul shook his head: 'Not heavy enough.' Finally David found a stereo amplifier, a heavy one! That was what Keres was looking for and together with his own purchases they reached 100 kgs and he was very happy. David baptised this amplifier 'Keres' and has kept it in his apartment in Moscow all these years. It is still working fine!

Before the last round of the Staunton tournament in Groningen 1946 Najdorf was taking bets for 500 guilders that he would beat Botvinnik in their game the next day. Not only would he win but he would 'pluck him like a chicken', and this was exactly what happened, just as Najdorf had predicted! Botvinnik never forgave Najdorf for this and when Reuben Fine pulled out of The Hague/Moscow tournament in 1948 for the vacant World Championship throne it would have been natural to have given this place to Najdorf. However, Botvinnik strongly opposed this suggestion and nothing came of it.

The evening before David had to play Najdorf in the Interzonal Tournament 1948 in Saltsjöbaden they played a series of five-minute games and David came out on top. He then exploited his victory to intimidate Najdorf the next day. After playing the Dutch Defence David's position was not as good as he had hoped. When both players were in time-trouble David suddenly proposed a draw, which came as a surprise to Najdorf. He refused with wild gestures... Then, although he had only a couple of minutes left for fifteen moves, David got up and started looking at some of the other games, while watching Najdorf out of the corner of his eye. Najdorf stopped looking at the position and stared at David in amazement; he was shocked! After a minute he beckoned David back to the table with both hands and agreed to accept the draw in a better position! David was a young player then. Later in life he never played such tricks on his opponents again.

The two adversaries in this story met again at the Argentina vs. USSR match playing first board for their countries between 16 and 25 March 1954. The match was staged in the Cervantes theatre and all seats were taken by an enthusiastic audience. It was a very great cultural event. At the opening ceremony President Juan Peron made the first move for Najdorf but as soon as Peron had left the stage Najdorf changed his move from 1 e4 to 1 d4. He shook his head: 'No, no, he made a mistake, that is not my move.'

Najdorf and David played their four games on the same chessboard that was used by Capablanca and Alekhine in their match for the World Championship in 1927. David won the first two games then lost a game. Then, although a pawn up, Najdorf proposed a draw in their last encounter. David declined because he felt that Najdorf should play on for a win. Then something very stranger happened. Najdorf left the table and went to find the captain of the Soviet team, grandmaster Viacheslav Ragozin, complaining that David had refused his offer of a draw! Ragozin called David to him and said in angry voice: 'You should accept immediately! You are winning this mini-match with Najdorf. What more do you want?' They shook hands and signed the peace on the spot!

Once, when David was playing a game with Smyslov for the 1944 Soviet Championship, he kept looking at his watch and finally decided to offer a draw. They exchanged a few words, Smyslov accepted the draw and both started to leave the playing hall. The arbiter however stopped them and said in a very surprised voice: 'Why a draw? There is no valid reason to decide the game as a draw; there still is a lot of play!' 'Yes but we are hungry and in five minutes the cafeteria closes and we will no longer be able to have a meal,' replied David. 'That is a perfectly valid reason,' the arbiter agreed! You can find this game on page 273.

Another tournament; again David was playing Smyslov and this time they agreed to a draw in 12 moves. A high chess official furiously told them that they should have continued to play. After all, the Soviet Chess Federation was paying them! David's answer became a classic in Soviet chess circles: 'Do you really believe that I will attack Smyslov for only three roubles a day?'

In his book *Achieving the Aim* Botvinnik gives his version of an incident that happened at the end of the first session of the ninth game during his match in 1951 with David Bronstein. He accuses Bronstein of not obeying a request from the arbiter, Karel Opocensky, to seal a move before the adjournment. He says that Bronstein pretended not to have heard what the arbiter said and violated the rules by not sealing as requested but executing the move on the board, thereby putting Botvinnik in the position of having to seal a move.

David Bronstein's version of events is quite different. From around move 30 both players were in great time-trouble. They had some idea how many moves had been made but were not sure. Although he had reached 40 moves, Botvinnik nevertheless made his 41st. At this moment both players had about one minute left on their clocks. Bronstein had heard Opocensky's request but the session playing time of five hours for the first 40 moves had not yet been reached and he was therefore within his rights to make another move. Opocensky then realised that he should not have asked David to seal a move *at that moment*. He waited until the five hours were used up and then politely asked Botvinnik to seal a move. Botvinnik refused: 'You should declare his move open,' and left the playing hall. The audience shouted 'shame' and whistled but Botvinnik ignored them.

In 1967 Lev Polugayevsky and David Bronstein played a game which was adjourned after Black's 41st move (see page 278). Polugayevsky spent all night analysing and when they came to resume this game the next day, David, sensing that his opponent had analysed extensively, deliberately avoided playing the best moves. Polugayevsky, taken completely by surprise, failed to find the best continuation and lost the game. In his book *Grandmaster Achievement* Polugayevsky now almost *blames* David for not having played correctly, thereby taking him out of his prepared variations!

In this book you will find games from David Bronstein's youth and his prime years, played in normal tournaments and in blitz and rapid tournaments. To show you that he can still be a dangerous opponent, some recent games have also been included, of which there are several played against computers – his latest love, although he played against the Soviet program M-20, later named Kaissa, as early as 1963 (page 278). In fact this was the second game. The first one David lost when he gave the program, rather overoptimistically, odds of a queen. Afterwards David became the friendly advisor on chess matters to the Kaissa team of programmers!

We've also included some draws. It is well-known that people are reluctant to play through games that have ended in a draw. However, we urge you to play through these anyway as they are remarkable and the result is of no importance. See for instance the game with Boleslavsky on page 219.

Some experimental games have also been selected. Games whereby the players' spoken thoughts were recorded on tape (with Tal, page 238) or several games played simultaneously against the same opponent (Vaganian and Tal, pages 182 and 282 respectively). Tal loved chess, particularly with an audience, and never refused David's invitations to play experimental chess for fun and fans.

Unfortunately, most of the games from David's early years have been lost. In 1941 he was ordered to leave Kiev as a conscript for the Red Army, taking only the clothes he was wearing. His mother left Kiev immediately, fleeing from the German Army, and when David returned home a couple of years later their home was empty. The earliest game on record is one that David played against Polyak in 1938 (page 71). It shows remarkable maturity for a 14-year-old boy.

When you play through these games you will see moves and ideas in the openings and strategic plans in the middlegame that look very familiar today, but please remember that, when these games were played, many of them were being introduced by David for the first time!

It was always my intention to include a table of results. This proved to be difficult as David Bronstein has hardly kept track of his achievements. When he made an attempt to compile a list of his results I noticed that he had completely forgotten to include the result of his World Championship match with Botvinnik! If he could forget to include this event, what others might he forget?! Therefore I can only promise that the list of results is as comprehensive as I could make it.

As said before, this book has been structured in such a way that it should be comprehensible to every chess amateur. It is not necessary to have a high rating. The comments have been kept as basic as possible and the number of variations has been limited, so as not to clutter your mind.

However, there are two notable exceptions: the game with Simagin (page 90) has been commented by Botvinnik and David has given his comments to those of Botvinnik. The result is a remarkable insight into this game.

For several weeks I had quite a fight with David as he did not want his game with Ljubojević (page 166) to be included in this book. He did not think that it was good enough! But I persisted and won when David discovered that Paul Keres had also annotated this game in 1973. After all, if Keres thought it worthwhile to give comments, it could not be *that* bad! The comments given in this game are a selection of those made by several other grandmasters over the years and some fresh ones by David. It would really be a pity to publish these games only with superficial annotations.

It was only by coincidence that this game was played at all. This was a hard time for David with no tournaments abroad and only a few of them at home. Finally he decided to write a letter to Dr Max Euwe, then President of the FIDE, asking him for help. The Dutchman kindly replied that he had very little influence but if a chance were to present itself he would do his best. And so he did when he made David first substitute for the Interzonal Tournaments in Leningrad and Petropolis.

However, this proved something of a poisoned chalice when Leonid Stein suddenly died. David was now to take his place. Of course he was shocked but what should he do? Refuse the invitation? After all he was paid a salary to play chess. He therefore decided to go to Brazil but made it known that he would not compete to qualify for the Candidates' Tournament as he did not want to take advantage of Stein's death.

David and I did not always see eye to eye on the selection of other games too. For instance, David did not want the game with Rojahn, Moscow Olympiad 1956, to be included. The reason? 'I am tired of this game.' Nevertheless I left it in (page 225). There were many such differences but I believe that in the end good compromises were made. Several games have been published before in books, albeit more than 20 years ago but I could not leave them out. Since we had until February 1995 to complete this book, we were also able to include some games played after David's 70th birthday.

We have used plain and simple English so only a basic knowledge of this language is required to be able to read this book. When a diagram is given this indicates that the position and the next move is of interest. I say 'of interest', not necessarily a good one!

I wish to thank Paul Boersma, Erik Bouwmans, Herman Grooten, Rob Hartoch, Lex Jongsma, Hans Ree, Max Pam and Minze bij de Weg for honouring David Bronstein in their respective columns on his 70th birthday and for their remarks and suggestions which made this book into what it is in its present form.

I would also like to thank Mariette Gilson, GM Genna Sosonko, Katja Serbina, Natascha Alikhashkin, Andrea Pearce, Rose-Marie and Peter Hannan for their co-operation. I am particularly grateful to FM Fred van der Vliet who found and corrected many mistakes, clarified variations and even suggested new ones. His personal database yielded a great deal of useful information and without his repeated and lengthy sessions of research at the Royal Dutch Library in The Hague, I would not have been able to compile an almost complete list of David Bronstein's most important results.

Last but not least I wish to thank Anne Fürstenberg for her patience with David and me!

The fresh comments and recollections in this book were dictated by David Bronstein; other material was taken from the books: *David Bronstein Chess Improviser* by Boris S. Vainstein, *200 Open Games* by David Bronstein, *Chess in the Eighties* by David Bronstein and Dr G. Smolyan, *International Grandmaster Tournament* (Zürich/Neuhausen 1953) by David Bronstein and *The Chess Self-Tutor* by David Bronstein. These make up for 98% of the contents of this book. The other 2% are from: *The World Chess Championship* (1951) by W. Winter and R.G. Wade, *The Oxford Companion to Chess* by David Hooper and Kenneth Whyld, *The Encyclopaedia of Chess* by Anne Sunnucks, *The Candidates' Tournament* for *the World Championship* (1956) by Dr M. Euwe and W.J. Mühring, *The Kings of Chess* by William Hartston, *The Chess Beat* by Larry Evans, *The World's Greatest Chess Games* by Reuben Fine, *Alekhine's Defence* by Thinkers' Press, *Chess in the USSR*, *Chess Herald*, *64*, *Chess Life & Review*, *The British Chess Magazine* and *Chess*, the famous magazine founded by B.H. Wood.

Why the title *The Sorcerer's Apprentice*? Play through the games, study them, and then play through them again until you begin to understand what you have seen. Then you will know that a *Sorcerer* has been at work and you have become his *Apprentice*!

I sincerely hope that many amateur chess players (and others) will get as much enjoyment out of the Chess Art that follows as the Artist must have had when he created it...

**Tom Fürstenberg**
Lasne, Belgium
1995

# A Word to the Reader

First, I would like to explain to you how this piece of chess literature came into your hands. In this connection I need to express my deepest thanks to the Dutch chess amateur Tom Fürstenberg. It was entirely his idea to bring together some of my games, 222 in total, in the highly original '40-50-60-70' format to commemorate my 70th birthday. I myself would never have been able to make this book because I always look for perfection in my comments and continually modify them. However, I know that perfection simply does not exist. With the help of Tom Fürstenberg I was able to finish my work.

I think that Tom Fürstenberg first had this idea four years ago when we met each other at the AEGON tournament in The Hague. After that tournament I was invited to stay at his house for a few days in order to take a rest. There I saw his collection of books and chess sets and he showed me an autograph book full of autographs, including mine, of the participants of the 1954 Chess Olympiad in Amsterdam. When I saw this book again after 35 years I remembered quite clearly having signed it because it was so nice. I had never seen one like this and have never seen one like it since!

Anyway, we talked a lot about chess. Then Tom Fürstenberg asked me to explain my main ideas of chess strategy and tactics and I showed him some of my most interesting games. To my surprise he liked my 'lectures' and after I had shown him many of my games he suddenly made me a proposition to collect my games into a book and make them available to a wider audience of chess fans. We started to work on this project every time I was in Belgium and spent a lot of time working on the comments, trying to make them as simple and easy to understand as possible, avoiding too technical and too professional analysis in order not to make them boring.

Herewith some suggestions on how you should read this book to get maximum enjoyment and benefit out of it. My advice to you is not only to read the often interesting stories but also to study the games carefully. I sincerely ask the reader not to think that my games are better than the games of any other grandmaster of my age. During my long career in chess we all have played a lot of games, most of them dull and not interesting, with the main goal to achieve a good result. But during these working days you are sometimes happy to produce an original idea in the opening, a sharp combination in the middlegame or to show neat technique in the endgame.

Please do not read the chess moves with your eyes only. No one amongst you would like to sing aloud the musical score of a conductor. You would not, I sincerely hope, read the libretto of an opera at home in a cosy living room with a glass of fine wine in front of a fire place, instead of going to the opera where the work is performed with live actors and singers. You would surely also prefer to go to a museum to see the real painting instead of leafing through a catalogue. Undoubtedly you would not cut poetry in several pieces but would prefer to enjoy a poem as a whole, unless...you are a professional musician, singer, painter or poet!

In this case there is no difference. You should not 'read' a chess creation but you should move the pieces on the chessboard and make move by move exactly as the work of Chess Art was created for the very first time. On your own chessboard with your own pieces. And in complete silence, to be able to follow closely the events as they unfold before your very eyes. The best way to do this is in three stages.

First, play through the whole game without hesitating more than a couple of seconds at each move. If you have the urge to pause longer – don't! Just make a mark in pencil and continue to play the game to the end. Then put the book aside, get a cup of tea or coffee, relax and try your best to recall from memory the spectacle you have just seen. Try to establish the reasons why certain decisions were made.

Second, play through the game again, somewhat slower this time, and mark in pencil everything that you did not see the first time.

Third, now go straight to those pencil marks and give your imaginative and creative energy free reign. Try to play better than my opponent and I. If you do not agree look closely at each decision, either for White or for Black, with a critical eye. If you look at a game like this you will discover a lot of new and useful knowledge which you can use for your own benefit. Write your findings in a notebook in order to look at them later when you are in a different mood, especially if you like the game. If, during stage one, you made no pencil marks at all, don't look at this game again. Go on to the next one that, hopefully, will give you more pleasure and satisfaction. It just means that it did not appeal to you. Although I consider chess an Art I would not blame you at all if you don't like a particular game. In a museum you cannot like every painting you see. As French gourmets say, taste is a very personal matter.

When I was learning to play chess, I studied thousands and thousands of games played by the older generation in exactly the same way and gained a lot from them.

With this book I trust that a further page in the history of chess has been added and I hope sincerely that the younger generation will find my games interesting and useful for their own development. The Sacred Hall of Chess Creativity is waiting for you!

When I came to the chess world everybody was impressed by the fantastic combinations in old chess books and the main interest for us in playing chess was to create something on the chessboard in a spiritual fight and co-operation with your opponent. Rating points did not exist and there was hardly any prize money. Of course we knew that somewhere grandmasters were talking about the World Championship but very few think that they can also be part of this.

To my own surprise I played an official match with the World Champion under the new FIDE system in the Spring of 1951.

In the years 1948-1951 Mikhail Botvinnik considered himself as the best player of all time! I set myself the task in this match to show that it was possible to play against him and not lose every game. We played 24 very interesting games and the result was 12-12.

As far as I am concerned this match was a complete victory for my chess ideas as from then on Botvinnik, obviously having become a wiser man, started to change his style and his results improved. Furthermore the younger generation of players studied and learnt a lot from my games and I cannot understand why, for more than 40 years, many chess journalists who have never played a serious chess match, criticised me for not winning the title. It seems that they know better than me what I like in chess!

I have been asked many, many times if I was obliged to lose the 23rd game and if there was a conspiracy against me to stop me from taking Botvinnik's title. A lot of nonsense has been written about this. The only thing that I am prepared to say about all this controversy is that I was subjected to strong psychological pressure from various sources and it was entirely up to me to yield to that pressure or not. Let's leave it at that.

I had reasons not to become the World Champion as in those times such a title meant that you were entering an official world of chess bureaucracy with many formal obligations. Such a position is not compatible with my character. Since my childhood I have enjoyed freedom and despite the country that I grew up in, I have tried to live all my years in this spirit and I am very happy that today I feel the same and can enjoy my freedom.

Also I think that it is not fair of Botvinnik to mention year after year that he did not crush me in the match only because he did not play a single game during the preceding three years and that he was rusty. I am convinced that he did not play because he did not want to reveal his opening secrets to his challenger and wanted to save his energy. He prevented me from studying any of his recent games and I could not prepare myself for this match as I would have liked to. On the other hand I had played more than hundred games in important tournaments in the three years before this match and Botvinnik had all the time and opportunity in the world to study my games and he prepared himself excellently.

When the 24th game was finished, many journalists came to the stage and asked Botvinnik to hold a press conference. The Champion agreed but 'forgot' to invite me to attend also. It so happened that neither before, during or after the match did the press ask me a single question about this contest!

Because Botvinnik, starting from the year 1931, was regarded as the best player of the USSR, everybody thought that he and only he had the right to be World Champion.

Despite the fact that in this long match Mikhail Botvinnik never showed any superiority over me, the English journalist and chess player Raymond Keene wrote: 'Bronstein would almost certainly have been no match for the Botvinnik of 1948.' I am wondering where he got this knowledge from. Prior to this match Botvinnik and I had played two games and the score was 1½-½ in my favour!

Then there is the question why, if I did not want to win the World Championship title, did I participate in so many FIDE qualification tournaments? The answer is very simple. In those days there were very few international tournaments and if one wanted to be respected by the Chess Federation it was necessary to play to prove that you are amongst the best.

By the way, did you know that the man who created this FIDE qualifying system never participated in it himself? When, during the AVRO tournament in 1938, Botvinnik was certain that he could no longer win the first prize, he challenged Dr Alekhine to a match for the title of World Champion. When that did not come about he tried again to arrange a match with Alekhine in 1945/46.

After Alekhine's death the throne was empty and in the Autumn of 1946, one day after the USSR vs. USA match was finished, Botvinnik invited Reshevsky, Smyslov, Dr Euwe, Keres and Fine to play a tournament for the World Championship without any further qualifying tournaments. Why Boleslavsky and Najdorf were not included is a complete mystery to me.

Further I still don't understand why it was necessary to play the subsequent The Hague/Moscow tournament in such a hurry in 1948. Why not play the Interzonal Tournament in The Hague and Moscow in May and then, a couple of months later, the Candidates' Tournament in Saltsjöbaden? For sure the participants would not all have been the same.

When Mikhail Botvinnik lost his title for the third time he should have played in the Candidates' Tournament in 1965 but rejected this proposition as unfair to him, claiming that he should have the right to play the 'traditional' revenge match with Petrosian as he had against Smyslov and Tal after having lost the title in their first encounters. It seems that he had created the qualifying system for others, not for himself!

Botvinnik was not ashamed at all of the fact that from the five official matches he played as defending World Champion, he did not win a single one of them but managed only two draws ...

I still wonder why people in general have respect only for World Champions and not for all chess players? Is it not clear that we all play the same game of chess? We all start from the same initial position, with White and Black and we like the same attacking plans, create the same defences, in short we are all using the same weapons.

When I published my book *International Grandmaster Tournament* (Candidates' Tournament, Neuhausen/Zürich 1953, T.F.), I annotated the games of all 14 grandmasters with great respect to them. Sometimes I think that this book is so popular because I speak about Chess Art, the beauty, the technique, common mistakes, strong and weak points of human characters, in short about all that makes chess so attractive.

Of course, as we grow older we make more mistakes as we cannot keep the tension and concentration up as we used to but our games are still interesting. After all World Champions only exist by virtue of those people who never had this title.

This is why the International Chess Federation, FIDE, when it was created in Paris on the 20th of July 1924 during the Olympic Games, took as their motto: *Gens Una Sumus* (we are all one family). You know of course that Pierre de Coubertin said: 'It is more important to participate than to win.' When we watch the Olympic Games we applaud all the participants, not just the Olympic Champions.

In chess tournaments at the highest level, where the tension is very great, the winners are awarded good prizes and there is nothing wrong with that. They need to study a great deal and have to prepare physically and mentally to make points, improve their rating and win tournaments. This does not mean that other grandmasters, who are not quite so strong, are not members of the world-wide family of chess players.

One of the beauties of chess is that most of the games which have been played during the last two centuries are not lost. Every amateur has at least a few chess books: not only about openings, middlegames and endgames but also tournament books.

When I play chess and, realising that my games will be published in a tournament book, I always try to vary my openings as much as possible, to invent new plans in attack and defence, to make experimental moves which are dangerous and exciting for both players and also for the audience. I believe that my greatest quality in the chess world is that I never play routine games. I judge the position again and again before every move, changing my strategy in reply to my opponent's moves, if necessary. Even in great time-trouble I never have any fear and bravely create combinations, sometimes good, sometimes risky. Probably, if I were to play more safely I would make more points in every tournament but then, where is the joy in that?

Chess on the highest level is not only a boardgame. It is much more. It is part of human civilisation. Both Dr Emanuel Lasker and Dr Max Euwe have described chess mainly as a fight. Also, it is interesting to study how a man thinks during a game of chess. I think that I made a substantial contribution to Chess Science when I started to take note of the times taken for each move by both players. I think that I have cemented a few bricks in the house of chess psychology by creating the phenomenon of time graphs. If interpreted correctly, they give a tremendous insight into the human character. Further I believe that my work as a journalist is as important as my games. Finally I am proud of the fact that I am not known for fights off the chessboard but only on it.

Besides playing for the World Championship, I have played more than 20 times for the championships of the USSR and Moscow, participated in many team competitions, travelled all over the world to play in strong international tournaments, given many lectures and simultaneous exhibitions, offered friendly advice to chess amateurs, and written many books and articles for more than 50 years. It is my belief that I have the right to be respected for these activities as I myself respect every amateur in the world.

We should never forget that we are all one big family of chess amateurs!

To conclude, I sincerely wish to thank all my Icelandic friends for making my 70th birthday an unforgettable one, just as they did 20 years ago when I celebrated my 50th birthday with them. On the 19th of February the Icelandic Chess Federation organised a party for me in their Icelandic Chess Palace.

**David Ionovich Bronstein**
Lasne, Belgium
1995

# Devik

I have heard the name 'Devik' since my childhood in the house where I grew up. My parents used this pet name to describe David.

My father made Devik's acquaintance in the Ukraine before the Second World War during a chess tournament. They immediately became friends in spite of the age difference – my father was then 20 and David only 15.

It seems that even then Devik must have had something unusual and mystifying in his personality that drew my father, not a very sociable man, to him. He decided that he must get to know this young boy, five years his junior. Later they often met each other at tournaments, sometimes even sharing a hotel room. They also started writing to each other regularly. It was a pity that later their paths did not cross as much as before but this was due to rather complicated circumstances beyond their control.

Thus, in our home Devik Bronstein was often talked about. I do not remember exactly what was said about Devik but I heard this name so much that it became strongly embedded in my memory. My mother has told me often that, even at the age of three, I liked to jump around the room singing loudly that I wanted to marry Devik Bronstein. It is obvious that, being so young, I did not appreciate the real meaning of these words. Evidently I just liked the sound of them, as a savage likes the sounds of a ritual. But perhaps, by pronouncing certain words, we arouse mysterious unknown forces which we don't understand and they start to move without our knowledge.

My first memories of Devik go back to 1950. When I was 4 years old we were travelling to the Ural mountains and made a stop in Moscow to change trains. Devik met us at the station, helped us with the luggage and sat with us in the train. I remember his large grey gabardine coat, very much en vogue at the time, in which Devik seemed to drown, his big hat, his spectacles and, above all, his gentle smile. Devik had bought a real chocolate bar with nuts for me. I was a terribly spoilt girl and, without saying 'thank you' I took it. Then, trying to pretend that it meant nothing to me, I carelessly started to play with this chocolate bar and held it between two fingers in front of the open train window. Suddenly I dropped it and it got stuck between the double glazing from where it was impossible to retrieve. I became very irritated and, when Devik tried to console me, I said something very rude and nasty. He was shocked and my parents were overcome with shame.

The next time I remember we met was when I was 8 years old. My parents and I went to visit Devik. At that time he had just moved to a room on Gorky street, nr. 25. I remember that the room was long and narrow, unlike anything I had seen before.

There were no signs of a regular style of household and family life. I sensed right away that this man had a totally different life from the one I was accustomed to. He prepared Turkish coffee for us on a small petroleum fired cooker in the old traditional way in a real copper coffee pot which he had bought somewhere in Yugoslavia.

Just recently I heard from Devik more details about this extremely interesting journey. He was one of the first Soviet citizens to set foot on Yugoslavian soil after many years of irreconcilable differences and hostilities between the two countries which now no longer exist. (In the autumn of 1954 David Bronstein opened the door for Krushchev, who visited Yugoslavia two months later, precisely as the American table-tennis players had opened the door for Nixon to come to China in 1972, T.F.).

While the adults drank coffee and talked, I looked around the room and my attention was caught by several large dolls. One of them was from India and had a garland of flowers (she is still in Devik's apartment in Moscow today).

I was particularly attracted by a doll with a beautiful, tanned face wearing a large straw hat. I did not say a single word but Devik did not miss the fascinated look in my eyes and said: 'I will offer you this doll as a gift.' For the duration of our stay I was on tenterhooks, afraid that Devik would forget his promise. When my parents and Devik finally got up and started to say goodbye, my pride prevented me from reminding Devik of his promise and I did not look at the doll any longer. Then Devik, smiling, picked up the doll from the sideboard and handed her to me, saying said that her name was Mona Lisa.

This doll lived with me for a very long time and I was almost in tears when someone broke her. However, I have kept her straw hat until this day.

My third memory of meeting Devik dates back to the winter of 1964. I was then 18 years old and a student at the Conservatory of Music. My mother took me for my holiday from Minsk (where we still live today) to Moscow. She suggested that we should visit Devik, probably to show off her grown-up daughter, and led me to his new apartment. He was then 40 years old. He greeted us with a knitted sports cap on his head (as he explained to my mother later – he was ashamed of his baldness in front of a young lady!) When Devik saw me, he surprised me when he said jokingly with a big smile that he now understood how some men can marry the daughter of their best friend!

Devik was alone at home and he immediately started showing me his books. I remember that he was very proud of some books, which he had bought abroad and secretly smuggled into the country. One of them was the American edition of the novel *For Whom the Bells Toll* by Ernest Hemingway which was strictly forbidden in the USSR at that time because of the different version of the Spanish Civil War given in that book compared to the official Soviet one.

Then Devik's wife Marina came home and we all drank tea and a typical adult conversation developed in which I did not really take part. The next day Devik telephoned us at the hotel where we were staying. I picked up the phone and, realising who was on the phone, wanted to pass him on to my mother. To my great surprise Devik said that he wanted to speak to me. I was lost and, being very shy, I did not know what to say to this older person whom I hardly knew. I mumbled a few incomprehensible words and handed the phone to my mother. I did not understand at all this man's attitude towards me.

It took another nineteen years until we met again. Meanwhile I had committed some errors in my life but fortunately for me, I managed to correct some of them and, like myself, Devik was also single again.

My father had meanwhile died tragically at the age of 58 when one winter's night he slipped on the icy sidewalk and broke his leg. He was in hospital for several days when an infection set in and he did not survive.

From 20 September to 15 October 1983, Devik played the Semi-Finals of the Soviet Championship in Minsk. Now it was he who came to visit us. Everything was decided surprisingly fast, simple and natural as happens when destiny brings two people together. And from this moment on I finally started to genuinely know Devik.

I remember how, in my childhood, my mother once took me to the cinema to see the famous Walt Disney film Bambi. At that time my mother remarked that Devik resembled Bambi. I never forgot this and later, many years later, my image of Devik always conjured up a young deer, indeed just like Bambi, with a clear and open look in his eyes, pure and innocent.

Even more astonishing is that this image was confirmed to me when we became closer. I have never met before a human so open to good and without defence against evil which has presented itself more than enough to Devik in all its forms.

The heavy boots of Soviet history have marched through his life as through those of everyone of his generation. First of all the arrest of his father in 1937 put a black spot on his future. Being the son of 'an enemy of the people' was an indelible stain on his personal record. Such a file decided the fate of every man in the Soviet Union and I can imagine that this was the reason why Devik did not go to university. He had dreams of becoming a mathematician.

In the summer of 1941, during the first weeks of the war, he left Kiev on foot. He has often remarked bitterly that, from then on, it was his destiny to live like a tramp, a vagabond. Yet, he admits, he saw his future as a gift of destiny as, logically, he should have died during the war. Only a few young men of the 1924 generation escaped this fate. In the spring of 1942 Devik was just saved by chance as a doctor of the Appeals Commission established that he was short-sighted and could not fulfil his military service. After many unbelievable adventures he arrived in Tbilisi, Georgia.

In spite of all the difficulties that exist in a time of war he remembers his stay in this city with warmth and humour. It is there that, as a representative of the elite of the Georgian youths (Devik, being Ukrainian, Jewish and never having been a member of Komsomol!), he was sent to Stalingrad to help rebuild a steel factory.

After the war was over Devik, already a famous chess master – the youngest in the world – was transferred to Moscow on the instigation of Boris Vainstein, President of the USSR Chess Federation. Vainstein, a highly educated man and very talented mathematician, was director of the department of economics in the NKVD working directly under Beria. He was also the chairman of the Dynamo Chess Club, the official sport society of the NKVD and this is how Devik became a member of this club.

Later, his ill-wishers blamed him for this from time to time but, except for being a formal member of Dynamo and receiving some official references when requested by the Soviet Sports Committee to obtain a passport to go abroad, he never benefited from this membership. He entered this society at the lowest rank in 1945 and left in 1984 without promotion for almost 40 years. When they side-lined Bronstein he was also stripped of his monthly allowance and instead received a small pension in his capacity as a sports instructor, but that is part of another story.

Thus Devik became a Muscovite instantaneously, albeit without a fixed place of abode. During the next few years he lived in the apartment of Boris Vainstein, who really did a lot to help him, where he had one room.

In the spring of 1944 Devik's father suddenly reappeared in Moscow from the camps, suffering, exhausted and sick. He had been released due to bad health. Devik now felt it was his humanitarian duty to help his parents, both helpless, lost in society. They became his main source of worry, almost like his children. Devik, not having seen his father for more than seven years, was glad to see him alive and wanted to help him in any way he could, trying to make him forget the ordeal he went through. It was forbidden for his parents to live within 100 kilometres of Moscow or Kiev. Devik found a place for them to live one hour by road outside the capital, while he himself wandered from one furnished room to another, occasionally also residing in simple hotel rooms in the city.

During those years he nevertheless managed to become a star in the world of chess and his name became more and more famous. From one tournament to another his ascent finally culminated in 1951 in a match with Mikhail Botvinnik for the ultimate crown.

This match was surrounded by many rumours which have not died down until this day. These rumours were superficial and none of them really got to the heart of the matter. Still today people regret the fact that Devik did not win this match.

There exists however an opinion that by not winning the title, Devik's chess career was over. I know how much he was hurt, not because he regretted that he never became

World Champion but because of the attitude of the people close to him. The truth is that Devik was afraid to be proclaimed the official World Champion!

It is obvious that his character is in total contradiction with having to carry such a title *in the Soviet Union*. Chess, in common with other sports, was considered by the State a way of confirming the superiority of the Soviet political system over all others. It was therefore necessary to have champions in all aspects of life in order to prove that socialism made a better world. World Champion was an official position in Soviet society and the personality of the champion had to be in harmony with this title. However, Devik's personality and character had hardly any of the attributes that would meet these criteria. *Nomina sunt odiosa* – we will not cite any names but it is difficult to imagine Devik, signing a very flattering telegram to the Ruler of the Communist party or even worse, embracing and kissing him!

Further, if 'the son of an enemy of the people', moreover being Jewish, had surreptitiously climbed to the top of the pyramid of the chess world it would have been considered a flaw in The System, especially if the family history of the new champion had been made public...

Few people knew that, when Devik played this match in the Tchaikovsky Hall, his parents were sitting in the first rank in the audience. As a former prisoner of several camps it was forbidden for his father to be in Moscow. Sitting close by in his loge was the powerful chief of the KGB General V. S. Abakumov. While Devik was playing he had to think constantly of this potentially dangerous situation. And, in spite of his subconscious desire not to become World Champion, Devik did not lose this match to Botvinnik whom he did not regard as such an exceptionally good player as most thought he was. The result was a draw thereby proving to the whole world that he had enormous talent and was amongst the very best grandmasters of all time.

Devik cherishes a letter which he received from Dr Max Euwe which started with the words: Dear Grandmaster and Co-Champion!

Devik has never had the title of *Ex*-World Champion, a title which would have given him certain benefits and would have assured him of financial security for the rest of his life. But he does not care about this because he has another scale of values.

Throughout his life Devik has been blamed by his colleagues for being rather impractical. His more realistic fellow grandmasters even had some anecdotes to tell about Devik like: 'what value has to be attached to goods that Bronstein will bring back to the Soviet Union?' The answer: 'It should be expensive, useless, preferably heavy and voluminous!'

However, there was some truth to this. When they brought back suitcases full of practical and useful items from abroad, he would bring back such 'bizarre' items as dictionaries and expensive books in various languages while in our country it was wiser to pretend to be ignorant and not to understand any foreign language.

Once, when in Amsterdam, he saw a very luxurious coffee service, rococo-style, in a very elegant shop and spent all the money he had with him on it. During the whole trip home to Moscow he kept it on his knees for fear of breaking it.

Recently we travelled for three months all over Europe and even reached Iceland. Devik surprised me when he showed me a small electric train which he keeps in the chess club in Reykjavik. He had bought it several years earlier to compensate somehow for the fact that there were no real trains in Iceland!

Devik has never tried to refute his reputation of being somewhat eccentric. In fact it seemed that he was even pleased with this as he could hide behind it. It gave him a feeling of safety. In the country in which he lived it was better to be considered somewhat strange than to be suspected of nonconformism. Nevertheless I believe that what seems strange to others is deeply connected with Devik's philosophy of life that everything that is useless and superfluous is in fact required in daily life for the human spirit.

Devik appreciated, then and now, nothing more than the spirit of freedom. Having lived all his life in a state where the word liberty had only a theoretical meaning and where in reality only slavery was cultivated, Devik managed to keep his spiritual freedom. For him no dogmas existed. His courageous and free spirit enabled him to glance at many things in life for the first time and make his own judgement.

This is how he plays chess; how he got his many innovative ideas how to organise chess. Let's take for example Active (Rapid) Chess. It was Devik who proposed this for the very first time when he wrote about it in his column in *Izvestia* many years ago and was its most ardent promoter. When this idea was finally accepted and people saw how attractive and even lucrative it could be, there were enterprising young players who declared, without any modesty, that chess started with them and proclaimed this idea as their own without any reference to its original creator, David Bronstein.

God will pass judgement on them, and not only on them, as David's problems started many years earlier.

As soon as this cannibalistic time was over, when one had to irrevocably occupy first place and nothing but first place at each and every tournament abroad in order to prove the incontestable strength of the Soviet school of chess, Devik was slowly but surely eliminated from the world of chess. The Soviet authorities decided who would participate in tournaments and who would play abroad and they did not like Devik, without any doubt considering him to be a stranger. Strictly speaking Devik was not a dissident but his inner freedom, his decent behaviour, his professional and human fairness were in striking contrast to the character of those who had imposed the Soviet System for many decades.

As Devik did not have the 'protection' of the title of *Ex*-World Champion, they were able to ignore him. They prevented him from participating in important tournaments abroad, even personal invitations were not honoured. Instead they proposed other players whose views they considered merited to be rewarded.

Devik told me that one day that he had lost his patience and turned to one of these superiors of the Soviet Chess Federation, Mr Baturinsky, to discuss this situation. Grandmaster Boris Spassky had nicknamed this man 'the black Colonel' for his notorious history as a prosecutor in the armed forces.

Baturinsky told Devik, while staring at the ceiling, that for a player of his present level one tournament a year was more than sufficient and that the personal invitations he was still receiving were of no importance at all. In reality he did not even get that one tournament! I know that Dr Max Euwe tried to help Devik but in vain.

One day the authorities found the right opportunity to eliminate Devik altogether. After the 1976 IBM tournament in Amsterdam, Victor Korchnoi chose not to return to the Soviet Union. Among the names of grandmasters that condemned Korchnoi for this, the one of Bronstein was missing. It was then that they remembered that he was a friend of Korchnoi and that he had helped him during his match with Anatoly Karpov, the flag-bearer of Soviet chess. This was sufficient to close the door to participation in tournaments in the West for the next 14 years. Devik continued to participate in local tournaments of minor importance with players of lesser strength and as a result his rating deteriorated but the quality of his games remained high. Now the officials told him that with such a rating he could no longer participate in prestigious tournaments.

A wind of change coincided with the appearance of *Perestroika* in 1986. The tight leash was slackened and Devik was allowed to play a tournament in Yugoslavia at the personal invitation of grandmaster Svetozar Gligorić and was able to renew ties with his old friends and make new ones.

Within a few years (very difficult ones for him) Devik accomplished the impossible – like a Phoenix he rose from the ashes and regained his popularity. He was one of the first to participate in the AEGON tournament in The Hague where he had to play exclusively against computers, contributing a great deal to the prestige and popularity of this event.

At the Donner Memorial tournament 1994, after the game Devik played against Velimirović (page 285, T.F), Vasily Smyslov said to me: 'Finally this is again the young imaginative Devik we used to know!'

In reality Devik *is* young and this can be confirmed by all who have met him during the last few years. His spirit is still flexible, his desire and thirst to create and discover new things is present as before in his best years.

When I think about Devik I realise that the majority of people are just there increasing the population in *quantity*. Far less are those who, by their sheer presence, increase the *quality* of mankind. I sincerely believe that he belongs in the latter category.

**Tatiana Boleslavskaya**
*Minsk, Belarus*
1995
Professor of the History and Theory of Music, Devik's
wife and daughter of grandmaster Isaac Boleslavsky

# 40 Recommendations for the Novice

1. No one has ever been able to study chess in its entirety, not even the World Champions, but everybody can play and receive a lot of enjoyment from it.

2. Play in chess takes place on a board, divided into 64 squares, half of which are light and half dark.

3. Before the battle commences the pieces and pawns occupy the following positions:

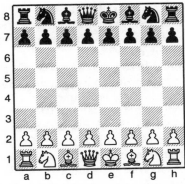

4. The winner is that one of the two players who is able to announce: 'check and mate (checkmate)' to the king of his opponent.

5. The rules of how the pieces move can be learnt by anyone who wishes to play within the space of an hour.

6. Friendly games of chess should be played at rapid tempo, say 15 minutes on the clock for each player. Half an hour per game is most convenient and a fair rate for creative play.

7. As in other forms of sport, a chess duel should consist of a small series of games, best of all mini-matches of four to six games.

8. Not more than two hours need be spent on such a mini-match. The bitterness of defeat will always be forgotten at the joyous moment of victory.

9. In the initial position any pawn has the choice of moving forward one or immediately two squares: only the knights can jump to the left or right, ending up in front of the rook's or bishop's pawns (the knight is also allowed to jump over the pieces or pawns of the opponent's army).

10. The most popular beginning of the game is to move two squares with the pawn (White always begins) in front of the king (e2-e4) if you like an attacking game. However, this is somewhat dangerous because tactical complications can arise almost immediately.

11. After the opening move of this king's pawn, not only the knights but also the queen, the bishop next to the king and the king itself (of course not all at once but one of the pieces at the player's discretion) can now make a move: the king – one square forward (to e2), the queen and bishop to any diagonal square (e2, f3, g4 and h5, and e2, d3, c4, b5 and a6 respectively).

12. The king's knight, besides going to the squares in front of the bishop's and rook's pawns (f3 and h3 respectively), can now also go to the square from where the pawn has just moved (e2). But whereas the bishop will move along the light-squared diagonals all the game, the queen, once she has gained more space, can move any number of squares in any direction, and the king – in any direction but only to a neighbouring square.

13. On the first move it is better to play the pawn in front of the queen (d2-d4) but better still is to play the king's knight towards the centre, occupying the square in front of the bishop's pawn (♘g1-f3).

14. By then advancing one square the pawn in front of the knight's former square (g2-g3) and then placing the bishop on the pawn's square (♗f1-g2), one can thus build the 'King's House'. Black can also use this method of course.

15. By castling kingside, whereby the king jumps two squares to the right (from e1 to g1) and then the rook in the corner is moved over the king and placed on the neighbouring square (from h1 to f1), one can complete the erection of a very solid defensive post for the king. Castling in this manner is written as 0-0.

16. Castling on the left is also possible when the space and between the queen's rook is clear and neither the king nor the rook have moved. The king jumps from e1 to c1 and the rook from a1 to d1. This is written as 0-0-0.

17. The opponent will not be able to prevent you from employing this technique of building the 'King's House' and, in order to breach your defences, he will now need to display a great deal more sharpness, resourcefulness, will-to-win, imagination etc., than after the popular but very risky (for novices) 'King's Pawn Opening' (e2-e4).

18. After completing the defensive line for your king you can advance the pawn in front of your queen one square (d2-d3), boldly preparing to attack with the queenside pawns or even with the king's pawn alone.

19. After the 'King's House' has been established you do not need to hurry to bring into battle the rook or the bishop and knight on your queenside – the bishop and knight are active even in their initial position while the rook in the corner should patiently await the opening of horizontal and vertical lines.

20. The queen should also be in no hurry to leave her initial position. She can perhaps be allowed to move to the king's former square (♕d1-e1) but only if the advance of the king's pawn needs to be supported from the rear.

21. All our pieces of advice are equally good both for the white and the black pieces and, of course, when the forces of the two sides come into contact, the players commanding the actions of their chess armies themselves can, as they think best, introduce modifications to these basic strategic plans.

22. In quiet positions the strongest piece is the queen since she moves any number of squares in any direction. The knight is roughly equivalent in strength to the bishop but the rook is rather stronger than the bishop and is clearly superior to the knight.

23. Two knights and a bishop are roughly equal to a queen but two bishops and a knight are slightly stronger than a queen.

24. Two rooks are superior in strength to a queen but only if they are actively placed and their actions co-ordinated.

25. On the scale of comparative values, three pawns compensate approximately a knight, four a bishop, five a rook and nine a queen. The king cannot be captured (checkmate ends the game) and is therefore of infinite value.

26. A pawn that has crossed the chess equator (the middle of the board) acquires a special privilege. If it wishes it can remove an enemy pawn from the board but only immediately after the latter has completed the 'double step' as only allowed in the initial position. In so doing the attacking pawn moves to the imaginary square where the opponent's pawn would have been had it made a 'single step' and the opponent's pawn must

be removed from the board. This method of one pawn taking another is called 'taking *en passant*'.

27. On reaching the last rank a pawn has to move off the battlefield and make way for another piece of the same colour, at the player's choice – queen, rook, bishop or knight, irrespective of the number of similar pieces already in the player's possession.

28. If there are no pawns and pieces remaining on the board except a lone queen or rook on your side, it is easy to announce 'checkmate'. It is slightly more difficult with just two bishops, very difficult with a bishop and a knight and impossible with two knights unless the opponent makes a blunder.

29. The 'King's House' can be breached in three stages: first, by attacking with pieces to weaken the pawn screen, then by attacking with pawns to create a breach in the defences and finally mounting a decisive offensive and piece invasion.

30. An attack can always be successfully parried or weakened if the attacking pieces are carefully exchanged.

31. You should not bring into play only your favourite piece but should seek a plan of action by which the pieces make moves in turn, creating a united group in attack and defence.

32. In the initial stage of study it is desirable not to move all pawns around the king whereas it is useful to advance pawns in the centre and on the opposite wing, creating greater space for your pieces and taking away safe squares from the opponent's pieces.

33. As the strong pieces disappear, the role of your king grows since it has less to fear. And when there are only pawns left on the board, the king can (and must) boldly go and attack the key squares of the board. In short, move in any direction towards the opponent's pawns if it is useful and/or necessary – to the support of your own pawns.

34. As the number of pieces is reduced, the role of the pawns grows and therefore one should be careful if and how to exchange them.

35. Pawns are capable themselves of breaching any defensive wall and should therefore not be given up for nothing.

36. For the sake of a rapid attack one can sometimes give up a pawn and, in exceptional cases, to win an extra move, while you are attacking, one may not begrudge a knight or a bishop.

37. For the sake of opening a diagonal for a bishop or a file for a rook it can sometimes be useful to give up one pawn.

38. Only when a position with a mating finish can clearly be seen should you pluck up courage and fearlessly sacrifice a rook or even your queen.

39. You should not continue playing in a position in which, by your own personal evaluation of the situation, there are no real hopes of saving the game. It is better to admit defeat, congratulate your opponent on winning and immediately offer him a new return game. In short, it is better not to await the bitter words 'check and mate'.

40. It is impossible to learn the openings from books but, by combining practical play with theoretical study, one can gradually understand the basic strategic plans and tactical ideas concealed behind the 'pages of opening moves' and the vast number of opening variations recommended in books taken from the tournament games of masters and grandmasters.

**David Ionovich Bronstein**

# 40 Combinations with Explanations

## (1) Bronstein,D – Morgulis,L

Pioneers Palace Championship,
Kiev, 1940

*[C26] Vienna Opening*

1 e4 e5 2 ♘c3 ♗c5 3 ♗c4 ♘f6 4 d3 d6 5 ♘a4 ♘bd7 6 ♘xc5 ♘xc5 7 ♘e2 c6 8 0-0 0-0 9 ♗g5 h6 10 ♗e3 ♘e6 11 f3 d5 12 ♗b3 a5 13 c3 b6 14 ♕e1 ♕c7 15 ♕f2 ♖b8 16 ♕h4 ♗a6 17 ♖ad1 ♘c5 18 ♗xh6 ♘e8 19 ♗e3 ♘xd3 20 exd5 cxd5 21 ♘g3 g6 22 ♗xd5 ♘f4 23 ♗xf4 exf4 24 ♘e4 ♗xf1 25 ♘g5 ♘f6 26 ♕h6 ♕e5 27 ♕xg6+ ♔h8 28 ♕h6+ ♔g8 29 ♗e4 ♗c4 30 ♗h7+ ♔h8 31 ♗d3+ ♔g8 32 ♗xc4 ♖b7 33 ♕g6+ ♔h8 34 ♗xf7 Black resigns.

Position after 23...e5xf4

**24 ♘g3-e4!**

Please note that all 40 combinations were taken from actual games played in important tournaments which demanded the utmost physical and intellectual effort.

With hindsight everything is simple but when sitting at the board it was not so easy to find 24 ♘e4 ♗xf1 25 ♘g5 ♔g7 26 ♕h7+ ♔f6 27 ♘e4+ ♔e5 28 g3 fxg3 29 ♕h4. Such a variation seems to be obvious after you learn more and more new methods of attack. Also, you have to respect the strategic and tactical ideas of your opponent. For instance, if instead of 28 ♕h6+ White plays 28 ♗xf7 Black then can answer 28...♗d3 and White's attack grinds to a halt. But I did not fall into this trap because we knew each other very well. We were about the same age and both liked to play an innovative style of chess. Every Sunday we used to come to the chess club as early as possible to play blitz chess. We must have played thousands and thousands of three-minute games. Morgulis, whose talent was undeniable, died suddenly of heart disease at a very young age in 1942.

# (2) Bronstein,D – Ratner,B

14th USSR Championship,
Moscow, 1945

*[B16] Caro-Kann Defence*

1 e4 c6 2 ♘c3 d5 3 ♘f3 dxe4 4 ♘xe4 ♘f6 5 ♘xf6+ gxf6 6 d4 ♗f5 7 ♗d3 ♗g6 8 ♗f4 e6 9 0-0 ♗d6 10 ♗g3 ♗xg3 11 hxg3 ♘d7 12 ♕d2 0-0 13 ♖ad1 ♔g7 14 ♖fe1 ♕c7 15 c4 ♘b6 16 b3 ♖fd8 17 ♕e3 ♖d7 18 g4 ♕d8 19 g3 c5 20 ♗xg6 hxg6 21 ♔g2 cxd4 22 ♘xd4 ♕f8 23 ♖h1 ♔g8 24 ♘xe6 ♖xd1 25 ♘xf8 ♖xh1 26 ♔xh1 ♖xf8 27 ♕e7 ♔g7 28 ♕xb7 ♘c8 29 ♕d7 Black resigns.

Position after 23...♔g7-g8

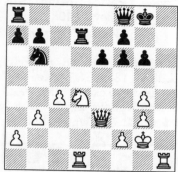

**24 ♘d4xe6!**

White's pieces are clearly more active than Black's. The rook on h1 has a strong influence on the open h-file. It could even give a check on h8 at the right moment. At the same time the centralised white knight strikes deep into the enemy camp, amongst others the square e6. In such cases we must find a way to increase the strength of the attack by means of a sacrifice.

It is not too difficult to find: 24 ♘xe6 fxe6 25 ♖xd7 ♘xd7 26 ♕xe6+ ♕f7 27 ♖h8+. If 24...♕e7 then 25 ♖h8+ ♔xh8 26 ♕h6+. The game took a different turn but the result was the same.

How was such a combination possible? The answer is simple. The black rook on a8 is not participating. Had it been on e8, the pressure on the h-file would have been much more difficult to exploit.

If this had been the case White might have taken action on the other wing to try to make use of the passive position of the black knight by playing 24 ♘b5 with the aim of taking on a7.

# (3) Bronstein,D – Koblentz,A

### 14th USSR Championship,
### Moscow, 1945
*[C35] King's Gambit Accepted*

1 e4 e5 2 f4 exf4 3 ♘f3 ♗e7 4 ♗c4 ♘f6 5 e5 ♘g4 6 0-0 d6 7 exd6 ♕xd6 8 d4 0-0 9 ♘c3 ♘e3 10 ♗xe3 fxe3 11 ♕d3 ♘c6 12 ♖ae1 ♗g4 13 ♖xe3 ♕h6 14 ♖ee1 ♗d6 15 ♘e5 ♘xe5 16 dxe5 ♗c5+ 17 ♔h1 ♗e6 18 ♘e4 ♗b6 19 c3 ♖ad8 20 ♕e2 ♖fe8 21 ♗xe6 ♖xe6 22 ♕f3 ♖e7 23 ♘g3 ♖ed7 24 ♘f5 ♕g5 25 ♕xb7 ♖d2 26 ♕f3 ♗c5 27 b4 ♗f8 28 ♘d4 ♔h8 29 ♘e6 Black resigns.

Position after 28...♔g8-h8

**29 ♘d4-e6!**

After 28...♔h8, it seems that Black has some compensation for the pawn: he has a rook on White's second rank, but to be objective, White's position is much better than Black's. The white pieces are very well placed but we have to be careful. If, for instance, the white queen takes the pawn on f7, Black's answer could be that his queen takes the pawn on g2 and gives mate.

We have to find another way to exploit the weakness of the pawn on f7. Although this pawn controls the square e6 it cannot leave the f-file as otherwise the white queen can sacrifice herself by taking the black bishop on f8 and after the black rook takes the queen, White's rook on f1 will give mate by taking the rook on f8.

The white knight therefore does not have to fear the black pawn on f7 when it goes to e6 and wins the exchange.

# (4) Pachman,L – Bronstein,D

Prague vs. Moscow Match,
4th round, Prague,1946,
*[E67] King's Indian Defence*

1 d4 ♘f6 2 c4 d6 3 ♘c3 e5 4 ♘f3 ♘bd7 5 g3 g6 6 ♗g2 ♗g7 7 0-0 0-0 8 b3 ♖e8 9 e4 exd4 10 ♘xd4 ♘c5 11 ♖e1 a5 12 ♗b2 a4 13 ♖c1 c6 14 ♗a1 axb3 15 axb3 ♕b6 16 h3 ♘fd7 17 ♖b1 ♘f8 18 ♔h2 h5 19 ♖e2 h4 20 ♖d2 ♖xa1 21 ♖xa1 ♗xd4 22 ♖xd4 ♘xb3 23 ♖xd6 ♕xf2 24 ♖a2 ♕xg3+ 25 ♔h1 ♕xc3 26 ♖a3 ♗xh3 27 ♖xb3 ♗xg2+ 28 ♔xg2 ♕xc4 29 ♖d4 ♕e6 30 ♖xb7 ♖a8 31 ♕e2 h3+ White resigns.

Position after 20 ♖e2-d2

**20...♖a8xa1!**

The diagram shows a complicated position which can be characterised as 'difficult', almost 'impossible'. However, a very simple method can assist us and that is to divide this position into several parts. Then we see that the group of pieces and pawns around the black king are in no danger whatsoever. On the opposite side there are two pawns in the line of sight of the bishop on c8 and the pawn on h4. The pawns on b3 and e4 also have to be defended. In Black's camp there are two undefended pawns but the pawn on d6 is not attacked and taking the h-pawn will only benefit Black as the white king's position becomes too open.

Now we shall see if Black can start an attack. After all it is his turn to move. The white knight in the centre appears to be very strong but in fact has no influence on its surroundings. White's only hope is his bishop on a1. To destroy the foundation of the white position Black should take the bishop on a1 with his rook.

# (5) Zita,F – Bronstein,D

Prague vs. Moscow Match,
6th round, Prague,1946,
*[E68] King's Indian Defence*

1 c4 e5 2 ♘c3 ♘f6 3 ♘f3 d6 4 d4 ♘bd7 5 g3 g6 6 ♗g2 ♗g7 7 0-0 0-0 8 b3 c6 9 ♗b2 ♖e8
10 e4 exd4 11 ♘xd4 ♕b6 12 ♕d2 ♘c5 13 ♖fe1 a5 14 ♖ab1 a4 15 ♗a1 axb3 16 axb3 ♘g4
17 h3 ♖xa1 18 ♖xa1 ♘xf2 19 ♖e3 ♘xh3+ 20 ♔h2 ♘f2 21 ♖f3 ♘cxe4 22 ♕f4 ♘g4+ 23
♔h1 f5 24 ♘xe4 ♖xe4 25 ♕xd6 ♖xd4 26 ♕b8 ♖d8 27 ♖a8 ♗e5 28 ♕a7 ♕b4 29 ♕g1 ♕f8
30 ♗h3 ♕h6 White resigns.

Position after 17 h2-h3

**17...♖a8xa1!**

There is clearly a conflict between the knight on g4 and the white h-pawn. The knight
has come too close to the white king and the h-pawn is asking the knight to retreat behind the demarcation line. What decision should Black take?

Of course retreating is the simplest but then we must ask ourselves why the black
knight went into the attack in the first place. Maybe we can create confusion amongst
White's defences and boldly take the pawn on f2 by playing 17...♘xf2. After 18 ♔xf2 can
we play 18...♘xb3 19 ♖xb3 ♗xd4+ 20 ♔f1 ♕xb3 or after 18 ♕xf2 play the other knight
to d3? Very tempting isn't it? But upon taking a closer look we see that if the rook on b3
is taken by the queen she leaves the bishop on d4 without any protection and after 21
♕xd4 White can put his hopes up again as he can now play ♘d5, with threats along the
diagonal a1-h8, not to mention ♘f6+. After 17... ♘xf2 White may also play 18 ♘a4!

That is why Black first takes the bishop on a1 with his rook and only then the knight
takes the pawn on f2.

# (6) Bronstein,D – Pachman,L

Moscow vs. Prague Match,
Moscow 1946
*[C88] Spanish Opening*

1 e4 e5 2 ♘f3 ♘c6 3 ♗b5 a6 4 ♗a4 ♘f6 5 0-0 ♗e7 6 ♖e1 b5 7 ♗b3 0-0 8 a4 ♗b7 9 d3 ♘a5
10 ♗a2 d6 11 c3 c5 12 ♘bd2 ♕c7 13 ♘f1 c4 14 ♗g5 cxd3 15 ♗xf6 ♗xf6 16 ♕xd3 ♘c4 17
b3 ♘b6 18 a5 ♘c8 19 b4 ♘e7 20 ♘e3 ♖fd8 21 ♖ac1 ♖ac8 22 ♖ed1 g6 23 ♘g4 ♗g7 24 ♘g5
d5 25 ♕f3 f5 26 exf5 ♘xf5 27 ♖xd5 ♔h8 28 ♖xd8+ ♖xd8 29 ♕h3 h5 30 ♘f7+ ♔h7 31
♘g5+ ♔h8 32 ♖e1 ♖d2 33 ♗e6 ♘e7 34 ♕e3 ♖c2 35 ♘gf7+ ♔g8 36 ♘gxe5 ♖xc3 37
♘g5+ ♔h8 38 ♘ef7+ ♔g8 39 ♘e5+ ♔h8 40 ♘gf7+ ♔h7 41 ♘g5+ ♔h8 42 ♘gf7+ ♔h7 43
♕f4 Black resigns.

Position after 26...♘e7xf5

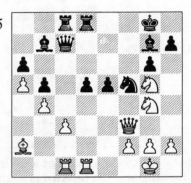

**27 ♖d1xd5!**

Everyone knows that the queen is stronger than a rook and that a rook is stronger
than a knight or a bishop but when we judge and evaluate a position it is sometimes essential to violate these materialistic calculations. The reason for such advice is the simple fact that a piece does not act on its own in the game. It makes an attack or organises
a defence *in co-ordination* with other pieces and pawns.

When using a little bit of fantasy or imagination it is often possible to find a move
which is useful for the whole chess army, even if this move leads to some material loss.
From my own experience I have learned that in a complicated middlegame position,
when pawns and pieces are engaged in battle, it is often wise to sacrifice a rook for an enemy bishop.

After Black's 26th move we have a perfect example of such a position. Of course White
can simply play 27 ♗xd5+ but then Black will play 27...♗xd5 and slow down White's attack. With 27 ♖xd5 White opens the vital diagonal a2-g8, but at the same time keeps his
strong attacking bishop and forces the black king to take refuge in the corner of the
board.

# (7) Bronstein,D – Kotov,A

### Moscow Championship 1946

*[B17] Caro-Kann Defence*

1 e4 c6 2 d4 d5 3 ♘c3 dxe4 4 ♘xe4 ♘d7 5 ♘f3 ♘gf6 6 ♘c3 e6 7 ♗d3 ♗e7 8 0-0 c5 9 ♕e2 cxd4 10 ♘xd4 0-0 11 ♗g5 ♘c5 12 ♖ad1 ♘xd3 13 ♖xd3 ♕c7 14 ♘db5 ♕c6 15 ♖fd1 b6 16 ♘d4 ♕c7 17 ♖g3 ♔h8 18 ♘cb5 ♕b7 19 ♕e5 a6 20 ♘c3 ♘d7 21 ♗h6 Black resigns.

Position after 20... ♘f6-d7

**21 ♗g5-h6!**

The white queen is under attack but nevertheless the white bishop takes a short step forward and, like in a fencing contest, says: 'touché'. Black resigns because mate cannot be avoided – 21...♘xe5 22 ♗xg7+ ♔g8 23 ♗xe5+ ♗g5 24 ♖xg5 mate! When the clocks were stopped grandmaster Kotov explained that he had only calculated the move 21 ♕xg7+.

When I later saw his book *Think Like a Grandmaster* I realised that he had looked at the variation 21 ♕xg7+ ♔xg7 22 ♗xe7+ ♔h8 23 ♘f5 f6 24 ♘h6 but there is a better line for Black: 23...exf5 24 ♖xd7 ♕c6 or 23 ♘c6 ♕c7 24 ♖xd7 ♕xg3 25 hxg3 ♗xd7 26 ♗f6+ and if 23...♕xc6 24 ♖xd7 then 24...e5 is possible.

It is noteworthy that one move earlier White missed an even more beautiful combination: 20 ♘d6 ♕d7 21 ♘c6 ♕xc6 22 ♗xf6 gxf6 (22...♗xf6 23 ♕xf6 gxf6 24 ♘xf7+ ♖xf7 25 ♖d8+) 23 ♕e3 ♕xc2 24 ♖c1 ♕g6 25 ♖xg6 fxg6 26 ♖c7 ♗xd6 27 ♕h6 ♗xc7 28 ♕xf8 mate. Black can avoid this disaster by playing 20...♕d5 but the endgame is in White's favour anyway.

Shortly after his book was published in England Alexander Kotov told me bravely: 'I have included quite a few of your chess articles in it.' 'Well,' I said 'if they are useful to the readers then I don't mind. I might even be pleased with such publicity.'

However, while putting this book together I was surprised to find that Black could have played 12...♕xd4 13 ♗xh7+ ♘xh7 14 ♖xd4 ♗xg5 with three pieces for the queen or, instead of taking the queen with the rook, 14 ♗xe7 ♕b4 and Black is better in both cases.

# (8) Bronstein,D – Dubinin,P

15th USSR Championship,
Leningrad, 1947

*[C39] King's Gambit Accepted*

1 e4 e5 2 f4 exf4 3 ♘f3 g5 4 h4 g4 5 ♘e5 h5 6 ♗c4 ♖h7 7 d4 ♗h6 8 ♘c3 ♘c6 9 ♘xf7 ♖xf7 10 ♗xf7+ ♔xf7 11 ♗xf4 ♗xf4 12 0-0 ♕xh4 13 ♖xf4+ ♔g7 14 ♕d2 d6 15 ♖af1 ♘d8 16 ♘d5 ♗d7 17 e5 dxe5 18 dxe5 ♗c6 19 e6 ♗xd5 20 ♖f7+ ♘xf7 21 ♖xf7+ ♔h8 22 ♕c3+ ♘f6 23 ♖xf6 ♕xf6 24 ♕xf6+ ♔h7 25 ♕f5+ ♔h6 26 ♕xd5 ♔g6 27 ♕d7 Black resigns.

Position after 18...♗d7-c6

**19 e5-e6!**

The move of the white pawn makes White's advantage decisive. The white rooks have the open f-file all to themselves, the white queen is in a waiting position, the white king is safe while Black's pawn on g4 is pinned by the rook. Black's queen looks dangerous but in reality she is not. Black's rook, bishop and knights do not really participate actively in the game.

The opening of this game was interesting: 1 e4 e5 2 f4 exf4 3 ♘f3 g5 4 h4 g4 5 ♘e5. All theoretical books judge the position as better for Black after 5...♘f6 6 ♘xg4 ♘xe4 7 d3 ♘g3 8 ♗xf4 ♘xh1 9 ♕e2+ ♕e7 10 ♘f6+ ♔d8 11 ♗xc7+ ♔xc7 12 ♘d5+ ♔d8 13 ♘xe7 ♗xe7. I had expected 5...♘f6 and after 6 ♘xg4 ♘xe4 I would have liked to play the discovery I made a long time ago: 7 ♘c3! My novelty brings a piece into action that I refer to as 'the lazy knight'. After 7...♘g3 8 ♘d5 ♗g7 9 d4 0-0 10 ♗xf4 ♘xh1 11 ♘h6+ ♔h8 (11...♗xh6 12 ♕g4+ ♔h8 13 ♗xh6 ♖g8 14 ♗g5) 13 ♕h5 we have an extremely interesting position. However, if Black had played 8...♗e7 I would not have known what to do.

I finally managed to put this idea into practice in 1994 in my game against Kim Åstrup, see page 285.

By the way, in the years 1945-47 I played the King's Gambit 10 times with White and achieved the perfect score of +10-0=0!

# (9) Bronstein,D – Panov,V

Moscow Championship, 1947

*[C30] King's Gambit Declined*

1 e4 e5 2 f4 ♗c5 3 ♘f3 d6 4 c3 ♗g4 5 fxe5 dxe5 6 ♕a4+ ♗d7 7 ♕c2 ♘c6 8 b4 ♗d6 9 ♗c4 ♘f6 10 d3 ♕e7 11 0-0 0-0-0 12 a4 a5 13 b5 ♘b8 14 ♘bd2 ♗g4 15 ♘b3 b6 16 ♗e3 ♘bd7 17 ♖ae1 ♗e6 18 ♗xe6 ♕xe6 19 ♔h1 ♕e7 20 ♘bd2 ♘g4 21 ♗g1 h5 22 ♘c4 g5 23 ♘xd6+ cxd6 24 ♘d2 f6 25 ♘c4 ♔b7 26 ♗xb6 ♘xb6 27 ♘xa5+ ♔c7 28 ♘c6 ♕e8 29 a5 ♘d7 30 b6+ ♔b7 31 a6+ ♔xb6 32 ♖b1+ Black resigns.

Position after 25...♔c8-b7

**26 ♗g1xb6!**

The dimensions of a chessboard are not large. Space is a very relative notion. You can play on a pocket chess set or on a demonstration board but in either case you will have no more than 64 squares at your disposal. It goes without saying that if you want to win the battle you will need to control as much space as possible. To achieve this it is logical to use far-reaching pieces such as bishops.

In this position the white bishop has found a very good square. As an extra security measure he defends the h2 square but at the same time attacks the square b6 near the enemy king. Normally an attack will be successful if carried out by several pieces at the same time. That is why the not so far-reaching knight has taken up his position on c4 to increase the pressure on the b6 pawn.

The sacrifice of the bishop destroys the defence around the black king and enables White to march on to the eighth rank with his two connected passed pawns on the queenside.

Panov was a very good chess master and journalist. In 1930 he wrote a wonderful book called *An Attack*. When he left *Izvestia* I took his place. When I did not achieve 12½-11½ in my World Championship match with Botvinnik in 1951 he was sad. 'You spoilt my chess column,' he said. 'I had already finished my article *New Young World Chess Champion* and had put a lot of effort into it.'

# (10) Bronstein,D – Szabo,L

Interzonal Tournament,
Saltsjöbaden, 1948
*[C04] French Defence*

1 e4 e6 2 d4 d5 3 ♘d2 ♘c6 4 ♘gf3 ♘f6 5 e5 ♘d7 6 ♘b3 f6 7 ♗b5 a6 8 ♗xc6 bxc6 9 0-0 c5 10 c4 dxc4 11 ♘a5 ♘b6 12 exf6 ♕xf6 13 dxc5 ♕f5 14 ♗g5 ♕xc5 15 ♕d8+ ♔f7 16 ♖ad1 ♗b7 17 ♘xb7 ♖xd8 18 ♘xc5 ♖d5 19 ♘e4 ♗d6 20 ♘c3 ♖a5 21 ♗c1 ♘a4 22 ♘xa4 ♖xa4 23 a3 c3 24 b3 ♖a5 25 ♖d3 ♖c5 26 ♗e3 ♖a5 27 ♖xc3 ♖xa3 28 ♗c5 ♖a5 29 b4 ♖a4 30 g3 a5 31 b5 ♖d8 32 ♗xd6 cxd6 33 ♖c7+ ♔f6 34 ♔g2 ♖a2 35 ♘d4 ♖e8 36 ♖e1 e5 37 b6 ♖b2 38 b7 Black resigns.

Position after 15...♔e8-f7

**16 ♖a1-d1!**

This position is very easy to judge: the black king has lost his right to castle, there are weaknesses in the positions of the black pawns and both Black's rooks and bishops are in their initial position. Furthermore, the white queen is very active on d8. Now the move 16 ♘c6 looks very promising. Black cannot take the knight because then the other knight gives a check, winning the black queen. However Black can defend better with 16...♗d7 17 ♘fe5+ ♔g8 18 ♘e7+ ♕xe7 19 ♗xe7 ♖xd8 20 ♗xd8 ♗d6 and despite the loss of the exchange Black's position is playable thanks to the strong pair of bishops. Or Black plays 16...♘d5 defending the pawn on c7 and the square e7, hoping to be able to play ...h6 as soon as possible.

That is why White did not move the knight and preferred to bring the reserve into battle. The move 16 ♖ad1 is justified by the variation: 16...♗b7 17 ♘xb7 ♖xd8 18 ♘xc5 ♖xd1 19 ♖xd1 ♗xc5 20 ♘e5+ ♔g8 21 ♖d8+ ♗f8 22 ♗e7. If Black tries to avoid this line, accepting the sacrifice of the knight with 16...♕xa5, then White continues the attack with 17 ♕xc7+ ♔g8 18 ♘e5 h6 19 ♖d8 e.g. 19...hxg5 (19...♔h7 20 ♗f6) 20 ♕f7+ ♔h7 21 ♕g6+ ♔g8 22 ♖xf8+ ♔xf8 23 ♕f7 mate.

Szabo avoided this line but lost a piece and should have resigned much earlier.

# (11) Barcza,G – Bronstein,D

Budapest vs. Moscow Match,
Budapest, 1949
*[A20] English Opening*

1 c4 e5 2 a3 ♘f6 3 d3 a5 4 ♘c3 d6 5 ♘f3 ♘bd7 6 e3 g6 7 ♗d2 ♗g7 8 b4 axb4 9 axb4 ♖xa1 10 ♕xa1 0-0 11 ♕a7 ♕e7 12 e4 c6 13 ♗e2 d5 14 cxd5 cxd5 15 ♕a4 b6 16 0-0 ♗b7 17 exd5 ♘xd5 18 ♘xd5 ♗xd5 19 ♕b5 ♕d6 20 ♖c1 h6 21 ♘e1 ♖d8 22 ♗f3 ♘f6 23 ♗xd5 ♘xd5 24 ♖c6 ♕d7 25 ♕c4 ♖a8 26 ♕c1 b5 27 h3 ♔h7 28 ♕c5 ♘f4 29 ♖c7 ♕f5 30 ♕c6 ♖a1 31 ♕e4 ♘xd3 32 ♕xf5 ♘xe1 33 ♔f1 ♘c2+ 34 ♗c1 ♖xc1+ 35 ♔e2 ♘d4+ 36 ♔d2 ♘b3+ White resigns.

Position after 31 ♕c6-e4

**31...♘f4xd3!**

    Both players' positions have weaknesses. One's first impression is that the white king is just about fine. Three pawns protect him and one of them has made an escape route. The knight on e1 is well protected by two white pieces.

    On the other side of the board is the black king who will have to keep the bishop close by his side as two pawns have moved forward rather frivolously. If White manages to exchange queens then there will be problems for the pawn on f7.

    Reasoning like this brings us to the conclusion that the white rook on c7 is more dangerous than the black one on a1. However, I believe that we have forgotten to take into account that it is Black's turn to make a move!

    If one considers the positions separately it often appears that each side is fine but when both armies clash it becomes clear that one of them is probably losing. We can only distinguish the difference if there is a good move available. In this case Black has such a move. After 31...♘xd3 32 ♕xf5 ♘xe1 White cannot prevent checkmate by the double check with ♘f3++. If White tries to save his queen with, for instance 33 ♕xf7, then 33...♘f3 is checkmate.

    The magic of chess!

# (12) Szily,I – Bronstein,D
### Moscow vs. Budapest Match,
### Moscow, 1949
### *[C63] Spanish Opening*

1 e4 e5 2 ♘f3 ♘c6 3 ♗b5 f5 4 exf5 e4 5 ♕e2 ♕e7 6 ♗xc6 bxc6 7 ♘d4 ♘f6 8 ♘c3 c5 9 ♘b3 d5 10 ♕b5+ ♕d7 11 ♕a5 ♕c6 12 ♘a4 ♖b8 13 d4 c4 14 ♘bc5 ♗d6 15 b3 0-0 16 h3 ♗xf5 17 ♗e3 ♘d7 18 ♕d2 ♘b6 19 ♘c3 ♕e8 20 a4 cxb3 21 cxb3 c6 22 ♘e2 ♘d7 23 ♕c3 ♗e6 24 0-0 ♗xh3 25 ♘g3 ♕g6 26 gxh3 ♗xg3 27 ♔h1 ♖h5 28 fxg3 ♕xh3+ 29 ♔g1 ♕xg3+ 30 ♔h1 ♖f3 31 ♖xf3 ♕xf3+ 32 ♔g1 ♘xc5 33 dxc5 ♕g3+ 34 ♔h1 ♖f8 35 ♕e1 ♕f3+ 36 ♔g1 ♖f6 37 ♗f2 ♖g6+ 38 ♔f1 ♕h3+ 39 ♔e2 ♕d3 mate.

Position after 24 0-0

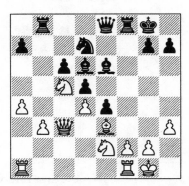

**24....♗e6xh3!**

If a chess player plays his rook's pawn up one square too early after having castled, there is always the danger that this pawn will be attacked.

Of course this pawn is protected by his neighbour but that one has its own task in protecting the king against checks from the North on the g-file by Black's rooks or Her Majesty the queen and may be reluctant to be distracted by what is going on next to him.

This is exactly what is happening here. Black sacrifices his bishop in order to open up the position around the white king. White refuses the gift but Black insists and will be victorious in the subsequent attack.

The black bishops initiated the attack but the black rooks made optimal use of the f-file. Earlier in the opening the black e-pawn courageously crossed the equator and played a decisive role from its outpost.

A perfect example of combining forces resulting in a sad fate for the white king. His bishop made the mistake of exchanging himself for a black knight.

# (13) Bronstein,D – Keres,P

Candidates' Tournament,
Budapest, 1950
*[C91] Spanish Opening*

1 e4 e5 2 ♘f3 ♘c6 3 ♗b5 a6 4 ♗a4 ♘f6 5 0-0 ♗e7 6 ♖e1 b5 7 ♗b3 0-0 8 d4 d6 9 c3 ♗g4
10 h3 ♗xf3 11 ♕xf3 exd4 12 ♕d1 dxc3 13 ♘xc3 ♘a5 14 ♗c2 ♖e8 15 f4 b4 16 ♘d5 ♘xd5
17 ♕xd5 c6 18 ♕d3 g6 19 ♔h1 ♗f8 20 ♖f1 ♗g7 21 ♗d2 c5 22 ♗a4 ♖f8 23 ♖ab1 ♕b6 24
f5 ♗d4 25 ♕g3 ♘c4 26 ♗h6 ♗g7 27 ♗xg7 ♔xg7 28 f6+ ♔h8 29 ♕g5 b3 30 axb3 ♕b4 31
bxc4 ♕xa4 32 ♖f4 ♕c2 33 ♕h6 Black resigns.

Position after 32...♕a4-c2

**33 ♕g5-h6!**

This position is a memorable one for me. I knew that if I won this last-round game,
then I would tie for first place with Boleslavsky in the first official FIDE Candidates'
Tournament in Budapest 1950. That is why I decided to play a very sharp move in a
well-known classical position.

The queen's move was the last one of this extraordinarily tense game. I think Black
rejected 26...♘xb2 because of 27 ♖xb2 ♗xb2 28 ♗b3 with several threats to the black
king. In my opinion, Black chose 26...♗g7 intending 27 ♗xg7 ♔xg7 28 f6+ ♔h8 29 ♕h4
g5 but in the heat of the battle he must have overlooked that White can block the pawn
on g6 with 29 ♕g5! If now 29... ♖g8 then 30 ♖f4 ♕d8 31 ♖h4 ♕f8 32 ♖h6 intending 33 ♕h4.

With my next move 30 axb3 I show respect for Paul Keres as it would be very childish
to play 30 ♖f4 bxa2 31 ♕h6 axb1♕+ 32 ♔h2 in a situation where the simple 30 axb3
♘e5 31 ♖f4 is quite sufficient.

I won this game and the subsequent match against Isaac Boleslavsky, earning me the
right to play a match for the World Championship.

# (14) Bronstein,D – Boleslavsky,I

Candidates' Play-off,
Game 1, Moscow, 1950
*[D89] Grünfeld Defence*

1 d4 ♘f6 2 c4 g6 3 ♘c3 d5 4 cxd5 ♘xd5 5 e4 ♘xc3 6 bxc3 c5 7 ♗c4 ♗g7 8 ♘e2 cxd4 9 cxd4 ♘c6 10 ♗e3 0-0 11 0-0 ♗g4 12 f3 ♘a5 13 ♗d3 ♗e6 14 d5 ♗xa1 15 ♕xa1 f6 16 ♗h6 ♕b6+ 17 ♔h1 ♖fd8 18 ♖b1 ♕c5 19 ♗d2 b6 20 ♗b4 ♕c7 21 ♖c1 ♕b7 22 ♕b1 ♖ab8 23 dxe6 ♘c6 24 ♗c3 ♘e5 25 ♗b5 ♖bc8 26 ♗xe5 ♖xc1+ 27 ♕xc1 fxe5 28 ♗d7 ♕a6 29 ♘g3 ♕xa2 30 h4 ♖f8 31 ♕g5 ♖f6 32 ♕xf6 Black resigns.

Position after 13...♗g4-e6

**14 d4-d5!**

What unusual facet of Black's position attracts our attention? The knight at the edge of the board, of course. Had it been on f6, the black king would not have had any worries. It is interesting to know how the knight came to a5. Most likely from c6 and if it wants to move, it will probably use the same square again. In order to keep the knight out of play we should try to get control over the square c6. Why then not push the white queen's pawn forward?

At the same time the black bishop will be driven away from the diagonal a2-e6. Such a simple move and yet so many words to explain the decision to move a pawn forward!

Have we forgotten that opening the diagonal a1-h8 allows the bishop to take the rook on a1? It is not necessarily a disaster to let a good bishop take a rook which is tucked away in a corner. The bishop won't be able to return to defend the black king.

Conclusion: we will play 14 d5 as after 14...♗xa1 15 ♕xa1 f6 Black will be totally passive and White's pieces can use their fantasy and knowledge to create a strong offensive.

# (15) Botvinnik,M – Bronstein,D

World Championship Match,
Game 11, Moscow, 1951
*[E17] Queen's Indian Defence*

1 d4 e6 2 ♘f3 ♘f6 3 c4 b6 4 g3 ♗b7 5 ♗g2 ♗e7 6 0-0 0-0 7 b3 d5 8 cxd5 exd5 9 ♗b2 ♘bd7 10 ♘c3 ♖e8 11 ♘e5 ♗f8 12 ♖c1 ♘xe5 13 dxe5 ♖xe5 14 ♘b5 ♖e7 15 ♗xf6 gxf6 16 e4 dxe4 17 ♕g4+ ♗g7 18 ♖fd1 ♕f8 19 ♘d4 ♗c8 20 ♕h4 f5 21 ♘c6 ♖e8 22 ♗h3 ♗h6 23 ♖c2 e3 24 fxe3 ♗xe3+ 25 ♔h1 ♗e6 26 ♗g2 a5 27 ♗f3 ♔h8 28 ♘d4 ♖ad8 29 ♖xc7 ♗d5 30 ♖e1 ♕d6 31 ♖c2 ♖e4 32 ♗xe4 ♗xe4+ 33 ♕xe4 fxe4 34 ♘f5 ♕b4 35 ♖xe3 ♖d1+ 36 ♔g2 ♖d2+ 37 ♖xd2 ♕xd2+ 38 ♔h3 ♕f2 39 ♔g4 f6 White resigns.

Position after 31 ♖c7-c2

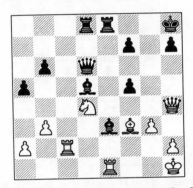

**31...♖e8-e4!**

It is simple to evaluate this position. The pieces of both players confront each other in the centre of the board where the pawns are gone. In this situation it is advisable to insure them well! The black pieces cover each other but the white ones are disjointed. Just a breeze will be sufficient to blow the royal stronghold apart. Where is the weakest link in White's position? That is clearly the diagonal h1-a8. There is just one bishop to defend it on f3 and he is not strong enough by himself to repel an attack. That is why Black can simply play his rook from e8 to e4.

It is worth mentioning that if White plays 30 ♖f1 ♕d6 31 ♘xf5 (31... ♕xc7? 32 ♕f6+!) then Black needs to see the hidden move 39...♖xg3+ (31...♗xf3+ 32 ♖xf3 ♕d1+ 33 ♔g2 ♖d2+ 34 ♔h3 ♖xh2+ 35 ♔xh2 ♕g1+ 36 ♔h3 ♕h1+ 37 ♔g4 ♖g8+ 38 ♔h5 ♖g5+ 39 ♔h6 ♖xg3+ 40 ♖xe3 ♖g6+ 41 ♔h5 ♕d1+). This variation was also mentioned in the Russian bulletin of the match by Paul Keres and Alexander Tolush.

# (16) Botvinnik,M – Bronstein,D

World Championship Match,
Game 17, Moscow, 1951
*[E45] Nimzo-Indian Defence*

1 d4 ♘f6 2 c4 e6 3 ♘c3 ♗b4 4 e3 b6 5 ♘ge2 ♗a6 6 a3 ♗e7 7 ♘g3 d5 8 cxd5 ♗xf1 9 ♘xf1 exd5 10 ♘g3 ♕d7 11 ♕f3 ♘c6 12 0-0 g6 13 ♗d2 0-0 14 ♘ce2 h5 15 ♖fc1 h4 16 ♘f1 ♘e4 17 ♘f4 a5 18 ♖c2 ♗d8 19 ♗e1 ♘e7 20 ♕e2 ♘d6 21 f3 g5 22 ♘d3 ♕e6 23 a4 ♘g6 24 h3 f5 25 ♗c3 ♗f6 26 ♖e1 ♖ae8 27 ♕d1 ♖f7 28 b3 ♖fe7 29 ♗b2 f4 30 ♘e5 ♗xe5 31 dxe5 ♘f7 32 exf4 ♘xf4 33 ♘h2 c5 34 ♘g4 d4 35 ♘f6+ ♕xf6 White resigns.

Position after 29 ♗c3-b2

**29...f5-f4!**

'If...' We often think in chess, 'If...'. If there was no white pawn on e3 it would make sense to contemplate sacrificing the black queen on e1. So if we can play 29...f4 to try and get this e3-pawn out of the way... But it cannot be that the best moves are so simple and easy to find. Who says that 29...f4 is the best move in this position? It is a move that should be considered and we think it is very useful. That is often sufficient reason to play it.

However, you're not always obliged to make the best move. Moves should be active, enterprising, sound and beautiful! If the adversaries follow this rule, it will be interesting for the spectators, especially if they play quickly. The spectators who followed this game back in 1951 were very grateful to the players. Although the first 27 moves were played slowly, the next 13 moves, until the time control, were rattled off at high speed since both players were in time trouble. Under those circumstances Black played 29...f4. White decided to block the e-file immediately and played 30 ♘e5 but after 30...♗xe5 31 dxe5 ♘f7 32 exf4 ♘xf4 White's hopes to breach Black's defences on the square f6 were in vain.

In this game I adopted the strategy of deliberately making moves that defy all logic. This had the effect of completely confusing Botvinnik. After the opening he was psychologically 'groggy'.

# (17) Bronstein,D – Botvinnik,M

World Championship Match,
Game 22, Moscow, 1951
*[A91] Dutch Defence*

1 d4 e6 2 c4 f5 3 g3 ♘f6 4 ♗g2 ♗e7 5 ♘c3 0-0 6 e3 d5 7 ♘ge2 c6 8 b3 ♘e4 9 0-0 ♘d7 10 ♗b2 ♘df6 11 ♕d3 g5 12 cxd5 exd5 13 f3 ♘xc3 14 ♗xc3 g4 15 fxg4 ♘xg4 16 ♗h3 ♘h6 17 ♘f4 ♗d6 18 b4 a6 19 a4 ♕e7 20 ♖ab1 b5 21 ♗g2 ♘g4 22 ♗d2 ♘f6 23 ♖b2 ♗d7 24 ♖a1 ♘e4 25 ♗e1 ♖fe8 26 ♕b3 ♔h8 27 ♖ba2 ♕f8 28 ♘d3 ♖ab8 29 axb5 axb5 30 ♖a7 ♖e7 31 ♘e5 ♗e8 32 g4 fxg4 33 ♗xe4 dxe4 34 ♗h4 ♖xe5 35 dxe5 ♗xe5 36 ♖f1 ♕g8 37 ♗g3 ♗g7 38 ♕xg8+ Black resigns.

Position after 36...♕f8-g8

**37 ♗h4-g3!**

What strikes us in this diagram is the active white rook on the 7th rank, the other rook on an open file and the good position of the white queen on b3. We further notice that both black bishops are not really participating in the game; the bishop on e8 is playing behind his own pawns and the other one is standing proudly on e5 but in reality he is not able to defend the diagonal a1-h8 permanently. For a moment we will ignore the strong bishop on h4 and play the queen, say to c2, to attack the e4-pawn. If Black then plays his bishop to g6 we can destroy his defence from another side with ♕xc6 with the threat ♗f6+.

Only now, with this idea in mind, we see in a bright moment that the queen does not have to leave at all but that we can attack immediately. Even if the black rook had been on c8 it would not have made a difference: 37 ♗g3 ♗g7 38 ♖xg7 ♕xb3 39 ♗e5 ♕xe3+ 40 ♔h1.

Don't forget, a bishop on an open diagonal and two rooks in the attack and you cannot go wrong! By winning games 21 and 22 I turned the wheels of fortune to my side: Now the score was 11½-10½. Just half a point more required and Botvinnik can no longer win the match ...

# (18) Tolush,A – Bronstein,D

USSR Team Championship,
Odessa, 1952

*[C08] French Defence*

1 d4 e6 2 e4 d5 3 ♘d2 c5 4 exd5 exd5 5 ♘gf3 c4 6 ♗e2 ♘c6 7 0-0 ♗d6 8 c3 ♘ge7 9 ♖e1 0-0 10 ♘f1 b5 11 ♗g5 b4 12 ♘e5 ♗xe5 13 dxe5 bxc3 14 bxc3 ♗e6 15 ♗f3 h6 16 ♗xe7 ♕xe7 17 ♕d2 ♖ab8 18 ♖ad1 ♖fd8 19 ♖e2 ♕c7 20 ♕e3 ♖d7 21 ♕f4 ♖bd8 22 g3 d4 23 ♗xc6 d3 24 ♖b2 ♕xc6 25 f3 ♕c5+ 26 ♕e3 ♕a5 27 ♖c1 ♖d5 28 f4 d2 29 ♖xd2 ♖xd2 30 ♘xd2 ♖d3 31 ♕f2 ♕d5 32 ♖c2 ♗h3 33 ♕e2 ♖e3 White resigns.

Position after 22 g2-g3

**22...d5-d4!**

The black pawn on d5 is ready to start an attack but as soon as you will move it you will simultaneously open the long diagonal for the white bishop. This bishop will capture the knight on c6 first and only then White's c-pawn will take Black's attacking pawn.

It all has its logic and in draughts, where capturing is obligatory, this way of judging the position would be perfectly correct. However, in chess the Goddess Caïssa left the possibility for players to make their own choice. Using this possibility the black d-pawn became the hero of a pretty combination by immediately taking another bold step forward. Later this stout pawn even penetrated to d2 where he sacrificed his life for the benefit of the other black pieces.

Looking back after so many years with a lot more experience I wonder whether the move 23...d3 was really the best. Is it not simpler to sacrifice this pawn immediately by playing 23...♕xc6 24 cxd4 ♕b6? Probably but a nice chess move is a gift from Caïssa and should be accepted with gratitude by the players for their personal enjoyment and for the audience.

# (19) Bronstein,D – Euwe,M

Candidates' Tournament,
Neuhausen/Zürich, 1953
*[E59] Nimzo-Indian Defence*

1 d4 ♘f6 2 c4 e6 3 ♘c3 ♗b4 4 e3 c5 5 ♗d3 d5 6 ♘f3 0-0 7 0-0 ♘c6 8 a3 ♗xc3 9 bxc3 dxc4 10 ♗xc4 ♕c7 11 ♗d3 e5 12 ♕c2 ♖e8 13 e4 exd4 14 cxd4 ♗g4 15 ♕xc5 ♘xe4 16 ♗xe4 ♖xe4 17 ♘g5 ♖e7 18 ♕c2 g6 19 ♘e4 ♗f5 20 ♘f6+ ♔g7 21 ♕d2 ♔xf6 22 d5 ♖d8 23 ♗b2+ ♘e5 24 f4 ♕c5+ 25 ♔h1 ♖xd5 26 fxe5+ ♔e6 27 ♕g5 ♔d7 28 ♖ac1 ♕b6 29 ♗c3 ♖e8 30 ♗b4 ♖exe5 31 ♕h4 a5 32 ♗e1 h5 33 ♗f2 ♕a6 34 ♗g3 ♖e4 35 ♖xf5 ♖xh4 36 ♖xd5+ ♔e6 37 ♖cd1 ♕c4 38 ♖d6+ ♔e7 39 ♖d7+ ♔f6 40 ♗xh4+ ♕xh4 41 ♖f1+ ♔g5 Draw agreed.

Position after 19...♗g4-f5

**20 ♘e4-f6+!**

In this position it is essential for us to know whose turn it is. If it were Black to move his knight could capture the pawn on d4 or his rook or bishop could take the knight on e4. But it is White's turn and the first thing that comes to mind is a check on f6. The black king can now attack the knight by going to g7. Sometimes it makes sense to sacrifice material to lure the enemy king into the open. Here White sacrifices a whole piece to achieve that. The black king cannot get back to g7 but must remain in the centre, assailed by the two rooks, queen and bishop. In this case Black found the only defence and the combination led to a friendly draw.

When this intellectual fight was published world-wide the famous master Dmitri Rovner from Leningrad published an article in which he indicated a more simple way to achieve the draw: 15... ♗xf3 16 gxf3 ♕d7 17 ♗e3 ♘xe4 18 ♗xe4 ♖xe4 19 fxe4 ♕g4+. But I still prefer the way chosen by Dr Max Euwe. Many years later I was told by Carel van den Berg that Dr Max Euwe liked this game very much. So did I.

# (20) Bronstein,D – Trifunović,P

### Olympiad, Amsterdam, 1954

*[E44] Nimzo-Indian Defence*

1 d4 ♘f6 2 c4 e6 3 ♘c3 ♗b4 4 e3 b6 5 ♘ge2 ♗b7 6 a3 ♗xc3+ 7 ♘xc3 0-0 8 ♗d3 c5 9 d5 exd5 10 cxd5 a6 11 0-0 d6 12 e4 ♘bd7 13 a4 ♕c7 14 ♘e2 ♖fe8 15 ♘g3 c4 16 ♗c2 b5 17 ♗e3 b4 18 ♖c1 a5 19 ♗d4 ♗a6 20 ♘f5 ♖e5 21 ♗d3 ♖xf5 22 exf5 ♘xd5 23 ♗e4 ♕c6 24 ♕f3 ♗b7 25 f6 ♖e8 26 ♗xh7+ ♔xh7 27 ♕h5+ ♔g8 28 fxg7 f6 29 ♕xe8+ ♔xg7 30 ♖xc4 ♕xc4 31 ♕xd7+ ♔g6 32 ♕g4+ ♔f7 33 b3 Black resigns.

Position after 20...♖e8-e5

**21 ♗c2-d3!**

The d-file acts as a sort of separation between the queen's and king's side. White has stopped the advance of Black's pawns on the queen's side. Black will not find it easy to fight against the white knight on f5. Moreover, White has put the pawn on d6 in a tight spot and has a perfect square for his bishop in the centre. Such a bishop is a feast for the eye. That is why Black proposed to exchange this bishop for a rook. If now 21 ♗xe5 Black will not be bothered any longer by the bishop and the d-pawn moves to a more active position on e5.

However, White is in no hurry. Black's position has been split in two and will disintegrate all by itself. After 21 ♗d3 Black decided to exchange his rook for a knight. That has temporarily weakened White's attack but the e-pawn, now on f5, is dreaming of an advance to the g-file.

In fairy tales a lot can happen!

# (21) Bilek,I – Bronstein,D

Hungary vs. USSR Match,
Budapest, 1955
*[B16] Caro-Kann Defence*

1 e4 c6 2 d4 d5 3 ♘c3 dxe4 4 ♘xe4 ♘f6 5 ♘xf6+ gxf6 6 c3 ♗f5 7 ♘e2 h5 8 ♘f4 h4 9 ♕f3 ♘d7 10 g4 hxg3 11 fxg3 e5 12 g4 ♗h7 13 ♘e2 exd4 14 cxd4 ♗b4+ 15 ♔f2 ♕e7 16 ♗g2 0-0-0 17 a3 ♗c5 18 ♗e3 ♘e5 19 dxe5 ♖d3 20 ♕xf6 ♕xf6+ 21 exf6 ♖xe3 22 ♖hc1 ♗b6 23 ♗f3 ♗e4 24 ♗xe4 ♖xe4+ White resigns.

Position after 17 a2-a3

**17...♗b4-c5!**

The black king is well protected while the white king has remained in the centre, wondering from which side the attack will come. If you forget for a minute that pawns not only move forward but also can play actively along a diagonal, then Black can contemplate a strong move such as 17...♘e5. Yes but what about the pawn on d4? It can take the knight on e5. Would it be possible to lure it away?

With a grain of imagination, a trifle of fantasy, a shade of calculation and a small risk we will seriously start to search and suddenly find the unexpected move 17...♗c5.

White declined the sacrifice of the bishop and unpinned the d4-pawn when he played 18 ♗e3 but then the move 18... ♘e5 was possible thereby increasing the power of the rook on d8. Now, being on e3, the bishop himself has become a target for Black.

With active play Black demonstrated clearly how bad the position of the white pieces really was.

# (22) Bronstein,D – Keres,P

Interzonal Tournament,
Gothenburg, 1955
*[E41] Nimzo-Indian Defence*

1 d4 ♘f6 2 c4 e6 3 ♘c3 ♗b4 4 e3 c5 5 ♗d3 b6 6 ♘ge2 ♗b7 7 0-0 cxd4 8 exd4 0-0 9 d5 h6 10 ♗c2 ♘a6 11 ♘b5 exd5 12 a3 ♗e7 13 ♘g3 dxc4 14 ♗xh6 gxh6 15 ♕d2 ♘h7 16 ♕xh6 f5 17 ♘xf5 ♖xf5 18 ♗xf5 ♘f8 19 ♖ad1 ♗g5 20 ♕h5 ♕f6 21 ♘d6 ♗c6 22 ♕g4 ♔h8 23 ♗e4 ♗h6 24 ♗xc6 dxc6 25 ♕xc4 ♘c5 26 b4 ♘ce6 27 ♕xc6 ♖b8 28 ♘e4 ♕g6 29 ♖d6 ♗g7 30 f4 ♕g4 31 h3 ♕e2 32 ♘g3 ♕e3+ 33 ♔h2 ♘d4 34 ♕d5 ♖e8 35 ♘h5 ♘e2 36 ♘xg7 ♕g3+ 37 ♔h1 ♘xf4 38 ♕f3 ♘e2 39 ♖h6+ Black resigns.

Position after 13...d5xc4

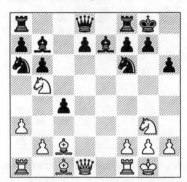

**14 ♗c1xh6!**

The chess army consists of eight pawns and seven pieces. Yes, seven pieces as the king has its own code of conduct. During the game he conforms to all wishes of the player and he is in fact a symbolic piece. The king cannot lose the battle, the player does that for him. Therefore it is essential that all wishes and desires of the chess pieces are taken seriously as they have gathered an enormous amount of experience over a very long period of time – since man started to record chess games!

My opponent knew very well that I could not afford to lose time by taking pawns but for reasons unknown to me he forgot about the bishop on c1. Probably he was focused on the variation: 14 ♘f5 ♖e8 15 ♘bd6 ♖e6 16 ♘xb7 ♕c7 etc. The unexpected sacrifice of a bishop promises a very strong attack. If now 14...♖e8 then the bishop will take a second pawn: 15 ♗xg7! That is why Black played 14...gxh6 but after 15 ♕d2!! the white attack unfolds by itself. After 15...♘c5 16 ♖ae1 ♘d3 17 ♗xd3 cxd3 18 ♕xh6 ♘h7 19 ♘f5 ♗f6 20 ♖e3 ♖e8 21 ♖g3+ ♔h8 22 ♖g7 or 18...♖e8 19 ♘f5 ♗f8 20 ♕g5+ ♔h7 21 ♘bd6 ♖e6 22 ♖e3 ♘g8 23 ♕h5+ ♘h6 24 ♘xh6 ♗xh6 25 ♕xf7+ ♔h8 26 ♖xe6 dxe6 27 ♕xb7 White has a superior position. In the final position Black would have liked to play 33...♘xf4, but then comes 34 ♖xh6+ ♘h7 (or 34...♔g8 35 ♕c4+ ♘4e6 36 ♖xf8+) 35 ♕d6! ♗xh6 36 ♘f5! ♕e8 37 ♕d4+ ♔g8 38 ♘xh6+.

This game was awarded the first brilliancy prize.

# (23) Bronstein,D – Geller,E

Interzonal Tournament,
Gothenburg, 1955
*[B31] Sicilian Defence*

1 e4 c5 2 ♘f3 ♘c6 3 ♗b5 g6 4 c3 ♗g7 5 d4 ♕b6 6 a4 cxd4 7 0-0 a6 8 ♗xc6 ♕xc6 9 cxd4 ♕xe4 10 ♘c3 ♕f5 11 ♖e1 d5 12 a5 ♗d7 13 ♕b3 ♘f6 14 ♖e5 ♕d3 15 ♖xe7+ ♔xe7 16 ♘xd5+ ♘xd5 17 ♕xd3 f6 18 ♗d2 ♔f7 19 ♕b3 ♗c6 20 ♘e1 ♖he8 21 ♘d3 ♖e6 22 ♖c1 ♗f8 23 ♖xc6 Black resigns.

Position after 14...♕f5-d3

**15 ♖e5xe7+!**

When evaluating a chess position the first thing we should look at is the position of the kings. In closed positions they can wait to castle but if the positions appear to be open then it is better for them to go into their hide-out as quickly as possible.

The position which we are evaluating here has to be considered as semi-open. The fact that the Black has not yet castled would not have been of great significance if the black queen were not on d3. It must be said that she did not go there voluntarily; she was lured there by White's rook. But Black's queen should also be partly blamed for his loss as she should have never undertaken the long journey to capture the white e-pawn. In doing so she opened the e-file for the white rook and now has to suffer for her recklessness.

Efim Geller tried to play this game against his own style but it never works. I have suffered myself many times like this.

# (24) Bronstein,D – Medina,A

Interzonal Tournament,
Gothenburg, 1955
*[D36] Queen's Gambit Declined*

1 d4 ♘f6 2 c4 e6 3 ♘c3 d5 4 cxd5 exd5 5 ♗g5 ♗e7 6 e3 c6 7 ♕c2 ♘bd7 8 ♗d3 ♘f8 9 ♘ge2 ♘e6 10 ♗h4 g6 11 0-0-0 ♘g7 12 f3 ♘f5 13 ♗f2 ♕a5 14 ♔b1 ♗e6 15 h3 0-0-0 16 e4 ♘g7 17 ♗g3 ♘ge8 18 ♗e5 ♖f8 19 ♘c1 dxe4 20 fxe4 ♘d7 21 ♗h2 ♘b8 22 d5 ♗d7 23 ♘b3 ♕b6 24 d6 Black resigns.

Position after 23...♕a5-b6

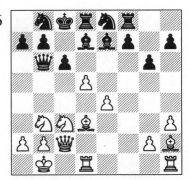

**24 d5-d6!**

There can be no doubt: White's position is harmonious. The sneaky bishop on h2 controls the diagonal all the way to b8, the rooks co-operate and can assist each other at any moment. Several strong pieces – the queen, two knights and a bishop – have gathered around the white king. The black king also has his supporters but they are obviously restricted in their movements. Although the movement of a knight, compared to a bishop, is more limited regarding the distance, it can exert better control at short distances.

In this example the white knights together control the squares a5, b5, c5, and d5 and a knight on d5 would be ideal to attack the black queen but presently that square is occupied by a white pawn. The obvious question is: Should not the pawn leave that square? Yes of course and that is how the move 24 d6 came about.

It sounds simple to come to that conclusion but it is not. If we want to find the best move but are somewhat inconsistent then the game of chess can be extremely difficult. Does 'a best move' really exist in a balanced position? The position is not balanced, Black has no space. White has several good moves, for instance 24 dxc6 or 24 ♘a4 or even 24 ♘b5 with the threat 25 ♗g1. However the move 24 d6 is the most aesthetic of all.

# (25) Bronstein,D – Sliwa,B

Alekhine Memorial Tournament,
Moscow, 1956
*[C75] Spanish Opening*

1 e4 e5 2 ♘f3 ♘c6 3 ♗b5 a6 4 ♗a4 d6 5 c3 ♗d7 6 d4 ♗e7 7 0-0 ♗f6 8 ♗e3 ♘ge7 9 ♘bd2
0-0 10 a3 ♘g6 11 b4 ♖e8 12 ♗c2 h6 13 ♘b3 ♗g5 14 ♘xg5 hxg5 15 g3 f6 16 ♕h5 ♘ce7 17
♘c5 ♗c6 18 ♗b3+ d5 19 ♖ad1 b6 20 ♘d3 exd4 21 ♗xd4 ♔f7 22 f4 ♖h8 23 ♕e2 gxf4 24
♘xf4 ♘xf4 25 ♖xf4 ♕c8 26 exd5 ♗xd5 27 ♗xf6 gxf6 28 ♖xd5 ♘xd5 29 ♗xd5+ Black resigns.

Position after 16...♘c6-e7

**17 ♘b3-c5!**

Let's take a quick look at the position: White's pieces are spread all over the board and
are controlling many squares. The black ones are very passive and Black's pawns on e5 and
g5 are easy targets. It is very likely that the f-pawn will start an attack. Not only will this
pawn become more active but it will also make way for the rook. Shall we therefore play
17 f4? Of course a good move but it is a pity to exchange a bishop for a knight: 17 f4 gxf4
18 gxf4 ♘xf4 19 ♗xf4 exf4 20 ♖xf4. Maybe 19 ♖xf4 exf4 20 ♗xf4? Or 19 ♗xf4 exf4 20 e5
to open the diagonal for the bishop on c2? In a good position there are often many possibilities and it is always difficult to make a choice. Maybe that is the reason why there are
chess players who prefer defensive positions with fewer possible moves, making it easier
to choose one.

In this game White decided to attack the pawn on e5 in a different way – with the available pawn on d4. After 17 ♘c5 it should be clear that if the knight is captured with the
pawn there is no defence against 23 ♕h7 after 17...dxc5 18 ♗b3+ c4 19 ♗xc4+ ♔f8 20
dxe5 ♗b5 21 ♗a2 ♗xf1 22 exf6. Taking the brave white pawn is also bad: 22...gxf6 23
♕h6 mate. Conclusion: even a defending centre pawn (on d6) is not always able to stop a
knight which crosses the equator from his own camp.

Such unexpected moves from both sides make a game of chess so particularly exciting
and interesting!

# (26) Bronstein,D – Golombek,H

### Alekhine Memorial Tournament,
### Moscow, 1956
*[E43] Nimzo-Indian Defence*

1 d4 ♘f6 2 c4 e6 3 ♘c3 ♗b4 4 ♘f3 b6 5 e3 ♗b7 6 ♗d3 ♘e4 7 0-0 ♗xc3 8 bxc3 0-0 9 ♘e1
f5 10 f3 ♘f6 11 a4 ♘c6 12 e4 fxe4 13 fxe4 e5 14 ♗g5 ♕e7 15 ♘c2 ♕d6 16 ♗h4 ♖ae8 17
♗g3 ♕e7 18 ♘e3 d6 19 ♗h4 ♘d8 20 ♘d5 ♗xd5 21 cxd5 c6 22 ♕b3 ♔h8 23 ♖ae1 h6 24
♕a3 g5 25 ♗g3 ♘d7 26 dxc6 ♘xc6 27 ♗b5 ♖xf1+ 28 ♖xf1 ♘cb8 29 ♗c4 ♖f8 30 ♖xf8+
♕xf8 31 dxe5 ♘c5 32 exd6 ♘xe4 33 d7 ♘c5 34 ♗e5+ ♔h7 35 ♗d3+ Black resigns.

Position after 32...♘c5xe4

**33 d6-d7!**

In such a wide open position two bishops are always better than two knights. White's
position appears to be so strong that he cannot lose this game unless he becomes terribly
careless, for example after 33 ♗e5+ ♔h7 34 ♗d3 ♕f2+. In this variation White just forgot that the bishop on g3 protects the square f2. And if White plays 34 ♕b2 instead of 34
♗d3 then Black has the good move 34...♘d7 at his disposal and White has to invent
something new. This is because the white queen is not centralised.

But what if...? Indeed, the pawn on d6 has a great desire to move on to the 8th rank, so
let's agree to a move by this pawn. At the same time the diagonal a3-f8 is opened and a
threat is created: ♕xf8+. Oh no, how is that possible? Black can now take the white
queen. Let's not panic, the conflict, after all, is just a chess game! A friendly contest in
strength, improvisation, wit and fantasy.

After having calmed down one can easily see that after 33 d7 ♕xa3 follows 34 d8♕+.
That is why the game took a different course.

# (27) Bronstein,D – Olafsson,F

Interzonal Tournament,
Portoroz, 1958
*[B90] Sicilian Defence*

1 e4 c5 2 ♘f3 d6 3 d4 cxd4 4 ♘xd4 ♘f6 5 ♘c3 a6 6 ♗c4 ♘bd7 7 a3 g6 8 h4 ♘e5 9 ♗b3
♗g7 10 ♗g5 ♕a5 11 ♕d2 ♗d7 12 ♗xf6 ♗xf6 13 ♘d5 ♕xd2+ 14 ♔xd2 ♖c8 15 ♘xf6+ exf6
16 ♖ad1 ♔e7 17 ♗d5 ♗c6 18 b3 ♗xd5 19 exd5 f5 20 c4 ♔d7 21 f3 h5 22 ♖c1 ♖c7 23 a4
♖e8 24.♖he1 ♔d8 25 ♖e2 ♘d7 26 ♖xe8+ ♔xe8 27 a5 ♘e5 28 ♘e2 ♔d7 29 ♔c3 ♖c8 30
♔d4 ♖e8 31 ♘f4 ♔e7 32 b4 ♔d7 33 ♖c2 ♔c7 34 ♖e2 ♔d7 35 c5 ♖c8 36 ♖xe5 dxe5+ 37
♔xe5 ♖e8+ 38 ♔f6 ♖e3 39 ♔xf7 ♖b3 40 ♘xg6 ♖xb4 41 ♘e5+ ♔c8 42 d6 ♖b2 43 ♔e8 ♖d2
44 ♘g6 ♔b8 45 g3 ♖d1 46 ♘e7 Black resigns.

Position after 35...♖e8-c8

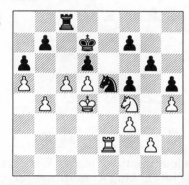

**36 ♖e2xe5!**

There cannot be any argument about the fact that Black's four pawns on the kingside have no future whatsoever as they will be stopped by White's h-pawn and knight on f4. On the other side of the board White has managed to cross the equator with his a-, c- and d-pawns and has firmly occupied square d4 with his king. The pawn on c5 exerts a steady pressure on d6 and forces the black king to be attentive. When the time is right the pawns are ready to march to the finish line and break the ribbon! The e-file is not occupied by any pawns but neither White nor Black have a chance to advance into the enemy camp. As Black has doubled pawns on the f-file White has in fact an extra pawn in the centre. With the resolute move 36 ♖xe5 White exchanges the passive rook for the strong black knight in the centre and activates his king. Now that the pawn on d6 has gone the role of the d5-pawn, supported by the c5-pawn, is dramatically increased.

For my play I was awarded the prize for the best endgame of the tournament.

# (28) Mukhin,V – Bronstein,D

USSR Team Championship,
Moscow, 1959
*[C27] Bishop's Opening*

1 e4 e5 2 ♗c4 ♘f6 3 ♘c3 ♘xe4 4 ♕h5 ♘d6 5 ♗b3 ♘c6 6 ♘b5 g6 7 ♕f3 f6 8 ♘xc7+ ♕xc7 9 ♕xf6 b6 10 ♕xh8 ♗b7 11 ♕xh7 0-0-0 12 ♘e2 ♘f5 13 d3 ♘cd4 14 ♘xd4 exd4 15 0-0 ♕c6 16 f3 ♕f6 17 ♕h3 ♗d6 18 ♕g4 ♖h8 19 g3 ♗xg3 20 hxg3 ♖h5 21 ♖f2 ♕h8 22 ♔g2 ♖h1+ 23 ♔f2 ♕e8 24 ♗d2 ♖xa1 25 ♕f4 ♕h8 26 ♗c1 ♕h5 27 g4 ♕h4+ 28 ♔e2 g5 29 ♕xg5 ♘g3+ 30 ♖xg3 ♕xg3 White resigns.

Position after 19 g2-g3

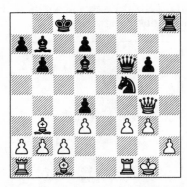

**19...♗d6xg3!**

This position clearly shows four groups of pieces. Which role can these groups play on the board? The bishops in the black 'king's group' are targeting the pawns around the white king but they are well-protected. The black knight can go to e3 but it will be captured there by White's bishop and the pawn will take the bishop. The position of the pawn has now been improved but where is the point that is best suited for a breakthrough?

If Black does not seize the opportunity to start an attack White will mobilise his reserves by playing ♗f4 and the Black attack will get bogged down. That is why Black decides to play for broke. Taking risks is an obvious part of the planned strategy.

After 19...♗xg3 20 hxg3 ♖h5 Black has cleared the square h8 for his queen to start a frontal attack along the open h-file.

# (29) Wexler,B – Bronstein,D

International Tournament,
Mar del Plata, 1960

*[A75] Modern Benoni Defence*

1 d4 ♘f6 2 c4 c5 3 d5 e6 4 ♘c3 exd5 5 cxd5 d6 6 e4 g6 7 ♘f3 a6 8 a4 ♗g4 9 ♗e2 ♗xf3 10 ♗xf3 ♘bd7 11 0-0 ♗g7 12 ♗f4 ♕b8 13 ♗e2 0-0 14 ♗g3 ♖e8 15 ♕c2 ♕c7 16 f4 c4 17 ♔h1 ♖ac8 18 a5 ♕d8 19 ♖fe1 ♖c5 20 ♖a4 ♖xa5 21 ♖xc4 b5 22 ♖b4 ♕b6 23 ♗f3 ♕c5 24 ♖b3 ♕c4 25 ♗e2 ♘xe4 26 ♗xc4 ♘xg3+ 27 hxg3 ♖xe1+ 28 ♔h2 ♖aa1 29 g4 ♖ac1 30 ♕f2 bxc4 31 ♖b7 ♗xc3 32 bxc3 ♖h1+ White resigns.

Position after 25 ♗f3-e2

**25...♘f6xe4!**

It is not easy to fathom this complicated position. There are many hidden difficulties. I believe that each chess-player has his own intuitive method of evaluating complicated positions. I myself often use stereotypical positions of the kings, the possibilities of the rooks to be active, the diagonals for the bishops, the intention of the pawns, etc. If we apply these criteria to this position it seems that the position of the black king is unassailable, barricaded behind his ramparts. Black's other pieces are also in excellent positions. White has two bishops and active pawns in the centre so Black should stay attentive; the move e5 must be prevented. However, Black's queen is attacked and a decision must be made to which square she will move. Possibly to d4 where she can create problems for White. There is another method of evaluation and that is to look at the relation between the pieces – using fantasy. As soon as White accepts the queen's sacrifice, the black knight takes the bishop on g3 and opens the road for the rook on e8 to the square e1. If White tries 30 ♕d3 then Black wins with 30...g5!

Before this game I had a friendly talk with our Ambassador to Argentina N. Alekseev and I promised him that I would try to win today with a queen's sacrifice. And so I did!

# (30) Bronstein,D – Geller,E

28th USSR Championship,
Moscow, 1961
*[E27] Nimzo-Indian Defence*

1 d4 ♘f6 2 c4 e6 3 ♘c3 ♗b4 4 a3 ♗xc3+ 5 bxc3 0-0 6 f3 d5 7 cxd5 exd5 8 e3 ♗f5 9 ♘e2 ♘bd7 10 ♘f4 c5 11 ♗d3 ♗xd3 12 ♕xd3 ♖e8 13 0-0 ♖c8 14 ♖b1 ♕a5 15 ♖xb7 ♘b6 16 g4 h6 17 h4 cxd4 18 g5 dxe3 19 gxf6 ♖xc3 20 ♕g6 Black resigns.

Position after 19...♖c8xc3

**20 ♕d3-g6!**

Let's evaluate in the usual way: the kings first. There are no pawns around the white king but he is well protected by White's pieces. The black king has the customary three pawns to defend him but their attention is demanded by the white pawn on f6. Normally such a pawn means a headache for the defending side and this position is no exception. Don't forget to take the white rook on b7 into account. Now it should not be too difficult to see that this white pawn and rook require assistance to continue the attack.

The decision could also have been forced by the white rook: 20 ♖xf7 but which decision leads to a quicker victory? Yes, 20 ♕g6.

Does that create a new problem? No, it just serves to start a discussion if one should play strongly or beautifully. It is not always possible to combine these criteria in one move.

What useful conclusion can we draw when looking at the diagram? Well, don't put a queen out of play to the side of the board, don't allow an enemy rook to the 7th rank and don't allow a pawn near your king's castle.

You may sometimes violate one or two of these rules but all three together is just too much!

# (31) Bronstein,D – Korchnoi,V

Moscow vs. Leningrad Match,
Leningrad, 1962
*[C83] Spanish Opening*

1 e4 e5 2 ♘f3 ♘c6 3 ♗b5 a6 4 ♗a4 ♘f6 5 0-0 ♘xe4 6 d4 b5 7 ♗b3 d5 8 dxe5 ♗e6 9 c3 ♗e7 10 ♗c2 0-0 11 ♕e2 f5 12 exf6 ♗xf6 13 ♘bd2 ♗f5 14 ♘xe4 ♗xe4 15 ♗xe4 dxe4 16 ♕xe4 ♕d7 17 ♗f4 ♖ae8 18 ♕c2 ♗h4 19 ♗g3 ♗xg3 20 hxg3 ♘e5 21 ♘xe5 ♖xe5 22 ♖fe1 ♖d5 23 ♖ad1 c5 24 a4 ♖d8 25 ♖xd5 ♕xd5 26 axb5 axb5 27 ♕e2 b4 28 cxb4 cxb4 29 ♕g4 b3 30 ♔h2 ♕f7 31 ♕g5 ♖d7 32 f3 h6 33 ♕e3 ♖d8 34 g4 ♔h8 35 ♕b6 ♖d2 36 ♕b8+ ♔h7 37 ♖e8 ♕xf3 38 ♖h8+ ♔g6 39 ♖xh6+ Black resigns.

Position after 38...♔h7-g6

**39 ♖h8xh6+!**

It is necessary to respect such a strong piece as the queen. To play with the queen is always easy. It is not necessary to remember where she is allowed to go and where not as she has the privilege of moving in every direction. But even the queen needs help if she wants to checkmate the king. She cannot do it by herself. In this position the queen is co-operating perfectly with the rook, which managed to approach the ramparts of the black king from behind. Black's move 37...♕xf3 was too risky (37...♕d7!).

It is safe to assume that White, when it is his turn to move, will move his queen to e8 to give a check and thus switch from the queenside to the kingside. If the black king would be obliged to go to g5 everything would go smoothly. White can use the routine way in this type of position: 39 ♕e8+ ♕f7 40 ♕e4+ ♔g5 41 ♔h3 ♕f4 42 ♕e7+ ♔g6 43 ♕e8+ ♕f7 44 ♕e4+ ♔g5 45 ♖a8 but where is the beauty?

Therefore, we have found another method to attack. By sacrificing the white rook the pawn on g4 and the queen together can capture the black queen: 39 ♖xh6+ ♔xh6 40 ♕h8+ ♔g5 41 ♕h5+ ♔f6 42 g5+. Or 39...gxh6 40 ♕g8+ ♔f6 41 ♕f8+.

# (32) Brzozka,P – Bronstein,D

Asztalos Memorial Tournament,
Miskolcz, 1963
*[A88] Dutch Defence*

1 c4 f5 2 ♘f3 ♘f6 3 g3 g6 4 ♗g2 ♗g7 5 0-0 0-0 6 d4 d6 7 ♘c3 c6 8 ♕c2 ♔h8 9 b3 ♘a6 10 ♗b2 ♘c7 11 ♖ad1 ♗d7 12 e3 ♕e8 13 ♖fe1 ♖d8 14 ♖d2 ♘h5 15 d5 ♕f7 16 dxc6 bxc6 17 ♘e2 c5 18 ♘f4 ♘f6 19 ♘g5 ♕g8 20 ♗c3 ♖de8 21 ♗a5 ♘e6 22 ♘gxe6 ♗xe6 23 ♘xe6 ♕xe6 24 ♕d3 ♘e4 25 ♕d5 ♕xd5 26 ♖xd5 ♗c3 27 ♖xc3 ♘xc3 28 ♖d2 ♘e4 29 ♖b2 a5 30 f3 ♘f6 31 ♔f2 ♖b8 32 ♔e2 ♖b6 33 ♔d3 e5 34 f4 e4+ 35 ♔c3 ♔g7 36 ♗f1 h5 37 h4 ♖fb8 38 ♗e2 a4 39 ♖eb1 a3 40 ♖d2 ♔f7 41 ♖bd1 ♔e7 42 ♖d5 ♘e8 43 ♖1d2 ♘c7 44 ♗d1 ♘a6 45 ♗c2 ♘b4 46 ♗b1 ♖a6 47 ♖d1 ♘xd5+ 48 ♖xd5 ♖xb3+ 49 ♔xb3 ♖b6+ 50 ♔c2 ♖b2+ 51 ♔c1 ♖e2 52 ♖d1 ♖xe3 53 ♖g1 ♖c3+ 54 ♔d2 ♖xc4 55 ♗c2 d5 56 ♖b1 d4 57 ♗d1 ♖c3 58 ♖b3 e3+ 59 ♔e2 ♖c1 60 ♖xa3 c4 61 ♖a7+ ♔d6 62 ♗a4 ♖h1 63 ♖d7+ ♔c5 64 ♖c7+ ♔b4 65 a3+ ♔c3 66 ♗b5 ♖h2+ 67 ♔f1 d3 68 ♖xc4+ ♔b2 69 ♔g1 e2 70 ♔xh2 e1♕ White resigns.

Position after 46 ♗c2-b1

**46...♖b6-a6!**

The position is closed with no play at all and a draw seems inevitable. However, in many positions there are nuances and one needs a lot of imagination to find them. Black now makes a very beautiful but mysterious move with the rook on b6. It puts White in zugzwang; the rook on d2 is the only piece that can still play. After 48 ♖xd5 Black's next seven rook moves are creating a tornado effect in the heart of the White position, especially 48...♖xb3+. It is probably the best rook move in the entire history of chess! If 49 axb3 then 49...a2 50 ♗xa2 ♖xa2 51 ♖d2 ♖a1 and Black has a better rook ending. Therefore 49 ♔xb3. However, all White's pawns will fall as ripe apples from a tree. The black pawns now decide the game. The king's pawn will become a queen.

## (33) Foguelman,A – Bronstein,D

Interzonal Tournament,
Amsterdam, 1964
*[D25] Queen's Gambit Accepted*

1 d4 d5 2 c4 dxc4 3 ♘f3 ♘f6 4 e3 ♗g4 5 ♗xc4 e6 6 ♕b3 ♗xf3 7 gxf3 c5 8 ♕xb7 ♘bd7 9 dxc5 ♗xc5 10 f4 0-0 11 0-0 ♘d5 12 ♖d1 ♖b8 13 ♕c6 ♕h4 14 ♘c3 ♖b6 15 ♕xd7 ♘xf4 16 ♘e2 ♘h3+ 17 ♔g2 ♘xf2 18 ♖d4 ♘g4 19 ♖f4 ♕xh2+ 20 ♔f1 ♗xe3 21 ♗d5 ♗xf4 White resigns.

Position after 14 ♘b1-c3

**14...♖b8-b6!**

Black is certainly better. His queen is in a menacing position and the white king is open. The white queen is far away and in no way dangerous for the black king which is well defended by the classical formation of three pawns and a rook. If Black does not act immediately White will play his bishop to f1 to create a defence around his king.

The manoeuvre 14...♖b6 fits well in Black's plan; the queen is lured away from the diagonal a8-h1 at the cost of a piece: 15 ♕xd7 which permits Black's knight on d5 to play: 15...♘xf4. If White now plays 16 ♗f1 then Black's attack is winning after 16...♕g4+ 17 ♔h1 ♕f3+ 18 ♔g1 e5 making way for the rook to g6 and if White plays 16 ♗e2 then 16...e5 17 exf4 ♖h6 18 h3 ♕g3+ 20 ♔h1 ♖xh3+. The rook came from b8 to h3 to deal the decisive blow. In every combination there is a piece which works harder than the others. The only problem is how to find this piece and put it to work!

Of course such an attack is only possible because White has omitted to play with his rook on a1 and his bishop on c1. In many instances these pieces are well positioned on their original squares but not when their king is badly protected and requires help, as in this case.

# (34) Bakulin,N – Bronstein,D

### 32nd USSR Championship,
### Kiev, 1964/65
### *[B16] Caro-Kann Defence*

1 e4 c6 2 d4 d5 3 ♘c3 dxe4 4 ♘xe4 ♘f6 5 ♘xf6+ gxf6 6 ♗e3 ♗f5 7 ♕d2 e6 8 ♘e2 ♘d7 9 ♘g3 ♗g6 10 ♗e2 ♕c7 11 0-0 h5 12 ♖fd1 h4 13 ♘f1 h3 14 g3 0-0-0 15 c4 c5 16 d5 e5 17 ♖ac1 f5 18 b4 ♗d6 19 f3 f4 20 ♗f2 ♖de8 21 ♔h1 ♖hg8 22 ♖e1 e4 23 ♗xc5 ♘xc5 24 bxc5 ♕xc5 25 ♗d1 ♘c7 26 gxf4 e3 27 ♕e2 ♗d3 28 ♕xd3 ♖g1+ 29 ♔xg1 e2+ 30 ♘e3 ♖xe3 31 ♕f5+ ♖e6+ 32 ♔h1 ♕f2 White resigns.

Position after 27 ♕d2-e2

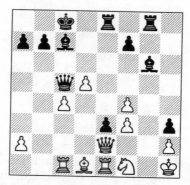

**27...♗g6-d3!**

In a game of chess all depends on your ability to see the connection between pieces and pawns, on your ability to exploit, to your own advantage, almost imperceptible weaknesses in the opponent's ranks.

When looking closer at the 'lines of force' of each black piece it can be easily established that the queen and the rook on g8 are radiating all the way towards a common point on g1, very close to the refuge of the white king and therefore of great interest to the black pieces. How strange that this important square is only guarded by the king himself. The logical conclusion is that the game will be over if queen and rook co-operate and one of them manages to get to g1. With this in mind it should be easy to discover the connection between the pieces 27...♗d3 28 ♕xd3 ♖g1+ 29 ♔xg1 e2+ and the path for the black queen to g1 is wide open. Now that the rook on g8 is no longer amongst us the queen alone may not seem so dangerous but with the pawn on h3 White is defenceless.

Do you like my play or are you in favour of the simple 27... ♗a5? There can be do discussion: the black bishop on c7 is much stronger than the white rook on e1.

The shortest way to a day of rest for the chess pieces is a sharp combination!

# (35) Mikenas,V – Bronstein,D

33rd USSR Championship,
Tallinn, 1965
*[A53] Old Indian Defence*

1 d4 ♘f6 2 c4 d6 3 ♘c3 c6 4 e4 e5 5 d5 ♗e7 6 ♗e2 0-0 7 ♘f3 ♘a6 8 0-0 ♗d7 9 ♘e1 ♕c8 10 ♘d3 ♗d8 11 f4 cxd5 12 cxd5 ♘c5 13 fxe5 ♘fxe4 14 ♘xe4 ♘xe4 15 ♗e3 ♗b6 16 ♗xb6 axb6 17 ♖f4 ♘c5 18 exd6 ♘xd3 19 ♕xd3 ♕c5+ 20 ♔h1 ♕xd6 21 ♖h4 h6 22 a3 ♖fe8 23 ♗f3 ♕e5 24 ♖b4 ♖xa3 White resigns.

Position after 24 ♖h4-b4

**24...♖a8xa3!**

When kings castle and have reached their hide-out they don't bother to think about defending themselves. After all, they are surrounded by pieces and pawns. However, when battles start to flare up then, in the heat of the clash, some pieces do not see the need to vary attacking moves with defensive ones here and there. To guard oneself against such forgetfulness it can be useful to spend a move in providing an escape route for the king should the need arise.

The black king has already created such a window and if a check occurs on the back rank he can flee to h7. In the white position there is no such refuge.

However, White spotted this and therefore did not play 24 ♖b1 (24...♕e1+ 25 ♕f1 ♕xh4). Instead he played his rook to b4 where it is defended by the pawn on a3, deciding to kill to birds with one stone: defending his pawn on b2 and attacking the pawn on b6.

The move 24...♖xa3 was a complete surprise for White. It is all over.

Such moves of beauty increase our interest in the game of chess.

# (36) Bronstein,D – Gligorić,S

50 years October Revolution Tournament,
Moscow, 1967
*[C85] Spanish Opening*

1 e4 e5 2 ♘f3 ♘c6 3 ♗b5 a6 4 ♗a4 ♘f6 5 0-0 ♗e7 6 ♗xc6 dxc6 7 d3 ♘d7 8 ♘bd2 0-0 9 ♘c4 f6 10 ♘h4 ♘c5 11 ♘f5 ♗xf5 12 exf5 ♖e8 13 b3 ♕d5 14 ♗b2 e4 15 ♘e3 ♕f7 16 d4 ♘d7 17 ♕g4 c5 18 ♕xe4 cxd4 19 ♗xd4 c6 20 ♖ad1 ♘c5 21 ♕g4 ♗f8 22 ♘c4 ♖ad8 23 ♗e3 b5 24 ♘d2 ♖d5 25 c4 ♖dd8 26 cxb5 cxb5 27 ♘f3 ♖d5 28 ♘d4 ♖ee5 29 ♖d2 ♕d7 30 ♖c1 b4 31 h3 ♘e4 32 ♖dc2 ♖xd4 33 ♖c7 ♕d5 34 ♗xd4 ♕xd4 35 ♖xg7+ ♗xg7 36 ♖c8+ ♔f7 37 ♕h5+ ♔e7 38 ♕e8+ ♔d6 39 ♖c6+ ♔d5 40 ♕d7+ Black resigns.

Position after 34...♕d5xd4

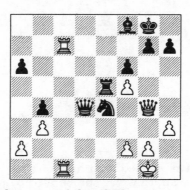

**35 ♖c7xg7+!**

What is a combination in the game of chess? There are many opinions and nobody has a uniform answer. Sometimes I think that a combination consists of a – not too long – series of moves with material sacrifices which contain a high element of risk. But if there is a risk why is such a string of moves considered to be forced? Because it only *appears* to be forced but in reality a combination contains many possibilities which are almost impossible to see while playing a tense game and which are, during subsequent analysis in a more relaxed atmosphere, still difficult to find.

The move 35 ♖xg7+ was the key move in White's combination. When I executed this move, almost without thinking, Svetozar Gligorić gave a start!

Why do I only speak for White? Black also strived to achieve this position and that is why he made his preceding sharp moves rather quickly. And why not; it appears that his king is completely safe. The move of the rook to g7 was a complete surprise for Black. He had completely overlooked that the pawn g7 might be weak. In fact this is not quite true. It is the bishop on g7, pinned by the white queen, which is weak.

By the way, in extreme time-trouble I missed a mate in one move with 39 ♕d8. However, much more importantly, Gligorić missed 33...♘c3!! after 33 ♖c7.

## (37) Bronstein,D – Winiwarter,L

International Tournament,
Krems, 1967
*[C86] Spanish Opening*

1 e4 e5 2 ♘f3 ♘c6 3 ♗b5 a6 4 ♗a4 ♘f6 5 0-0 ♗e7 6 ♕e2 b5 7 ♗b3 d6 8 c3 ♗g4 9 h3 ♗h5
10 d3 0-0 11 ♘bd2 ♘a5 12 ♗c2 c5 13 ♖e1 ♘d7 14 g4 ♗g6 15 ♘f1 f6 16 ♘e3 ♗f7 17 d4
♖e8 18 d5 c4 19 b4 ♘b7 20 a4 ♕c7 21 a5 g6 22 h4 ♔g7 23 ♔g2 h6 24 ♖h1 ♖h8 25 h5 g5
26 ♘f5+ ♔f8 27 ♗e3 ♖h7 28 ♘d2 ♗g8 29 f3 ♗d8 30 ♗f2 ♗e7 31 ♖hc1 ♗d8 32 ♕f1 ♗f7
33 ♗d1 ♗e8 34 ♗e2 ♖c8 35 ♘e3 ♘b8 36 ♘dxc4 bxc4 37 ♘xc4 ♗b5 38 ♘b6 ♗xe2 39 ♕xe2
♗e7 40 ♘xc8 ♕xc8 41 ♗a7 ♘d7 42 ♕xa6 Black resigns.

Position after 35...♘d7-b8

**36 ♘d2xc4!**

It is not too difficult to judge this position. Three of White's pawns have crossed into enemy territory where they have blocked Black's pawns and are exerting control over the squares b6, c6, e6 and g6. However, it is not easy for White to approach the black pieces neither diagonally or vertically. Only if... Maybe an advantageous exchange of a knight against two pawns is possible. The black pieces are very restricted in their movements and are impeding each other. A big advantage in space can often change... into a decisive attack if the sacrifice of a piece succeeds in creating mobile pawns.

This is precisely what White did in this game. Black resigned because his pawn chain a6-b5-c4 had completely disintegrated. White's pawns on a5, b4 and c3 were ready to march forward for a decisive attack. White was in no hurry to sacrifice the knight but the square c4 was the only square where it could be done. White prepared the breakthrough first by closing the centre with 18 d5 and then both wings with 21 a5 followed by 25 h5. If you play through the game attentively you will notice that, before taking decisive action, White reorganised his troops very efficiently.

# (38) Bronstein,D – Tal,M

USSR Team Championship,
Riga, 1968
*[C32] King's Gambit Declined*

1 e4 e5 2 f4 d5 3 exd5 e4 4 d3 ♘f6 5 dxe4 ♘xe4 6 ♘f3 ♗c5 7 ♕e2 ♗f5 8 ♘c3 ♕e7 9 ♗e3 ♘xc3 10 ♗xc5 ♘xe2 11 ♗xe7 ♘xf4 12 ♗a3 ♘d7 13 0-0-0 ♗e4 14 ♘g5 ♗xd5 15 g3 ♗xh1 16 gxf4 c5 17 ♗c4 ♗c6 18 ♘xf7 b5 19 ♘d6+ ♚e7 20 ♘xb5 ♖hf8 21 ♘d4 ♗g2 22 ♘e6 ♖f5 23 ♖g1 ♗e4 24 ♘c7 ♖d8 25 ♖xg7+ ♚f6 26 ♖f7+ ♚g6 27 ♖e7 ♘f6 28 ♘e6 ♖c8 29 b3 ♖h5 30 ♘g5 ♗d5 31 ♗d3+ ♚h6 32 ♗b2 c4 33 ♗f5 c3 34 ♗xc8 cxb2+ 35 ♚xb2 ♖xh2 36 ♖xa7 ♖f2 37 ♖a4 ♚g6 38 ♖d4 h5 39 a4 h4 40 a5 ♗g2 41 a6 ♘h5 42 ♗b7 ♘xf4 43 ♖xf4 Black resigns.

Position after 14...♗e4xd5

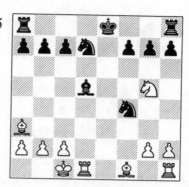

**15 g2-g3!**

There are eleven pawns on the board which have yet to make a move! Apparently the pieces were so fascinated that they denied the pawns the right to move. The other five pawns have disappeared and we must assume that they played one or the other role. What do we have on the board now? An open file right through the middle of the board and a black king who got stuck in the centre. Yes Black's position does not look good. White was searching for a beautiful move, hopefully decisive, and his attention was drawn to the move 15 g3. After the black bishop took the rook on h1 and the white pawn took the knight on f4, White had good hopes to win in a few moves. After all, he has two strong bishops, a knight in an attacking position and the possibility to give a check with a rook. What else can one wish for? Alas, in reality a long drawn-out battle took place. Credit should be paid to the move 16...c5. It eliminated the power of White's a3-bishop.

It is difficult to explain why Mikhail Tal did not play 20...♗xb5 21 ♗xb5 ♖d8. Does White really have an advantage after 22 ♗xd7 ♖xd7 23 ♗xc5+?

Instead of 17 ♗c4? White should have tried, 17 ♘xf7 ♖f8 18 ♘g5 with many new threats.

# (39) Polugayevsky,L – Bronstein,D

39th USSR Championship,
Leningrad, 1971
*[A34] English Opening*

1 c4 c5 2 ♘f3 ♘f6 3 ♘c3 d5 4 cxd5 ♘xd5 5 g3 g6 6 ♕b3 ♘b4 7 ♘e4 ♗g7 8 ♘xc5 ♕a5 9 a3 ♘4c6 10 ♕c4 b5 11 ♕h4 b4 12 ♘d3 ♗a6 13 ♗g2 ♗d7 14 0-0 ♖c8 15 ♘de1 ♘c5 16 ♘c2 ♘b3 17 ♖b1 ♕c5 18 ♘e3 ♘cd4 19 ♘xd4 ♘xd4 20 ♖e1 ♗b5 21 axb4 ♕d6 22 ♗f1 0-0 23 ♕e4 e6 24 b3 f5 25 ♕f4 e5 26 ♕g5 ♗xe2 27 ♗g2 ♗d3 28 ♖a1 e4 29 ♘c4 ♕d7 30 ♗b2 ♗xc4 31 ♗xd4 ♗xd4 32 bxc4 ♗xa1 33 ♖xa1 ♖xc4 34 ♗f1 ♖d4 35 ♖a6 ♔g7 36 b5 ♖xd2 37 ♖xa7 ♕xa7 38 ♕xd2 ♕b6 39 ♕c3+ ♕f6 40 ♕c5 ♖d8 41 b6 ♕d6 42 ♕c3+ ♕d4 43 ♕c6 ♖d6 44 ♕c7+ ♖d7 45 ♕c6 ♕d6 46 ♕c3+ ♕f6 47 ♕c5 ♖b7 48 ♕b5 ♕xb6 49 ♕e5+ ♕f6 White resigns.

Position after 7 ♘c3-e4

**7...♗f8-g7!**

When a chess player thinks about his next move he always considers what would be his opponent's move if it was his turn. In this position the answer is simple: 8 ♕c3 of course, to attack the rook on h8. If the rook moves Black loses the privilege of castling. To play 8...f6 is not the solution as the pawns no longer form a defensive shield for the king should Black wish to castle. If we intend to castle the natural move for Black is now 7...♗g7. But then White will take the pawn on c5 with his knight. That's no disaster! The knight has already lost two tempi and will lose another one. Then the knight must make one or two further moves to get back to his own camp. Meanwhile Black can castle and prepare an attack. That is exactly what happened in this game. Let this be a lesson: don't waste tempi.

When I prepared for this game I noticed that in his game with Semyon Furman, Lev Polugayevsky was going after the pawn on c5. Would he do it again? When he did I was very surprised. I was careful to avoid his home preparations and managed to win.

# (40) Pohla,H – Bronstein,D

### 1st Paul Keres Memorial Tournament,
### Tallinn, 1977
### [C91] Spanish Opening

1 e4 e5 2 ♘f3 ♘c6 3 ♗b5 a6 4 ♗a4 ♘f6 5 d4 ♗e7 6 0-0 0-0 7 ♖e1 b5 8 ♗b3 d6 9 c3 ♗g4 10 ♗e3 exd4 11 cxd4 ♘a5 12 ♗c2 c5 13 ♘bd2 cxd4 14 ♗xd4 ♘c6 15 ♘b3 ♖c8 16 h3 ♗h5 17 ♖c1 a5 18 ♗d3 ♘e5 19 ♖xc8 ♕xc8 20 ♗xe5 dxe5 21 ♗xb5 ♕e6 22 ♖e3 a4 23 ♗xa4 ♕a6 24 ♘bd2 ♗c5 25 ♖e1 ♕a7 26 ♖e2 ♗xf3 27 ♘xf3 ♗xf2+ 28 ♔h2 ♘h5 29 ♕d7 ♗g3+ 30 ♔h1 ♕a8 31 ♗b3 ♗f4 32 ♖c2 ♘g3+ 33 ♔g1 ♕a6 White resigns.

Position after 27 ♘d2xf3

**27...♗c5xf2+!**

When Paul Keres died, the tournament was renamed to honour him. He was one of my best friends and he had originally created this tournament. We all sorely missed him. My personal tribute to him was to play every day a different variation which he used to play himself.

In this game I played the Chigorin variation which Paul Keres often played against me with Black. Taking the pawns on f7 and f2 with check is a well-known theme. Here the f2 pawn is defended by the rook and the king. To take this pawn does not seem the right thing to do. In such cases the role of Black's other pieces must be looked at. Possibly they can be of assistance. After 27...♗xf2+ 28 ♖xf2 the rook is pinned by the queen on a7 and therefore the black knight can get away with taking the pawn of e4.

Now, with the combined forces of three black pieces, Black can start the attack on the white king. Taking on f2 renders the defence of the square g3 impossible as it was already weakened earlier by the move h3. In turn the black knight and bishop occupy g3 and are preparing the last move of the black queen.

David Bronstein's talent for chess was already evident in his childhood. His *curriculum vitae* resembles very much those of other famous Soviet grandmasters who received their first lessons in chess clubs which form part of the Palaces of Pioneers. His path started in Kiev and developed under the leadership of the experienced trainer A. Konstantinopolsky.

People began to speak about the 14-year-old Bronstein when he won a tournament in which six of the strongest adults from Kiev and six of the strongest schoolboys participated. A year later he shared the 2nd-4th prize in the Kiev adult championship and in 1940 he took 2nd place behind Boleslavsky in the championship of Ukraine. This success gave the young player the right to carry the title of master. It was then that I saw the games of Bronstein and I was very much impressed. Surely, at that time I could not guess that I was looking at games of the future challenger for the ultimate crown.

Several years passed and at the 13th championship of the Soviet Union I met David Ionovich at the chess board for the first time. Our game ended in a draw but it was a very lively game. In this tournament Bronstein occupied a very modest 15th place but managed to beat Mikhail Botvinnik. In the next championship he managed 3rd place and came close to the title of grandmaster.

The first ever Interzonal Tournament was held in 1948. A young player, who made his name not only by achieving good sporting successes but also by his bright individual style of play, was designated to play in this tournament. Bronstein played brilliantly and won the tournament without a single loss! He was awarded the title of grandmaster. At the 16th and 17th championship of the Soviet Union he shared first and second places.

It was during this period that the first qualifying tournaments took place under the auspices of the FIDE as they still do today. The first double round Candidates' Tournament took place in Budapest in 1950 with 10 players. Isaac Boleslavsky played superbly but faltered towards the end. Bronstein managed to catch him and they shared first and second place. The subsequent play-off was won by Bronstein who thereby obtained the right to cross swords with the World Champion. Botvinnik had brilliantly won his title during the famous tournament held in 1948 in The Hague and Moscow and was at the pinnacle of his chess career. Very few gave the young challenger much of a chance. The match itself however was a very tense and close struggle.

Bronstein was leading by one point with just two games remaining in the match, but in the 23rd game he was extremely unlucky, allowing the champion to equalise the score and to keep his title. It seems to me that this match was the most important competition in the chess life of Bronstein.

Bronstein then won the Interzonal Tournament of 1955, again without a single loss. He managed to win a most interesting game against second prize winner grandmaster Paul Keres. The game was recognised as the most beautiful game of the tournament (see page 50, T.F.).

David Ionovich owes his wide popularity not only to his successes and his strength but also because of his shining, innovative and original style of play. Bronstein distinguishes himself by his rich fantasy. When playing against him one always has to be prepared for the unexpected. His combinative talent shines very bright, his attacks, as a rule, are well-founded and for this reason are extremely dangerous.

David Bronstein's interest in the art of chess has many facets: his participation in tournaments and matches, in his analytical work, in his blitz chess games and even in his simultaneous exhibitions. Every time he appears on the stage he draws the attention of all, his friends, his admirers and his fellow-grandmasters, at home and abroad.

A particular bright page in his chess biography is undoubtedly his literary and journalistic activities. His book *International Grandmaster Tournament* (Candidates' Tournament, Neuhausen/Zürich 1953, T.F.) is a golden treasure in chess literature thanks to his profound knowledge of grandmaster chess and the ability to explain it in his original style to his readers. His numerous articles are refreshing and interesting. The grandmaster has a permanent column in the newspaper *Izvestia* communicating to his readers all the latest and most interesting events that are happening in the world of chess.

On the threshold of his 50th birthday he successfully participated in the Interzonal Tournament at Petropolis, achieving 6th place, proving that he was still amongst the strongest grandmasters in the world. The game that he played with grandmaster Ljubojević (see page 166 T.F.) was nominated for and awarded the brilliancy prize. The enterprising and attacking style that the Soviet grandmaster demonstrated in this game not only delighted the spectators but also all other participants in this tournament.

Together with all the admirers of chess art I congratulate David Ionovich Bronstein and I wish him with all my heart many more creative successes.

**Vasily Smyslov**, Ex-World Champion
and member of the editorial board of the magazine *64* where
this article was published for the first time in February 1974.

# 50 Games with Comments

## (1) Polyak,E – Bronstein,D

Adults & Juniors Tournament,
Kiev, 1938

*[D10] Slav Defence*

The Kiev tournament was intended to be an exhibition performance for both the best local adults (excluding masters) and the most promising young chess stars. I was then only a second category player, just 14 years old, but I played well, without fear, and managed to take first place, two points ahead of the second player. For this result I was promoted to the first category.

This game is very instructive. Just one month earlier Polyak had brilliantly taken first place in a strong tournament held in Moscow amongst the best first category players in the USSR. In this tournament he played several times successfully 4 ♕c2 in the Slav Defence. That is probably the reason why he was a little careless in our game.

Polyak often gave lectures at the Kiev Junior Chess Club and in this game of teacher against pupil he of course played for a win.

**1 d4**

By playing this move White is threatening to push the pawn to d5; at the same time the pawn on d4 keeps control of the squares c5 and e5 across the chessboard equator. This is the line that divides the battlefield.

**1 ... d5**

Black stops White's plan and simultaneously takes control of the squares c4 and e4.

**2 c4**

The battle for the centre has started.

**2 ... c6**

One of the best defences in this type of opening.

**3 e3 ♘f6**
**4 ♕c2**

The intention of this move is to prevent Black from developing his bishop to the square f5.

**4 ... g6**

With this move Black indicates he wishes to develop his bishop to f5 at any cost. At the same time he creates space for the other bishop on g7, after which Black is ready to castle.

**5 ♗d3 ♗g7**
**6 ♘f3 0-0**
**7 b3?**

White prepares to develop the bishop to b2 but more solid is first to put the white king into shelter by castling. It is interesting to see that during the whole game the white king forgets to castle and pays the price for this neglect. So remember, castle as soon as possible before starting any complications in the centre.

**7 ... c5!**

Very logical: Black attacks the centre pawn. The best reply for White would have been to castle.

**8 dxc5**

By accepting the pawn sacrifice White loses a vital tempo. In chess, but also in real day-to-day life, time can be very important.

Also possible was 8 cxd5 cxd4 9 e4 and if 9...♘xe4 10 ♗xe4 d3 11 ♕xd3 ♗xa1 12 ♘c3 and the black bishop cannot come back to g7, which weakens the black squares around the black king. For defensive purposes the black bishop may be more valuable than the white rook. With some imagination White can start a menacing attack.

**8 ... dxc4**
**9 ♗xc4 ♗f5**
**10 ♕e2 *(D)***
**10 ... ♘e4**
**11 ♘d4 ♘c6**

Of course it would be unwise to try to win a pawn by giving up the dark-squared bishop by playing 11...♗xd4 12 exd4 ♕xd4 13 ♗b2 ♕xc5 because White's bishops will become very strong and after 14 0-0 White has a promising attack.

Premature is 14 g4 ♗d7 15 ♕xe4 ♗c6 16 ♕f4 ♗xh1 17 ♕h6 because Black can close the diagonal by playing 17...e5.

| 12 | ♘xc6 | bxc6 |
|----|------|------|
| 13 | ♗b2  | ♕a5+ |
| 14 | ♔f1  |      |

Now the white king has lost the right to castle. This helps Black to continue the attack. It is not only the king that suffers but also the rook in the corner on h1 does not feel very comfortable. On the other hand the black rooks will become very active.

| 14 | ... | ♖ad8! |
|----|-----|-------|

The pawn is not going anywhere. The rooks should control the only open file on the board. White now tries to improve the position of his king and queen by exchanging the dark-squared bishops.

| 15 | ♗xg7 | ♔xg7 |
|----|------|------|

| 16 | ♕b2+ | ♔g8 |
|----|------|-----|
| 17 | b4   | ♕a4 |
| 18 | ♔e2  |     |

If White had predicted my reply he would of course have forced a draw by playing 18 ♘c3 ♘d2+ 19 ♔e2 (19 ♕xd2 ♕xb4 20 ♗xf7+ ♔xf7 21 ♖e1 ♖d3 22 ♖c1 ♖fd8) 19...♘xc4 20 ♘xa4 ♘xb2 21 ♘xb2 ♖b8 22 a3 a5 23 ♘d3 ♗xd3+ 24 ♔xd3 axb4 25 axb4 ♖xb4 26 ♖hb1.

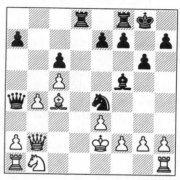

| 18 | ... | ♗e6! |
|----|-----|------|

This was Black's intention. Many years later a similar move was made by the young Bobby Fischer in his famous game with Donald Byrne.

| 19 | ♗xe6 |
|----|------|

This move is forced because if 19 ♕b3 then 19...♘xc5! 20 ♕xa4 ♗xc4+ winning a piece. 19 ♖c1 is unwise because of 19...♗xc4+ 20 ♖xc4 ♕d1 mate. Also, after 19 ♗d3 Black can play 19...♘xc5! If now 20 bxc5 then 20...♕g4+ and if 20 ♘c3 then 20...♘xd3 21 ♘xa4 ♘xb2 22 ♘xb2 ♖b8 23 a3 a5 and Black has a strong initiative.

| 19 | ... | ♕b5+ |
|----|-----|------|

Another possibility was 19...fxe6 20 f4 ♕b5+ 21 ♔f3 ♕d3 but the text move is simpler.

| 20 | ♔e1 | fxe6 (D) |
|----|-----|----------|
| 21 | ♘c3 | ♘xc3?    |

Black did not see the move 21...♘xf2! 22 ♕xf2 ♕d3 23 ♕b2 ♕xe3+, etc. Also good for Black is 21... ♘xf2! 22 ♘xb5 ♘d3+ 23 ♔d2, etc.

| 22 | ♕xc3 | ♖d3 |
|----|------|-----|
| 23 | a4   | ♕a6 |
| 24 | ♕c2  |     |

After the continuation 24 b5 ♖xc3 25 bxa6 ♖c2 26 ♖f1 ♖b8 the ending is also in Black's favour.

| | | |
|---|---|---|
| 24 | ... | ♖fd8 |
| 25 | h4 | ♕b7! |

Now that the black rooks have obtained full control of the d-file the main task for Black is to breach White's defences with his queen.

**26 ♖b1**

White should have played 26 ♔e2 and if 26...♕xb4 then 27 ♖hd1, but Black does better to answer 26...♕a6 and look for another way to win. Now there is no defence for the white king. Black wins easily.

| | | |
|---|---|---|
| 26 | ... | ♕d7 |

| | | |
|---|---|---|
| 27 | h5 | g5 |
| 28 | ♖h3 | ♖d2 |
| 29 | ♕b3 | ♖d3 |
| 30 | ♕c2 | ♕d5 |
| 31 | ♖g3 | |

If 31 ♔f1 then 31...♖d2 32 ♕c1 ♕d3+ 33 ♔g1 ♕e2 threatening ...♕xf2+ and ...♖d1.

| | | |
|---|---|---|
| 31 | ... | ♖d2 |
| 32 | ♕b3 | ♕f5 |
| 33 | ♖f3 | ♕e4 |

| | | |
|---|---|---|
| 34 | ♖c1 | ♖8d3 |
| 35 | ♖c3 | ♖d5 |
| 36 | b5 | ♕h4 |

**White resigns**

When the two kings returned to their initial positions we started to analyse and were both pleased with a good fight.

# (2) Belavenets,S – Bronstein,D

### 13th USSR Championship, Semi-Final, Rostov-on-Don, 1941

*[E67] King's Indian Defence*

In May 1941 I was finally awarded the title Master of Chess. At the age of 17 years probably the youngest master, not only in the USSR but in the whole world. At the same time I received an invitation to play in the Semi-Final of the Soviet Championship. This created a problem for me as I was in the last year of school and my final exams would coincide with this tournament.

Therefore the Director of the School boys Chess and Draughts Club, Semyon Jakovlevich Natov, requested permission from the authorities of the Kiev Educational Council for me to take my examinations within a fortnight instead of over the normal period of one month.

The teachers were kind to me and I easily passed all my exams on the different subjects. I received my diploma, filled in the application form for the Kiev University to study mathematics (together with languages my favourite subject) and arrived in Rostov-on-Don just in time for the first round.

Now I am not certain that I needed to hurry with my school examinations as war was in the air and in fact started 10 days later. This prevented me from entering the Kiev University but the desire to study mathematics never deserted me. Probably this is the reason why I like to play against computers and respect very much the people who write the programs.

| | | |
|---|---|---|
| 1 | d4 | ♘f6 |
| 2 | c4 | d6 |
| 3 | ♘c3 | e5 |

**4    ♘f3**

After 4 dxe5 dxe5 5 ♕xd8+ ♚xd8 6 ♘f3 ♘bd7 7 ♗g5 ♚e8 8 ♘b5 ♗d6 Black is fine. The pawn on e5 is stronger than the one on c4.

**4    ...    ♘bd7**
**5    g3**

A little stronger is 5 ♗g5 ♗e7 6 e3.

**5    ...    g6**
**6    ♗g2    ♗g7**
**7    0-0    0-0**

White is slightly better. His pieces are more developed.

**8    b3    ♖e8**
**9    e3    c6**

The key move in many variations of the King's Indian Defence. The pawn opens the way for the queen.

**10    ♕c2    ♕a5**

To prevent ♗a3 but also looking at f5 and h5 to put pressure on the squares d3, f3 and h3 which were weakened by the pawn moves to e3 and g3.

**11    a4    ♘f8**
**12    ♗a3    ♗f5**
**13    ♕b2**

If 13 e4 then 13...exd4.

**13    ...    ♖ad8**
**14    ♖fd1**

**14    ...    e4**

It is always useful to cross the equator with a centre pawn.

**15    ♘d2    ♘e6**
**16    b4    ♕c7**
**17    ♖db1**

White's pawn attack on the queenside looks dangerous.

**17    ...    ♕d7!**

A very clever move! After 18 b5 Black can answer 18...c5 and if then 19 b6, the reply is 19...a6.

**18    c5**

To prevent Black from playing 18...c5 himself.

**18    ...    ♘g5!**

But Black is not playing 18...d5 because he is planning to use this square for his knight.

**19    cxd6    ♗h3!**

Initiating a direct attack against the white king.

**20    ♗h1    ♕f5**
**21    ♘e2    ♘d5!**

All the white pieces are badly placed while the black ones are now in ideal positions. There is no defence against the threat 22...♗g4.

**22    b5**

If 22 ♘f4 then 22...♘xf4 23 exf4 e3 24 fxe3 ♖xe3 and wins.

**22    ...    ♗g4**
**23    ♚f1    ♘xe3+**
**24    ♚e1    ♘f3+**
**White resigns**

After the game my opponent, who was the Chairman of the Qualification Commission of the Soviet Chess Federation, was silent for a minute. Then he smiled and said to me: 'I see that we made the right decision when we promoted you to the rank of master.'

Many years later I heard that Sergey Belavenets had consulted with Vasily Smyslov on this matter, who had strongly recommended awarding me this title.

In January 1941 I sent a notebook to Moscow with 17 of my games played in the Ukrainian Championship where I qualified for the master title with 11½ out of 17.

By winning this game I passed another examination and so did the King's Indian Defence!

Several days after this game was played the tournament was stopped as the German troops crossed the frontier into the USSR.

Before we left we had a dinner together and Belavenets told me in a soft voice that he believed that he would not survive the war. Sadly I never saw him again as his premonition came true. He was killed on the battlefield on 7 March 1942 near Novgorod at the age of 32.

However, his chess career was continued by his daughter Ludmilla, a well-known children's chess teacher who also had a program on Soviet television for many years. She became the women's correspondence chess World Champion in 1993.

## (3) Tolush,A – Bronstein,D

13th USSR Championship, Moscow, 1944
*[E61] King's Indian Defence*

This game was played in the first round and was my first in a USSR Championship. Also it was my first tournament game in Moscow.

With my limited knowledge of openings I decided to stick to my favourite King's Indian Defence.

| 1 | d4 | ♘f6 |
|---|----|-----|
| 2 | c4 | d6 |
| 3 | ♘c3 | e5 |

| 4 | e3 | ♘bd7 |
|---|----|------|
| 5 | ♘f3 | g6 |
| 6 | ♗e2 | ♗g7 |
| 7 | b3 | 0-0 |
| 8 | ♗b2 | ♖e8 |
| 9 | ♕c2 | c6 |
| 10 | 0-0 | ♕a5 |

Preventing 11 ♗a3. It is easy to see that this game goes along the same track as the previous one with Belavenets.

| 11 | ♖fd1 | ♘f8 |
|----|------|-----|
| 12 | a3 | e4 |
| 13 | ♘d2 | ♗f5 |
| 14 | b4 | ♕c7 |
| 15 | ♘f1 | d5 |
| 16 | cxd5 |  |

A little premature. Also possible was 16 b5 with a4 and a5 to follow.

| 16 | ... | cxd5 |
|----|-----|------|
| 17 | ♕b3 | ♖ed8 |

I remember now that I was proud of myself that I resisted the temptation to move the rook from a8 to d8. The rook needs to be on a8 in case the a-pawn requires protection.

| 18 | ♖dc1 | ♕e7 |
|----|------|-----|
| 19 | a4 | h5 |
| 20 | a5 | h4 |
| 21 | ♗a3 |  |

If White wants to stop the advance of Black's h-pawn with 21 h3 then Black's plan could be 21...♗e6 and 22...♘h5 in order to threaten ...f5 and ...f4.

| 21 | ... | h3 |
|----|-----|-----|
| 22 | g3 | ♘8h7 |
| 23 | ♘d2 | ♘g5 *(D)* |

Black's play is classic: the h-pawn creates weaknesses in the position of White's

pawns and Black's pieces will try to find a passage through the white line of defence.

| 24 | b5 | ♕e6 |
|----|----|-----|
| 25 | ♘a4 | ♗g4 |
| 26 | ♕d1 | ♕f5 |
| 27 | ♗e7 | ♗xe2 |
| 28 | ♕xe2 | ♖dc8 |

One of the most difficult problems of playing chess is to co-ordinate attacking moves with defensive ones. It was necessary to stop the white rook from coming to the 7th rank.

| 29 | ♗xf6 | ♗xf6 |
|----|------|------|
| 30 | ♘c5 | b6 |
| 31 | axb6 | axb6 |
| 32 | ♖xa8 | ♖xa8 |
| 33 | ♘a6 | ♗e7 |

**34    ♔f1**

Despite time-trouble White avoids 34 ♖c6? ♗b4! 35 ♘f1 (35 ♘xb4 ♖a1+ 36 ♘f1 ♕f3) 35...♘f3+ 36 ♔h1 ♗d5 with the intention of playing ...♘e1, ...♘d3 and ...♗e1.

**34    ...                    ♖c8!**

Only now does the sleeping rook wake up and at precisely the right time comes actively into play.

Now White understood that the manoeuvre with the knight c3-a4-c5-a6 was in vain and it is not possible to protect both the g2 square and the c-file.

| 35 | ♕d1 | ♖xc1 |
|----|-----|------|
| 36 | ♕xc1 | |

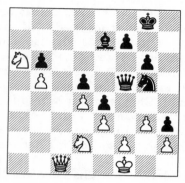

**36    ...                    ♔g7**

A natural looking move but more logical would have been 36...♘f3 37 ♘xf3 ♕xf3. If White plays 38 ♕c8+ ♔g7 39 ♕xh3 then Black can exploit the mobility of his bishop with 39...♕h1+! 40 ♔e2 ♕b1 41 ♕f1 (41 ♕d7 ♕d3+ 42 ♔e1 ♗a3) 41...♕xb5+ 42 ♔e1 ♕a5+ 43 ♔d1 ♕a1+ 44 ♔e2 ♕xa6+. Now the win is slightly more difficult.

| 37 | ♕c7 | ♗f6 |
|----|-----|------|
| 38 | ♘b4 | ♘f3 |
| 39 | ♘xf3 | ♕xf3 |
| 40 | ♔e1 | ♕h1+ |

**White resigns**

# (4) Bronstein,D – Botvinnik,M

### 13th USSR Championship,
### Moscow, 1944

*[C92] Spanish Opening*

This game was played in the fourth round. The tournament took place in June, exactly three years after the Semi-Final in Rostov-on-Don was stopped. In February 1944 I unexpectedly received an invitation to go from Stalingrad, where I was working on the reconstruction of a big steel factory, to Baku to play in the Semi-Final of the 13th Soviet Championship. In spite of losing the last two games I qualified for the Final.

In the first round of the Final I had won a beautiful game against Alexander Tolush, of course using my favourite King's Indian Defence.

Now I had to play against the most famous Soviet chess player, but this held no fears for me. The sharp combinative play of the Kiev Chess School was much more interesting than the classic strategy used by Mikhail Botvinnik. It should be mentioned that the best Ukrainian amateur chess player Dr Fedor Parfenovich Bohatirchuk defeated Botvinnik at least three times in their personal encounters. It was a severe blow to me when it was disclosed after the war that the Ukrainian ultra-nationalist Bohatirchuk was a staunch supporter of the German policies when they occupied Kiev. He escaped with the Nazi invaders when they were kicked out of the USSR by the Red Army and found a refuge in Canada.

Of course, young chess players preferred to follow the tactical and dynamic style of the amateur Bohatirchuk than the dull professional style of Botvinnik.

Amongst many others, it were Bohatirchuk's games which convinced me that the Spanish Opening is very strong for White and that the King's Indian Defence was perfectly playable for Black.

| | | |
|---|---|---|
| 1 | e4 | e5 |
| 2 | ♘f3 | ♘c6 |
| 3 | ♗b5 | a6 |
| 4 | ♗a4 | ♘f6 |
| 5 | 0-0 | ♗e7 |
| 6 | ♖e1 | b5 |
| 7 | ♗b3 | d6 |
| 8 | c3 | 0-0 |
| 9 | h3 | ♗e6 *(D)* |

A famous variation often played by Mikhail Chigorin.

| | | |
|---|---|---|
| 10 | d4 | ♗xb3 |
| 11 | ♕xb3 | exd4 |
| 12 | ♘xd4 | |

Opening the way for the f-pawn but better would have been 12 cxd4 d5 13 e5 ♘e4 14 ♘bd2 and if 14...♗b4 then 15 ♘xe4 ♗xe1 16 ♗g5! with wild complications.

| | | |
|---|---|---|
| 12 | ... | ♘xd4 |
| 13 | cxd4 | c5 |

| | | |
|---|---|---|
| 14 | dxc5 | |

Better was 14 ♘d2 and 15 ♘f3

| | | |
|---|---|---|
| 14 | ... | dxc5 |
| 15 | e5 | ♘d7 |
| 16 | a4 | c4 |
| 17 | ♕g3 | |

It looks as if White has a strong attack but my judgement was too optimistic. Botvinnik finds a good answer, probably part of his homework.

| | | |
|---|---|---|
| 17 | ... | ♖e8 |
| 18 | ♖d1 | |

A waste of time. More logical would have been 18 ♗h6 ♗f8 19 ♘c3 with an equal game. Now White's pieces on the queenside will not be developed for a long time.

| | | |
|---|---|---|
| 18 | ... | ♗h4 |
| 19 | ♕g4 | |

An invitation to take the pawn on e5 with the intention of playing 19...♘xe5 20 ♖xd8 ♗xf2+ 21 ♔f1 ♘xg4 22 ♖xa8 ♖xa8 23 hxg4 but Black can play much better – 21...♖axd8 22 ♕e2 (or 22 ♕f5) 22...♗g3. These simple variations I missed when I put my rook on d1.

After 19 ♕f4 Black plays 19...♕e7 20 g3 ♘xe5 21 gxh4 ♕b7 22 ♘d2 ♖ad8 with a strong attack.

| 19 | ... | ♗xf2+ |

A strong move. Now White should give up all his ambitions and fight for a draw.

| 20 | ♔xf2 |

If 20 ♔f1 then Black has the strong reply 20...f5! For example: 21 ♕xf5 ♖f8 22 ♕xd7 (22 ♕e6+ ♔h8 23 ♖xd7 ♕h4 with a strong attack) 22...♗d4+! and if 21 ♕f3 then 21...♗b6 22 e6 ♖xe6 23 ♖xd7 ♕xd7 24 ♕xa8+ ♖e8 25 ♕f3 ♕d4, etc.

| 20 | ... | ♘xe5 |
| 21 | ♖xd8 | ♘xg4+ |
| 22 | hxg4 | ♖axd8 |

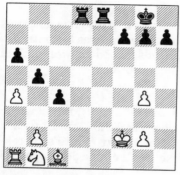

The sky has cleared and we have an unusual position. What is the correct plan for White? If 23 axb5 axb5 24 ♘c3 b4 25 ♘e2 ♖a8 then the black pawns have great mobility. Therefore White decides to stop them.

| 23 | axb5 | axb5 |
| 24 | ♗d2 | ♖d3 |
| 25 | ♖a5 | ♖b3 |
| 26 | ♗c1 |

Of course not 26 ♗c3 because after 26...b4 27 ♘d2 bxc3 28 ♘xb3 cxb2 29 ♘d2 c3 30 ♘b1 c2 and White cannot stop Black from queening.

| 26 | ... | f6 |
| 27 | ♖a3 | ♖d3 |
| 28 | ♖xd3 | cxd3 |
| 29 | ♗e3 |

Now that the black queenside pawns cannot make any progress they are not so strong but still, Black has the initiative. I guess that Botvinnik was very surprised by my accurate defensive moves. I wish I had played this quality of endgame after the adjournments during my match in 1951. Botvinnik repeated for many years that he saved his title only because I was very bad in simple endgames.

| 29 | ... | ♖e4 |

With the clear desire to win in a few moves. Much stronger and also more logical looks the simple move 29... ♔f7 to bring the strongest piece on the board into play. Then Black has the choice of playing ...g5, ...♔g6 and ...h5 or to bring the king closer to the centre with ...♔f7-e6-d5. I am not certain that, with my limited experience of tournament play, I would have found the best defence. And, one might ask, is it at all possible to stop the black king from coming to d5?

| 30 | ♔f3 | ♖b4 |
| 31 | ♗c1 | g5 |
| 32 | g3 | ♖c4 |
| 33 | ♗e3 |

White has successfully created a fortress on the queenside and the best for Black was to accept a draw by repetition of moves: 33...♖b4 34 ♗c1 ♖c4 etc. In time-trouble Botvinnik makes a sharp move which gives both sides a passed pawn but the white one will turn out to be the stronger of the two.

| 33 | ... | h5?? |
| 34 | gxh5 | g4+ |
| 35 | ♔f2 | ♖c2+ |
| 36 | ♘d2 | ♖xb2 |

Botvinnik judged this position as better for Black because of the possibility of playing ...b5-b4-b3-b2-b1♕. However, it

is obvious that he completely overlooked White's next move. He must have forgotten that the pawn on g4 had left g5 and no longer controlled the f4 square.

| 37 | ♗f4 | ♖a2 |
|----|-----|-----|
| 38 | ♔e3 | ♖a3 |
| 39 | ♔d4 | ♔f7 |
| 40 | ♔e4? | |

Losing a vital tempo. 40 h6 immediately was better.

| 40 | ... | b4! |
|----|-----|-----|
| 41 | ♔d4! | |

At this point the game was adjourned. What was Botvinnik's sealed move?

There were two considerations: if Black plays 41...♖c3 then it looks like a draw but after 41...♖a5 White has good chances. Even now, many years later, I am not certain whether Botvinnik was playing for a win or for a draw. The logical plan for Black is to attack the bishop on f4 with his rook. Then I can't see how White can make any progress.

| 41 | ... | ♖a5 |
|----|-----|-----|
| 42 | h6 | ♖b5 |
| 43 | ♔c4 | ♖b6 |

| 44 | ♔c5 | |
|----|-----|-----|

If instead 44 ♔xd3 then 44...b3 45 ♔c3 b2 46 ♔c2 ♖b5 leading to an easy draw for Black.

| 45 | ... | ♖b7 |
|----|-----|-----|
| 45 | ♘b3 | ♔g6 |
| 46 | ♔c4 | ♖b6 |
| 47 | ♘c5 | ♔h7 |
| 48 | ♔b3 | |

Now all Black's pawns are stopped and the black rook is passive. The black king must prevent the white pawn from making the journey h6-h7-h8♕.

| 48 | ... | d2 |
|----|-----|-----|
| 49 | ♗xd2 | ♖d6 |
| 50 | ♗f4 | ♖d1 |
| 51 | ♘e4 | ♔g6 |
| 52 | ♘f2 | ♖b1+ |

If 52...f5 then White obtains the e5 square for his knight, winning easily.

| 53 | ♔c2 | ♖a1 |
|----|-----|-----|
| 54 | ♔b2 | ♖a3 |

| 55 | ♘xg4 | ♖c3 |
|----|------|-----|
| 56 | ♘e3 | ♖d3 |
| 57 | ♘c2 | ♖d8 |

| 58 | ♘xb4 | ♚f5 |
| 59 | ♘c6 | ♖d7 |
| 60 | ♚c3 | ♚e4 |
| 61 | ♚c4 | ♚f5 |
| 62 | ♘d4+ | ♚e4? |

The black king neglected his task (see the comment on move 48). There was no need for him to be so active. After 62...♚g6, despite the fact that Black has lost three pawns, it is still not clear how White can win. After Botvinnik's mistake in this simple endgame, White wins in two moves with a short but nice combination.

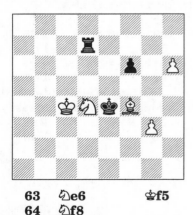

| 63 | ♘e6 | ♚f5 |
| 64 | ♘f8 | |

After having made this move I went away to get a cup of tea. When I came back I could not find my table, Botvinnik was nowhere to be seen. I asked the arbiter what had happened. He said that Black had resigned in the meantime and that they had prepared our table and board for two other players to continue an adjourned game from a previous round!

It is obvious why Botvinnik decided to resign: 64...♖d8 65 ♗d6 ♖xd6 66 h7.

# (5) Bronstein,D – Kan,I

14th USSR Championship,
Moscow, 1945
*[C34] King's Gambit Accepted*

There is not a single true chess player in the world whose heart does not beat faster at the sound of the words: 'gambit play'.

In the first instance our delight is for the legendary King's Gambit. Why so much delight? No other opening offers such wide possibilities for creative initiative; in no other opening are so many difficult problems created in the very first moves; no other opening moves allow the players to confront each other straight away in open fighting and to unfold the battle over the whole of the board. In many branches of the King's Gambit both players feel the desire to try and win not by collecting material but by using the strength of their own imagination.

It is no secret that any talented player must be in his soul an artist and what could be dearer to his heart and soul than the victory of the subtle forces of reason over crude material strength! My love for the King's Gambit can be seen in precisely those terms.

| 1 | e4 | e5 |
| 2 | f4 | exf4 |
| 3 | ♘f3 | ♘f6 |
| 4 | e5 | ♘h5 |
| 5 | d4 | g5 |

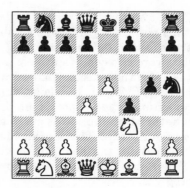

| 6 | h4 | |

A typical attack in this opening, but it was better to start with the move 6 g4 and only after 6...♞g7 then 7 h4 and the white attack will be very promising. Now the game enters a wild combinative stage favouring Black.

| 6 | ... | g4 |
| 7 | ♞g5 | d5! |

An excellent move and a classical reaction in this opening, opening a window for the bishop on c8 and stopping White's intention of taking the pawn on g4 with his queen. Also ...♞g3 now becomes a genuine threat.

**8 exd6**

White eyes the diagonal c4 to f7 for his bishop but it was better to play 8 ♝e2 ♞g3 (8...h6 9 ♞xf7 ♚xf7 10 ♝xg4 ♞g3 11 ♜h3) 9 ♝xg4 ♞xh1 and now White has the choice, either to play 10 ♝xf4 or the sharp 10 ♝h5!

| 8 | ... | ♝xd6 |
| 9 | ♝c4 | ♞g3 |
| 10 | ♝xf7+ | ♚f8 |

| 11 | ♝e6 | ♛e7 |
| 12 | d5 | ♞xh1 |

If 12...h6 then 13 ♛d4 ♛g7 14 ♝xc8 ♛xd4 15 ♞e6+ ♚e7 16 ♞xd4 ♜xc8 17 ♜g1 and Black is a pawn up but White has compensation. With hindsight it was better to play 11...h6 instead of 11...♛e7.

**13 ♛xg4 h6 (D)**

Today this position looks unusual but in the last century it was quite normal for White and Black to play like this. Black has defended cleverly and now the best solution for White is to play 14 ♛f5+ ♚e8 15 ♛g6+ ♚f8 16 ♛f5+ forcing a draw. It is dangerous for Black to play 14...♚g7 because after 15 b4 ♝xb4+ 16 ♚d1 ♞f2+ 17

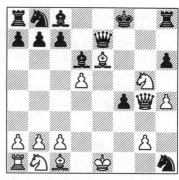

♚e2 ♛f6 18 ♝b2 or 17...hxg5 18 ♝b2+ ♚h6 19 ♝f6 the white attack becomes irresistible. It would have been a pity to finish the game so early. Therefore White decides to go for a new adventure.

The plan is clear: whoever succeeds first in awakening his sleeping queenside will be the winner of the battle.

Also we should not forget that at the expense of a rook White has a strong, well protected piece on e6 but his king is rather exposed.

| 14 | ♞e4 | ♝xe6 |
| 15 | dxe6 | ♞c6 |

If 15...♛g7 then 16 ♛f5+ ♚e7 17 ♞bc3 ♞c6 18 ♞d5+ ♚d8 19 ♞xd6 cxd6 20 ♝xf4 ♜f8 21 ♛d3.

| 16 | ♝xf4 | ♛g7 |
| 17 | ♝xd6+ | cxd6 |
| 18 | ♛f4+ | ♚e8 |
| 19 | ♞bc3 | |

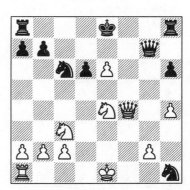

Black has a rook more and looking at the position we have the impression that the win is easy for Black. After for instance: 19...0-0-0 (of course not 19...♛e5 20 ♛f7+ ♚d8 21 ♛d7 mate) 20 0-0-0 ♛e5

21 ♕xe5 dxe5 (21...♘xe5 22 ♘d5) 22 ♖xh1 ♖he8 23 g4 ♖xe6 Black has stopped White's attack. But have we forgotten that the black king has already moved: ...♔e8-f8-e8 and lost the right to castle? This is why the 'lazy knight' appearing on c3 still keeps the position unclear.

| 19 | ... | ♖f8 |
|----|-----|-----|
| 20 | ♕e3 | ♕d4 |
| 21 | ♕xd4 | ♘xd4 |
| 22 | 0-0-0 | ♘f2 |

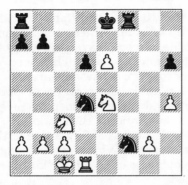

Black's knights are very active. White has to find a good move to retain chances of a draw. By now both players were in serious time-trouble: about 18 moves had to be made in two minutes. In such cases the younger player is always luckier.

| 23 | ♘xd6+ | ♔e7 |
|----|-------|-----|
| 24 | ♖xd4 | ♖ad8 |
| 25 | ♘db5 | a6 |
| 26 | ♖xd8 | ♖xd8 |
| 27 | ♘c7 | |

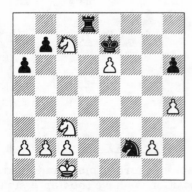

Suddenly the white pawn on e6 becomes very strong. This is the result of the 'positional' move 25...a6. After 25...♖xd4 26 ♘xd4 ♖d8 27 ♘ce2 ♘e4 28 c3 ♖f8 Black is still somewhat better but the logical result would probably be a draw.

| 27 | ... | ♖d4 |
|----|-----|-----|
| 28 | ♘3d5+ | ♔d6 |
| 29 | c3 | ♖e4 |
| 30 | e7 | ♘g4 |

| 31 | e8♕ | ♖xe8 |
|----|-----|------|
| 32 | ♘xe8+ | ♔xd5 |

It is remarkable that this wild opening has transformed into a simple knight ending with two extra pawns for White.

| 33 | ♔d2 | ♔e5 |
|----|-----|-----|
| 34 | ♘g7 | ♘f6 |
| 35 | ♔e3 | ♘d5+ |
| 36 | ♔f3 | |

**Black resigns**

Half a century later I still have fond memories of my opponent. He had played in tournaments with Dr Emanuel Lasker, Jose Raul Capablanca, Dr Max Euwe and Rudolf Spielmann.

When the traditional match Ukraine vs. Moscow was played in Kiev in 1937 I went with the other boys to the station to meet the Moscow team. We were very proud to walk with them through many streets to take them to their hotel.

Later we played some very good games and had many interesting conversations. For some time Kan was vice-president of the Central Chess Club.

This game was played one month after the war was over and many chess enthusiasts, most of them still in army uniforms, filled the theatre. I felt obliged to play as sharply as possible to fulfil the wish of the audience to see good romantic chess.

## (6) Bronstein,D – Goldberg,G

14th USSR Championship,
Moscow, 1945
*[B72] Sicilian Defence*

My opponent in this game was a fine positional player who had known Botvinnik since childhood and they were life-long friends. In one of his books Botvinnik says that Goldberg helped him in the second half of his match with Salo Flohr which started disastrously (Flohr +2) but ended in a draw: +2-2=8. Flohr, who used to lose on average one game each year, suddenly lost two in one week! There must have been a reason for this and there was! Goldberg's help was instrumental in finding a shop where Flohr could 'buy' a beautiful fur coat very cheaply!

Goldberg was also Botvinnik's second during the return match against Smyslov in 1958. In game 15 of that match, in a totally winning position, Botvinnik 'forgot' his clock and lost on time. Goldberg was very surprised. I asked him why he had not tried to draw Botvinnik's attention to the clock by making a noise or a gesture. He told me that he had so much faith in Botvinnik that he was convinced that he would make a move in time!

| 1 | e4 | c5 |
| 2 | ♘f3 | d6 |
| 3 | d4 | cxd4 |

In principle, it is unwise to exchange a pawn in the centre for one on the flank but White has the compensation of being able to put a knight in the centre.

| 4 | ♘xd4 | ♘f6 |
| 5 | ♘c3 | g6 |

The Dragon, one of the most controversial variations of the Sicilian. Black creates a safe home for the king but the pawns on e7 and d6 remain passive for a long time.

| 6 | ♗e2 | ♗g7 |
| 7 | ♗e3 | |

Also possible is 7 ♘b3 0-0 8 g4 ♘c6 9 g5 ♘d7 10 h4. I played this line in one of my games during the Ukrainian Championship in 1940 and also in my game with Viacheslav Ragozin in the 1944 USSR Championship. I still like this line but it is obviously very sharp and when one plays in a competition it is usually better to be a little prudent.

However, Black will start an attack in the centre and on the queenside, while White will not yet be fully able to exploit the opening of the h-file.

| 7 | ... | 0-0 |
| 8 | f4 | a6 |
| 9 | ♗f3 | ♕c7 |

In connection with ...a6 it seems better to play 9...e5 10 ♘de2 b5 here.

| 10 | ♘d5 | |

To exchange the knight on f6 which is defending h7.

| 10 | ... | ♘xd5 |
| 11 | exd5 | b5 |

| 12 | h4 | |

White starts the attack on the kingside as early as possible. Black has several ways to defend his position, so it is difficult to calculate all the consequences. White's aim is very clear: to open the h-file for the rook. Of course it is safer to play first 12 ♕e2, castle queenside and only then play h4. However, in White's position there is also a weakness, the pawn on d5, and White tries to distract Black's attention away from it.

| 12 | ... | ♘d7 |
| 13 | h5 | ♘b6 |

Still looking at the pawn on d5 and threatening to go to c4 but the knight is needed on f6 to defend h7. After 13...♘f6 White would have played 14 hxg6 hxg6 and 15 ♕d3 in order to play f5.

**14    c3**

Now the bishop is no longer required to protect the knight.

| 14 | ... | ♗b7 |
|----|-----|-----|
| 15 | hxg6 | hxg6 |

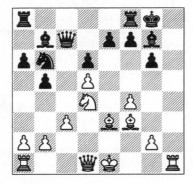

**16    f5**

The idea of this move is to open the diagonal for the bishop on e3. An experienced player knows that in such positions it may be useful to exchange bishops by playing ♗h6.

| 16 | ... | ♞xd5 |
|----|-----|------|

Both players have achieved their goals. White has opened the h-file and Black has captured White's weak pawn on d5. If 16...♗xd5 then White has a choice. Either 17 ♗h6 ♗xh6 18 ♖xh6 ♔g7 19 ♖xg6+ fxg6 20 ♗xd5 etc., or 17 fxg6 ♗xf3 18 gxf7+ ♔xf7 (18...♖xf7 19 ♞xf3) 19 ♞xf3 or 17 ♞xb5 axb5 18 ♗xd5 ♞xd5 19 ♕xd5 ♕c4.

| 17 | ♗xd5 | ♗xd5 |
|----|------|------|
| 18 | ♕g4 | ♖fc8 |
| 19 | ♕h4 | ♔f8 |
| 20 | ♗h6 | ♗xh6 |
| 21 | ♕xh6+ | ♔e8 |
| 22 | fxg6 | ♔d7 |
| 23 | ♕h3+ | |

To prevent the king from escaping to the queenside. If for instance now 23...e6 then 24 0-0 and White's rooks will become extremely powerful on f1 and e1.

| 23 | ... | ♗e6 |
|----|-----|-----|
| 24 | ♕e3 (D) | |
| 24 | ... | ♕c4 |

An active defence. If he has a chance Black could now play ...♖c5 and ...♖e5. Also ...b4 is a threat.

| 25 | a3 |
|----|----|

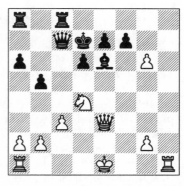

Preventing ...b4 and setting a trap. If now 25...a5 then 26 g7 b4 27 axb4 axb4 28 ♖xa8 ♖xa8 29 ♖h8 and White wins.

Also, after 25...a5 26 g7 ♖c5 White can play 27 ♖h8! ♖e5 28 ♕xe5 dxe5 29 ♖xa8 exd4 30 ♖d1! and wins.

| 25 | ... | fxg6 |
|----|-----|------|
| 26 | 0-0-0 | |

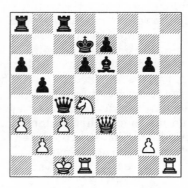

Castling is often an attacking move! Now White's rooks can improve their positions still further on e1 or h7 and the knight is unassailable on d4. 26...♖c5 is impossible due to 27 ♞xe6 ♕xe6 28 ♕xc5.

| 26 | ... | ♖f8 |
|----|-----|-----|

Certainly better would have been the continuation 26...♗g8 27 ♖he1 ♖e8 28 ♞f3 ♔c7 (28...♕a2 29 ♕b6 ♖ac8 30 ♞e5+) but Goldberg did not see the intention of White's b-pawn.

| 27 | b3 | ♕d5 |
|----|-----|------|
| 28 | ♖he1 | ♖f6 (D) |
| 29 | ♞xe6! | ♕xe6 |

If 29...♖xe6 then 30 ♖xd5 ♖xe3 31 ♖xe3.

| 30 | ♕b6 | ♖c8 |
|----|-----|------|
| 31 | ♖xe6 | ♖xe6 |
| 32 | ♔d2 | ♖c5 |

With one rook for the queen it is better to resign, even in time-trouble.

| | | |
|---|---|---|
| 33 | ♕b7+ | ♔e8 |
| 34 | ♖f1 | ♖ee5 |
| 35 | b4 | ♖c4 |
| 36 | ♕xa6 | ♔d7 |
| 37 | ♖e1 | ♖c6 |
| 38 | ♕a8 | ♖c8 |
| 39 | ♕xc8+ | ♔xc8 |
| 40 | ♖xe5 | dxe5 |
| 41 | c4 | bxc4 |
| 42 | ♔c3 | e4 |
| 43 | ♔xc4 | |

**Black resigns**

## (7) Bronstein,D – Katetov,M

Match Prague vs. Moscow,
Prague, 1946
*[C19] French Defence*

This was my first game as Moscow Champion so I was very excited and wanted to play my best. When I lost this game I was not surprised. On many occasions I used to lose in the first round, though eventually I managed to get rid of this habit.

Later on Katetov stopped playing chess and concentrated on his main interest in life – mathematics. His main scientific achievement is in topology, especially in the theory of dimensions. At the end of the fifties he was a rector at the Charles University of Prague. When his term as rector had finished, the leaders of the Czech Chess Union asked him to concentrate fully on chess and told him that in this way 'he could be more useful' for socialist Czechoslovakia than as a mathematician.

However, Professor Katetov stuck to his mathematics and organised colloquia with such topics as mathematical psychology and cosmology.

Since the early sixties Katetov has been a member of the Czechoslovak (now Czech) Academy of Science which was, and still is, a very honourable function. After the Velvet Revolution in 1989 he became a member of the collective leadership of the academy.

| | | |
|---|---|---|
| 1 | e4 | e6 |
| 2 | d4 | d5 |
| 3 | ♘c3 | ♗b4 |
| 4 | e5 | ♘e7 |
| 5 | ♘f3 | c5 |
| 6 | a3 | ♗xc3+ |
| 7 | bxc3 | ♕a5 |
| 8 | ♗d2 | c4 |
| 9 | h4 | |

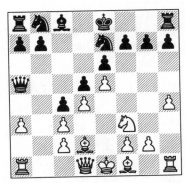

I start the attack as early as possible. Nowadays this move is very popular in this type of position.

| | | |
|---|---|---|
| 9 | ... | ♘bc6 |
| 10 | h5 | |

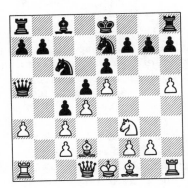

| 10 | ... | h6 |
| 11 | g4 | ♗d7 |
| 12 | ♘h4 | 0-0-0 |

White's plan was to launch an attack with f4 and f5 but it is not easy to realise this. My opponent, the Prague Champion, found the correct moment to start a counterattack with ...f6.

Probably better is 13 f4 f6 14 ♘f3 fxe5 15 ♘xe5 ♘xe5 16 dxe5. At a later stage of the game the white knight is out of play on h4.

| 13 | ♗g2 | f6 |
| 14 | f4 | fxe5 |
| 15 | fxe5 | ♖df8 |

| 16 | ♕e2 | ♘d8 |

Black is bringing the knight to a much better square. White must now decide where to put his king in safety.

| 17 | a4 | ♗e8 |
| 18 | ♗f3 | ♘f7 (D) |
| 19 | 0-0 | ♘g5 |
| 20 | ♗g2 | ♖xf1+ |
| 21 | ♕xf1 | ♘c6 |

With the obvious idea of taking the d4 pawn. The general opinion that bishops are better than knights does not apply in this position as the typical pawn chains in the centre have closed the diagonals.

| 22 | ♕f2 | ♘b8 |
| 23 | ♖f1 | |

A sharp move. White decided to leave the a-pawn without protection and increase the activity on the kingside.

It is worth mentioning that in the ensuing fight Black did not have time to capture the white a-pawn and this chess soldier became a witness to the resignation of his king.

| 23 | ... | ♘d7 |
| 24 | ♗xg5 | |

It is time to force the position. If for instance 24 ♕e1 then 24...♘b6 and when the knight takes a4 the pawn on c3 will be under great pressure. So White decided to also sacrifice the c3 pawn and to activate his knight on h4.

| 24 | ... | hxg5 |
| 25 | ♘f3 | ♕xc3 |
| 26 | ♘xg5 | ♖f8 |
| 27 | ♗f3 | ♗f7 |

| 28 | ♔g2 | |

Also possible was 28 ♗xd5 exd5 29 ♘xf7 with a draw by perpetual check after 29...♖xf7 30 ♕xf7 ♕g3+. White overestimates the strength of the centre pawns and underestimated the defensive powers of the black pieces.

| 28 | ... | ♗g8 |
| 29 | ♖h1 | ♘b8 |

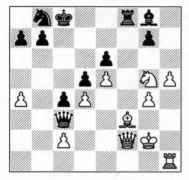

I am too lazy to count how often the knight has used this square for organising the defence.

**30 h6**

To activate White's rook. Now it looks as if White has a winning attack as the main battle will be around the e6 pawn. The black queen is out of play, Black's other pieces are passive on the last rank and the lone rook cannot create an adequate defence by itself.

| 30 | ... | gxh6 |
| 31 | ♖xh6 | ♘c6 |
| 32 | ♖f6 | ♖e8 |

**33 ♗xd5**

Starting a combination to keep the balance, or so White thinks. If White remains passive, e.g. 33 ♖f4, Black can start playing the pawns on the queenside.

| 33 | ... | exd5 |
| 34 | ♖f8 | |

White had this position in mind when he played 33 ♗xd5.

| 34 | ... | ♖d8 |

A clever defence.

| 35 | ♕f5+ | ♔c7 |

Stronger than 35...♔b8 36 ♖xd8+ ♘xd8 37 ♕f6 ♕a5 38 e6.

| 36 | ♖xg8 | ♖xg8 |

White thought that it was not possible to play this move.

| 37 | ♕f7+ | ♘e7! |

A totally unexpected move! Both players were in time-trouble. Alternatively, Black could have played 37...♔b6 and after 38 ♕xg8 taken the pawns on c2 (with check) and a4 and then pushed the c4 pawn but it seems that Black might have been worried about the advance of White's e-pawn.

| 38 | ♕xe7+ | ♔b8 |
| 39 | ♔f1 | |

An innovative defence! The knight on g5 was in danger. The immediate 39 ♘e6 loses after 39...♖xg4+.

| 39 | ... | ♕xd4 |
|----|-----|------|
| 40 | ♕d6+ | ♔a8 |
| 41 | ♘e6 | ♕d1+ |
| 42 | ♔f2 | ♕xc2+ |
| 43 | ♔g3 | ♕d3+ |
| 44 | ♔f2 | ♕d2+ |
| 45 | ♔f3 | ♕c3+ |
| 46 | ♔f4 | ♕c1+ |
| 47 | ♔f3 | ♕f1+ |
| 48 | ♔e3 | ♕g1+ |
| 49 | ♔d2 | c3+ |

After this tense battle Black is the first to give a decisive check.

| 50 | ♔d3 | ♕g3+ |
|----|-----|------|
| 51 | ♔c2 | ♕f2+ |

**White resigns**

Out of the next five games I scored 4½ points.

A month before this match the Soviet Chess Federation had created the possibility for the winning master playing in the Moscow Championship of 1946 to achieve a grandmaster norm. Before the last round I was a full point ahead of Vladimir Simagin and when I drew my game with Andor Lilienthal I became champion of Moscow. As I had already made my first norm by taking third place in the Soviet Championship in 1945 I was expecting to receive official ratification of the title of grandmaster.

However, the decision of the Federation was delayed but I was told before the Moscow half of the Moscow vs. Prague match, that if I were to win all six games I would receive the grandmaster title after all. Although I fulfilled this condition I was still not awarded the title!

Furthermore, two years later, the Soviet Chess Federation, together with other national federations, had to submit a list to FIDE of 30 candidates – their choice of participants to play in the Interzonal Tournament of 1948 in Saltsjöbaden, Sweden but my name was not on it!

It was apparent that someone with power in the high echelon of bureaucrats neither liked my character nor my style of play. (It seems to me that this 'bureaucrat', already at that time, thought that young Bronstein would pose a threat to him. T.F.).

## (8) Bronstein,D – Kottnauer,C

Match Prague vs. Moscow,
Prague, 1946
*[B50] Sicilian Defence*

Besides chess, Čenek Kottnauer had many other interests in life. He was especially good at water polo and was a member of the Czechoslovakian national team. In the fifties he moved to England where I met him a few years ago. We had a long and pleasant talk.

| 1 | e4 | c5 |
|----|-----|------|
| 2 | ♘f3 | d6 |
| 3 | c3 | |

This move is very logical. White is preparing d4 to create a strong pawn centre.

| 3 | ... | ♘f6 |

| 4 | ♗b5+ | ♗d7 |

| 5 | ♗xd7+ | ♕xd7 |
|---|--------|------|
| 6 | d3 | |

If White plays 6 ♕e2 then Black can answer 6...♕g4.

| 6 | ... | e6 |
|---|-----|-----|
| 7 | 0-0 | ♗e7 |
| 8 | ♕e2 | 0-0 |
| 9 | d4 | |

The two white pawns in the centre are more active than the black ones on d6 and e6.

| 9 | ... | ♘c6 |
|----|------|------|
| 10 | ♖d1 | cxd4 |
| 11 | cxd4 | d5 |

A classical attack against the white centre pawns, preventing White from playing 12 d5 himself and opening the diagonal for the bishop on e7.

| 12 | e5 | ♘e4 |
|----|-----|------|

| 13 | ♘e1 |
|----|------|

White violates the rule of fast development. Probably 13 ♗e3 and 14 ♘bd2 would have been somewhat safer but White tries to exploit the exposed position of the black knight on e4. This is a little naïve because before playing 12...♘e4 Black had obviously calculated that the knight would be safe there.

| 13 | ... | f6 |
|----|-----|------|
| 14 | f3 | ♘g5 |
| 15 | ♘c3 | fxe5 |

If 15...♘xd4 16 ♖xd4 ♗c5 17 ♗e3 fxe5 18 ♖dd1 ♗xe3+ 19 ♕xe3 ♘f7 20 f4 and White is winning.

| 16 | dxe5 | ♕e8 *(D)* |
|----|-------|------|
| 17 | f4 | |

The key move of White's plan. Now it seems that the black knight must retreat

to f7, but Black decided to play more sharply, trying to exploit the better development of his pieces.

| 17 | ... | ♕g6! |
|----|-----|------|

A very clever move. The main idea is 18 fxg5 ♗c5+ 19 ♔h1 ♖f2 20 ♕d3 ♘b4 21 ♕b5 (if 21 ♕xg6 then 21...♖f1 is mate) 21...♖af8 22 ♘f3 ♖8xf3 23 gxf3 ♕h5 and mate cannot be avoided. There is a common saying in chess that if a combination is very beautiful then in many cases it has a hidden refutation and that is exactly the case in this game.

| 18 | fxg5 | ♗c5+ |
|----|-------|------|
| 19 | ♗e3! | ♗xe3+ |
| 20 | ♕xe3 | d4 |
| 21 | ♖xd4 | ♘xd4 |
| 22 | ♕xd4 | ♕xg5 |
| 23 | ♘e4 | ♕h6 |
| 24 | ♘f3 | |

White has refuted Black's combination and successfully placed his knight in a central position. However, there are many open lines for Black's rooks, so White still needs to play carefully.

| 24 | ... | ♖ac8 |
|----|-----|------|

| 25 | ♘c3 | ♖cd8 |
|----|------|------|
| 26 | ♕e4 | |

It is always a pleasure to have the queen centrally placed like this.

| 27 | ... | ♖d7 |

| 27 | ♖f1 | a6 |
|----|------|------|
| 28 | h3 | |

A shelter for the king.

| 28 | ... | ♕f4 |
|----|------|------|
| 29 | ♕e2 | |

An exchange of queens is not in White's favour.

| 29 | ... | ♖c8 |
|----|------|------|
| 30 | ♔h1 | h6 |
| 31 | ♕f2 | ♕b4 |
| 32 | a3 | ♕c4 |
| 33 | ♖e1 | ♖f8 |

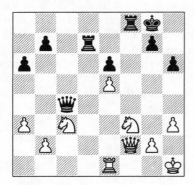

**34 ♖e4**

After several defensive moves White now transfers the rook to a strong position on g4 in order to start a direct attack on g7.

| 34 | ... | ♕c6 |
|----|------|------|
| 35 | ♔h2 | ♖d3 |
| 36 | ♕e2 | ♖fd8 |
| 37 | ♖g4 | ♕c7 |

**38 ♘e4**

The white knight eyes the outpost on g6 and simultaneously creates a new threat: 39 ♘f6+ ♔h8 40 ♕e4 gxf6 41 ♕g6 ♖3d7 42 ♕xh6+ ♖h7 43 ♕xf6+.

| 38 | ... | ♔h8 |
|----|------|------|
| 39 | ♘d6 | ♖d5 |
| 40 | ♕e4 | |

Note that e4 has been a transit square for all of White's attacking pieces.

| 40 | ... | ♖f8 |
|----|------|------|
| 41 | ♘h4 | ♖f1 |

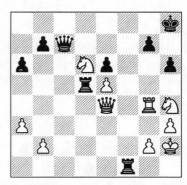

Black now intends to play ...♕b6 and ...♕g1+ with the possibility of a perpetual check. How can White meet this challenge?

**42 ♘e8**

Like this!

**Black resigns**

Many years later I am still pleased with my artistic discovery. If now 42...♕b6 then White will announce mate in three by sacrificing his queen: 43 ♕h7+ ♔xh7 44 ♖xg7+ ♔h8 45 ♘g6 mate.

# (9) Bronstein,D – Simagin,V

15th USSR Championship, Semi-Final, Leningrad, 1946
*[D94] Slav Defence*

(In the January issue 1947 of *Chess in the USSR* Botvinnik annotated this game. Of course his notes are of grandmaster quality but when Bronstein adds his thoughts and comments to those of Botvinnik one does indeed get quite a different view of the events that follow – T.F.)

| 1 | d4 | d5 |

| 2 | c4 | c6 |
|---|---|---|
| 3 | ♘f3 | ♘f6 |
| 4 | ♘c3 | g6 |

**Botvinnik**: It is well-known that this move is rarely played because of the reply 5 ♗f4. However, White prefers to play the Schlechter variation.

| 5 | e3 | ♗g7 |
|---|---|---|
| 6 | ♗d3 | 0-0 |
| 7 | 0-0 | c5 |

**Botvinnik**: This move was played by Paul Keres in his game with Georgy Lisitsin, Moscow 1940.

| 8 | dxc5 | dxc4 |
|---|---|---|
| 9 | ♗xc4 | ♘bd7 |
| 10 | e4 | ♘xc5 |

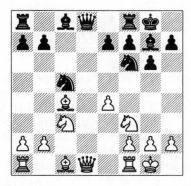

**11 e5**

**Botvinnik**: Also good was 11 ♕e2.

**11 ... ♘g4**

**Botvinnik**: If now 11...♕xd1 12 ♖xd1 ♘g4 then 13 ♗f4 ♗e6 14 ♘d5 ♔h8 15 h3 ♘h6 and White has the better chances.

**12 ♗g5**

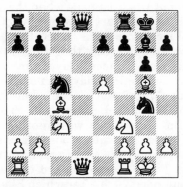

**Botvinnik**: One of several possibilities. The pawn on e5 limits Black's bishop and

knight on g4. Tempting was therefore 12 ♕e2 and after 13 h3 White would have had a clear advantage. Now, although Black can capture the disagreeable pawn, he gets a cramped position because of the weak pawn on e7 and the bad position of his queen.

**Bronstein**: Indeed, the development of the queen to e2 is very tempting but the bishop's move seemed even stronger to me. White selects the pawn e7 as a target and sacrifices the pawn on e5 to achieve that goal, opening the e-file for the rook. But the queen is better on d2 than on e2 because if the black bishop leaves g7 the square h6 will be an ideal place for her to start an attack.

**12 ... ♘xe5**

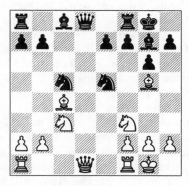

**13 ♘xe5**

**Botvinnik**: 13 ♕xd8 ♖xd8 14 ♗xe7 ♘xf3+ 15 gxf3 ♖d4 does not lead to any real advantage for White but the logical move 13 ♘d5! does. If Black replied with 13...♗g4 as Simagin intended, then not 14 ♘xe7+ ♔h8 15 ♘xg6+ fxg6 16 ♗xd8 ♖axd8 17 ♕c2 ♘xf3+ with a strong attack for Black but 14 ♗xe7 ♗xf3 15 gxf3 ♕c8 16 ♗xf8 ♕xf8 (16...♕h3 17 ♗e2 ♘xf3+ 18 ♗xf3 ♗e5 19 ♘f6+ and 20 ♘g4) 17 ♕e2 and it is doubtful if Black can obtain sufficient compensation for the exchange. So Black gets the chance to play the bishop to d6 to support e7 but his position remains difficult.

**Bronstein**: Yes, White would win the exchange but the resulting position after 13...♗g4 14 ♗xe7 ♗xf3 15 gxf3 ♕c8 16 ♗xf8 ♕h3 17 ♗e2 ♖xf8 18 f4 would have to be judged equal regardless of White's material advantage. A sharp fight looms ahead in which Black's chances are not worse.

The purpose of the attack on the e7 pawn is not to win the exchange (with White's pawn formation around his king destroyed) but to divert the black pieces away from vital positions: the rook from f8 defending f7 and the bishop from g7 protecting h6. With the move 13 ♘d5 this goal is only achieved partially.

| 13 | ... | ♗xe5 |
| 14 | ♘d5 | |

**Bronstein**: I could have grabbed material with 14 ♕xd8 ♖xd8 15 ♗xe7 ♖d4 16 ♗xf7+ ♔xf7 17 ♗xc5 ♖c4 18 ♗e3 ♗e6 but the outcome of the resulting endgame would be a draw, in spite of the extra pawn.

| 14 | ... | ♗d6 |
| 15 | ♖e1 | ♘e6 |

**Botvinnik**: Simagin defends very accurately. The natural 15...♗e6 would lead to a disaster after 16 ♗h6 ♖e8 17 ♕d4 f6 18 ♖xe6 ♘xe6 19 ♘f4.

| 16 | ♗h4 | ♗d7 |

**Bronstein**: Here the middlegame starts. Black has defended well and not only managed to fend off White's somewhat wild attack but to keep the extra pawn. From now on the fight will be extremely complicated.

| 17 | ♕d2 | ♖c8 |

**Bronstein**: Instead, Black could have played 17...♗c6 with the intention of exchanging the knight. And, although the variation 18 ♖ad1 ♗xd5 19 ♗xd5 ♔g7 20 ♗xb7 ♖b8 21 ♗f3 (21 ♗d5 ♗b4) would

lead to some advantage for White, it would relieve some of the pressure on the black position.

Black chooses a complicated and, for both players, difficult method.

| 18 | ♗b3 | ♔g7 |
| 19 | ♖ad1 | ♖e8 |

| 20 | ♘e3 | |

**Botvinnik**: White has strong pressure for the pawn; especially as the knight on d5 restricts Black's game. With 20 f4 White would have retained all the advantages. Instead, White chooses to retreat the knight from its centralised position. Black gets some breathing space and liberates himself from White's stranglehold.

**Bronstein**: I would like to point out that quiet defending moves along the lines of 18...♔g7 and 19...♖e8 are in the style of Wilhelm Steinitz who stated that the king is a strong piece which is quite capable of defending itself. Surely, in this case it is only a half-truth. The king controls the h6 square but what happens when the southwesterly winds start blowing along the diagonal from square a1 to h8? But are we not prepared to accept that the first check by the white queen, say from the b2 square, is lethal? Today I am of the opinion that a3, ♗a2 and b4 would have been a good plan to launch a strong attack.

At the time there was another move that I liked. It is quite possible that if I had had to play the game again, say in the sixties, I would have indeed chosen the recommended 20 f4 after which Black has to be careful not to fall into some sort of zugzwang!

Let's examine the variation 20 f4 ♗c6. The sacrifice 21 ♖xe6 immediately is not sound because of 21...fxe6 22 ♕d4+ ♔f7 23 ♘e3 ♕b6 24 ♕d2 ♗c5 25 ♗f2 ♖cd8 or after inserting the move 21 ♕c3+ ♔g8 22 ♖xe6 because of 22...♗xd5. If Black were to reply 20...♘c5 then thunderbolts and lightning would be the result: 21 ♕d4+ ♔g8 22 ♖xe7 ♗xe7 23 ♗xe7 ♖xe7 24 ♘f6+ ♔f8 (24...♔g7 25 ♘e8++ ♔h6 26 ♕g7+ ♔h5 27 ♘f6+) 25 ♘xh7+ ♔g8 26 ♘f6+ ♔f8 27 ♘h5 ♖e6 28 ♗xe6 ♘xe6 29 ♕h8+ ♔e7 30 ♕f6+ ♔e8 31 ♕h8+ ♔e7 (31...♘f8 32 ♘f6+ ♔e7 33 ♘g8+ ♔e8 34 ♕e5+ ♘e6 35 ♘f6+) 32 ♕f6+ ♔e8 and both players would have earned a well-deserved fighting draw!

After 19...♖e8 the black knight is no longer obliged to guard the pawn on e7. White must be ready for such a turn of events and prepare, to the best of his ability, an adequate reply to the move ...♘c5.

What changes in the position after such a plausible move? First, the white queen has the ideal square d4. Second, the bishop on b3 will get the diagonal a2-g8 (when the knight on d5 moves away!). Third, the influence of the white rook on e1 will be expanded all the way to e7! So the move ...♘c5 will give White solid advantages but even if Black does not intend to play like this, can we force him (to play ...♘c5)? We can! For this purpose the move 20 ♘e3 is excellent. In view of the threat 21 ♘g4 and 22 ♕h6+ Black must play 20...♘c5 (after all, he cannot play 20...h5? because of either 21 ♗g3 ♗xg3 22 hxg3 ♘c5 23 ♘f5+ gxf5 24 ♕g5+ ♔h7 ♗xf7 or 21 ♘c4 ♖xc4 22 ♗xc4).

**20 ... ♘c5 (D)**

**Bronstein**: We cannot break through Black's defence with quiet manoeuvres. In such positions a sacrifice is necessary. One has to be courageous to make a sacrifice as there always is an element of risk in it.

Botvinnik once said that a combination is a 'forced variation with a sacrifice'. Maybe so but this statement is not complete. One should add that a sacrifice is always risky.

What if the sacrifice is absolutely correct and the consequences can be calculated with mathematical precision? I just don't know. But if you think that a sequence of moves with sacrifices, which have no risk element at all in them, should not be called a combination but a 'technical manoeuvre' I will agree.

However, in practice this does not exist and do you know why? Because, if the sacrifice does not contain an element of risk, it is not a sacrifice but just a simple exchange. Maybe a very complicated one but still an exchange. I feel that my thoughts are not so straight forward and if sooner or later someone will challenge me on this then we'll start a theoretical discussion.

Let's get back to the position. Of all white pieces the bishop on b3 is 'predestined' for a sacrifice. I already had the idea of a sacrifice on f7 when there were still two knights – a white one and a black one – on this diagonal.

In short, we will sacrifice the bishop on f7! But when is the right moment? This is the most difficult part of any combination. A sacrifice should be made when all circumstances are favourable. But to create such circumstances one should try to be clever and use one's imagination. For instance, it would be nice if the black queen was in an active position, say on b6 or c7, so if the knight went to d5 White would win a tempo and open up a path to h6 for his queen. Then we can assume that a favourable situation has presented itself on the board.

That is precisely why I played 20 ♘e3 – to provoke the reply 20...♘c5. Then I played the bishop along the a2-g8 diagonal to see if Black would exploit the fact that the white knight no longer controlled the squares b6 and c7.

According to my understanding and feeling that is how every player who likes combinations thinks when an attack begins to take shape.

**21    ♗c4**

**Bronstein**: Does it not seem strange that the bishop moves to a square where it can be attacked and captured by a pawn? Surely 21 ♗d5 seemed safer. The threat 22 ♘c4 would be maintained and a new one – 22 b4 ♘a6 23 ♗xb7 – would be created. However, during a game players make their moves while there is a clock ticking beside the board and in order to create a little extra time to be able to check the upcoming sacrifice, White played ♗c4. Certainly Simagin now took some time to calculate the consequences of 21...b5 22 ♗xb5. However, this combination would not work after 22...♗xb5 23 ♘g4 ♚h8.

The move 21 ♗c4 enables Black to save the pawn on b7 but after 21... b5 22 ♗d5 f6 the fight for the square f7 would be over.

However, a new fight would then have erupted for the squares d6, e6 and f6, albeit of a quieter nature.

**21    ...            b5**
**22    ♗d5           ♛c7**

**Botvinnik**: Courageously played! Simpler and probably better would have been 22...f6 with a solid position and an extra pawn. Now White can, by sacrificing a bishop, launch an attack against the black king with all his pieces.

**Bronstein**: During his entire chess career Simagin did not only make courageous sacrifices of pawns and pieces, he also gratefully accepted them! That is why he did not choose the solid move 22...f6 but the trickier 22...♛c7 as if he wanted to say: 'Do you want to sacrifice? Good luck! Have you calculated all the variations? I have and I don't see a dangerous attack. I know that your queen can break through to h7 but I will play my bishop to g7 and your queen will not be able to take my pawn on g6. I will know how to defend this pawn from b6. And watch out! Don't underestimate my resources when I play my

rook to h8. It could well be that your queen will be trapped. But if you decide to sacrifice – go ahead!'

I understood Simagin's challenge and decided to go for the subsequent dazzling complications and combinations.

Running ahead of events, everything went exactly as Simagin had predicted in his secret thoughts. And, because of the annoying 'coincidence' that the black rook was on c8 and, unfortunately, not on a8, Black should have won this game.

Yet, dear reader, you will say that White won. But I, the cocky commentator trying to justify my point of view, say that it could have turned just the other way!

**23    ♗xf7!**

**Botvinnik**: Undoubtedly White's best chance.

**23    ...           ♚xf7**
**24    ♘d5**

**Bronstein**: Many years ago I started to note the time used for each move by my opponents and by myself and to draw graphs accordingly. Often I was asked what conclusions one can draw from these graphs. Many! Having analysed a great number of games like this, I am convinced that if a player takes a positional decision in a very complicated position, he almost always rechecks his previous calculations with every subsequent move and uses more and more time to do it.

The paradox is that if the same player takes a combinative decision he will not look at previous calculations anymore after a couple of moves and thus not recalculate variations over and over again. He will just courageously execute the subsequent moves, no longer relying on precise calculations but steering a course by his judgement of the position. He will execute the next two, three moves with great speed, following the chosen path.

And you, grandmaster, the reader will ask me, do you not have any doubts with each move? Do you not check more than once, hoping to find something that was previously overlooked?

Correct – I have this deficiency! But I speak not about me but about others. I am an exception to the general rule and I am fully aware of it, a bad exception!

**24    ...    ♕b8**

**Bronstein**: As Simagin is convinced that his previous calculations are perfect, he abandons the pawn on e7 by retreating his queen to b8. Obviously Black is certain that the variation 25 ♕h6 ♗xh2+ 26 ♔h1 (or 26 ♔f1) 26...♗e5 27 ♘xe7 ♗g7 28 ♕xh7 ♕b6 will lead to a better position for Black. But the pawn on e7 is the gate to the black king's fortress and the decision to abandon this pawn without a fight is wrong. While the move 24...♕b8 spoils Black's position, the ungainly looking retreat to d8 guarantees Black at least a draw and White has no better than to strive for a peaceful conclusion. The main variation is 24...♕d8 25 ♕h6 ♔g8 26 f4 ♖c6 (if 26...♘e6 or 26...♗e6 then 27 f5!) 27 ♔h1 (or 27 f5 immediately with the idea 27...♗xf5 28 ♗f6 exf6 29 ♖xe8+ ♕xe8 30 ♘xf6+) 27...♘e6 28 f5 ♘g7 29 f6 ♘f5 30 fxe7 ♗xe7 31 ♘xe7+ ♘xe7 32 ♕d2 ♖c7 33 ♕d6 recapturing the piece.

**25    ♕h6    ♗xh2+!**

**Botvinnik**: Black's position appears to be critical but Simagin finds an excellent counter chance. It appears that there is no other defence, e.g. 25...♘e6 26 ♖xe6 ♔xe6 (26...♗xe6 27 ♕xh7+ ♔f8 28 ♗g5) 27 ♕xh7 ♗c6 28 ♘xe7; or 25...♖h8 26 ♗xe7 ♗e5 27 ♖xe5 ♕xe5 28 ♗f6 ♕xf6 29 ♘xf6 ♔xf6 30 ♕f4+.

**Bronstein**: Yes, after 25...♘e6 26 ♖xe6 ♗xe6? 27 ♕xh7+ the result is clear but how to continue after 26...♔xe6! 27 ♕xh7 ♗c6 28 ♘xe7 ♖xe7 29 ♗xe7 ♖h8 here?

**26    ♔f1**

**Botvinnik**: Probably White did not like the continuation 26 ♔h1 ♗e5 27 ♕xh7+ ♔g7 28 ♘xe7 ♖h8 29 ♕xg6+ ♔f8 but without justification because by playing 30 g3 (30...♖xh4+ 31 gxh4 ♕f4 32 ♖xd7 ♘xd7 33 ♕e6, etc.) with the threat ♖d1-d5-f5+, White obtains an irresistible attack. However, in this variation Black can improve his play with 28...♖c6! and reach equality. White now fans the smouldering fire into a full blaze.

**Bronstein**: The move 26 ♔f1 can be easily explained. In the above variation given by Botvinnik, instead of 28 ♘xe7, White can play 28 ♖xe7+ ♖xe7 29 ♘xe7 but after 29... ♖h8 30 ♕xg6+ ♔f8 White can only dream of playing ♗f6.

Now this move, ♗h4-f6, will be possible because the bishop is not pinned as it would be if the king had been on h1.

**26    ...    ♗e5**

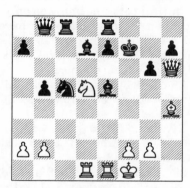

**27    ♘xe7**

**Botvinnik**: Too cautious. White cannot avoid taking the h-pawn anyway.

**27    ...    ♗g7**
**28    ♕xh7    ♕b6**

**Botvinnik**: Here Simagin was terribly unlucky. He had surmounted many hurdles, finding many difficult moves in order to reach a better position and now he loses all that with one move... Black did not want to separate himself from the g6 pawn but it was time to go for the counterattack.

Interestingly, 28...♖c6 would have given White the better chances after 29 ♗g3 but after 28...♕h2 White would find himself in almost insurmountable difficulties.

In any case Black would not have to lose the game, for example 29 ♕xg6+ ♔f8 30 ♗f6 ♕h1+ 31 ♔e2 ♕h6; or 29 ♖xd7 ♕h1+ 30 ♔e2 ♕xg2; or 29 f3 ♕h1+ 30 ♔f2 ♘d3+ 31 ♔g3 ♘xe1; or 29 ♖e3 (29 ♖e5 ♕h1+ 30 ♔e2 ♕xg2) 29...♕h1+ 30 ♔e2 ♗g4+ 31 ♖f3+ ♗xf3+ 32 gxf3 ♖xe7+.

**Bronstein**: When I played 27 ♘xe7 I was under the impression that I had discovered a combination of timeless beauty: 28...♕h2 29 ♕xg6+ ♔f8 30 ♖xd7! ♘xd7 31 ♕e6 with the deadly threats 32 ♕g8 mate and 32 ♘g6 mate. Black cannot thwart both threats. I especially like the variation: 31... ♕h1+ 32 ♔e2 ♕xh4 33 ♘g6 mate. Because of her desire and obligation to serve her king, the white queen is pinned! By the way, the move 28...♖c6 which Botvinnik mentioned can be met with 29 ♖e3 with the threat ♖f3+. Also his recommendation 29 ♗g3 loses in one move after 29...♕xg3. If I had known that my beautiful combination was only an illusion then I would certainly have preferred 27 ♕xh7+ instead of 27 ♘xe7. Then, after 27...♗g7 28 ♖xe7+ ♖xe7 29 ♘xe7, Black has no defence:

a) 29...♖h8 30 ♕xg6+ ♔f8 31 ♗f6 ♘e6 32 ♗xg7+ ♘xg7 33 ♕f6+ ♔e8 34 ♘g6 ♖h1+ 35 ♔e2.

b) 29...♕h2 30 ♕xg6+ ♔f8 31 ♗g3 ♕h1+ 32 ♔e2 ♕h6 33 ♕xh6 ♗xh6 34 ♘xc8 ♗xc8 35 ♖d8+.

c) 29...♕b6 30 ♘xc8 ♗xc8 31 ♖d8.

d) 29...♗f5 30 ♘xf5 gxf5 31 ♕xf5+ ♔g8 32 ♗e7 ♘a4 (32...♕c7 33 ♗xc5 ♕xc5 34 ♖d8+ ♗f8 35 ♕xc8) 33 ♕e6+ ♔h7 34 ♖d5 ♖c1+ 35 ♔e2 ♕h2 36 ♕e4+

**29 ♘xc8**

**Black resigns**

**Botvinnik**: Black resigned not a moment too soon; 29...♗xc8 30 ♖xe8 or 29...♖xc8 30 ♖e7+ is hopeless.

**Bronstein**: Perhaps the reader will expect me to blame time-trouble for our oversights? After all, how many opportunities have not been missed due to time-trouble? Not so. I love time-trouble! During these minutes and seconds the scientific side of the game of chess disappears and on the stage remain two human beings

who are either lucky or unlucky. If the exciting minutes and seconds of time-trouble had not been present in this game I would never have played 27 ♘xe7 but would have taken the h7 pawn with the queen with check and then the pawn on e7 with the rook and also with check (see comments after Black's 28th move). When Simagin played 28...♕b6 his intention was to protect the g6 pawn but it was a mistake, which is understandable when one considers that both players were tired after such a tense battle.

When the clocks were stopped one could read nothing on the face of either player. We completed and signed both scoresheets and handed them silently to the arbiter. It was Simagin who spoke first. Almost apologetically he said: 'I did not see the move 29 ♘xc8.' I also became talkative: 'Why did you not give me the opportunity to execute my planned combination with sacrifices and fireworks? Why did you not play your queen to h2?' 'Which sacrifices, what fireworks?' exclaimed Simagin, 'This is what I wanted to play but I felt sorry for my pawn on g6. Also, your move 29 ♘xc8 I totally overlooked. Otherwise I would of course have played 28...♕h2. Now show me what fireworks you had in mind,' he said and impatiently put the queen on h2 and I showed him 28...♕h2 29 ♖xd7 ♘xd7 30 ♕xg6+ ♔f8 31 ♕e6 ♕h1+ 32 ♔e2 ♕xh4 (32...♕xg2 33 ♕g8 mate) 33 ♘xg6 mate. 'Indeed, that is very beautiful,' he said.

That same evening we started to analyse this game which still reeked of gunpowder and found that my combination, although beautiful, could not be realised. Instead of the move 29...♘xd7 Black can play 29...♕h1+ 30 ♔e2 ♕xg2 and if 29 ♕xg6+ ♔f8 30 ♖xd7 ♕h1+ 31 ♔e2 ♕xh4.

My opponent was sorry to refute such a nice combination and we both used all our imagination trying to rehabilitate it, but unfortunately in vain. We tried to take the g6 pawn like this, like that, to take the bishop on d7, to leave him in peace.

We tried all roads for the white rook – ♖d1-d4, ♖e1-e4, ♖e1-e8 – but without any success. The secret of the survival of the black king could be summed up as follows: if White takes the pawn on g6 then the black queen will take the bishop on h4 but if White first takes the bishop on d7 then the black queen will take the pawn on g2 after having given a check on h1 forcing the king to step in front of his rook and to pin the knight on e7. We concluded that the game was interesting but the combination incorrect.

Today, nearly half a century after the game was played, it is time to say a little more. The move 23 ♗xf7 was a complete surprise for Simagin. He looked at the bishop for about eight minutes and was upset by the fact that he had given me such a chance. After the game we very much enjoyed analysing together.

About a quarter of a century after I made this story for the *Chess in the USSR* magazine, I don't want to change the style of the comments I made then. They were created for people with imagination. Of course, Simagin, being himself a very talented combinative player, must have seen the possibility of the sacrifice on f7 but when I actually made it he was nevertheless surprised. Instead of defending himself calmly he started to play very fast and counterattacked. For the reader who is interested in Simagin's short chess career, I can recommend his own book *Selected Games*. I was very pleased to receive some credit when he wrote in his preface to this book that I had persuaded him to make his fine games available to a wider audience. It is a pity that his book has only been translated into Spanish and not into any other languages. Simagin, a player with a highly original, unique and imaginative style of play, lived all his life in Moscow and played for the famous club Spartak. He was a chess philosopher and a very educated personality with a great love for literature. He never gave his brain time to rest.

Simagin died suddenly of a heart attack during the tournament at Kislovodsk on the 25th September 1968. A few days before this tragic event we had a long and friendly talk and Vladimir Pavlovich told me: 'David, you cannot even imagine how many chess activities I am involved in for my chess club Spartak Moscow: especially for chess amateurs. Not only playing for them but also giving lectures, simultaneous exhibitions, answering many questions, holding consultations, etc. But now I am very tired and don't feel well at all.'

A few years ago the Spartak Moscow Chess Club received a gift from their Sports Society: space in a building right in the centre of the city! Unfortunately they missed a unique opportunity to honour their illustrious former member.

I sincerely hope that, one day, they will change their name to the V. P. Simagin Chess Club!

The chess world should remember Vladimir Simagin as a real friend, a brilliant player and highly educated philosopher.

## (10) Zagoryansky,E – Bronstein,D

### Moscow Championship, 1947
*[A80] Dutch Defence*

My opponent in this game, Evgeny Alexandrovich Zagoryansky, was a very intelligent man, educated in high society and a real Prince. His family even owned a village, about 50 kilometres outside of Moscow called Zagoryanskaya, which still exists to this day. Of course, after 1917 his family lost their possessions and privileges. I know for instance that, because of his noble background, he was not allowed to go to university and sometimes had to work as a trench digger.

Because of his great intellect, elegant manners and handsome physical appearance he was chosen to represent the Soviet Chess Federation in America during the radio-match USSR vs. USA in 1945. However, at the last moment, his passport 'was not ready' and he was replaced by a member of the Soviet Embassy in Washington.

Besides chess he had a great talent for literature. He wrote several books but few were published – the material was too sensitive.

He wrote a brilliant book about the famous American chess player Paul Morphy but it was never translated into any other language. Also he was famous as a very skilled card player, probably one of the best in the USSR, and loved to attend horse races.

He was never called by his full name Hmell-Zagoryansky but all chess players knew who was meant if one referred to 'The Prince'. He was very pleased about it, as this, and his dignity, were the only things he managed to save after the Revolution of 1917.

| 1 | d4 | e6 |
|---|-----|-----|
| 2 | ♘f3 | f5 |
| 3 | g3 | ♘f6 |
| 4 | ♗g2 | ♗b4+ |

Black doesn't lose a tempo if White now plays c3 as this square will no longer be available to the knight on b1.

| 5 | ♘bd2 | 0-0 |
|---|------|------|
| 6 | 0-0 | ♘c6 |
| 7 | ♘e1 | ♗xd2 |

A very strong move. The threat was 8 c3 ♗e7 9 e4. If 7...d5 then, after 8 ♘d3, the other white knight can go to f3 keeping the e5 square under control.

I once lost a beautifully played game to Zagoryansky in the Semi-Final of the 14th USSR Championship in Moscow 1945 and that is the reason why I was now very careful.

| 8 | ♕xd2 |
|---|------|

White's position is better. Black has problems with his development and should try to play ...d6 and ...e5 to make his bishop active.

| 8 | ... | d6 |
|---|-----|-----|
| 9 | b3 | ♕e8 |

For better mobility. Supporting a possible e5 but, now that the bishop will go to b2, it is no longer advisable to open the diagonal for this bishop. Black has another plan.

| 10 | ♗b2 | ♗d7 |
|----|------|------|
| 11 | ♘d3 | a5 |
| 12 | a3 | a4 |
| 13 | b4 | ♖b8 |
| 14 | c4 | ♘e7 |
| 15 | f3 | ♕g6 |
| 16 | ♖ae1 | |

White has made all necessary preparations to destroy the black pawn formation by advancing the pawn e2-e4-e5. Black should now be creative. That is why he plays actively on the queenside, trying to control the white squares.

| 16 | ... | b5 |
|----|-----|-----|

To restrict the bishop on b2.

| 17 | ♖c1 | bxc4 |
|----|------|-------|
| 18 | ♖xc4 | ♘ed5 |
| 19 | ♖e1 | ♗b5 |
| 20 | ♖cc1 | c6 |

| 21 | e4 | fxe4 |
|----|------|-------|
| 22 | fxe4 | ♘b6 |

Both sides have achieved their goals. White has created a strong pawn centre and Black has built a good defensive position on the white squares.

| 23 | ♘f4 | ♕h6 |
|----|------|------|
| 24 | ♖cd1 | |

To be able to play d5 and take on e6.

| 24 | ... | ♘c4 |
|----|-----|------|

25 &#9819;c3 e5

Suddenly Black makes a long planned move to restrict the influence of the bishop on b2.

26 &#9816;h3 &#9816;g4

Another black knight finds a good square across the equator.

27 &#9815;c1 &#9819;h5
28 &#9820;f1

28 ... h6

A clever move which looks quite innocent but in reality is a trap.

29 &#9820;xf8+ &#9820;xf8
30 &#9820;f1 &#9820;xf1+
31 &#9815;xf1 &#9816;xa3!

This cunning move was hidden behind the smoke screen of 28...h6. Therefore I could make it without much hesitation. To create such a position from a rather suspicious opening requires a lot of energy and time. If I had not been in severe time-trouble at this moment I would have undoubtedly found the move 31...&#9816;ce3, more direct and certainly more beautiful.

32 &#9819;f3 &#9816;c2

Now the knight arrives on the strong central square d4. The fight is effectively over.

| | | |
|---|---|---|
| 33 | dxe5 | dxe5 |
| 34 | &#9815;xb5 | cxb5 |
| 35 | &#9819;f1 | &#9816;d4 |
| 36 | &#9812;g2 | a3 |
| 37 | &#9815;d2 | a2 |
| 38 | &#9819;a1 (D) | |
| 38 | ... | &#9816;e3+ |
| 39 | &#9812;g1 | &#9819;e2 |
| 40 | &#9819;xa2+ | &#9812;h7 |

**White resigns**

# (11) Bronstein,D – Tartakower,S

Interzonal Tournament,
Saltsjöbaden, 1948
*[B10] Caro-Kann Defence*

This game was played in the last round and the result was important to me and even more to the Soviet Chess Federation because the Hungarian grandmaster Laszlo Szabo and myself were leading the battle for first place. It happened that I won and he lost (to Erik Lundin).

That is how I took the first place in my first international tournament. Perhaps it is worth mentioning that the second international tournament I played was not until the winter of 1953/54, at Hastings, three years after my match for the highest chess title. That was the reality of the Cold War period.

On the 24th of August 1948 the Sport Committee of the USSR officially awarded me the title of grandmaster of the USSR; the eleventh person to receive it.

Actually this is not quite correct, I was the twelfth! In 1929 Boris Verlinsky from Odessa had become champion of the USSR and was awarded the grandmaster title.

Several years later he was stripped of it to enable the authorities to make Botvinnik the first *official* grandmaster of the USSR!

It was very exciting to play against Dr Savielly Tartakower, the chess hero of my youth. I liked very much not only the books of this outstanding artist but also his style of play and his behaviour during his complicated and difficult life.

Although being a pure amateur in chess he always played on even terms with the best professionals. In my opinion his beautiful games are very much underrated. His brilliant books and journalistic achievements drew most of the attention away from his games.

Also we should not forget that during the Second World War Dr Xavier (he changed his first name when he moved to France) Tartakower joined the French resistance movement with General de Gaulle under the name of Lieutenant Cartier. Several times he was dropped by parachute behind enemy lines on secret missions.

| 1 | e4 | c6 |
| 2 | ♘f3 | d6 |
| 3 | d4 | ♗g4 |

In 1948 this move looked strange but today it is very common.

| 4 | h3! |

The bishop is stronger than the knight.

| 4 | ... | ♗h5 |
| 5 | ♗e3 | ♘f6 |
| 6 | ♘bd2 | ♘bd7 |
| 7 | c3 | ♗g6 |

In many positions where Black has played ...d6 and ...♘bd7 his bishop is blocked on c8. The unusual manoeuvre ...♗c8-g4-h5-g6 transforms this bishop into a very active piece. Now the pawn on e4 is under attack.

**8    e5**

White begins an early attack, trying to exploit the frozen position of the bishop on f8.

| 8 | ... | ♘d5 |

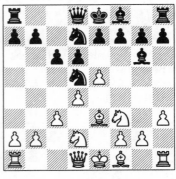

| 9 | e6 |

A temporary pawn sacrifice with the same idea mentioned before but now it is also directed against the pawn on e7.

| 9 | ... | fxe6 |
| 10 | ♗e2 | e5 |
| 11 | dxe5 | ♘xe5 |
| 12 | ♘xe5 | dxe5 |
| 13 | ♗h5 |

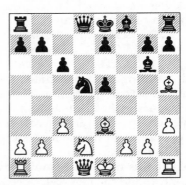

Now White fights for control of the e4 square for his knight. If 13 ♗g4 then Black can play 13...e6 14 ♗xe6 ♕f6 15 ♗g4 ♘xe3 16 fxe3 ♗c5 with active play.

| 13 | ... | ♘xe3 |
| 14 | ♗xg6+ | hxg6 |
| 15 | fxe3 | ♕d3 |
| 16 | ♕f3 | e6 |

Black has defended with great skill and now White has to make a decision whether to put a knight on e4 or to castle queenside. Today, after half a century of experience, I would have chosen one of these moves but at that time I was proud to make a purely technical move after which,

I was sure, I could not lose. Whether one can win such a position depends on having some luck. Black has four isolated pawns but they can easily be protected.

| | | |
|---|---|---|
| 17 | ♕e4 | ♕xe4 |
| 18 | ♘xe4 | ♗e7 |

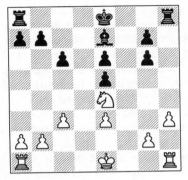

**19 ♔e2!**
White's king could castle either side but decides to stay in the centre.

| | | |
|---|---|---|
| 19 | ... | ♖d8 |
| 20 | ♖ad1 | 0-0 |
| 21 | ♖xd8 | ♖xd8 |
| 22 | ♖f1 | |

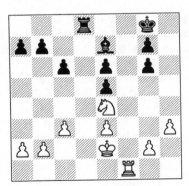

This move keeps the black king out of the centre but it is not clear how White can make any progress. Now it is Black who starts to play for a win! His next move creates a weakness on c6 which is partly responsible for White's success in the endgame.

| | | |
|---|---|---|
| 22 | ... | b6 |
| 23 | ♘f2 | ♖d5 |
| 24 | ♘d3 | ♗f6 |
| 25 | ♘b4 | ♖b5 |
| 26 | a4 | ♖c5 |

**27 e4!**
Another pawn comes to e4. Suddenly the active black rook is trapped between the white and black pawns. Black planned 27...a5 28 ♘d3 ♖c4 but this does not work because instead of saving his knight, White can play more bravely 28 ♔d3 axb4 29 cxb4 and the black rook is lost.

| | | |
|---|---|---|
| 27 | ... | b5 |
| 28 | a5 | ♗d8 |
| 29 | ♖a1 | ♖c4 |
| 30 | ♔d3 | ♗e7 |
| 31 | ♘a6! | ♖a4 |
| 32 | ♖xa4 | bxa4 |

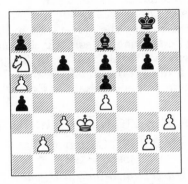

Black has managed to save his rook but at a cost: his pawn formation on the queenside. Black's pawns do not support each other because they are disconnected and it is only a matter of time before the white knight gobbles up all the black pawns.

The problem of keeping seven pawns alive, all completely isolated, some doubled, could not even be solved by the ingenious brain of Dr Tartakower.

| | | |
|---|---|---|
| 33 | ♘b8 | a3 |
| 34 | bxa3 | ♗xa3 |
| 35 | ♘xc6 | ♗c5 |
| 36 | ♔c4 | ♗g1 |
| 37 | ♔b5 | ♔f7 |
| 38 | ♔a6 | ♔f6 |
| 39 | ♘xa7 | ♔g5 |
| 40 | g3 | ♗f2 |
| 41 | c4 | ♔f6 |
| 42 | ♘c8 | ♗xg3 |
| 43 | c5 | ♔f7 |
| 44 | ♔b6 | ♔e8 |
| 45 | a6 | |

**Black resigns**

Spectators watching the last round saw more than chess-playing. While I was far from my board, walking around to see the position on the boards of Szabo and Boleslavsky, I saw a spectator, obviously drunk, come to our table and throw the clock and all the pieces on the ground. Dr Tartakower successfully defended himself by making a strategic retreat. The police intervened and order was quickly restored. Later it was established that the man was from Lithuania and was protesting against 'the Russians' who had sent his sister to Siberia. The attack was therefore directed at me, but not Dr Tartakower.

This incident was widely discussed in the press and by the players. Even the always silent Isaac Boleslavsky had something to say: 'If this man really is against the Russians, why did he attack David Bronstein and not Alexander Kotov?'

# (12) Bronstein,D – Furman,S

### 16th USSR Championship, Moscow, 1948
### *[E51] Nimzo-Indian Defence*

This tournament was played in November, just two months after I had won the Interzonal Tournament, and it was of course important for me to defend my new position in the chess world as a grandmaster. This particular game was played towards the end of the tournament and was of great importance to both players. Alexander Kotov and I were fighting for first place, which was a small sensation, with Semyon Furman following us closely. Later, when I recognised the logical play of Furman, I invited him to be my assistant during preparation for the match in 1951. Also, I took him abroad as my second to the Interzonal Tournament in Gothenburg in 1955 and the Candidates' Tournament in Amsterdam 1956. It is a well-known fact that Victor Korchnoi also spent a lot of time analysing many aspects of chess theory with him in a friendly and open way. When Furman started to work with Anatoly Karpov, I was not surprised by the

young grandmaster's success, showing a brilliant understanding of grandmaster strategy. It was obvious that Furman had passed on to him a lot of the knowledge acquired during his earlier years.

It should also be said that Furman had very good analytical powers and was able to look deeply into the games of other grandmasters, disclosing the secrets of their success. After he made comments on several of the games I played in the Interzonal Tournament of 1955, he surprised me with a very neat observation: 'I now know how you manage to win so many games,' he said. 'You manoeuvre your pieces in such a way that the opponent can never attack them in one move and even if they can there might be a hidden trick. Besides, you can see the intention of your opponent most of the time and act accordingly.' Of course he was right!

However the game that follows is an exception.

According to Isaac Boleslavsky, who deeply annotated this game for *Chess in the USSR*, it was the most complex and mind-boggling of the 16th USSR Championship. With pure logic I had achieved a winning position by move 24 but, sensing that there was more than an elementary win, I looked for complications and beauty and, with some luck, found both!

| | | |
|---|---|---|
| 1 | d4 | ♘f6 |
| 2 | c4 | e6 |
| 3 | ♘c3 | ♗b4 |
| 4 | e3 | d5 |
| 5 | a3 | ♗e7 |
| 6 | ♘f3 | 0-0 |
| 7 | ♗d3 | b6 |
| 8 | 0-0 | c5 |
| 9 | b3 | ♗b7 |
| 10 | ♗b2 | ♘c6 |

The game has transposed into a variation of the Queen's Gambit with the difference that the white pawn stands on a3. This factor has both positive and negative significance: the square b4 is inaccessible to the black knight but White's b3 pawn is slightly weakened so that the natural 11 ♕e2 can be answered by 11...♘a5 with an attack on the b3 pawn. To be considered was 11 ♕c2; the continuation chosen by White should not have given him an advantage.

**11    cxd5         exd5?**

This is a serious positional mistake, after which Black finds himself in a difficult situation. With hanging c- and d-pawns the black knight at c6 turns out to be very badly placed. It blocks the defence of the c5 pawn by the rook and the defence of the d5 pawn by the bishop and if the knight moves away, say to a5, the important square e5 remains in White's hands. The normal position for Black's knight, when he has hanging pawns, is on the d7 square where it defends the c5 pawn and controls the square e5. Black should of course have captured on d5 with his knight and after 11...♘xd5 12 ♘xd5 ♕xd5 13 ♕c2 ♕h5 he stands no worse.

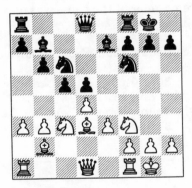

**12    ♘e2!**

This subtle move reinforces the d4-pawn and threatens the unpleasant transfer of the white knight to f5. It is very difficult for him to obtain any play. Probably best was 12...a5 followed by the sacrifice of the pawn at a4; in this case the c-pawn would have become a passed pawn and Black could have hoped for counterplay. After the following natural but poor move things become even worse for Black.

**12    ...          ♘e4**
**13    dxc5         bxc5**
**14    ♕c2          ♕b6**
**15    ♘g3**

After 15 ♘f4 Black can play 15...♘a5 16 ♘xd5 ♗xd5 17 ♗xe4 ♗xe4 18 ♕xe4 ♖fe8 and Black recaptures his pawn. Black's

hanging pawns in the centre are very weak.

**15    ...          f5**
**16    ♘h5          ♖f7**
**17    ♖ab1!**

Before setting up decisive pressure on the d5 pawn White deprives Black of his last counter-chance: an attack on the b3 pawn. In addition he now threatens b3-b4 in some instances.

But maybe also possible was 17 ♖fd1 ♘a5 18 ♘e5 ♘xb3 19 ♖ab1 c4 20 ♗xc4 dxc4 21 ♕xc4 ♖af8 22 ♘xf7 ♖xf7 23 ♗d4.

**17    ...          ♖d8**
**18    ♖fd1         ♖d6**
**19    ♘f4          ♔h8**

This turns out to be a tactical mistake but also 19...a5, to prevent b4, does not help, e.g. 20 ♗f1 ♘d8 21 b4 axb4 22 axb4 cxb4 23 ♘e5 ♖f8 24 ♗d4 ♕a5 25 ♖a1 and the black queen is lost.

**20    ♗f1          ♕d8**

This loses a pawn but Black's position is already hopeless. If 20...♘d8 there would have followed 21 b4 c4 22 ♗e5 ♖d7 23 ♗d4 and 24 ♘e5.

**21    ♘xd5**

21 ♖xd5 is even simpler: the double capture on d5 allows ♗c4: 21...♖xd5 22 ♘xd5 ♕xd5 23 ♗c4 ♕d7 24 ♗xf7.

**21    ...          ♗h4**

Black carries out his only threat. After the simple 22 g3 it is doubtful whether he could have exploited the weakening of the a8-h1 diagonal which White wrongly feared. White prefers another move which forces the exchange of a knight for a bishop which cannot be bad.

| 22 | ♘xh4 | ♛xh4 |
|---|---|---|
| 23 | ♘f4 | ♖fd7 |
| 24 | ♘h3? | |

Now Black succeeds in creating great complications. Instead, after 24 ♖xd6 ♖xd6 25 ♘h3, White would have won without any difficulty, for example: 25...♖d2 26 ♛c4 ♖xf2 27 ♛f7, or 25...♖g6 26 ♛c4 ♛xh3 27 ♛f7.

| 24 | ... | ♘d2! |
|---|---|---|
| 25 | ♛xf5 | |

Looking directly to f8 but the simple 25 ♛xc5 would have been stronger.

Now the knight cannot capture either bishop or rook since the rook on d6 will be attacked twice. On the other hand 26 ♖xd2 is threatened. Certainly an interesting point.

| 25 | ... | ♘e7 |
|---|---|---|
| 26 | ♛f7 | |

Not 26 ♛f8+ ♘g8 27 ♖bc1 since after 27...♖g6 Black's attack is irresistible.

| 26 | ... | ♛h6 |
|---|---|---|
| 27 | f4 | |

Exploiting the fact that the black pieces are tied up. If 27...♘xb1? then 28 ♖xd6 ♖xd6 29 ♛xe7 with an easy win. White acquires the extremely important g5 square for his knight.

| 27 | ... | ♘g8 |
|---|---|---|

**28 ♛f8**

A safe move but one which almost cost me half a point. We both had less than two minutes for 13 moves. Although I prepared 28 ♘g5! while playing f4, even with so little time, you cannot only trust your intuition; some calculation is required. 28 ♘g5!:

a) 28...♘xb1 29 ♖xd6 ♖xd6 30 ♛xg7+ ♛xg7 ♘f7 mate.

b) 28...♛xg5 29 ♛xd7 and White wins.

c) 28...♗d5 29 ♗xg7+ ♛xg7 30 ♛xg7+ ♔xg7 31 ♖xd2.

d) 28...♛g6 29 ♛xg6 hxg6 30 ♗e2.

e) 28...♘xf1 29 ♛xg7+ ♛xg7 30 ♖xd6 ♘f6 (if 30...♛xb2 then 31 ♖xb2 ♖xd6 32 ♘f7+ ♔g7 33 ♘xd6 ♗a6 34 ♘e8+ ♔f7 35 ♘c7 ♗d3 36 ♖f2 ♘xe3 37 ♖f3) 31 ♗xf6 ♖xd6 32 ♗xg7+ ♔xg7 33 ♔xf1 with an easy win.

| 28 | ... | ♘xb1 |
|---|---|---|

The capture of the rook turns out to be much more dangerous for Black than it appears at first sight. In view of the fact that he was already in serious time-trouble 28...♘xf1 was more prudent, leading after 29 ♖xd6 ♖xd6 31 ♖xf1 ♖d2 31 ♖f2 ♖d1+ to a draw by repetition of moves. The remainder of the game was played at lightning speed.

| 29 | ♖xd6 | ♖xd6 |
|---|---|---|

Of course not 29...♛xd6 because of 30 ♗xg7+.

| 30 | ♘g5 | ♗d5 |
|---|---|---|

30...♖d7 fails to 31 ♘f7+ ♖xf7 32 ♛xf7 with the double threat of ♛xb7 or ♗c4.

| 31 | e4 | ♗xb3 |
|---|---|---|
| 32 | e5 | |

**32 ... ♖d1**

This move with the black rook looks natural but it loses immediately. Furman did not realise how dangerous the march of the e-pawn was. If he had had a minute more he would no doubt have chosen 32...♖d7, hoping for 33 ♛f5 ♖d1! 34 e6 ♗xe6 35 ♘xe6 ♘d2, but if White should strengthen the attack by the natural move 33 h4 it is still not easy to stop his f-pawn from marching to f7. If 32...♖b6 or 32...♖d7 then 33 h4 with the intention of pushing the e- and f-pawns forward.

**33 e6!**

It is interesting to follow the advance of the pawn from e3 to e6 with continuous threats.

**33 ... ♗xe6**
**34 ♘xe6 ♖d4**

Desperation. On 34...♖d7 White wins by 35 ♘xg7 ♖xg7 36 ♗c4.

**35 ♗xd4 cxd4**
**36 ♘g5**

### Black lost on time

During the time scramble the moves were made at lightning speed and the demonstration boards, operated by junior players, could not keep pace. However, afterwards the game was replayed for the audience. It was then that for the first and last time in my life I heard some chess enthusiasts shout: 'Bravo, bis! Bravo, bis!' like after a concert!

By winning this game I increased my lead and eventually shared first place with Alexander Kotov. First it was suggested that we should contest a match but then it was decided that we should share the title USSR Champion.

I believe it was the first time that the winners of national championships (in all sports) received a gold medal and the Sports Committee spent a little more money making two of them!

Furman, who was half a point behind us, took third place, received a bronze medal and made his first grandmaster norm.

# (13) Bronstein,D – Ilivitsky,G

### 16th USSR Championship, Moscow, 1948

*[D28] Queen's Gambit Declined*

If I had not won the Interzonal in 1948 I would not have played in this 16th USSR Championship. I had played in the Semi-Final in Leningrad in the Autumn of 1947, shared third and fourth place and did not qualify for the Final. When I received the grandmaster title by winning the Interzonal Tournament in the summer of 1948, the Soviet Chess Federation found a place for me.

I know that the general opinion is that the Soviet Championships at that time were the strongest tournaments in the world. But this could also be said about the Semi-Finals. The quality of chess was very high in the USSR for many years. I also would like to say that the Soviet Championships then were not as they are today, just making the most points. It was a kind of intellectual show and the participants were expected to show the beauty of chess art. We always played in a little theatre on the stage with the audience sitting in chairs like during a concert. The tournament lasted about one month. We played at least four games a week; 40 moves in 2½ hours, two days for adjournments and one free day. It was of course tiring but very interesting. The games started about 5 p.m. and very soon the hall filled up with chess lovers. They came each day and many faithful fans came every year. The admirers could follow the games on large demonstration boards. It was a great pleasure to see nine or ten games being played at the same time by the best players in the world. Also, during the games, you could participate in a simul or listen to explanations by a grandmaster. Also special bulletins with games were available and many newspapers gave reports every day. The results were broadcast on radio during the main news. In addition, five minutes after midnight there was a special, detailed broadcast. That is why chess and chess players were so popular. It was not orchestrated by the government, it was genuine enthusiasm! Of course when you feel such big respect from the audience you feel an obligation to play for them.

This, however, does not make it easier on the players. But it was a pleasure to play in such surroundings and ambience. So even if today some names are not so well-known abroad, they were all very strong players of course. There were no computers and they all played at their own strength. I was happy to play in more than 20 Soviet finals and I think that it helped me to understand chess. Needless to say there were only small prizes in these tournaments. It was an honour to participate and applause from the audience was sufficient reward. With a good result you had a chance to be sent abroad so it was very important to achieve just that.

In this game Black lost several tempi in the opening and gave White the opportunity to make a sharp move by putting his knight on d5.

This sacrifice gave White two strong passed pawns. White played his knight to f5 and when both rooks came to the 7th rank it was easy to find the decisive combination.

| 1 | c4 | ♘f6 |
| 2 | ♘c3 | e6 |
| 3 | d4 | d5 |
| 4 | ♘f3 | c5 |
| 5 | cxd5 | ♘xd5 |
| 6 | e3 | |

Immediately 6 e4 is also possible.

| 6 | ... | ♘c6 |

It is not advisable to play ...a6 and ...b5 now. If Black had wanted to play these moves the knight should have gone to d7.

| 7 | ♗c4 | ♘f6 |
| 8 | 0-0 | a6 |
| 9 | ♕e2 | b5 |
| 10 | ♗b3 | ♗e7 |
| 11 | ♖d1 | 0-0 |
| 12 | dxc5 | ♕c7 |
| 13 | e4! | |

Threatening e5. After 13...♗xc5 follows 14 e5 ♘g4 15 ♘e4! Now Black cannot play 15. ...♘cxe5 because of 16 ♘xe5 ♘xe5 17 ♗f4 ♗e7 18 ♖ac1 with strong attacking chances for White. Therefore ...

| 13 | ... | ♘d7 *(D)* |
| 14 | ♘d5 | exd5 |
| 15 | exd5 | ♘xc5 |
| 16 | dxc6 | ♗d6 |
| 17 | ♗c2 | |

Both bishops are eyeing the black king!

| 17 | ... | ♕xc6 |

| 18 | b4 | |

After 18 ♘g5 h6 19 ♘e4! ♖e8 20 ♖xd6 ♕xd6 21 ♘f6+ gxf6 22 ♕xe8+ ♔g7 23 ♗xh6+ ♔xh6 24 ♕h8+, etc.

| 18 | ... | ♘b7 |
| 19 | ♗b2 | ♕c4 |
| 20 | ♗d3 | ♕f4 |
| 21 | g3 | ♕g4 |
| 22 | a3 | ♗f5 |
| 23 | ♗xf5 | ♕xf5 |

Black has defended well but the exchange of bishops has weakened the white squares. The queen will assist the knight into play.

| 24 | ♘h4 | ♕e6 |
| 25 | ♕f3 | ♖ab8 |
| 26 | ♘f5 | ♗e5 |
| 27 | ♗xe5 | ♕xe5 |
| 28 | ♖ac1 | ♖fe8 |

| 29 | ♖d7! | ♘d8 |
| 30 | ♖cc7! | ♖b6? |

Providing White with the opportunity to conclude with a pretty combination but in any case no king can resist two rooks on the 7th rank supported by a knight.

| 31 | ♖c8! | ♖b8 |

**32    Ⓡcxd8!       Ⓦe1+**

Now, after 33 ♔g2 Ⓡbxd8 34 ♘h6+ ♔h8 35 ♘xf7+ ♔g8 the black queen is safe but the white knight simply takes the black rook. It is easy to see that if Black had played 32...Ⓡbxd8 or 32...Ⓡexd8 then 33 ♘h6+ gxh6 34 Ⓦxf7+ ♔h8 35 Ⓦxh7 is mate.

**33    ♔g2**

**Black resigns**

# (14) Bronstein,D – Boleslavsky,I

Candidates' Play-off,
7th game, Moscow,1950
*[E21] Nimzo-Indian Defence*

I remember how in the winter of 1938 a young student from Dnepropetrovsk created a sensation in the Ukrainian Championship, played in Kiev. The tournament hall was overcrowded with spectators who followed with great interest the very lovely style of this young candidate master. He played with fantastic speed and was winning almost every game. He took first prize and later won the Ukrainian Championship twice more. I was also in the audience and his beautiful conceptions on the board impressed me very much. The following year I also played in the Ukrainian Championship and then, despite some age difference, we became friends. We found that we had many common interests besides chess. In later years we often played in the same tournaments. We also analysed a lot together and of course did not keep any secrets from each other in the openings. This is why in this match it was very difficult for me to play with the black pieces. After his first move 1 e4 Isaac Boleslavsky always obtained a better position. I remember that in the second game of this match, after Isaac Boleslavsky had made his first move, I thought for a long time (I was told afterwards for some 50 minutes!) trying to find something better and I came up with 1...♘f6. In this game I had White so the first move was easier to make. I did not play 1 e4 because I did not feel like playing a French or Sicilian which we had extensively analysed together.

Also, I need to say that contrary to the general opinion, I did not use a single day for theoretical preparation. I spent the month before the match in the famous Latvian holiday resort of Jurmala in the House of Literature. It is easy to explain why I was there. The young lady that I had fallen in love with earlier that year was sent by her office to be a summer teacher in a children's camp near Jurmala. All the free time we had we used to be together.

At the same time there was a championship of the All Union Spartak Club and Alexey Suetin, the author of a book about the life and games of Isaac Boleslavsky, saw me every day without an assistant, chessboard or chess book. I was looking on this contest as a friendly one.

During the Budapest Candidates' Tournament Boleslavsky and I had discussed the chances of the next challenger and my friend, who had lost seven games to Botvinnik without winning a single one, was of the opinion that a fight against Botvinnik was hopeless. Once he had had a chance to checkmate Botvinnik in a few moves but missed the opportunity.

Of course I had a completely different opinion. I argued that Botvinnik was very strong but one could still play against him successfully. I was sure that I could demonstrate that his strategy was far from perfect.

Isaac Boleslavsky was leading in the Candidates' Tournament but after a talk he had with Boris Vainstein he decided to slow down to allow me to tie for first place with him. Vainstein would try to arrange a tournament with Botvinnik, Boleslavsky and myself for the World Championship. Alas, it did not come about and we had to meet in a play-off for the right to challenge Botvinnik.

The whole atmosphere in the Soviet chess world was that Botvinnik was the best player during the last two decades and he deserved the title of World Champion. One was almost afraid to take it away from him!

Playing for the title of World Champion is the dream of every chess player but deep inside me, subconsciously, I must have had no real ambition to win. Otherwise I cannot explain why I did not win the match when, only two games from the end, all the odds were in my favour.

After the match Botvinnik himself gave evidence to this opinion despite the result of 12-12 and the obvious fact that he saved his title only in the last game, he simply explained his 'bad' result like this: 'I have not played chess for three years. This is why I played below my normal strength but my opponent is a good player. He is particularly strong when the game is transforming from the opening to the middlegame and in addition he conducts an attack against the enemy king very well.'

Botvinnik did not explain why, during almost two months of play, he did not succeed in winning a single game during the first five hours of play. Four out of his five wins were achieved after the adjournment. I lost three completely even endgames as a result of bad homework. On the other hand he lost four games before the first time control.

Anyhow, even if I had won this match, I am not sure that I would have been able to call myself World Champion for long because the rules, created by Botvinnik, gave him the right to join the next World Championship contest and play for the title in a tournament with three participants; the present World Champion, his new challenger and Botvinnik himself. I think that if you cannot defend your title in the same way that you get it you're not a real World Champion.

In the match with Isaac Boleslavsky I was successful in the first and in the seventh games. I also had an easy win in the fifth game but made some weak moves after the adjournment and the game ended in a draw. It was in the sixth game that I played the famous Marshall Attack in the Spanish Opening and managed an easy draw with Black. Then I started to play less strongly and after 12 games, the score was 6-6. We played a very sharp 13th game (see page 219) and while playing through the moves it should be clear that neither of us was too much concerned about the final result. I did not care about Black's passed pawns and Black very freely sacrificed his queen for my knight.

The match was decided in game 14 after Boleslavsky repeated the sacrifice of two pawns from game 12; in the meantime I had found a refutation in home analysis.

Now, many years later, I think I might have made a mistake in winning this match, but most likely I saved my friend from a certain defeat, possibly even humiliation.

By not winning the title I have put a shadow on my chess career and it is a little sad that I have had to read and hear for more than 40 years that I am not a good player. It seems that all my other achievements in chess have been ignored.

Isaac Boleslavsky and I were able to play excellent technical chess but we only used it in time-trouble and during thousands and thousands of blitz games which we played for our own pleasure. However, during tournaments we always tried to use our fantasy, to create and solve difficult problems, finding and refuting new strategies or just to find single moves.

We were paid a (very small) salary specially to make a spiritual show for the audience. Also, the Soviet Chess Federation insisted that it was not nice to play purely technical chess.

This match was played in the Central Chess Club of the Soviet Railworkers where most of the Soviet Championships were played. The arbiter at this event was a man of honour who had great personal courage, Nikolai Mikhailovich Zubariev.

The conditions of play were normal for such matches with one exception: no prize money! To be able to spend more money on food we accepted the proposition one of the editors of the *Evening Moscow* newspaper, Alexander Vasilievich Stepanov, to give comments to our games for a special bulletin which he was publishing. We agreed that comments would be supplied by the winner and, in case of a draw, by the player with the white pieces.

By the way, it took the Soviet Chess Federation more than twenty days to inform FIDE of the result of our match!

| 1 | d4 | ♘f6 |
|---|----|-----|
| 2 | c4 | e6 |
| 3 | ♘c3 | ♗b4 |
| 4 | ♘f3 | |

White does not care if Black decides to exchange his bishop for the knight as his b-pawn will come closer to the centre. This simple move with the king's knight was a favourite of the former Kiev player Efim Bogoljubow, the winner of the 1925 Moscow tournament who later, in 1929 and again in 1934, tried unsuccessfully to take the chess crown from Dr Alekhine.

| 4 | ... | d6 |
|---|-----|-----|
| 5 | ♕b3 | |

Before making the decision how to conduct his pawns White is curious to see whether Black will exchange his bishop or not. Also possible was 5 ♗g5 pinning in return the black knight.

Many years ago, I think in 1960, during the Soviet Championship in Leningrad, I was thinking about my opening in the next game with Korchnoi. As he often played 1 c4 ♘f6 2 ♘f3 e6 3 ♘c3 I decided to try 3...♗b4 and if 4 d4 then 4...d6. Then, using my fantasy, I was dreaming of a nice combination after 5 ♗g5 h6 6 ♗h4 ♕e7! 7 ♕a4+? ♘c6 8 d5 exd5 9 cxd5 ♕e4 10 ♘d2 ♕xh4 11 dxc6 0-0 12 a3 ♘g4 13 g3 ♕f6 14 axb4 ♕xf2+ 15 ♔d1 b5 16 ♕b3 ♗e6 17 ♕a3 ♘e3+ 18 ♔c1 ♕e1+ 19 ♘d1 ♕xd1 mate.

After the tournament I gave a lecture in the Chigorin Chess Club and told the audience about this and used the expression 'chess dream'. Later I read in a book that I saw this variation during my sleep!

| 5 | ... | a5 |
|---|-----|------|
| 6 | g3 | ♘c6 |
| 7 | ♗g2 | ♘e4 |
| 8 | 0-0 | ♗xc3 |
| 9 | bxc3 | 0-0 |
| 10 | ♘e1 | f5 (D) |

Black has broken the white pawn chain and established a strong outpost for his

king's knight in the centre but he has paid a high price for this. The moves 5...a5 and 10...f5 have created weaknesses and White can now take advantage of these by starting a pawn attack.

| 11 | f3 | ♘f6 |
|----|-----|------|
| 12 | a4 | ♕e7 |

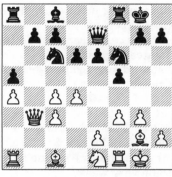

| 13 | c5 | d5 |
|----|-----|-----|

It would not have been wise to play 13...dxc5 because after 14 ♗a3 the white bishop gets a fine diagonal. Now that Black has created the triangle d5-e6-f5 with his pawns it is better for White to exchange his bishop for Black's knight. Thus he prevents Black from defending the e5 square and also increases the power of the bishop on g2.

| 14 | ♗g5 | h6 |
|----|------|------|
| 15 | ♗xf6 | ♕xf6 |
| 16 | ♘d3 | b6! |

Black tries to start an attack first. If he waits any longer then the white pawn on e2 will establish an offensive position on e4.

| 17 | cxb6 | ♖b8 |
|----|------|------|
| 18 | ♕a3 | ♖xb6 |
| 19 | f4! | ♗a6 |

| 20 | ♘c5 | ♕e7 |
|----|-----|-----|

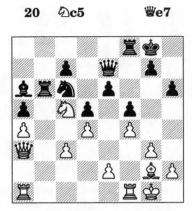

The first impression is that Boleslavsky has successfully solved all of his problems. The influence of the white bishop on g2 is limited by the pawn on d5, the b-file is under Black's control and with his next move he could improve the position of his bishop by moving it to c4. In 999 out of a 1000 cases this judgement would be correct, but this is an exception! White's next move violates the classic rule that a strong knight should not exchange itself for a weak bishop.

**21    ♘xa6!!**

Not at all expected by Black. If now 21...♕xa3 22 ♖xa3 ♖xa6 then after 23 ♖b1 ♖b6 24 ♖b5 ♖fb8 25 ♖c5 ♔f7 27 e3 ♔e7 24 c4 it is obvious that the strong pawn on d5 has become very weak.

In the above variation it was also possible to play 23 e3 ♖b6 24 c4 ♘b4 25 ♖c1 maintaining some pressure but I prefer the variation with the active rook on c5.

The motive of the pawn on c3 threatening to move to c4, indirectly supported by the bishop on g2, will be a factor during the next 19 moves. When White finally makes this move his advantage becomes overwhelming.

It was not easy at all to find a weakness in Boleslavsky's superb classical strategy.

My decision to play this type of attack was based on the events in our fifth game of this match. In that game, by making logically attacking manoeuvres, I had obtained an advantage in space which I transformed into a winning endgame.

**21    ...             ♖xa6**

| 22 | ♕c5! | ♖b8 |
|----|------|-----|
| 23 | ♖fb1 |     |

This is the maximum that can be achieved for now. The threat is 24 ♖b5 and in case of 23...♖ab6 the variation 24 ♖xb6 ♖xb6 25 c4 dxc4 26 ♖c1 does not look good for Black.

**23    ...             ♕xc5**

More accurate was 23...♖xb1+ 24 ♖xb1 ♕xc5 25 dxc5 ♔f8 and Black's defensive task would have been easier.

| 24 | dxc5 | ♔f8 |
|----|------|-----|
| 25 | ♖b5  | ♖aa8 |
| 26 | ♔f2  | ♔e7 |
| 27 | ♔e3  | ♖g8 |
| 28 | ♖ab1 |     |

**28    ...             ♖gb8**

Just when Black should undertake a counter offensive he decides to avoid any activity and to wait for the adjournment. Probably Black did not like the variation: 28...g5 29 fxg5 hxg5 30 c4 ♘b4 31 cxd5 ♘xd5 (31...exd5 32 ♖1xb4 axb4 33 ♗xd5) 32 ♗xd5 exd5 33 ♔d4 ♖h8 34 ♖b7 ♖c8 35 ♖1b3 ♖xh2 36 ♖e3+ ♔d7 37 ♔xd5.

During the game we both favoured the white position but now, well after the event, the game appears to be a clear draw to me; a fair result!

| 29 | ♔d3 | ♔d7 |
| 30 | e3 | ♔e7 |
| 31 | ♔d2 | ♖c8 |
| 32 | ♗f3 | g6 |
| 33 | ♗e2 | h5 |

This move can be understood as an invitation to play 34 h4, but how can White then break the strong chain of black pawns?

| 34 | h3 | ♖g8 |
| 35 | ♖b7 | ♖gc8 |

**36  g4**

White picked up what Black refused to take, i.e. to start an attack with the pawns on the kingside. The opening of extra files may be useful for the white bishop or even for his rooks.

| 36 | ... | hxg4 |
| 37 | hxg4 | ♘d8 |
| 38 | ♖7b2 | ♘f7 |
| 39 | g5 | ♔d7 |

**40  c4**

Just before the adjournment White finally makes the move which he has been wanting to make for such a long time. The key to this attack lies in the sealed move.

| 40 | ... | dxc4 |

After 40...c6? White will play 41 cxd5 exd5 and 42 e4!! opening useful diagonals for his bishop.

| 41 | ♗f3 |

The sealed move. The bishop returns to its main diagonal.

| 41 | ... | ♖a7 |
| 42 | ♔c3 | c6 |
| 43 | ♖h2 |

Now that both white rooks have taken control of the board the outcome of the battle becomes clear. However, in a long and tiring match one needs to solve many problems before being able to sign the score-sheet with a win.

| 43 | ... | ♔e7 |
| 44 | ♗e2 | ♔f8 |
| 45 | ♗xc4 | ♖e8 |
| 46 | ♖b6 | ♖c7 |
| 47 | ♖a6 | ♔g7 |
| 48 | ♖xa5 | e5 |

Black is now also trying to create more space for his rooks but it is too little too late.

| 49 | ♖h3 | ♖d7 |
| 50 | ♗b3 | exf4 |
| 51 | exf4 | ♖e4 |
| 52 | ♖a8 | ♖xf4 *(D)* |
| 53 | ♗xf7 |

Transforming the game into a winning rook ending. The passed pawn on the a-file will decide the game. Of course some good technique is still required.

| 53 | ... | ♖xf7 |

| 54 | ♖ah8 | ♖f3+ |
|----|-------|-------|
| 55 | ♖xf3 | ♔xh8 |
| 56 | a5    | ♖a7   |
| 57 | ♔b4   | ♔g7   |
| 58 | ♖a3   | ♖a6   |
| 59 | ♖d3   | ♔f7   |

| 60 | ♖d6   | ♔g7 |
|----|-------|-----|
| 61 | ♖d7+  | ♔g8 |
| 62 | ♔a4   | ♔f8 |
| 63 | ♖b7   | f4  |
| 64 | ♖b4   | ♔e7 |
| 65 | ♖xf4  | ♔e6 |
| 66 | ♖f6+  | ♔d5 |
| 67 | ♔b4   |     |

**Black resigns**

# (15) Reshevsky,S – Bronstein,D

Candidates' Tournament,
Neuhausen/Zurich, 1953
*[E68] King's Indian Defence*

The life of Sammy Reshevsky is well-known. He started to play chess at a very young age and was a brilliant prodigy. He then stopped playing for a while to work at his education but then returned and for many years was amongst the best players in the world. It is no secret that he regarded himself to be of equal strength to the World Champion. In 1955, during the USSR vs. USA match in Moscow, the American Ambassador held a reception. During this event Reshevsky asked a high Soviet official for permission to play a match for the World Championship with Botvinnik. (The high Soviet official was Krushchev – T.F.) The diplomatic answer was that this was a matter for the Soviet Chess Federation to decide.

They did not want to organise a match outside of FIDE for the title but suggested that Reshevsky could play a match of 24 games against me in December 1956 and January 1957. The match was to be played in Moscow and New York for a total prize fund of $ 6,000 ($ 3,600 to the winner). Unfortunately the events in October of 1956 in Hungary prevented this match from taking place.

During the Candidates' Tournament of 1953 Reshevsky played without a second, just as I did. For both of us the conditions were even. We did all the preparation ourselves. I decided to play my favourite King's Indian Defence.

The evening before this game I was told by the heads of our delegation that, after evaluating the situation in the tournament, they had come to the conclusion that I could win against Reshevsky and I was ordered to do so. I came to the game, sat down at the table and never moved again until the game was adjourned! Of course I was fortunate to win, mostly because Reshevsky always avoided simple moves and was also playing for a win. One of the seconds at this tournament, Master M. Beilin, wrote such a good story about this game that it was published in *Molodaja Gvardija*, one of the largest literary magazines in the USSR.

| 1 | d4  | ♘f6 |
|---|-----|-----|
| 2 | c4  | g6  |
| 3 | g3  | ♗g7 |
| 4 | ♗g2 | 0-0 |

| 5 | ♘c3 | d6 |
|---|------|-----|
| 6 | ♘f3 | ♘bd7 |

This move has the disadvantage that the knight restricts the bishop but rook and bishop are on ideal squares in this King's Indian variation. However, Black has somewhat less space than White.

| 7 | 0-0 | e5 |
|---|-----|-----|
| 8 | e4 | ♖e8 |

The normal move in this position is 8...c6 but 8...♖e8 avoids any preparation by White. If now 9 d5 then Black answers 9...♘c5 10 ♕c2 a5.

| 9 | h3 | exd4 |
|----|---------|------|
| 10 | ♘xd4 | ♘c5 |
| 11 | ♖e1 | a5 |
| 12 | ♕c2 | |

Why not 12 ♘db5 to prevent ...c6? Black could play 12...♗e6 13 ♘d5 ♗xd5 14 exd5 ♖xe1+ 15 ♕xe1 ♘d3 16 ♕e2 ♘xc1 17 ♖xc1 ♕d7 and if 13 b3 then 13...c6 14 ♘xd6 ♘fxe4! Or 13...♕d7 14 ♔h2 ♖ad8 and then ...c6.

| 12 | ... | c6 |
|----|-----|-----|

There was no sense in trying to win a pawn with 12...♘fxe4 13 ♘xe4 ♗xd4 15 ♗g5 ♕d7 16 ♘f6+ ♗xf6 and Black's most valuable piece would disappear from the board.

| 13 | ♗e3 | ♘fd7 |
|----|--------|------|
| 14 | ♖ad1 | a4 |
| 15 | ♘de2 | |

White has played logically.

| 15 | ... | ♕a5 |
|----|-----|------|

A surprise for White. If he plays now 16 ♖xd6 then 16...♘e5 17 b3 ♗xh3 18 ♗xh3 ♘f3+ 19 ♔f1 ♘xe1 20 ♔xe1 ♘xe4 21 ♖d3 ♖ad8.

Now the theoretical line is finished and the real struggle starts.

| 16 | ♗f1 | ♘e5 |
|----|------|------|
| 17 | ♘d4 | a3 |

Always a useful move in this kind of position, as it could become important in the endgame.

| 18 | f4 | ♘ed7 |
|----|--------|------|
| 19 | b3 | ♘a6 |
| 20 | ♗f2 | ♘dc5 |
| 21 | ♖e3 | ♘b4 |
| 22 | ♕e2 | ♗d7 |
| 23 | e5 | dxe5 |
| 24 | fxe5 | ♖ad8 |

Now the time is right to bring the rook on a8 into the centre.

| 25 | g4 | ♘e6 |
|----|--------|------|
| 26 | ♗h4 | |

With this move White created some very interesting complications.

Does he really plan to give away his bishop for Black's rook?

Is Black willing to exchange his bishop for White's rook?

Let's see what happens.

| 26 | ... | ♘xd4 |
|----|--------|------|
| 27 | ♖xd4 | ♕c5 |

Now 27...♗xe5 is not so effective because White would not fall into the obvious trap 28 ♗xd8? ♗xd4! 29 ♗xa5 ♖xe3 but would choose the simple line 28 ♖de4 f6 29 ♖xe5 ♖xe5 30 ♖xe5 fxe5 31 ♗xd8 ♕xd8 32 ♕xe5.

| 28 | ♖de4 | ♗h6 |
|----|--------|-----------|
| 29 | ♔h1 | ♗e6! (D) |
| 30 | g5 | ♗g7 |
| 31 | ♖f4 | ♗f5 |
| 32 | ♘e4 | |

Now it is White's turn to create a nice trap for Black.

On 32...♕xe5? follows immediately 33 ♖xf5! ♕xf5 34 ♘f6+ and if 33...gxf5 White plays 34 ♘f6+ ♗xf6 35 gxf6! ♕xe3 36 ♕g2+! A brilliant conception which clearly indicates that Reshevsky's ambitions were not unfounded!

| 32 | ... | ♗xe4+ |
|----|-----|-------|
| 33 | ♖fxe4 | ♘a6 |
| 34 | e6 | fxe6 |
| 35 | ♖xe6 | ♖f8 |

At this moment I clearly remembered my instructions: play to win. The only possibility to achieve this was to avoid simplification. By this time we were both in great time-trouble.

| 36 | ♖e7 | ♗d4 |
|----|-----|-----|
| 37 | ♖3e6 | ♕f5 |
| 38 | ♖e8! | |

This is the only move! If 38 ♔g2? then 38...♘c5!

| 38 | ... | ♘c5! |
|----|-----|------|

38...♘c7 was sufficient but Black plays for a win! If now 39 ♖6e7 then Black replies 39...♘xb3 (40 axb3 a2) winning a key

pawn and destroying White's pawn chain on the queenside.

| 39 | ♖xd8 | ♘xe6 |
|----|------|------|
| 40 | ♖xf8+ | ♔xf8 |

At this point the game was adjourned and White sealed his move. He no longer has any winning chances.

| 41 | ♗g3 | |
|----|-----|--|

White's best chance. If he has time to protect the pawn on g5 by playing h3-h4 then his bishops may become active. Now it appears that the pawn on g5 is protected indirectly: 41...♘xg5 42 ♗d6+ ♔g7 43 ♕e7+ ♘f7 44 ♕f8+ ♔f6 45 ♕e7+ with perpetual check.

| 41 | ... | ♕xg5! |
|----|-----|-------|
| 42 | ♕xe6 | ♕xg3 |

| 43 | ♕c8+ | ♔e7 |
|----|------|-----|
| 44 | ♕g4 | |

This is the crucial point of the game. In a chess struggle one needs some luck. If now 44 ♕xb7+ then 44...♔d8 45 ♕a8+ ♔c7 and the white queen has no more checks.

| 44 | ... | ♕c3 |
|----|-----|-----|
| 45 | ♔g2 | ♕b2+ |
| 46 | ♕e2+ | ♔d6 |
| 47 | ♔f3 | ♗c5 |

White cannot take on b2 because the black king will get through to c1. If the white king tries to prevent this then one of Black's pawns on the kingside will promote to a queen.

| 48 | ♔e4 | ♕d4+ |
|----|-----|------|
| 49 | ♔f3 | ♕f6+ |
| 50 | ♔g2 | ♔c7 |
| 51 | ♕f3 | ♕b2+ |
| 52 | ♕e2 | ♕d4 |
| 53 | ♔f3 (D) | |

| 53 | ... | h5 |
|----|-----|-----|
| 54 | ♔g2 | g5 |
| 55 | ♔g3 | ♕f4+ |
| 56 | ♔g2 | g4 |
| 57 | hxg4 | hxg4 |
| 58 | ♔h1 | ♔b6 |
| 59 | ♔g2 | ♔c7 |
| 60 | ♔h1 | ♗d6 |
| 61 | ♔g1 | ♔b6 |
| 62 | ♕g2 | ♗c5+ |
| 63 | ♔h1 | ♕h6+ |
| 64 | ♕h2 | ♕e3 |
| 65 | b4 | ♗d4 |

**White resigns**

To tell the truth, Reshevsky didn't resign but simply waited for his flag to fall. He has no moves. After 66 c5+ ♔a7 67 ♕g2 g3 he is in complete zugzwang.

## (16) Bronstein,D – Panno,O

Olympiad, Amsterdam, 1954
*[A53] Old Indian Defence*

This was my first visit to Holland, not knowing that I would return many, many times. I cherish the most pleasant memories of my month-long stay in Amsterdam.

Of course in Russia we had learned about the special relationship between our two countries going back all the way to our Tsar Peter The Great who lived in Holland for a while, but actually to see the country is quite something else.

The Olympiad was originally scheduled to take place in Argentina but due to financial difficulties the organisers had to inform FIDE that they could not fulfil it. It was grandmaster Lodewijk Prins who,

almost single-handedly, organised it in Amsterdam at very short notice. Not only did he do it perfectly, he also played for the Dutch team and achieved a memorable, fully deserved victory over Kotov.

The event took place in the famous and still existing Apollo Hall. The playing conditions were excellent and although there were many spectators every day they watched in silence and did not come too close to our tables.

I remember that one day a young man came up to me – how he had come to the area where the players were I don't know – and asked me to sign his autograph book. When Tom Fürstenberg – that is who this young man was – showed me this autograph book almost 40 years later, I clearly remember having signed it because it is difficult to forget such a nice book! Besides, in those days we were rarely asked for autographs.

The hospitality of the Dutch people was fantastic and, contrary to the opinion of some journalists, Soviet diplomats imposed no restrictions on whom we could talk to and what we could see.

Towards the end our team was well ahead on points and we could afford to relax somewhat.

It was then that I was allowed to play on the first board in our match against Holland and I had the privilege to play with Dr Max Euwe.

Our game ended in a draw after I managed to find a good defence against his attack.

| 1 | d4 | ♘f6 |
|---|-----|------|
| 2 | c4 | d6 |
| 3 | ♘c3 | e5 |
| 4 | dxe5 | dxe5 *(D)* |

This game was played in the seventh round of the final and to increase our lead over Argentina all of us, Botvinnik, Smyslov, Keres and myself (on the third board) had decided to play extra solid chess in order not to give the slightest chance to our adversaries.

This explains my choice of opening in this game. I did not know then that the new World Junior Champion was extremely

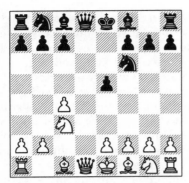

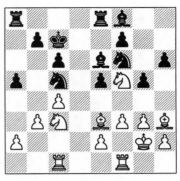

strong in positional play and that this game was going to be much more tense than I had anticipated.

| 5 | ♕xd8+ | ♚xd8 |
|---|---|---|
| 6 | ♘f3 | ♘bd7 |
| 7 | g3 | c6 |
| 8 | ♗h3 | ♗d6 |
| 9 | ♗e3 | h6 |
| 10 | 0-0 | ♖e8 |
| 11 | ♘h4 | ♗f8 |

**12 b3**

A simple defence against the threat 12...g5 13 ♘f5 ♘b6 14 f3 ♘xc4.

| 12 | ... | g5 |
|---|---|---|
| 13 | ♘f5 | ♘c5 |
| 14 | f3 | ♚c7 |
| 15 | ♖ac1 | a5 |
| 16 | ♚g2 | ♗e6 (D) |

Black avoids moving the b-pawn because after 16...b6 17 ♖c2 ♗e6 18 ♖b1 and then a3, b4, etc., the white pawns might become dangerous.

| 17 | ♘g7 | ♗xg7 |
|---|---|---|
| 18 | ♗xc5 | ♘d7 |
| 19 | ♗xe6 | ♖xe6 |
| 20 | ♗f2 | ♗f8 |

| 21 | ♘d5+ | ♚d8 |
|---|---|---|
| 22 | ♘b6 | |

If 22 ♘e3 then 22...a4 opening the a-file for the rook in the corner. Also White's pawn on b3 may become a target for the black pieces.

With the text move White keeps the black rook in a passive position and hopes to be able to go for Black's pawn on a5 at a later stage.

| 22 | ... | ♘xb6 |
|---|---|---|
| 23 | ♗xb6+ | ♚e8 |
| 24 | c5 | ♗e7 |
| 25 | ♖cd1 | |

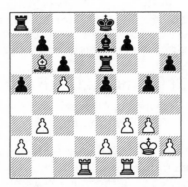

**25 ... f6**

By creating some sort of Maginot line with his pawns Black hopes that he will be able to defend some weak squares with his king. However, he can only take small steps at a time and could be out of breath quickly. In case of 25...♗d8 26 ♖d2 ♗xb6 27 cxb6 ♖a6 28 ♖fd1 ♖xb6 29 ♖d8+ ♚e7 30 ♖1d7+ ♚f6 31 ♖c7 ♚g7 32 ♖8d7 ♖f6 33 ♖xb7 ♖xb7 34 ♖xb7 White still has some pressure although Black could most likely save half a point.

| 26 | e4 | ♗d8 |
|----|------|------|
| 27 | ♗xd8 | ♖xd8 |
| 28 | ♖xd8+ | ♔xd8 |
| 29 | ♖d1+ | ♔e8 |

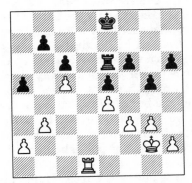

When a chess player finds himself in a position like this one he often starts to think: 'Can I win if the rooks disappear from the board? Can my king find a path through to the enemy pawns?'

In fact in this case there are two paths: a long one ♔g2-f2-e2-d2-c2-b2-a3-a4 and a shorter one ♔g2-h3-g4-f5. That is why the latter takes preference.

| 30 | h4 | ♖e7 |
|----|-----|------|

After the continuation 30...gxh4 31 gxh4 h5 the white king will be forced to make the long march. But instead of 31 gxh4 White could push his pawn to g4: 31 g4 h5 32 gxh5 ♖e7 33 ♔h3 ♖g7 34 ♖d2 ♖g3+ 35 ♔xh4 ♖xf3 36 h6 when he would have excellent chances.

That is why Black preferred to play a passive move. However, it is well-known that in a rook ending, usually the side with the most active rook wins.

Black might also have tried 30...h5 hoping that White will not play 31 g4 hxg4 32 h5 gxf3+ 33 ♔xf3 and the white king is ready to attack, not to mention the powerful pawn on h5.

| 31 | ♖d6 | |
|----|-----|--|

Of course this is a good move but much stronger would have been 31 h5 immediately. The game had been very tense up to here and in my quest for the most logical moves I had used all but two minutes of my time. This explains our far from perfect play for the next ten moves.

Black could have created some counterplay by 31... gxh4 32 g4 h5 33 ♖xf6 hxg4 34 fxg4 ♖f7.

| 31 | ... | ♔f7 |
|----|------|------|
| 32 | h5 | g4 |
| 33 | fxg4 | ♖e6 |
| 34 | ♖d8 | ♖e8 |

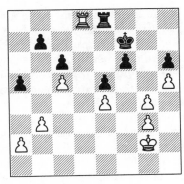

| 35 | ♖d2 | |
|----|-----|--|

There was no time to calculate the consequences of exchanging the rooks. In king and pawn endings there are always hidden traps.

At home it is easy to imagine that the white king is on c4 and the black one on a7. As there is no time to go to a4 White should move his b-pawn. And what if the black king comes to a6? Then a modest move with the a-pawn is necessary.

However, during a very serious chess game your vision might be different, not so clear. Our human abilities are limited, not only by space and time but also in quantity of mental energy.

And, be frank, would you pay so much respect to some tiny soldier on a2?

That is why White avoided exchanging rooks but now the win is far from easy.

I believe that Panno allowed me to take a full point for the Soviet team by playing too passively.

| 35 | ... | ♔e7 |
|----|------|------|
| 36 | ♔f3 | ♖g8 |
| 37 | ♖d1 | ♖g7 |
| 38 | ♖b1 | ♖g8 |
| 39 | b4 | axb4 |
| 40 | ♖xb4 | ♖b8 |
| 41 | a4 | ♔e6 |
| 42 | g5 | fxg5 |

| 43 | a5 | Rf8+ |
| 44 | Kg4 | Rf7 |
| 45 | Rb6 | Rc7 |
| 46 | a6 | bxa6 |
| 47 | Rxa6 | Kf6 |
| 48 | Ra8 | |
| | **Black resigns** | |

Only Julio Bolbochan salvaged a draw, playing White, against Vasily Smyslov. Paul Keres beat Herman Pilnik and Mikhail Botvinnik, remembering his humiliating defeat against Miguel Najdorf in Groningen 1946, took an honest revenge. Our team won the Olympiad by a margin of seven points!

Two years later Oscar Panno returned to Amsterdam and played great artistic chess in the Candidates' Tournament. When he returned to Argentina after the event he took home with him a beauty prize, not for a game he had played, but a Dutch girl named Willy Bink as his wife!

# (17) Bisguier,A – Bronstein,D

Interzonal Tournament,
Gothenburg, 1955
*[A82] Dutch Defence*

I met Arthur Bisguier for the first time during the Olympiad in Helsinki in 1952. It is difficult to believe that during this tense political climate we became friends and were openly talking to each other in the tournament hall.

We also went on a sight-seeing tour together. Arthur told me that he very much liked literature and writing. In the following years we kept our friendship going, mostly from a distance but we were always very pleased when we got the chance to play together. If I remember correctly we played in two national USSR vs. USA matches in 1954 and 1955 respectively, in Gothenburg 1955, Moscow 1962, Zagreb in 1965, Tallinn 1971 and 1981 and in several Chess Olympiads. In 1993 we met again in Las Vegas where we spent a lot of time together sitting around yellow chess tables, brown dinner tables and, Arthur

always being a very lucky man, around the green gaming tables!

About 20 years ago Arthur Bisguier and Paul Benkö played a match of four games with new rules. The board was set-up without the pieces; only the pawns were in their original positions on the 2nd and 7th ranks. Instead of making a move, each player in turn was allowed to put a piece of his choosing on the board anywhere on the 1st and 8th ranks. When all pieces were on the board White could make his first move. I was honoured to be called the inventor of this novelty although I got the idea from a letter published in *British Chess Magazine* in 1945 or 1946. All four games were published in the Dutch magazine *Schaakbulletin*.

Nowadays Bobby Fischer proposes 'shuffle chess.' (See page 271 for David Bronstein's latest innovation! T.F.)

| 1 | d4 | f5 |
| 2 | e4 | fxe4 |

This gambit is named after the great English player Howard Staunton. Yes, he avoided a match with Paul Morphy but on the other hand he wrote excellent comments to the works of William Shakespeare.

Which is of more cultural value?

| 3 | Nd2 | |

A new move. Arthur was very proud of this novelty and said: 'It is a gift for you, David.'

| 3 | ... | Nf6 |
| 4 | g4 | d5 |
| 5 | g5 | Nfd7! |

On 5...Ng8 White could play 6 f3 Bf5 7 fxe4 dxe4 8 Nc4 when he stands better. White has more space and Black is underdeveloped.

| 6 | f3 | e5 |
| 7 | fxe4 *(D)* | |
| 7 | ... | Qxg5 |

Better would have been 7...Nc6 8 exd5 Nxd4 9 Ne4 Nc5 10 Bg2 Bf5 or 9 c3 Qxg5 10 cxd4 Qh4+ 11 Ke2 Qg4+ 12 Ke1 Qh4+ with a draw.

| 8 | Ngf3 | Qh5 |
| 9 | exd5 | Bd6 |
| 10 | Ne4 | 0-0 |

**11 &g2 &g4**

Black is playing for combinations. It would have been much better to continue 11...&f6 in order to activate the bishop on c8.

**12 &e2 &b4+**
**13 c3**

**13 ... exd4**
**14 &xd4**

After 14 cxb4 White didn't like 14...d3, for instance 15 h3 &g6.

**14 ... &h4+**
**15 &d1 &e7**

It is not easy to evaluate such an unusual position, even for a strong computer. Both White's knights dominate the centre, Black's queen is not 'developed' and there is no clear answer to the question as to who has the so-called 'advantage'. It is a real chess position and all you need to do is fight!

**16 &g3 &c5**
**17 &f3 &a4+**
**18 b3 &d7**

The bishop is cut off once more!

**19 &c2 &f6**
**20 &a3 &ba6**
**21 &d4 &f7!**

Threatening 22...&g6+ and 23...&d3+ if White plays 23 &b2.

**22 &e4 &e8**

Black prepares to take back on f6 with the pawn but the pressure on e4 has to be increased first. The pin is annoying.

The threat is 23...&xd4 24 cxd4 &xe4 25 &xe4 &f5.

**23 &hf1**

White has prevented ...&f5 and the bishop on f6 can no longer move but Black sets a trap. Now he should pin the white knight on e4.

**23 ... &g6**
**24 &ae1 (D)**
**24 ... &h3!!**

Black intended this move when he played 22...&e8. If now 25 &xh3 then 25...&xe4, if 25 &h1 then 25...&xf1 and if 25 &g1 then 25...&xg2. It appears that the rook on a8 is not developed but it is performing an important task; supporting the rook on e8.

A similar move was made by Dr Alekhine in his famous game with Karel Opočensky in Prague 1942.

| 25 | ♖xf6 | ♕xg2 |
|----|------|------|
| 26 | ♖f4  | ♖xe4 |
| 27 | ♖xe4 | ♘xe4 |
| 28 | ♕xg2 | ♗xg2 |
| 29 | ♖e2  | ♗h1  |
| 30 | ♖e1  |      |

White has found the best defence which shows how deeply the move 24...♗h3 had to be calculated!

| 30 | ... | ♘f2 |
|----|-----|-----|
| 31 | ♘e6 | ♗xd5 |

**White resigns**

## (18) Unzicker,W – Bronstein,D

Interzonal Tournament,
Gothenburg, 1955
*[B92] Sicilian Defence*

This was my second Interzonal Tournament and I was lucky enough to make a double and win them both without losing a game. In chess literature it is often said that in 1947 the FIDE created a new, very fair, cycle of competition called the World Championship.

I doubt whether this was good for Chess Art and from my own experience I can say that it is far from being fair. No, I am not talking about my match for the World Championship in 1951 when the Champion had the right not to win a single game and could retain his title by making 24 draws. My remark is completely different. In the Interzonal Tournament of 1948 we were fighting for the first five

places which would mean qualification for the Candidates' Tournament. When the tournament was finished, FIDE increased the number of qualifiers from five to ten. All five participants in The Hague/Moscow tournament of 1948 received the right to play in the next Candidates' Tournament. When in the Candidates' Tournament of 1953 Keres, Reshevsky and myself shared the second place, FIDE awarded us the right to play a tournament between us to decide who would play in the next Interzonal Tournament...

Only after my protest did FIDE change its mind and ask us to play for one place in the next Candidates' Tournament.

In the Interzonal Tournament in 1958, when I finished jointly half a point behind the winners, FIDE did not increase the number of players for the next Candidates' Tournament.

Meanwhile Botvinnik had created a rule, which was accepted by FIDE, that no more than three players from the USSR could qualify from the Candidates' Tournament. By introducing such a 'clever' idea he could narrow down his most dangerous opponents to only three. Another non-chess move by 'the champion of all time'.

I am not going so far as to say that the FIDE system made no sense at all. During the AVRO tournament in 1938 it was generally accepted that the best players at that time were Dr Alekhine, Capablanca, Dr Euwe, Keres, Fine, Reshevsky, Flohr and Botvinnik.

On this basis Botvinnik invited Dr Euwe, Keres, Reshevsky, Fine and Smyslov in September 1946 to sign an agreement concerning the World Championship.

They played (without Fine but also without Najdorf and Boleslavsky) in the famous 'The Hague-Moscow' tournament in 1948. Nobody had any doubts that these five were the best players at the time.

Why then did we need a FIDE system at all?

In his book *The History of Chess* grandmaster Harry Golombek even suggested a new way to measure the success of a grandmaster. He said that, despite the fact that in the AVRO tournament the first and second places were shared by Keres and Fine, the really impressive candidate for the World Championship title was Botvinnik.

Maybe with this statement Golombek was trying to justify the secret negotiations that were going on at the time between Dr Alekhine and Botvinnik...

After the Interzonal Tournament in Amsterdam 1964, where I managed sixth place, FIDE, according to new rules, eliminated me together with Stein and gave these places to Reshevsky and Portisch, who had finished behind us.

Thirty years later I still remember that, after the tournament was finished, I protested to FIDE and suggested increasing the number of people who could play in the Candidates' matches by playing one extra round. This proposition was on the agenda at the FIDE congress in Tel-Aviv during the Olympiad there, but despite official support from several chess federations, it was rejected on the basis that you cannot change the rules of qualification while the three-year cycle is in progress.

I have only one question now: What about the Interzonal Tournament in 1948 when the rules were changed **after** the tournament?!?!

Now it is time to say how I came to play in Gothenburg. About two or three months before the tournament I received a telephone call from Paul Keres in the middle of the night. After apologies for calling so late he asked me only one question: 'David, what do you have against Gothenburg?' We understood each other immediately and so I answered without any hesitation: 'Nothing. Let's go and play in this Interzonal Tournament. As I understand from your question, Gothenburg must be a wonderful town.'

'Thank you,' said Keres and so we had managed to create an opportunity to go abroad again!

This is the only reason why we refused to play with Reshevsky for a place in the next Candidates' Tournament and therefore Reshevsky's qualification was automatic. Unfortunately, he did not use this opportunity and to this day I do not know why.

When I took first place in Gothenburg the number of qualifiers was also five but after the tournament was finished, FIDE again allowed four more losers to play in the Candidates' Tournament in Amsterdam 1956!

Now, can we really call the FIDE system fair?

| 1 | e4 | c5! |
| 2 | ♘f3 | d6! |
| 3 | d4 | cxd4 |
| 4 | ♘xd4 | ♘f6 |
| 5 | ♘c3 | a6! |

This opening is known as the Najdorf variation, though Karel Opočensky played it before Najdorf did!

| 6 | ♗e2 | e5 |

This move intends to drive the knight away from the centre and to stop the advance of the e-pawn, hoping to eventually play ...d5.

| 7 | ♘b3 | ♗e7 |
| 8 | 0-0 | 0-0 |
| 9 | ♗e3 | ♕c7 |
| 10 | a4 | b6! |
| 11 | ♕d2 | ♗e6 |
| 12 | ♖fd1 | ♖c8 |

To prevent ♘d5: if now 13 ♘d5 then 13...♗xd5 14 exd5 ♕xc2.

| 13 | ♕e1 | ♕b7 |
| 14 | ♖d2 | ♘bd7 |
| 15 | f3 | |

| 15 | ... | d5! |

This move is always welcomed by Black in the Sicilian Defence. But quite a few defensive and preparatory moves need to be made before one finally has the opportunity to attack White's most important pawn – the king's pawn.

| 16 | exd5 | ♘xd5 |
| 17 | ♘xd5 | ♗xd5 |
| 18 | ♖ad1 | ♘f6 |
| 19 | ♘c1 | |

| 19 | ... | e4! |

Now the time has come to cross into 'no man's land' to attack f3 to make g2 a target.

| 20 | ♕f2 | ♗c5 |
| 21 | ♗xc5 | bxc5 |
| 22 | ♕e3 | ♖e8 |
| 23 | f4 | c4! |

Another black pawn joins the attack with the clear intention of disrupting the white pawn chain and create new weaknesses on White's half of the board.

| 24 | b3 | ♖ac8 |
| 25 | h3 | |

| 25 | ... | ♗e6! |

Making d5 available to the knight.

| 26 | ♔h2 | |

If 26 g4 then Black could play 26...♘d5 27 ♕xe4 ♕b6+ 28 ♕d4 ♕b8 29 ♖f1 cxb3 30 cxb3 ♖cd8 31 ♖dd1 g5!

| 26 | ... | ♕c7 |
| 27 | ♖d6 | a5! |
| 28 | bxc4 | ♗xc4 |
| 29 | ♘b3 | ♗xe2 |
| 30 | ♕xe2 | |

| 30 | ... | e3! |

A very active pawn indeed. Was it already dreaming about the fairy tale in which pawns are sometimes transformed into queens? Most likely yes but what about the queen on e2? How can a lonely pawn move such a strong piece out of the way? He cannot and it is obvious that some assistance is required.

| 31 | ♖6d4 | ♘e4 |
| 32 | ♕f3 | ♘g5 |
| 33 | ♕g4 | ♘e6 |
| 34 | ♖e4 | h5 |

Attacking the queen and creating an escape route for the king.

| 35 | ♕f3 | ♘g5 |

It was simpler to take the f-pawn with the knight, but in time-trouble I did not see it and made a more natural move.

| 36 | ♖xe8+ | ♖xe8 |
| 37 | ♕g3 | ♕xc2 |
| 38 | ♖d5 (D) | |
| 38 | ... | e2! |

In severe time-trouble I no longer had time to calculate and had to rely entirely on my intuition. If now 39 ♘d4 then Black replies 39...♕e4.

| 39 | ♖xg5 | e1♕! |

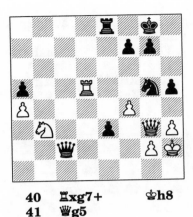

| 40 | ♖xg7+ | ♚h8 |
| 41 | ♕g5 | |

It appears that White arrives first.

| 41 | ... | ♕xg2+!! |

No, it's Black!

| 42 | ♕xg2 | ♖e2 |

**White resigns**

## (19) Bronstein,D – Evans,L

Match USSR vs. USA,
Moscow, 1955
*[C78] Spanish Opening*

September 1995 is exactly 50 years since the first meeting of the national teams of the USA and USSR. I was then only 21 years old, and thanks to my excellent result in the 14th USSR Championship, I was honoured to be a member of our team.

On the 10th board I played two very interesting games with the American master Anthony Santasiere.

The match, played by radio, lasted four days and the result was sensational: the winners of four Olympiads, the Americans,

lost by 4½-15½. More important was the attention this friendly event received by the media. The newspapers were full of chess news and the American Ambassador to the USSR received the Soviet team and delegation at a reception at his embassy, just 200 metres from the Kremlin walls.

It was to be my first visit to 'terra incognita'. I did not know the etiquette very well and decided to stay in the background. Mr Averell Harriman noticed me standing in a corner of a big hall, came over to me, took me by the arm and asked: 'Would you like a glass of whisky with ice or soda?' The only thing I recognised was the word 'ice' so I said: 'yes please'. When he handed me my glass I saw a drink with an unfamiliar colour and smell but decided to go for it. I closed my eyes and took a few sips. Nothing happened; I survived! From that moment onwards whisky became a favourite drink of mine – amongst others of course!

Then Mr Harriman proposed a toast to our two countries as being friendly and close neighbours!

Before the match in 1955 I was suddenly invited to go and see the Chairman of the Committee of Soviet Physical Culture and Sport – chess came under their protection – Mr Nikolai Nikolayevich Romanov.

The conversation lasted less than a minute: 'David Ionovich, I beg of you, please play seriously against the American team tomorrow. In our Soviet Championships you can experiment as much as you like but this match is important. Will you do that?'

I did not have to think about my answer: 'Of course.' I was pleased that I was not obliged to stop my experiments altogether!

| 1 | e4 | e5 |
| 2 | ♘f3 | ♘c6 |
| 3 | ♗b5 | a6 |
| 4 | ♗a4 | ♘f6 |
| 5 | 0-0 | b5 |
| 6 | ♗b3 | d6 *(D)* |

A direct invitation to play 7 ♘g5. Then, after 7...d5 8 exd5 ♘d4 9 ♖e1 (or 9 ♕e1)

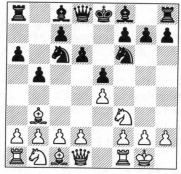

9...♘xb3 10 ♖xe5+ (or 10 ♕xe5+) 10...♗e7 11 axb3 0-0, Black has excellent attacking possibilities in spite of being two pawns down. The white queenside is still undeveloped and the pawn on d5 will fall. However, it is unwise for White to accept this present. An article about this variation was published in 1939 in *Chess in the USSR*.

| | | |
|---|---|---|
| 7 | c3 | ♘a5 |
| 8 | ♗c2 | c5 |
| 9 | d4 | ♕c7 |
| 10 | ♘bd2 | g6 |

Up to here the players have followed the well-known path of the Chigorin system in the Spanish Opening.

If Black had now played 10...♗e7 and then castled the game would have become a positional struggle.

However, Larry Evans, being a very inventive combinative player, found a new way of solving the opening problems. He combined two systems of great chess thinkers: Steinitz and Chigorin.

His intention is good but the black king is still in the centre and this gives White

an opportunity to start a sharp attack against Black's pawns.

| | | |
|---|---|---|
| 11 | b4 | cxb4 |
| 12 | cxb4 | ♘c6 |
| 13 | ♗b2 | ♗g7 |
| 14 | ♖c1 | ♗b7 |
| 15 | ♗b3 | ♕e7 |

There is a classical rule in chess which says that you can keep your king in the centre but only in a closed position. But if the position is even semi-open, then you can always expect a nasty surprise.

| | | |
|---|---|---|
| 16 | ♖xc6 | ... |

Starting an attack and taking advantage of the fact that the pawn on f7 is not protected by a rook.

| | | |
|---|---|---|
| 16 | ... | ♗xc6 |
| 17 | dxe5 | ♘h5 |

Evans, a very strong grandmaster, had probably calculated up to this point when he played 10...g6. I can only assume that he had underestimated the power of White's next moves.

| | | |
|---|---|---|
| 18 | g4 | ♘f4 |
| 19 | exd6 | ♕d7 |

Black is threatening to take the g-pawn with his queen. It seems that White needs to change his strategy and must now defend instead of continuing the attack.

Luckily there is a move that does both!

| | | |
|---|---|---|
| 20 | ♘e5 | ♘h3+ |
| 21 | ♔h1 | ♗xe5 |
| 22 | ♗xe5 | f6 |
| 23 | ♗g3 | ♔f8 |
| 24 | ♔g2 | ♘g5 |
| 25 | h4 | ♘f7 |
| 26 | ♕a1 | ♘e5 |
| 27 | g5 | ♖e8 |
| 28 | ♕d4 | ♕g4 |

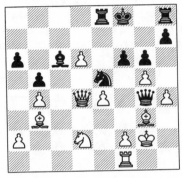

The black queen has finally come to g4, but only for one move. The rest of the game is only of interest because both of us were in great time-trouble. We played at lightning speed until the end because we did not know how many moves had been made.

| | | |
|---|---|---|
| 29 | f3 | ♕d7 |
| 30 | gxf6 | ♘f7 |
| 31 | e5 | g5 |
| 32 | ♖e1 | gxh4 |
| 33 | e6 | ♕c8 |
| 34 | ♕xh4 | ♖xe6 |
| 35 | ♖xe6 | ♗e8 |
| 36 | ♖e7 | ♕c1 |
| 37 | ♖xe8+ | ♔xe8 |
| 38 | ♕e4+ | ♔d8 |
| 39 | ♕e7+ | ♔c8 |
| 40 | ♗e6+ | ♔b8 |
| 41 | ♕c7+ | ♕xc7 |
| 42 | dxc7+ | ♔b7 |
| 43 | ♗xf7 | ♖f8 |
| 44 | ♗d5+ | |

**Black resigns**

This game with Evans was, I am sad to say, played in the last friendly match between the teams of the United States and the USSR.

When Evans was 17 years old he had written a book with 50 of my best games and indicated that, in his opinion, I would be the next World Champion.

## (20) Aloni,I – Bronstein,D

Olympiad, Moscow, 1956
*[E85] King's Indian Defence*

The following story and comments (except where indicated otherwise) are excerpts from an article in the *British Chess Magazine*, no.5, 1967 by Raaphy Persitz:

There is a Greek saying, ascribed to the poet Archilochus, that goes: 'The fox knows many things but the hedgehog knows one big thing.' If applied to chess players the difference between fox and hedgehog corresponds more or less to the distinction between strategists and tacticians; between those who rely primarily upon their judgement and those who trust their intuition. The former are hedgehogs, the latter are foxes.

Hedgehogs are orderly and determined creatures. They think in bold, broad terms and are intent on getting to the heart of things.

In contrast, foxes are curious beasts, loving the many possible continuations, the complexity of combinations and thriving upon uncertainty. True foxes often create exceptional circumstances where rules are, as it were, made to be disregarded. They are always on the look-out for situations in which material and positional values are so confused, so blurred, that an objective appraisal becomes meaningless.

Thus Averbakh, Euwe, Fine, Flohr, Gligorić, Kottnauer, Nimzowitsch, Olafsson, Pachman, Panno, Petrosian, Portisch, Réti, Rubinstein, Smyslov, Steinitz, Taimanov and Tarrasch, to make a random selection, are all, in varying degrees, hedgehogs; whilst Alexander, Bronstein, Chigorin,

Czerniak, Geller, Korchnoi, Kotov, Lasker, Larsen, Marshall, Najdorf, Pillsbury, Reshevsky, Pirc, Spielmann, Szabo, Tal and Tartakower are foxes.

It would not be very purposeful to explain in detail the distinction. After all, there are foxes – and there are foxes!

Indeed, not even all hedgehogs look or think alike. And there exist numerous cases that cannot be clearly put into one or the other category; independent, classless animals who go about their own way, stubbornly refusing to be confined into cramped, precisely defined cases: Alekhine, Botvinnik, Capablanca, Keres, Spassky and Stein are but a few members of this group.

Hedgehog or fox? Fox or hedgehog? Both beasts have shown themselves capable of equally noble exploits.

In the following brief and fierce duel, two worthy arch-foxes confront each other at their fighting best. It is a breathtaking cut-and-thrust battle which does credit to both. In the end, the more creative, more resourceful, more profound fox, Bronstein, scores a memorable victory over the cunning and tenacious fox, Aloni.

Being one of Bronstein's most imaginative efforts I dare say this encounter (which for some obscure reason has not attracted the attention it deserves) will find admirers even amongst the dourest and most resolute of hedgehogs.

| | | |
|---|---|---|
| 1 | d4 | ♘f6 |
| 2 | c4 | g6 |
| 3 | ♘c3 | ♗g7 |
| 4 | e4 | d6 |

The King's Indian Defence has become one of the most formidable replies to 1 d4. Its popularity is no small measure due to pioneering work by Bronstein and Boleslavsky in the forties.

**5 f3**

The Sämisch Attack. White intends to castle on the queenside and to attack on the kingside.

| | | |
|---|---|---|
| 5 | ... | e5 |
| 6 | ♘ge2 | |

6 d5 is more committal while the simplifying 6 dxe5 dxe5 7 ♕xd8+ ♔xd8 poses no problems for the black king: he will find a safe place on c7 after ...c6. White must then take care that Black does not get control over the square d4.

| | | |
|---|---|---|
| 6 | ... | 0-0 |
| 7 | ♗e3 | |

With Black having castled and played ...e5 White may consider 7 ♗g5 here.

| | | |
|---|---|---|
| 7 | ... | ♘bd7 |
| 8 | ♕d2 | a6 |
| 9 | g4? | |

**Bronstein**: Premature. It is better to play d5 first to stabilise the centre and to accept the pawn sacrifice after 9...♘h5 10 g4 ♘f4 11 ♘xf4 exf4 12 ♗xf4 ♘e5 13 ♗e2.

| | | |
|---|---|---|
| 9 | ... | exd4! |

The thematic reaction to an ill-prepared wing demonstration: a timely counterattack in the centre.

**10 ♘xd4**

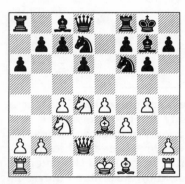

**Bronstein**: Many years ago positions of this kind were judged without any doubt as favourable for White. White has control of the centre and has prepared the attack h2-h4-h5. The new dynamic school questions such routine statements. Today preference is given to the player who has the initiative on both wings. In his famous book about Indian Openings, published in 1925, Dr Tartakower says that opening strategy is changing. Instead of *occupying* the centre one should try to *attack* it. This is exactly the strategy I followed in this important game.

| | | |
|---|---|---|
| 10 | ... | c5! |

A daring decision: Black deliberately weakens his pawn on d6 and renounces control of the central square d5 in order to increase the power of his pieces. It will become apparent that the advantages of this plan will outweigh the disadvantages.

| 11 | ♘c2 | ♘e5! |
| 12 | ♗e2 | ♗e6! |

The action is shifting from the kingside to the queenside, which represents a moral victory for Black and indicates how ill-timed 9 g4 was.

| 13 | ♘a3 | ♘fd7! |

Preparing either ...f5 or ...♘c6-d4.

**Bronstein**: The last four moves are typical in many variations in the King's Indian Defence. The pawn on d6 is sacrificed for an active deployment of the black pieces.

| 14 | 0-0-0 |

**Bronstein**: White accepts the challenge. If White castles kingside, then Black can make an active move with his queen to h4, trying to organise an attack against the weakened white pawns.

| 14 | ... | b5! |

Black's target is now on the queenside and he opens lines at the cost of three pawns in order to take the white king by storm.

| 15 | cxb5 | axb5 |
| 16 | ♘cxb5 (D) |

| 16 | ... | c4! |
| 17 | ♕xd6 | ♕a5 |

**Bronstein**: Better was 17...c3 at once because now White can play 18 ♗d2. During the game both players were of the opinion that after 18...c3 19 ♗xc3 ♖fc8 20 ♔b1 ♖xc3, etc., Black has a very strong attack. This is why White is trying to avoid this variation with the move 18 ♗d4. If now 18...c3 then White can safely play 19 ♘xc3.

| 18 | ♗d4? | ♖fc8 |

**Bronstein**: This move was very surprising for White because his bishop now finds a shelter on c3 from the cold Polar wind.

| 19 | ♗c3 |

| 19 | ... | ♘d3+! |

**Bronstein**: However, the icy wind has shifted and is now blowing from the North-East!

| 20 | ♗xd3 | ♗xc3 |
| 21 | ♘xc3 | cxd3 |
| 22 | ♖xd3 (D) |

**Bronstein**: White has three extra pawns but as compensation Black has a lot of space for his pieces.

Now the black knight enters into play and announces with a big fanfare the final attack.

| 22 | ... | ♘e5 |
| 23 | ♖e3 | ♖d8! |
| 24 | ♕e7 | ♖d7 |
| 25 | ♕f6 | ♕c5! |

The crowning point of the combination initiated by 19...♘d3+. White is allowed no time to regroup.

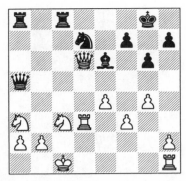

**Bronstein**: All of Black's pieces are ideally placed, even the rook on a8 although he has yet to make a move! (And will not in this game! T.F.).

**26    ♘c2**

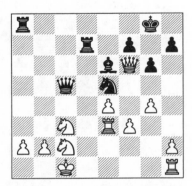

**26    ...        ♘d3+**

**Bronstein**: It is not often that knights work like twins but on moves 19 and 26 they both give check to the white king, making identical moves.

| 27 | ♖xd3 | ♖xd3 |
|----|------|------|
| 28 | a3 | ♕f2 |
| 29 | ♖e1 | ♖d2 |

**White resigns**

Games like this can leave one with mixed feelings: on the one hand a sense of satisfaction at being just good enough to appreciate their beauty; on the other hand a sense of despondency stemming from the realisation I shall never live to play like Bronstein.

This, perhaps, is just as well: what a dull place our world would be if all its inhabitants could play chess like Bronstein, paint like Rembrandt, or make love like Casanova...!

**Bronstein:** This game was played during the first match between Israel and the USSR. We played on four boards and if one remembers that this match took place in September 1956 it is easy to understand that there was great tension on every board.

I was happy to score the winning point for my team as the other three boards had finished in a draw. Also, I was proud of this victory against this very strong combinative player, many times champion of Israel.

## (21) Spassky,B – Bronstein,D
Candidates' Tournament,
Amsterdam/Leeuwarden, 1956
*[E80] King's Indian Defence*

Spassky came to this tournament only hours after having become the new World Junior Champion, so I decided to play a sharp game. It was not our first encounter. During the Soviet Championship in 1947, I was invited to visit a junior chess club and then had a chance to meet for the first time two talented players, Victor Korchnoi and Boris Spassky. I did not reject the invitation to play two five-minute games with Spassky. Although he lost both, he impressed me very much with his concentration and logical moves.

In the Autumn of 1993, when I visited Paris for several days I paid a visit to the Caïssa Chess Club to meet the legendary Mme Chantal Chaudé de Silans again and to have the pleasure of presenting this brilliant French lady with a beauty prize – flowers from the best gardens of France! Our friendship dates back to the Women's World Championship held in Moscow, December 1949 and we have since met many times.

The next evening I was pleased that Spassky, who had heard that I was in Paris, immediately came to see me. We had a long talk and often referred to our first meeting. We have played many fine games but I never managed to win and I know why. I always tried to disrupt his logical play right from the opening. This worked against others such as Botvinnik but it failed against Spassky!

| 1 | d4 | ♘f6 |
|---|-----|------|
| 2 | c4 | g6 |
| 3 | ♘c3 | ♗g7 |
| 4 | e4 | d6 |
| 5 | f3 | e5 |
| 6 | d5 | ♘h5 |
| 7 | ♗e3 | ♘a6 |
| 8 | ♕d2 | ♕h4+ |
| 9 | g3 | |

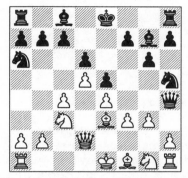

To an amateur some of Black's moves seem unorthodox, but in chess 2+2 is not always 4! If White had played 9 ♗f2 then 9...♕e7.

| 9 | ... | ♘xg3!!! |

Dr Max Euwe in the tournament book: 'An extremely deep and highly original conception whereby Black sacrifices his queen for the pair of bishops and a couple of pawns! A most enterprising combination. Everybody knows that the queen is much stronger than two bishops in the endgame.

'It is very difficult to judge the correctness of this sacrifice but one thing is certain: if there is a player in the world who could make such a conception work, it can only be Bronstein! It is a pity that he failed; maybe he was not in form that day.'

| 10 | ♕f2 | ♘xf1 |
|----|------|------|
| 11 | ♕xh4 | ♘xe3 (D) |
| 12 | ♔f2 | ♘xc4 |
| 13 | b3 | ♘b6 |

More active would have been 13...♘a3 and ...♘b4.

| 14 | ♘ge2 | f5 |

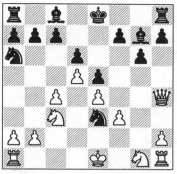

| 15 | ♖hg1 | 0-0 |
|----|-------|-----|
| 16 | ♔g2 | ♗d7 |

Black has an excellent pawn formation.

| 17 | a4 | ♗f6 |
|----|------|------|
| 18 | ♕g3 | ♘b4 |
| 19 | a5 | ♘c8 |

So far all of Black's plans have been successful. If now 20 h4 there could follow: 20...♘e7 21 ♖h1 ♘c2 22 ♖ac1 ♘e3+ 23 ♔f2 f4 24 ♕g1 ♖f7 25 h5 g5 26 h6 ♔h8 and later ...♖g8 with the intention of opening more scope for both bishops by playing ...g4.

| 20 | exf5? | |

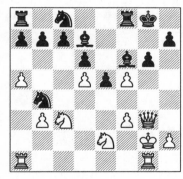

| 20 | ... | ♗xf5? |

Not the best move from either player. Black had at least a draw with 20...♘e7, for instance 21 ♘e4 ♘xf5 22 ♘xf6+ ♖xf6 23 ♕g5 ♖af8 followed by ...♘xd5 or ...♘d3. White cannot play 21 fxg6 because after 21...♘f5! Black has a winning attack. For instance 22 ♕e1 (22 ♕f2 ♘d3) 22...♘c2 or even worse 22 gxh7++ ♔h8 23 ♕e1 ♘d3 24 ♕d2 ♘h4+ and the idea of the queen's sacrifice is fully justified after 25 ♔g3 ♖g8+!!

| 21 | Ra4 |
|----|-----|

Black completely overlooked this move but he continues to fight and put up strong resistance.

| 21 | ... | ♘d3 |
|----|-----|-----|

Better was 21...♘a6 right away.

| 22 | Rc4 | ♘c5 |
|----|-----|-----|
| 23 | ♘e4 | ♘a6 |
| 24 | ♘xf6+ | Rxf6 |
| 25 | f4 | e4 |
| 26 | ♘c3 | ♘e7 |
| 27 | Re1 | Raf8 |

Drawing all the pieces into the attack. Possibly only Spassky could win such a position.

| 28 | b4 | c6 |
|----|-----|-----|
| 29 | ♘xe4 | ♗xe4+ |
| 30 | Rcxe4 | ♘xd5 |

Black originally sacrificed his queen to obtain the pair of bishops. All that now remains are two knights!

| 31 | Re8 | ♘ac7 |
|----|-----|-----|
| 32 | Rxf8+ | ♔xf8 |
| 33 | ♔h1 | Rf5 |
| 34 | ♕h4 | ♘f6 |
| 35 | ♕f2 | ♘b5 |

Black tries to construct a fortress but he is disillusioned and has no fighting spirit left.

| 36 | ♕e2 | ♘d5 |
|----|-----|-----|

| 37 | a6 | bxa6 |
|----|-----|------|

The fortress turns out to be a 'Hollywood Village' with many entry gates and no protection.

| 38 | ♕e8+ | ♔g7 |
|----|------|-----|
| 39 | ♕xc6 | ♔h6 |
| 40 | ♕xa6 | ♘xb4 |
| 41 | ♕b7 | ♘d3 |

| 42 | Re7 | ♘xf4 |
|----|-----|------|
| 43 | Rxh7+ | ♔g5 |
| 44 | ♕e7+ | ♔g4 |
| 45 | ♕e3 | ♔g5 |
| 46 | h4+ | ♔g4 |
| 47 | ♔h2 | ♘h5 |

A fight to the very end!

| 48 | Rh6 |
|----|-----|

**Black resigns**

I was very pleased to read many nice compliments about my play in this game but best of all I liked George Koltanowski's statement in his article in *Chess Life & Review* that a player who is brave enough to sacrifice his queen for two bishops in top-level competition should not harbour any hopes of ever becoming World Champion!

For me, a player such as Koltanowski, who at the age of 90 can still give **simultaneous blindfold** exhibitions is a *real* champion!

The best evidence that chess is not a sport but an intellectual Art is the fact that in the next generation of amateurs there might always be an admirer of beauty who finds an improvement of your attack and plays another immortal game.

Such a game was played on 6 June 1965 for the Hastings Chess Club championship between H.G. Rhodes (white) and A. Learner (black).

Here is the game, played with great energy and a lot of imagination.

1 d4 ♘f6 2 c4 d6 3 ♘c3 e5 4 d5 g6 5 e4 ♗g7 6 f3 ♘a6 7 ♗e3 ♘h5 8 ♕d2 ♕h4+ 9 g3 ♘xg3 10 ♕f2 ♘xf1 11 ♕xh4 ♘xe3 12 ♔e2 ♘c2 13 Rc1 ♘d4+ 14 ♔d1 0-0 15 ♘ce2

f5 16 ♘xd4 exd4 17 ♘h3 fxe4 18 fxe4 ♘c5 19 ♘f2 d3 20 b4 ♖xf2 21 bxc5 ♖g2 22 h3 ♗d7 23 c6 bxc6 24 ♕e7 ♗h6 25 ♕xd7 ♖d2+ 26 ♔e1 ♖e2+ 27 ♔d1 ♖f8 28 ♖b1 ♖d2+ 29 ♔e1 ♖e2+ 30 ♔d1 ♖ef2 31 ♔e1 ♗d2+ 32 ♔d1 ♗c3 33 ♖e1 ♖f1 White resigns.

'Bravo!' as Dr Tartakower used to say in such cases!

# (22) Bronstein,D – Nezhmetdinov,R

24th USSR Championship, Moscow, 1957

*[C76] Spanish Opening*

By education Rashid Nezhmetdinov was a fantastically good mathematician and science probably lost a great mind. Besides chess he also loved to play draughts and was unique in the fact that he was equally good at both. For many years he won Russian Championships in both disciplines!

By playing in a sharp attacking style he produced many brilliant combinations. His creative energy was dangerous to every opponent, even Mikhail Tal suffered. In my library I have two editions of Nezhmetdinov's best games and I can recommend these to anyone. By the way, Nezhmetdinov also gave blindfold simultaneous exhibitions in chess **and** draughts *at the same time*! A real genius.

| | | |
|---|---|---|
| 1 | e4 | e5 |
| 2 | ♘f3 | ♘c6 |
| 3 | ♗b5 | a6 |
| 4 | ♗a4 | d6 |

One of the best defences. However, it gives White a choice of how to play.

If 5 0-0 ♗g4 6 h3 ♗h5 7 c3 ♕f6, Fischer discovered that 8 g4! ♗g6 9 d4 ♗xe4 10 ♘bd2 wins for White. Or 5 ♗xc6+ bxc6 6 d4 f6 7 ♘c3 ♗e6 8 ♗e3 ♘e7 9 ♕d3 ♖b8 10 0-0-0 and White has more space. Also 5 d4 b5 6 ♗b3 ♘xd4 7 ♘xd4 exd4 and now 8 ♗d5 or 8 c3 (not 8 ♕xd4 c5 9 ♕d5 ♗e6 10 ♕c6+ ♗d7 11 ♕d5 c4) and White has a long-lasting initiative.

| | | |
|---|---|---|
| 5 | c3 | ♗d7 |

As my opponent was an excellent combinative player I had expected 5...f5,

which Capablanca once played against Réti. I had prepared 6 exf5 ♗xf5 7 d4 e4 8 0-0 exf3 9 ♖e1+ with a strong attack.

Long ago, after the 14th USSR Championship in 1945, I wrote an article about the openings played in this tournament and made the prediction that in future one of the new champions would probably use such a method of attack. Is it possible that I foresaw the appearance of Mikhail Tal?!

| | | |
|---|---|---|
| 6 | d4 | g6 |
| 7 | 0-0 | ♗g7 |
| 8 | a3! | |

A logical move but it is not as simple as it looks. In some cases it enables White to start an attack with b4.

| | | |
|---|---|---|
| 8 | ... | ♘ge7 |
| 9 | ♗e3 | 0-0 |
| 10 | ♘bd2 | ♕e8 |

To make space for the rook on a8.

| | | |
|---|---|---|
| 11 | ♗b3 | ♔h8 |
| 12 | dxe5 | dxe5 |

Black must keep control of d4.

| | | |
|---|---|---|
| 13 | ♘h4! | |

To enable the f-pawn to join in the attack.

| | | |
|---|---|---|
| 13 | ... | f6 |
| 14 | g3 | ♗h3 |
| 15 | ♖e1 | ♖d8 |
| 16 | ♕e2 | f5 |
| 17 | f4! | |

| | | |
|---|---|---|
| 17 | ... | exf4? |

According to his style of play as Nezhmetdinov always felt at home in long combinations, but he failed to see White's strong 23rd move.

In my view the best line for Black would have been 17...fxe4 18 ♘xe4 ♘d5 19 ♗c5 exf4.

| 18 | &xf4 | fxe4 |
|----|------|------|
| 19 | ⊘xe4 | ⊘d5 |
| 20 | &g5! | |

The following complications are in White's favour.

| 20 | ... | ⊘d4! |
|----|-----|------|
| 21 | cxd4 | &xd4+ |
| 22 | ⊗h1 | ⊘e3! |

**23    &c2!!**

The refutation of Black's combination.

| 23 | ... | ⊘g4 |
|----|-----|-----|
| 24 | ⊘f3 | ♛c6 |
| 25 | &xd8 | ♜xf3 |
| 26 | ♛xf3 | ⊘f2+ *(D)* |
| 27 | ♛xf2! | &xf2 |
| 28 | &f6+ | ⊗g8 |
| 29 | &b3+ | ⊗f8 |
| 30 | ♜ad1 | &xe1 |
| 31 | ♜d8+ | ♛e8 |
| 32 | ♜xe8+ | ⊗xe8 |
| 33 | &c3 | &xc3 |
| 34 | ⊘xc3 | ⊗e7 |
| 35 | ⊗g1 | c5 |
| 36 | a4 | |

**Black resigns**

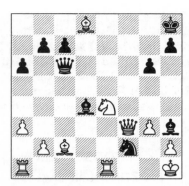

# (23) Bronstein,D – Bilek,I

International Tournament,
Gotha, September 1957
*[B30] Sicilian Defence*

During my active chess career – which is far from over – I have played with many Hungarian players. The explanation is very easy. Having been born in the Ukraine, I find Hungary very similar and always grab invitations to play there with both hands. The first time I went to Hungary was in 1949 for the match Budapest vs. Moscow. I still have many friends in Hungary and I feel a little sorry that the last time I played there dates back to the year 1989.

The tournament in the German town of Gotha assembled a strong field of players and I was satisfied that I managed to take first place. The prize money was very low but the spirit of the tournament was very friendly throughout and every participant was respected.

I was a guest of Professor Herbert Grätz, who later was the organiser of the Leipzig Olympiad in 1960. We had many friendly discussions about everything, even such difficult subjects as the Second World War.

After the tournament we made a trip together in his car and I got the chance to visit several towns, including Berlin and Leipzig, giving simultaneous exhibitions and lectures. To my chess literature and political knowledge I managed to add some practical geographical education about Germany.

One day, I did not feel well and Professor Grätz took me to a Soviet military hospital. While I was waiting for help he came to me with a very serious expression on his face and said: 'I congratulate you as a representative of mighty Russia – Soviet scientists have launched a rocket and put a satellite named Sputnik in orbit. I never thought that you could do it before the Americans.' It was the 4th of October 1957 and that news soon spread all over the world.

| | | |
|---|---|---|
| 1 | e4 | c5 |
| 2 | ♘f3 | ♘c6 |
| 3 | ♗b5 | |

An active move, creating some problems for Black. The idea behind this move is that a centre pawn should not be exchanged against one on the flank. White is ready to castle while Black's kingside is still frozen. In some variations White can take on c6, destroying the connections between the black pawns.

| | | |
|---|---|---|
| 3 | ... | ♘f6 |
| 4 | ♕e2 | g6 |
| 5 | c3 | |

It is well known that two pawns in the centre are strong.

| | | |
|---|---|---|
| 5 | ... | ♗g7 |
| 6 | 0-0 | 0-0 |
| 7 | d4 | cxd4 |
| 8 | cxd4 | d5 |

A classic example of how to attack a strong centre.

| | | |
|---|---|---|
| 9 | e5 | ♘e4 |
| 10 | ♗e3 | |

Not 10 ♘c3 because Black can answer 10...♗g4. The text leaves open the choice as to whether the knight should go to d2 or c3; even ♘fd2 can be considered here. 10...♗g4 is not strong because of White's reply 11 h3! ♗xf3? 12 gxf3 and the knight is lost.

| | | |
|---|---|---|
| 10 | ... | f6! |

To break up White's strong centre.

| | | |
|---|---|---|
| 11 | exf6 | exf6 |
| 12 | ♘c3 | |

Here 12...♘xc3 13 bxc3 only strengthens White's position and frees White's bishop and knight.

| | | |
|---|---|---|
| 12 | ... | a6 |

Not 12...f5 because of 13 ♘xd5 but if 12...♗e6 13 ♖ac1 and if now 13...f5 then 14 ♗xc6 bxc6 15 ♗f4 and the bishop on e6 is very bad.

| | | |
|---|---|---|
| 13 | ♗d3 | ♘xc3 |
| 14 | bxc3 | |

This position should be judged as better for White. The reason is that the two white pawns in the centre are stronger than the isolated black pawn on d5 and in addition White can also create pressure on the open b-file. Also, the bishop on g7 is passive.

| | | |
|---|---|---|
| 14 | ... | ♘e7 |
| 15 | a4 | |

To prevent 15...b5.

| | | |
|---|---|---|
| 15 | ... | ♗f5 |
| 16 | ♖fb1! | ♕d7 |
| 17 | ♘e1 | ♖f7 |

Black cannot exchange bishops as otherwise the white knight will be too strong on c5.

| | | |
|---|---|---|
| 18 | ♗d2 | ♗f8 |
| 19 | ♕f3 | |

Improving the position of the queen.

| | | |
|---|---|---|
| 19 | ... | ♗g4 |
| 20 | ♕g3 | ♘c6 |
| 21 | ♘c2 | ♖e8 |
| 22 | ♘e3 | ♗e6 (D) |
| 23 | h4! | |

The time has come to play actively! All White's pieces including the rooks are ready for action. Probably the best move now would have been to put the king on h8 but Black prefers another defence.

| | | |
|---|---|---|
| 23 | ... | ♘e7 |
| 24 | ♖e1! | ♖c8 |
| 25 | ♖ab1! | |

The rook lays a smoke-screen for a nice combination. It is interesting to see how the rooks manoeuvre on the first rank to find the best position to support the attack.

| 25 | ... | ♖c6 |
| 26 | h5 | |

This pawn heralds an all-out attack.

| 26 | ... | ♘f5 |
| 27 | ♘xf5 | ♗xf5 |
| 28 | hxg6 | hxg6 |

| 29 | ♖xb7!! | |

This is what White prepared when he played 26 h5

| 29 | ... | ♕xb7 |
| 30 | ♗xf5 | |

Black's position is in shambles.

| 30 | ... | ♖e7 |

Black's only chance is to weaken White's attack by exchanging rooks. Of course, White does not allow it.

| 31 | ♕xg6+ | ♗g7 |
| 32 | ♖b1! | ♖b6 |
| 33 | ♖f1! | ♔f8 |
| 34 | g3! | |

The king will make a passage for the rook to manoeuvre to create threats.

| 34 | ... | ♖e2 |
| 35 | ♗c1 | ♕e7 |
| 36 | ♔g2 | ♖c6 |

Black cannot exchange the rooks by playing 36...♖e1 as White will force mate by 37 ♖xe1 ♕xe1 38 ♗a3+ ♔g8 39 ♕h7+ ♔f7 40 ♕h5+ ♔g8 41 ♗h7+ ♔h8 42 ♗g6+, etc., a typical case of co-ordination between queen and bishop.

| 37 | ♖h1! | ♖xc3 |
| 38 | ♗f4 | |

Now ♖b1 is the threat and it is interesting to see that both black rooks and the queen are losing the battle for the open file against the lone rook! If now 38...♖b2, then the pretty move 39 ♖e1 decides (see previous comments).

| 38 | ... | ♖a3 |
| 39 | ♖c1! | |

**Black resigns**

# (24) Bronstein,D – Palmiotto,F

Olympiad, Munich, 1958
*[B09] Pirc Defence*

This was to be my last Olympiad. Altogether I played four times for my country, winning four gold medals. In all other sports, if you win a gold medal, you can call yourself an Olympic Champion forever. Maybe it is time to introduce this rule in chess. First you can be an Olympic Champion but if not everybody likes it then, after two years, you can call yourself an ex-Olympic Champion! It is not easy to win a gold medal playing on four boards even if you are a member of a magic team consisting of Botvinnik, Keres, Smyslov, Tal and Petrosian but then it is only a 'team competition'. Of course, the main advantage of being a member of such a team is that in the mornings you get together and discuss openings and strategy and in the evenings you consult each other about adjourned positions. (Unfortunately there is no defence against such practices.) However, at the board you are entirely on your own.

| 1 | e4 | d6 |
| 2 | d4 | ♘f6 |

| | | |
|---|---|---|
| 3 | ♘c3 | g6 |
| 4 | f4 | ♗g7 |
| 5 | ♘f3 | 0-0 |
| 6 | e5 | ♘fd7 |
| 7 | h4! | |

Attack!

| | | |
|---|---|---|
| 7 | ... | c5 |
| 8 | h5! | cxd4 |
| 9 | ♕xd4 | dxe5 |
| 10 | ♕f2 | exf4 |

Here Black offered a draw which was politely declined!

| | | |
|---|---|---|
| 11 | hxg6! | hxg6 |

White has saved time by not developing the rook on a1 and the bishop on c1.

| | | |
|---|---|---|
| 12 | ♗xf4! | ♘f6 |
| 13 | ♕h4 | ♕a5 |
| 14 | ♘g5 | ♗g4 |

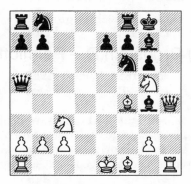

| | | |
|---|---|---|
| 15 | ♗d3! | ♘bd7 |
| 16 | 0-0!! | |

This was a surprise for Palmiotto. Another possibility was the plan of ♔d2, ♖h2 and ♖ah1.

| | | |
|---|---|---|
| 16 | ... | ♗h5 |
| 17 | ♖ae1 | e5 |
| 18 | ♗d2 | ♕c5+ |
| 19 | ♗e3 | ♕c6 |
| 20 | ♗b5 | ♕c7 (D) |
| 21 | ♗e2 | ♗xe2 |
| 22 | ♖xe2 | ♖fc8 |
| 23 | ♘ce4 | ♔f8 |
| 24 | ♘xf6 | ♘xf6 |
| 25 | ♖xf6 | ♗xf6 |
| 26 | ♘h7+ | ♔e7 |
| 27 | ♕xf6+ | ♔e8 |
| 28 | ♖d2 | a5 |
| 29 | ♕g7 | |

**Black resigns**

This game was played in the match USSR vs. Italy and being myself a follower of the famous classical Italian chess school I started an early attack with pawns intending to show that even in the semi-open openings one can create an attack in combinative style. Indeed, the classical Italian chess school is immortal.

Many years later, in 1990, I was invited to play in a tournament in Rome. Quite unexpectedly, for me that is, Botvinnik arrived. I asked the organisers if he was going to play. 'No,' they said 'he is here to receive the Giacomo-Greco-prize.' I asked them if he had ever played a game in the style of the Italian School. 'No,' they replied, 'but he wrote in one of his books that Greco was a great player.'

Now, five years later, I am still very much amused by such naïveté and wonder if those Italian officials have ever seen any of my games!

# (25) Bronstein,D – Liberzon,V

28th USSR Championship,
Leningrad, 1960
*[C18] French Defence*

This tournament was not very successful for me, in spite of the fact that I played several good games, for instance with Leonid Shamkovich when, for once in my life, I castled queenside in the King's Indian Defence and finished the game with a nice queen sacrifice (see page 279).

Also I remember games I lost, especially one, to Spassky. I don't need to give it here because it is in every collection of brilliant games. I have only one excuse for losing this game; it was played the day after I had celebrated my birthday!!

The French Defence, used by my opponent in this game, was an fantastic invention by a group of French players. They used it for the first time in a correspondence game against British players in the last century.

As thousands and thousands of games have been lost because of the strong white bishop on c4 attacking the black pawn on f7, the French discovered a brilliant remedy: play 1...e6 instead of 1...e5 and White should have no longer any expectations for a quick victory.

Black can attack White's pawn on e4 with 2...d5 and usually a tense fight develops. However, Black must make a concession or two. He permits the white pawn to occupy an outpost on the square e5. From here it exerts pressure on Black's position and in many cases closes the centre. Further he has a disadvantage in space in the centre and should therefore try to look for counterplay on the wings.

Although White usually gets an advantage, the French Defence is still playable with Black by resourceful players.

In this game the reader can see for himself the many problems that White has to solve to break through Black's defences in order to be successful in the end.

A very tense positional struggle develops, full of tactical nuances. The light-squared white bishop turns out to be much more useful than his black counterpart, mainly because of the pawns on d4 and d5.

| 1 | e4 | e6 |
| 2 | d4 | d5 |
| 3 | ♘c3 | ♗b4 |
| 4 | e5 | c5 |
| 5 | a3 | ♗xc3+ |
| 6 | bxc3 | ♘e7 |
| 7 | ♕g4 | ♘f5 |
| 8 | ♗d3 | h5 |
| 9 | ♕f4 | |

Nowadays the move 9 ♕h3 is considered stronger. The computer Hitech, programmed by former correspondence chess

World Champion Professor Hans Berliner, played this move against me during the AEGON tournament in The Hague, Holland, 1993.

| 9 | ... | cxd4 |
| 10 | cxd4 | ♕h4 |

| 11 | ♕xh4! | ♘xh4 |
| 12 | g3! | ♘f5 |
| 13 | ♘e2 | ♘c6 |
| 14 | ♗b2 | ♘a5 |
| 15 | f3! | ♗d7 |
| 16 | ♔f2 | ♘c4 |
| 17 | ♗c1 | |

Black's knight is the only well-placed piece. Note that the rook on a1 and bishop on c1 are in their original positions. However, White's advantage is on the kingside.

| 17 | ... | ♖c8 |
| 18 | g4! | ♘e7 |
| 19 | gxh5! | ♖xh5 |
| 20 | h4! | ♗a4 |
| 21 | ♘g3 | ♖h8 |
| 22 | h5! | ♘a5 |
| 23 | ♖a2 | ♘ac6 |
| 24 | ♖b2 | b6 |
| 25 | ♗g5 | ♘g8 |
| 26 | ♗d2 | ♘h6 |
| 27 | ♖h4 | ♘e7 (D) |
| 28 | ♗xh6!! | |

White could not allow ♘f5.

| 28 | ... | ♖xh6 |
| 29 | ♖g4 | ♔f8 |
| 30 | ♔e3 | ♖c3 |
| 31 | ♖a2 | ♖c7 |

White's bishop is better than Black's. The white attack will become strong as soon as his rooks start to co-operate with one another.

| 32 | ♔d2 | f5 |
| 33 | exf6 | ♖xf6 |

Not 33...gxf6 as the white h-pawn will become too dangerous.

| 34 | f4 | ♘g8 |
| 35 | ♔e3 | ♗e8 |
| 36 | ♖g5 | ♖cf7 |

| 37 | f5!! | ♘h6 |
| 38 | fxe6 | ♖xe6+ |
| 39 | ♔d2 | ♗c6 |
| 40 | ♖a1 | ♖f3 |

The adjourned position.

| 41 | ♖g1 | ♖f2+ |

| 42 | ♔d1 | ♖e7 |
| 43 | ♘e2 | ♘g8 |
| 44 | ♘g3 | ♘h6 |
| 45 | ♔c1 | ♖c7 |
| 46 | ♖e1 | ♖g2 |

46...♖f6 was necessary.

| 47 | ♗g6 | ♘f7 |
| 48 | ♖g4 | ♗b5 |
| 49 | ♖e3 | ♘d6 |
| 50 | ♖f3+ | ♔g8 |

| 51 | h6!! | gxh6 |
| 52 | ♖f6!! | ♖g1+ |
| 53 | ♔b2 | ♘c4+ |
| 54 | ♔a2 | ♖g7 |
| 55 | ♘f5! | |

**Black resigns**

## (26) Veresov,G – Bronstein,D

USSR Team Championship,
Moscow, 1960

*[E11] Bogo-Indian Defence*

The Soviet Team Championship was an annual event. Once every four years it formed part of the Sport Olympiad of the USSR.

Immediately after the Olympiad was finished in the summer of 1967, I went to the Dynamo Sports Club and found all the officials very busy and excited. They tried to find a mistake in the calculations of the points gathered from about 50 different kinds of sport.

The problem was that the Dynamo Sports Club was losing the Olympiad to the world famous Soviet Army Sports Club, by just one point. I was following their discussions and suddenly an ingenious idea came to me and I asked modestly: 'Excuse me please but how many points did you count for my performance?' 'David, why are you asking such a question. Of course we know that you won the Olympiad with the Moscow team. We gave you the maximum number of points.' 'What do you mean for the win,' I asked: 'I am the **double** winner.' Suddenly they all fell silent and I continued: 'This year the competition is also the Championship of the USSR, so I received an extra gold medal.'

You should have seen the happy faces all around!

With my extra points, the Dynamo Sports Club overtook the Soviet Army Sports Club and achieved first place.

This assured me a steady income for the next two years and the exclusive permission to have my holidays, during all four seasons of the year, at the football training camp of Dynamo outside Moscow in very nice surroundings!

| 1 | d4 | e6 |
| 2 | c4 | ♝b4+ |

Paul Keres played this move in his game with Dr Max Euwe in the first round of the famous AVRO tournament in Holland, in November 1938.

The participants not only played chess but travelled each day to another town where the next round was to be held!

| 3 | ♝d2 | a5 |
| 4 | ♞f3 | |

If 4 e4, then 4...d6 and ...e5. Also 4...d5 immediately is possible.

| 4 | ... | ♞f6 |
| 5 | ♞c3 | d6 |
| 6 | ♛c2 | ♞c6 |

Now 6...c5 is not so good because the b6 square will become very weak.

| 7 | g3 | e5 |
| 8 | dxe5 | dxe5 |
| 9 | 0-0-0 | *(D)* |

White should play 9 a3 here and, depending on Black's response, decide on which side to castle.

| 9 | ... | ♝xc3 |
| 10 | ♝xc3 | ♛e7 |

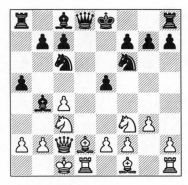

| 11 | ♝g2 | |

Now it was necessary to play 11 a3.

| 11 | ... | ♞b4!! |

The beginning of a strategically very deep conception.

| 12 | ♛a4+ | ♝d7 |
| 13 | ♛a3 | ♝c6! |

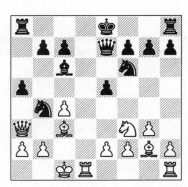

This position was judged by Veresov as better for White as Black now loses a pawn. From my side, it looks better for Black as he has targets to attack in the white position: some weak squares near the white king, and the pawn on e2. Very favourable for Black is the fact that the white queen is completely out of play.

| 14 | ♝xe5 | 0-0 |
| 15 | ♝xf6 | ♛xf6 |
| 16 | ♖d2 | ♝e4! |

The start of a very ingenious plan. I had seen this idea before in some chess compositions and was pleased to be able to put my knowledge into practice.

| 17 | ♖hd1 | |

White still has no idea what will hit him.

| 17 | ... | h6!! |

Raaphy Persitz was so impressed with this modest but cunning move that he wrote an article in *British Chess Magazine* with many compliments for my invention.

| 18 | ♗h3 | ♗h7!! |

Only now does White see the threat of ...♕g6 but it is too late. There is no defence.

The diagram looks like a typographical error. In such positions the white king is usually on g1.

| 19 | ♖d7 | ♖fe8!! |
| 20 | ♔d2 | ♗f5! |

A neat finish. If now 21 ♗xf5 ♕xf5 22 ♔e1 then 22...♘c2+ with a lethal fork.

| 21 | ♕c3 | ♗xh3 |
| 22 | ♕xf6 | gxf6 |

**White resigns**

You ought to know that Veresov was very anti-Semitic. He lived in Minsk and was a real enemy of Isaac Boleslavsky.

# (27) Bronstein,D – Fischer,R

International Tournament,
Mar del Plata, 1960

*[D01] Lewickiego Attack*

Lewickiego Attack? Yes, in old books it was called just that! I do not feel any inclination to call this the Veresov Attack as it is done nowadays. Although he played this line quite often, he should not be honoured by having an opening named after him.

Many years ago, the Mar del Plata tournament became an annual event in Argentina and I believe that Najdorf won it about ten times. I travelled to Argentina with

Boris Spassky. Luckily for us, our flight was delayed in London due to adverse weather conditions and I used this chance to show Boris the London nightlife.

When we arrived in Buenos Aires, we discovered Bobby Fischer's name on the list of participants.

The next morning, when we went to the station to go to Mar del Plata, Bobby was waving to me from the train and I had the pleasure of introducing Boris Spassky to the great American player. They became friends instantly and have remained so until this day.

In the tournament they were both fighting for first place. I managed to make a draw with Spassky and in this game I was also playing for a draw. At one moment I had a chance to win but I missed it.

| 1 | d4 | ♘f6 |
| 2 | ♘c3 | d5 |
| 3 | ♗g5 | ♗f5 |
| 4 | e3 | e6 |
| 5 | ♗d3 | ♗xd3 |
| 6 | ♕xd3 | c5 |

| 7 | ♗xf6 | gxf6 |
| 8 | dxc5 | ♘d7 |

Here 8...f5 is not so good because of 9 0-0-0 ♘d7 10 g4 fxg4 11 e4.

| 9 | e4 | dxe4 |
| 10 | ♕xe4 | ♘xc5 |
| 11 | ♕f3 | |

Bobby Fischer thought for about 15 minutes and played the 'simple' but very strong...

| 11 | ... | ♗g7! |

From such moves one can distinguish a good player from an excellent one.

| 12 | ♘ge2 | 0-0 |
|----|------|-----|
| 13 | g4   | b5  |
| 14 | ♘g3  | ♘a4! |
| 15 | ♘xa4 |     |

If 15 ♘e4, then 15...f5 16 gxf5 ♗xb2 17 ♖d1 (17 f6 ♔h8 18 ♖d1 ♕a5+ 19 ♔f1 b4) 17...♕h4.

| 15 | ...  | bxa4 |
|----|------|------|
| 16 | 0-0  | ♖c8  |
| 17 | ♖ac1 | ♕d4  |
| 18 | b3   |      |

| 18 | ...  | ♕b2  |
|----|------|------|
| 19 | bxa4 | ♖xc2 |
| 20 | ♖xc2 | ♕xc2 |
| 21 | ♕b3  | ♕g6  |

Now Black plays for a win but underestimates White's resources.

| 22 | h3   | ♗h6  |
|----|------|------|
| 23 | ♕f3  | ♖d8  |
| 24 | ♖d1  | ♖xd1+ |
| 25 | ♕xd1 | f5   |

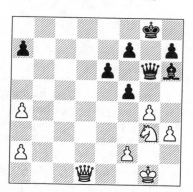

It seems that Black has seized the initiative but now White has a fine queen manoeuvre.

| 26 | ♕d8+ | ♗f8 |
|----|------|-----|

| 27 | gxf5 | exf5 |
|----|------|------|
| 28 | ♕b8  | ♕h6  |
| 29 | ♘xf5 | ♕xh3 |

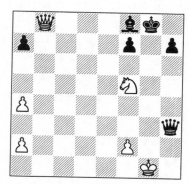

This is the position that Fischer wanted to achieve but it is White's move.

| 30 | ♘e7+! | ♔g7 |
|----|-------|-----|
| 31 | ♕e5+! | f6  |
| 32 | ♘f5+! | ♔f7 |

The only move. Fischer obviously overlooked that after 32...♔g6 there is a check by the queen from e8. If the black king takes the knight, there will be another check with the queen from c8. Black now has to defend.

| 33 | ♕d5+ | ♔g6 |
|----|------|-----|
| 34 | ♘e3  | ♕h5 |
| 35 | ♕g8+ | ♗g7 |
| 36 | ♕e8+ | ♔h6 |
| 37 | ♕d7  | ♕g6+ |
| 38 | ♔f1  | ♗f8 |

| 39 | ♕xa7 | ♕d3+ |
|----|------|------|
| 40 | ♔g2  | ♕e4+ |
| 41 | ♔g1  | ♕g6+ |
| 42 | ♔f1  | ♕d3+ |
| 43 | ♔g2  | ♕e4+ |

44 f3 &#9813;d3

Here the game was adjourned for a couple of hours to enable the players to have a meal.

45 &#9813;d4 &#9813;e2+
46 &#9818;g3 &#9813;e1+
47 &#9818;g4

Fischer had defended brilliantly and I was no longer trying to win but here I should have played 47 &#9818;f4 &#9813;h4+ 48 &#9816;g4+ &#9818;g7 49 &#9813;d7+ to push the black king into the corner. Now it is time for the black queen to show her power in Fischer's hands.

47 ... &#9813;g1+
48 &#9818;f5 &#9813;g6+
49 &#9818;e6 &#9813;e8+
50 &#9818;d5 &#9813;a8+
51 &#9818;e6 &#9813;e8+
52 &#9818;f5 &#9813;g6+
53 &#9818;f4 &#9813;g5+
54 &#9818;e4 &#9818;g6!

An excellent defensive move.

55 f4 &#9813;g1
56 &#9813;d7 &#9813;h1+

57 &#9818;d3 &#9813;b1+
58 &#9818;e2 &#9813;xa2+
59 &#9818;f3 &#9813;a1!

Threatening ...&#9813;h1+ and keeping an eye on the pawns on a4 and f6, utterly unafraid of all possible checks with the queen, the knight or the pawn on f5. A perfect move!

60 &#9813;g4+ &#9818;f7
61 &#9813;h5+ &#9818;g7
62 a5 &#9813;c3
63 &#9813;g4+ &#9818;h8
64 &#9813;e6 &#9815;c5
65 &#9813;e8+

**Draw agreed**

# (28) Tal,M – Bronstein,D

29th USSR Championship,
Baku, 1961
*[B01] Scandinavian Defence*

This opening is not very popular these days. Why? Is any other first move better? By attacking White's centre pawn, Black puts his cards on the table immediately.

Throughout my life I have been, and still am, very interested in psychology in general and particularly in chess thinking. It was a mystery to me why sometimes masters made strange moves in the opening stage when they have plenty of time and then the same masters play brilliantly in time-trouble. About 40 years ago I started to write down the time used by players and soon started to record times in my own games. Now I have a very large collection of games with the time used for each move. I have written several articles in different chess magazines about this. Over the years I published hundreds of games played in World Championship matches together with the time used for each move, in my chess column in the newspaper *Izvestia*.

My intention was to increase the understanding of chess not only for amateurs but also for scientists who are trying to understand how the human brain works. I think I have succeeded because I have received many letters from my readers.

For me personally it is now absolutely clear why we think for a short or long time and why we make mistakes.

The main ingredient of a chess struggle is the tension which develops between two players, whether it concerns a five-minute game or a conventional game. In this game it is very illustrative to see how Tal apparently played the first seven moves with great confidence, accepting my pawn sacrifice. With his next five moves he tried to justify this decision. With hindsight one can see that from moves 18 to 24 Tal used a lot of time, trying to reduce the pressure of the black pieces, but it was in vain. It would have been better to use this amount of time, about one hour, to play the opening more carefully. This is only one example and the reader who is interested in this aspect of chess should start recording times; it might well be that his chess improves immediately.

The times, noted in brackets, are in minutes and were recorded by myself during the game.

| 1 | e4 (0) | d5 (2) |
| 2 | exd5 (0) | ♘f6 (0) |

The main line, 2...♛xd5 3 ♘c3 ♛a5 4 ♘f3 ♘f6 5 d4 ♝g4 6 h3, gives White an advantage in space. This is why I prefer the waiting move 2...♘f6. Anyhow, White can keep some pressure by playing simply 3 d4 ♘xd5 4 ♘f3 ♝f5 5 ♝d3 ♝xd3 6 ♛xd3 e6, etc. Tal prefers to transpose the opening into the Panov variation of the Caro-Kann.

| 3 | c4 (3) | c6 (2) |
| 4 | d4 (0) | cxd5 (0) |
| 5 | ♘c3 (0) | g6 (10) |
| 6 | ♛b3 (2) | ♝g7 (1) |
| 7 | cxd5 (0) | 0-0 (2) |

What compensation does Black have? He has made a safe house for his king and is free to start an attack.

| 8 | ♘f3 (11) | ♘bd7 (3) |
| 9 | ♝g5 (1) | ♘b6 (3) |
| 10 | ♝c4 (4) | ♝f5 (5) |
| 11 | ♖d1 (10) | ♘e4! (16) (D) |

This is the refutation of White's play. White has lost tempi by mistakenly trying to protect the extra pawn on d5.

| 12 | 0-0 (11) | ♘xc3 (22) |

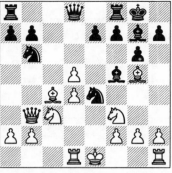

| 13 | bxc3 (0) | ♖c8 (2) |
| 14 | ♝b5 (4) | h6! (8) |
| 15 | ♝h4 (8) | g5! (5) |
| 16 | ♝g3 (0) | ♛xd5 (1) |

It is easy to see that White's plan has failed. Tal now tries to gain time and to put his knight on e5 but Black reacts perfectly by pinning the knight.

| 17 | ♛b4 (0) | ♝g4 (4) |
| 18 | ♖fe1 (19) | ♝xf3 (5) |
| 19 | gxf3 (0) | e6! (2) |

This is probably the winning move. The white pawn formation around the king is destroyed and the other pawns are not much better.

| 20 | ♗d3 (6) | ♛xf3 (4) |
| 21 | ♖d2 (28) | ♖fd8 (10) |
| 22 | ♖e3 (18) | ♛c6 (1) |
| 23 | ♗b5 (0) | ♛d5 (1) |
| 24 | ♖de2 (15) | ♞c4 (10) |
| 25 | ♗xc4 (0) | ♖xc4 (0) |
| 26 | ♛b2 (0) | ♖dc8 (2) |
| 27 | ♗e5 (3) | ♗xe5 (2) |
| 28 | ♖xe5 (0) | ♛c6 (1) |

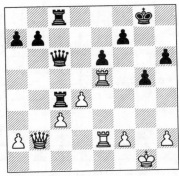

White tries to activate his rooks but in reality the black rooks are dominating the game.

| 29 | ♖2e3 (5) | b6 (5) |
| 30 | ♛a3 (1) | ♖xc3 (1) |
| 31 | ♛xa7 (0) | ♖xe3 (2) |
| 32 | ♖xe3 (0) | ♖a8 (2) |

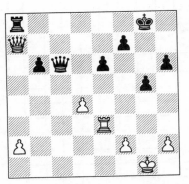

| 33 | ♖c3 (0) | ♛e4 (0) |
| 34 | ♛c7 (0) | ♖xa2 (1) |
| 35 | ♖c1 (0) | ♛xd4 (1) |
| 36 | ♛g3 (0) | ♚g7 (2) |
| 37 | h4 (0) | ♛xh4 (5) |
| 38 | ♛c3+ (0) | ♚g6 (1) |
| 39 | ♛d3+ (0) | ♚h5 (0) |

| 40 | ♛e3 (0) | ♖a4 (4) |

**White resigns**

Total time used:
White: 2.29 Black: 2.28
(See Time Graph on the next page)

# (29) Bronstein,D – Shamkovich,L

Moscow Championship,
September 1961
*[B01] Scandinavian Defence*

Leonid Shamkovich is a player of my generation. He lived in Leningrad and I in Kiev. We have played many games of which all have been interesting, with sharp moves, attack and defence.

Shamkovich is very proud of his knowledge of the classical chess heritage. He has written many theoretical articles about chess openings and has introduced many novelties. His play is very logical and full of nuances. The book which he published many years ago about the art of sacrifice in chess is one of the best in chess literature and I can heartily recommend it.

About a quarter of a century ago, Shamkovich changed his place of residence and made a successful chess debut in his new country, the USA. When I was in New York in 1993 he invited me for dinner at his home and I saw for myself the many prizes which he had won in top US tournaments. It was nice to see that he is still 'young' and full of energy. It was also a pleasure for me to hear that he wants to write a book about some of my games. I hope he will not forget and I look forward to the first edition!

| 1 | e4 | d5 |
| 2 | exd5 | ♞f6 |
| 3 | d4 | ♞xd5 |
| 4 | ♞f3 | ♗f5 |
| 5 | a3 | e6 |
| 6 | c4 | ♞b6 |
| 7 | ♞c3 | ♗e7 (D) |

Now ♗e2 and 0-0 is a good plan but White should play more actively. Black has two weaknesses: b7 and g7. How can White exploit them?

## Time Graph Tal,M-Bronstein,D

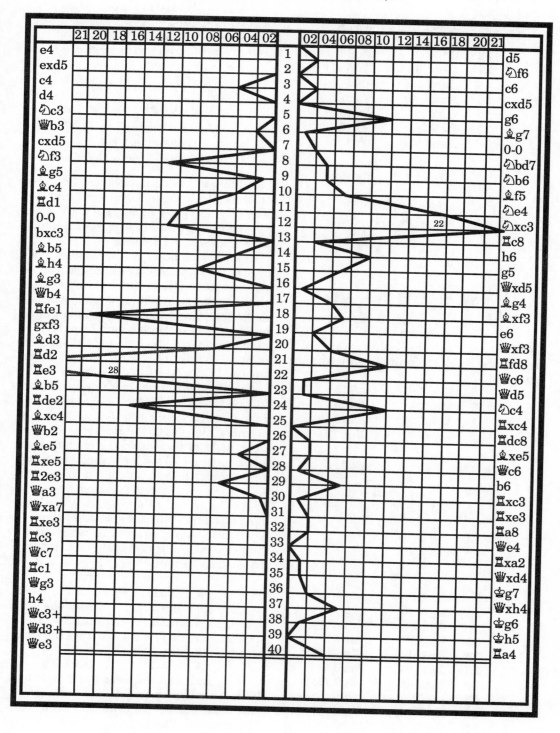

| White (Tal) | Move | Black (Bronstein) |
|---|---|---|
| e4 | 1 | d5 |
| exd5 | 2 | ♘f6 |
| c4 | 3 | c6 |
| d4 | 4 | cxd5 |
| ♘c3 | 5 | g6 |
| ♕b3 | 6 | ♗g7 |
| cxd5 | 7 | 0-0 |
| ♘f3 | 8 | ♘bd7 |
| ♗g5 | 9 | ♘b6 |
| ♗c4 | 10 | ♗f5 |
| ♖d1 | 11 | ♘e4 |
| 0-0 | 12 | ♘xc3 |
| bxc3 | 13 | ♖c8 |
| ♗b5 | 14 | h6 |
| ♗h4 | 15 | g5 |
| ♗g3 | 16 | ♕xd5 |
| ♕b4 | 17 | ♗g4 |
| ♖fe1 | 18 | ♗xf3 |
| gxf3 | 19 | e6 |
| ♗d3 | 20 | ♕xf3 |
| ♖d2 | 21 | ♖fd8 |
| ♖e3 | 22 | ♕c6 |
| ♗b5 | 23 | ♕d5 |
| ♖de2 | 24 | ♘c4 |
| ♗xc4 | 25 | ♖xc4 |
| ♕b2 | 26 | ♖dc8 |
| ♗e5 | 27 | ♗xe5 |
| ♖xe5 | 28 | ♕c6 |
| ♖2e3 | 29 | b6 |
| ♕a3 | 30 | ♖xc3 |
| ♕xa7 | 31 | ♖xe3 |
| ♖xe3 | 32 | ♖a8 |
| ♖c3 | 33 | ♕e4 |
| ♕c7 | 34 | ♖xa2 |
| ♖c1 | 35 | ♕xd4 |
| ♕g3 | 36 | ♔g7 |
| h4 | 37 | ♕xh4 |
| ♕c3+ | 38 | ♔g6 |
| ♕d3+ | 39 | ♔h5 |
| ♕e3 | 40 | ♖a4 |

**8 ♕b3**

Pressure against b7.

| 8 | ... | ♕c8 |
| 9 | c5 | ♘6d7 |
| 10 | ♗f4 | ♘f6 |
| 11 | ♗c4 | c6 |
| 12 | 0-0 | |

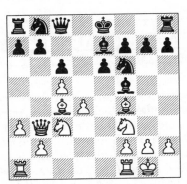

All White's pieces are active, while Black has not yet completed his development.

**12 ... ♘d5**

Logical but not good.

**13 ♗xd5**

This opens the e-file as after 13...cxd5 comes 14 ♘b5.

| 13 | ... | exd5 |
| 14 | ♖ae1! | ♗e6 |
| 15 | ♗g5 | ♗xg5 |

Not 15...f6 because of 16 ♖e3 and ♖fe1.

| 16 | ♘xg5 | 0-0 |
| 17 | ♘e2 | ♘a6 |
| 18 | ♘g3 | h6 |

If 18...♘c7 then 19 ♕d3 g6 20 f4 f5 21 ♖e5 followed by ♖fe1 and the bishop on e6 has become a pawn.

**19 ♘xe6**

Another good plan is ♘f3, followed by ♘e5 and f4.

| 19 | ... | fxe6 |
| 20 | f4 | ♕d7 |
| 21 | ♖e5! | ♖f7 |

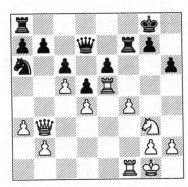

| 22 | f5 | exf5 |
| 23 | ♘xf5 | ♖af8 |
| 24 | g4 | |

In the game Alekhine-Euwe, Amsterdam 1936, Alekhine defended his knight on f5 with the same move.

| 24 | ... | ♕d8 |
| 25 | ♖fe1! | ♕g5 |
| 26 | ♕g3 | ♔h7 |
| 27 | h4 | ♕g6 |

**28 ♔g2**

According to Steinitz's theory the king is a strong piece in the middlegame. Here he joins his army before starting the final attack.

**28 ... h5**

The only defence against 29 h5 ♕g5 and 30 ♘d6 etc. However, now the pawn on h5 becomes a target.

**29 ♘e7 ♖xe7**

Again the only move. If 29...♕xg4 then 30 ♕xg4 hxg4 31 ♖h5 mate and if 29...♖f2+ then 30 ♔g1 with the same threat ♖xh5+.

| | | |
|---|---|---|
| 30 | ♖xe7 | hxg4 |
| 31 | ♕e5 | g3 |
| 32 | ♕g5 | ♖f2+ |
| 33 | ♔xg3 | ♕xg5+ |
| 34 | hxg5 | ♖xb2 |
| 35 | ♖7e6! | ♘c7 |
| 36 | ♖h1+! | ♔g8 |
| 37 | ♖e7! | ♘b5 |
| 38 | ♖h8+! | ♔xh8 |
| 39 | g6 | ♖b3+ |
| 40 | ♔g4 | |

**Black resigns**

## (30) Cherepkov,A – Bronstein,D

28th USSR Championship,
Moscow, 1961
*[C80] Spanish Opening*

Alexander Vasilievich Cherepkov returned to his native town of Leningrad after having served in the Red Army as a brave soldier during all four years of the Great Patriotic (Second World) War. For his contribution in evicting the troops of Nazi Germany he received many honourable decorations.

Some time later, when peace had returned to our country, he decided to pay tribute to his hobby-horse: chess! He was a coach for young chess players of the Leningrad Junior Chess Club for many years.

Not so long ago I had a pleasant chat with Korchnoi about the chess talent of this man of great honour and dignity.

It is such a pity that, although having been several times Champion of Leningrad, Cherepkov never had the chance to play in strong international tournaments outside the USSR. I am convinced that this is the only reason why he was not able to join the ranks of grandmasters.

We met twice over the board, first in the 28th USSR Championship in Moscow 1961 and then in the USSR Championship Semi-Final in Jaroslavl 1982.

Will we still get a third chance this century?

This game hinges around my 29th move ...e3!! It took me all of 15 minutes to think it out. The idea of the combination with the rook sacrifice had matured much earlier but I wanted to check all the details one more time. This, by the way, is the basic reason for my constantly getting into time-trouble. For although double-checking never did anybody any harm, one must be reasonable about it. I wonder how many delightful combinations I have ruined in my many years of tournament play only because of the fact that I noticed a counter-combination for my opponent, a combination which he was most likely not even thinking about and, more often the case, which just was not there at all! The excess of fantasy!

This is precisely what happened in this game.

| | | |
|---|---|---|
| 1 | e4 | e5 |
| 2 | ♘f3 | ♘c6 |
| 3 | ♗b5 | a6 |
| 4 | ♗a4 | ♘f6 |
| 5 | 0-0 | ♘xe4 |

During my school years this variation was often played by Dr Euwe. I remember one game with Dr Alekhine from their match in 1935 when Alekhine sacrificed a pawn in the opening and Euwe fearlessly took it: 6 d4 b5 7 ♗b3 d5 8 dxe5 ♗e6 9 c3 ♗e7 10 a4 b4 11 ♘d4 ♘xe5 12 f4. I had analysed this variation in depth myself and found that after the theoretical recommendation 12...♗g4 White can keep the initiative after 13 ♕c2 ♘g6 14 f5 ♘e5 15 ♗f4. But if Black plays 13...c5 then the chances are even. It was important in the strange old days to think for yourself and not just wait for a new floppy disk!

| | | |
|---|---|---|
| 6 | d4 | b5 |
| 7 | ♗b3 | d5 |
| 8 | ♘xe5 | |

This was a surprise for me. In those days everyone played 8 dxe5 in this position and the text is very rarely played. I had played it myself in a game against the famous opening expert grandmaster Ludek Pachman during the Interzonal Tournament in Portorož 1958 and managed to win in a very instructive fashion: 1 e4 e5

2 ♘f3 ♘c6 3 ♗b5 a6 4 ♗a4 ♘f6 5 0-0 ♘xe4
6 d4 b5 7 ♗b3 d5 8 ♘xe5 ♘xe5 9 dxe5 c6
10 c3 ♗f5 11 ♗c2 ♕d7 12 a4 ♖c8 13 axb5
axb5 14 ♗e3 ♘c5 15 ♘d2 ♗xc2 16 ♕xc2
♗e7 17 f4 0-0 18 f5 ♖fe8 19 ♗d4 ♗f8 20
♖f3 ♘e4 21 ♘xe4 dxe4 22 ♕xe4 c5 23 ♗f2
♗d6 24 ♖d1 ♕e7 25 e6 fxe6 26 ♗h4 ♕c7
27 f6 and Black resigned.

The most surprising thing for me was
the fact that the move 8 ♘xe5 does not exist in the big four-volume opening books
by ... Ludek Pachman!

I did not know of this game at the time
and just played it because this move looks
more logical than 8 dxe5 as it clears the
path for the f-pawn and the knight on f3
can no longer be pinned by Black's bishop.

| 8 | ... | ♘xe5 |
| 9 | dxe5 | ♗b7? |

Too optimistic. Black has hopes of acti-
vating this bishop if and when he can play
...d4. However, the bishop leaves its good
post on c8 and loses control over the g4
square. Better would have been 9...c6 and
only then to decide if the bishop needs to
move at all.

| 10 | c3 | ♗c5 |
| 11 | ♕g4! | |

Cherepkov notices my mistake and starts
a very dangerous attack.

| 11 | ... | ♕e7 |
| 12 | ♘d2! | ♕xe5 |
| 13 | ♘xe4 | dxe4 |
| 14 | ♗f4 | ♕f6 |
| 15 | ♖ad1! *(D)* | |

Perfect play in the classical tradition of
Anderssen, Morphy and Pillsbury! All of
White's forces are placed in the centre and

despite the fact that Black has an extra
pawn, White has a slight advantage.

| 15 | ... | 0-0 |
| 16 | ♗xc7 | ♖ae8 |

A good defensive move. Black is preparing to push the e-pawn (see the note to
move 9). That is why this rook was played
and not the on f8. That one has to keep an
eye on f7.

| 17 | ♗f4 | |

More active would have been 17 ♕h5
♕c6 18 ♗g3 and if 18...e3 then simply 19
♗d5 exf2+ 20 ♗xf2.

| 17 | ... | ♗e7 |

Also a passive move. After 17...♗c8 18
♕h5 ♕b6 Black can soon expect to play
...♗e6 and all of Black's defensive problems would have been solved. However,
without any justification he was playing
for a win.

| 18 | ♗e3 | ♖d8 |
| 19 | ♖d4 | ♖xd4 |
| 20 | ♗xd4 | ♕g5 |
| 21 | ♕d7 | ♗a8 |

White is better. Black hopes to be able
to play e3 at some stage and to capture the
pawn on g2.

| 22 | ♗e3 | ♕f6 |
| 23 | ♖d1! | h5 |
| 24 | ♕c7 | ♖e8 |
| 25 | ♖d7 *(D)* | |

Looks as strong as it is but a move like
25 h4, creating an emergency exit for the
king and threatening 26 ♗g5, should have
seriously been taken into consideration.
After 25...♕xh4 26 ♖d7 Black needs to
find a solution to the threat of 27 ♗c5 by
playing for instance 26...♕f6. If now 27
♗c5 then 27...e3 (finally!) 28 ♗xe3 ♕g6

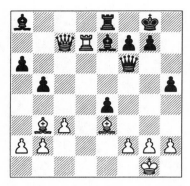

and Black's queen together with the bishop on a8 can stop the white attack.

**25      ...           ♗c6!**

Not 25...♔f8 because of 26 ♖xe7. Also ♗c5 is a threat.

**26   ♗d4          ♛h6**
**27   ♗e3          ♛f6**

A draw by repetition of moves? No, perhaps another day.

**28   ♗g5?         ♛xg5**
**29   ♛xc6**

**29   ...           e3!!**

The beginning of a brilliant combination. This move is now possible because of White's 28th move.

The art of a practical chess fight is mainly the ability to make the right move at the right moment. That is the case with this pawn move. It creates great complications, pouring oil on the fire. The passive 29...♔f8 is hopeless.

**30   ♖d5?** *(D)*

To be honest, I also would have played this move, especially when in severe time-trouble. Being a very imaginative player himself, Cherepkov was not worried about

30...exf2+ and must have thought that I had blundered the rook on e8.

Of course, after the normal defensive move 30 ♖d1 the game ends in a draw: 30...exf2+ 31 ♔f1 ♔f8 32 ♛f3 ♛f6 33 ♛xf6 (33 ♛xh5 g6 34 ♛h6+ ♔g8 35 ♖d7 ♗c5) 33...♗xf6 34 ♖d7 ♖e7 35 ♖d8+ ♖e7 36 ♖d7 etc.

**30   ...           e2**

I was also in severe time-trouble and by moving the black pawn forward I was just trusting my own intuition. Anyhow, it was too late to look for another move. The rook on e8 is lost in any case.

**31   ♛xe8+        ♔h7**
**32   ♗c2+         g6!**

This is the only chance for Black to play for a win because if 32... f5 then 33 ♗xf5+ ♛xf5 34 ♛xh5+ ♔g8 35 ♛xe2 ♛xd5 and a draw is the most likely outcome.

**33   ♛xf7+        ♔h6**
**34   g3?**

White should have played 34 ♖d1 exd1♛+ 35 ♗xd1 ♛d2 36 g3 ♛xd1+ 37 ♔g2 ♛d8 38 h4, when he has slight chances of

a draw, but who is playing for a draw in this game?!

Now I could have won in one move by promoting my pawn on e2 to a queen.

**34    ...    ♕c1+?**

It is a well-known fact that during a practical game, players often do not check variations entirely but just trust each other. That is what happened here. Of course I saw the move 34...e1♕+ but what should I do after the continuation 35 ♔g2 ♕g4 36 ♖d8 here?

Being very short of time I failed to discover the idea 36...♕h3+ 37 ♔f3 ♕h1+ 38 ♔e3 ♕e6+ and settled for four moves with easy to find checks – a treasure in time-trouble.

**35    ♔g2    ♕f1+**
**36    ♔f3**

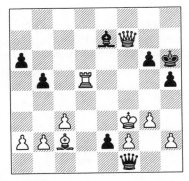

**36    ...    e1♘+**
**37    ♔e3**

Now, after so many years have passed, who can say what Black was hoping for? In time-trouble I may just have overlooked this move and only considered 37 ♔e4 ♕e2+ 38 ♔d4 ♘xc2 or 38 ♔f4 ♘g2 and checkmate in both variations.

**37    ...    ♘xc2+**
**38    ♔d2** (D)

Now the white king is in a safe place and it is obvious that all Black's winning variations were illusions.

**38    ...    ♘b4**

Here Cherepkov had barely a few seconds left on his clock. He saw the variation 39...gxh5 40 ♕e6+ and without hesitation played...

**39    ♖xh5+?**

...throwing away a much deserved win. After 39 ♕f4+ g5 40 ♖d6+ ♗xd6 41 ♕xd6+ ♔g7 42 ♕e5+ ♔g6 43 ♕e6+ ♔g7 44 ♕f5 ♘xa2 45 ♕xg5+ ♔f7 46 ♕xh5+ White can exchange queens and should win easily because of his passed pawns.

Maybe White could also win Black's knight with some clever queen checks.

**39    ...    ♔xh5!**

White thought that Black could only play 39... gxh5 after which he intended 40 ♕e6+ winning easily.

**40    ♕h7+    ♔g4!**

Another nasty surprise for White as, at first sight, it seems totally illogical to abandon the pawn on g6. White only counted on 40... ♔g5 after which he would capture Black's bishop and knight.

After the game, we looked at some variations. The Leningrad master admitted to not having seen all of them. Instead, he was confident of victory, in spite of the fact that he was very short of time. However, he knew that he had to sacrifice his rook on h5 as the black king would be exposed. He was convinced that a mating variation would present itself. So, when I promoted the pawn to a knight he executed his following moves instantly.

**41    cxb4    ♗xb4+**
**White resigns**

This game gave us both a lot of intellectual pleasure. I specifically remember how surprised we both were when we suddenly discovered that after the moves 34...e1♕+ 35 ♔g2 ♕g4 White needs to find a defence against 36...♕h3+ 37 ♔xh3 ♕f1 mate and for the same reason it is not wise to play 36 h3.

I hope that this game will give you, the reader, as much pleasure as it did the spectators in the theatre who gave us a warm applause.

## (31) Bakulin,N – Bronstein,D

### Moscow Championship, 1961
*[B04] Alekhine's Defence*

It has always been a challenge to play in the Moscow Championship. Although the participants are not always well-known players they are all of grandmaster strength and one uses a lot of energy and has to be very concentrated to fight for one of the top places. I played more than 10 times in this championship and successfully took or shared first place in 1946, 1947, 1953, 1957, 1961, 1968 and 1982. In 1947 I shared the first place with Simagin and Ravinsky but two weeks later I came only 2nd in the play-off when Simagin won the title.

I also shared first place in 1968 and, according to the rules, the winners were required to play a play-off match of four games. However Tigran Petrosian refused to play against me, saying that in this way I would be able to play a match with the World Champion without having qualified to do so through the FIDE system!

I am especially proud of my first title in 1946 and the last one in 1982. In my first I finished ahead of Smyslov and the last was played as the Moscow Open Championship, dedicated to 60 years existence of the Soviet Union, with 12 grandmasters from various Republics. I shared the first place with Naum Rashkovsky.

| 1 | e4 | ♘f6 |
|---|----|----|
| 2 | e5 | ♘d5 |
| 3 | d4 | d6 |
| 4 | ♘f3 | g6 |

This variation was played by Fischer against Spassky in game 13 in Reykjavik 1972. I think it was the best game of the match for both sides.

| 5 | c4 | ♘b6 |
|---|----|----|
| 6 | b3 | ♗g7! |
| 7 | ♗b2 | 0-0 |

| 8 | ♗e2 | dxe5 |
|---|----|----|

The position in the centre should be made clear before deciding how to develop on the queenside.

| 9 | ♘xe5 | |
|---|------|--|

If 9 dxe5, then 9...♕xd1+ 10 ♗xd1 ♘c6 11 a3 ♗g4 12 ♘bd2 ♘d7.

| 9 | ... | c5 |
|---|-----|----|
| 10 | f4 | ♘c6 |
| 11 | dxc5 | ♕xd1+ |
| 12 | ♔xd1 | ♘d7 |

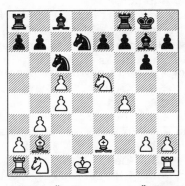

| 13 | ♘c3 | ♘dxe5 |
|----|-----|-------|
| 14 | fxe5 | ♗xe5! |
| 15 | ♔e1 | ♘b4 |

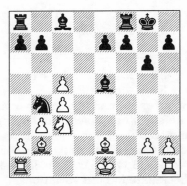

The white king tries to find a safe place but it is too late: he won't find it!

| 16 | ♔f2 | ♗d4+! |
|----|-----|-------|
| 17 | ♔g3 | |

Note how well 'developed' Black's rook on a8 and bishop on c8 are. There are no better squares for them than the ones they are on right now!

| 17 | ... | f5 |
|----|-----|----|

The pawn on c5 is unimportant.

| 18 | ♘a4 | f4+ |
|----|-----|-----|

| 19 | ♔f3 | ♗e3! |
|----|-----|------|
| 20 | ♖hd1 | h5 |
| 21 | h3 | e5 |

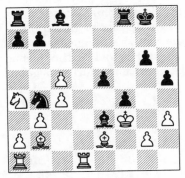

Black's e- and f-pawns are heading towards the other side of the board!

| 22 | ♘c3 |  |

If 22 ♗xe5 then 22...b6 23 ♘c3 ♗b7+ 24 ♘d5 ♖ae8 25 ♗c3 ♘xd5 26 cxd5 ♗xc5.

| 22 | ... | ♘c2 |
| 23 | ♘e4 |  |

White has to try to stop the advance of Black's g-pawn. Not 23 ♖ab1 because of 23...♘d4+ 24 ♖xd4 exd4 25 ♘d5 g5.

| 23 | ... | ♘xa1 |
| 24 | ♗xa1 | ♗f5 |
| 25 | ♖d6 | ♖ae8 |
| 26 | ♗c3 | g5 |
| 27 | ♗d3 | g4+ |
| 28 | ♔e2 |  |

The pawn on c5 could already have been taken on move 17. Now it will be removed by means of a beautiful sacrifice of a bishop! Often such moves look easy but we should not forget that they must be well prepared beforehand.

| 28 | ... | ♗xc5! |
| 29 | ♘xc5 | e4 |
| 30 | ♗c2 | f3+ |
| 31 | ♔f1 |  |

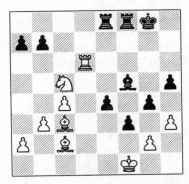

| 31 | ... | gxh3 |
| 32 | ♖h6 | fxg2+ |

The last four moves with Black's pawns illustrate clearly that the famous French musician and chess champion François-André Danican Philidor was perfectly correct in his statement that pawns are the soul of chess. I have played many games using the ideas of the great French player and I also believe that combinations are the soul of chess!

| 33 | ♔g1 | ♗h7! |

Contrary to pawns, pieces can and do move backwards (although I have new ideas in this respect, see page 271).

| 34 | ♗f6 | b6 |
| 35 | ♘d7 | ♖f7 |
| 36 | c5 | ♖xd7 |
| 37 | b4 | ♖e6 |
| 38 | ♗b3 | ♔f8 |
| 39 | ♔h2 | ♖xf6 |
| 40 | ♖xf6+ | ♔g7 |

**White resigns**

# (32) Bronstein,D – Korzin,V

Moscow Championship, 1961
*[D36] Queen's Gambit Declined*

In Moscow there are thousands of real chess fans who play well and have a good understanding of chess. The games in the Moscow Championship are played in the evenings so there is always a large crowd which comes after a hard day's work is finished to get intellectual pleasure from master play. I always felt the obligation to play for my fans and show them many different aspects of chess.

In this game I chose a dull opening variation but later found a possibility for a nice combination. I especially like the last three moves with my queen.

| 1 | d4 | d5 |
|---|-----|------|
| 2 | c4 | e6 |
| 3 | ♘c3 | ♘f6 |
| 4 | ♗g5 | ♘bd7 |
| 5 | cxd5 | exd5 |

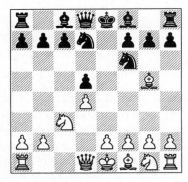

**6 e3**

Not 6 ♘xd5 because of 6...♘xd5 7 ♗xd8 ♗b4+.

| 6 | ... | c6 |
|---|------|------|
| 7 | ♗d3 | ♗e7 |
| 8 | ♕c2 | |

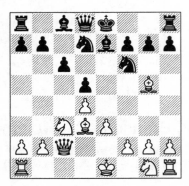

White delays the development of his kingside in order to see what Black will do. After 8... 0-0 9 ♘f3 ♖e8 10 g4 ♘f8 the move 11 h3 is attractive. The defence chosen by Black has a weakness: it is too slow.

His idea is to transfer his knight to g7 and then to play ♗f5, exchanging his 'bad' bishop for White's 'good' bishop. This would work if White plays ♘f3 next move, but White leaves this square for his pawn and it prevents Black's intention.

By the way, this defence was often used by Korzin and he told me that he had never lost a game with it...until this game!

| 8 | ... | ♘f8 |
|----|------|------|
| 9 | ♘ge2 | ♘e6 |
| 10 | ♗h4 | g6 |
| 11 | 0-0-0 | ♘g7 |
| 12 | f3 | 0-0 |
| 13 | h3 | ♘fe8 |
| 14 | ♗f2 | f5 |

| 15 | ♘f4 | ♘e6 |
|----|------|------|
| 16 | ♘ce2 | ♗h4 |
| 17 | g3 | ♘xf4 |
| 18 | ♘xf4 | ♗g5 |

After the first attempt by Black to exchange his light-squared bishop (see the comment to move 8), he finds another way to create a defence around his king with the assistance of his dark-squared bishop.

Now White needs to find the best way to get to the black king. From experience I know that there is only one way: to push the pawns forward and sacrifice a piece at the right moment in order to win a decisive tempo, exactly as in this game.

It is interesting to see the difference between the moves 19 and 22. First, White retreats the knight because it is under attack by the black bishop and then he does not care anymore and lets the black bishop do what he intended in the first place.

| 19 | ♘g2 | ♘g7 |
|----|------|------|
| 20 | h4 | ♗e7 |
| 21 | ♘f4 | ♗d6 |
| 22 | h5 | ♗xf4 |

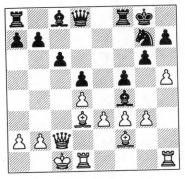

**23 hxg6! ♗c7**

It would have been much better to play 23...hxg6 but it was difficult to resist the temptation to keep the extra piece.

**24 ♖xh7 ♕g5**

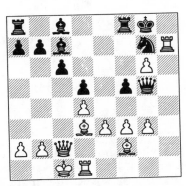

Is White's position good? Yes, because in exchange for the knight White can start a dangerous attack by doubling his rooks on the h-file, a thematic example.

| 25 | ♖dh1 | ♕xg6 |
|----|------|------|
| 26 | ♖7h6 | ♕g5 |
| 27 | g4 | ♗d7 |
| 28 | f4 | ♗xf4 |

If Black plays 28...♕xg4 then 29 ♖g1 ♕f3 30 ♖g3.

| 29 | exf4 | ♕xf4+ |
|----|------|------|
| 30 | ♔b1 | ♕xg4 |

It seems that Black can save himself with ...♔f7 but it is White to move. He will now slalom his queen decisively into the heart of the black position.

My opponent, a brilliant musician, very much appreciated this artistic touch. After the game we analysed with great pleasure, forgetting about the result.

| 31 | ♕c5!! | ♖ae8 |
|----|------|------|
| 32 | ♕d6 | ♗c8 |
| 33 | ♕c7 | |

**Black resigns**

# (33) Aronin,L – Bronstein,D

### Estonian Masters Tournament, Tartu, 1962
### [B28] *Sicilian Defence*

In the summer of 1962 the Estonian Chess Federation invited me to play in a tournament with Estonian masters. This took place in one of the buildings of the world famous Tartu University where we had a room at our disposal.

My opponent in this game was also a guest. We both came from Moscow, had played several games before and knew each other quite well. Our first encounter, which ended in a draw, dates back to the

Semi-Final of the USSR Championship in
1945.

Lev Solomonovich Aronin played successfully many times in USSR Championships but never managed to actually
become the champion. He never received
the title of grandmaster which he deserved without any doubt. Also, his name
was removed from the list of participants
of the Interzonal Tournament 1952 in
Stockholm in favour of another player, a
high-ranking member of the USSR Chess
Federation (Kotov, T.F.). It turned out that
this player was to be the winner of the
tournament with a record score.

In the 22nd USSR Championship played
in 1955 Aronin had a totally winning position in the last round against Vasily Smyslov and therefore did not seriously analyse
the adjourned position. He missed a hidden, very neat, drawing variation found by
Smyslov, who had done his homework brilliantly, and had to settle for a draw, missing qualification by half a point for the
Interzonal Tournament in 1955.

Aronin's style of play reminds me of
Botvinnik and Furman, very positional and
safe but occasionally also using his combinative talent.

| 1 | e4 | c5! |
|---|----|-----|
| 2 | ♘f3 | a6! |
| 3 | ♗e2 | d6! |
| 4 | 0-0 | ♘f6 |
| 5 | ♘c3 | e5! |

As White still has not played d4, Black
now prevents it. However, the e5-pawn
could become a target for f2-f4 later.

| 6 | d3 | ♗e7 |
|---|----|-----|
| 7 | ♘d2 | 0-0 |
| 8 | f4 | exf4! |
| 9 | ♘f3 | |

Now a sort of King's Gambit has come
on the board.

| 9 | ... | d5! |
|---|-----|-----|
| 10 | ♗xf4 | ♘c6 |

Not 10...dxe4 because White's bishop
will become active on c4.

| 11 | e5 | ♘e8 |
|----|-----|-----|
| 12 | ♔h1 | ♘c7 |
| 13 | ♕d2 | ♗f5 |
| 14 | ♖ae1 | ♘e6 |

| 15 | ♗g3 | ♗g6 |
|----|-----|-----|
| 16 | ♗d1 | b5! |

Starting an attack.

| 17 | ♘e2 | c4! |
|----|-----|-----|
| 18 | d4 | b4! |
| 19 | c3 | ♕a5 |
| 20 | ♗h4 | ♖ab8 |
| 21 | ♗xe7 | ♘xe7 |
| 22 | ♘g5 | ♘c7 |
| 23 | ♘f4 | h6! |
| 24 | ♘xg6 | fxg6 |
| 25 | ♖xf8+ | ♖xf8 |
| 26 | cxb4 | ♕xa2 |

My queen took this pawn and not the one
on b4 because I had found a nice combination.

| 27 | ♘f3 | ♘b5 |
|----|-----|-----|
| 28 | ♕c2 | a5! |

This is where the combination begins.
It is based on the following variation: 31
♕d7? ♕xe1+ 32 ♘xe1 ♖f1 mate. Now
White is forced to accept the sacrifice of a
knight but Black gets very mobile passed
pawns in return.

| 29 | ♕a4 | ♕xb2 |

| 30 | ♕xb5 | ♕xb4 |
|----|------|------|
| 31 | ♕xb4 | axb4 |
| 32 | ♔g1 | b3 |
| 33 | ♔f2 | g5 |
| 34 | h3 | ♖a8 |

White is lost. However, while trying to win in the most beautiful way I created problems for myself.

There are several easy ways of winning for Black besides the one I chose.

| 35 | g4 | ♖a2+ |
|----|------|------|
| 36 | ♔e3 | ♘g6 |
| 37 | ♘d2 | ♖a1 |
| 38 | ♘f3 | ♘f4 |
| 39 | ♔d2 | ♘d3 |
| 40 | ♖g1 | ♖a2+ |
| 41 | ♔c3 | ♘f2 |
| 42 | ♔b4 | ♘e4 |
| 43 | ♖e1 | ♖a8 |
| 44 | ♖xe4 | dxe4 |
| 45 | ♘d2 | ♖a1 |
| 46 | ♗e2 | b2 |
| 47 | ♔c3 | |

| 47 | ... | b1♕ |
|----|------|------|
| 48 | ♘xb1 | ♖xb1 |

| 49 | ♗xc4+ | ♔f8 |
|----|------|------|
| 50 | d5 | |

Without mistakes, chess is not interesting. Routine games can be played by computers but human mistakes create very unusual situations and it is always a challenge to find a way out of trouble. In this particular endgame, by a sudden turn of events, White obtains two mobile passed pawns. Supported by the bishop they may become dangerous. Now Black has to decide if he still wants to play for a win or will settle for a draw. This is a very rare case where I calculated very deeply and decided to play for a win, albeit by balancing on the edge of an abyss.

| 50 | ... | ♖d1 |
|----|------|------|
| 51 | ♔c2 | ♖a1 |
| 52 | d6 | |

If the white king attacks the rook, the answer will be the same. The intention is to push the e-pawn forward as soon as possible.

| 52 | ... | ♖a5 |
|----|------|------|
| 53 | e6 | ♖c5 |

The manoeuvres of the black rook have a defensive but also an attacking purpose. They increase the power of the e-pawn by attacking the bishop and at the same time preventing it from giving a possible check on b5.

| 54 | ♔b3 | e3! |
|----|------|------|
| 55 | e7+ | ♔e8 |
| 56 | ♗d3 | ♔d7 |
| 57 | ♗g6 | ♖e5 |
| 58 | ♔c2 | e2! *(D)* |
| 59 | e8♕+ | ♖xe8 |
| 60 | ♗xe8+ | ♔xe8 |

| 61 | ⌱d2 | ⌱d7 |
| 62 | ⌱xe2 | ⌱xd6 |
| 63 | ⌱d2 | ⌱e5 |
| 64 | ⌱e3 | |

**64** ... **g6!**

Without this tempo the game would be drawn. Now White can no longer retain the opposition. Examples like this can be found in every good book on endgames.

| 65 | ⌱f3 | ⌱d4 |
| 66 | ⌱f2 | ⌱e4 |
| 67 | ⌱e2 | ⌱f4 |
| 68 | ⌱f2 | h5! |
| 69 | gxh5 | gxh5 |
| 70 | ⌱g2 | ⌱e3 |
| 71 | ⌱g3 | h4+! |

**White resigns**

# (34) Bronstein,D – Darga,K

Interzonal Tournament,
Amsterdam, 1964

*[D31] Queen's Gambit Declined*

This was my first and only game with Klaus Darga. We had the common destiny to be reserve players during the match between the USSR vs. The Rest of the World which was played in Belgrade in the Spring of 1970. In four rounds, we never played a single game!

This game I remember as the game where, in time-trouble, I had to make a move every second, but each move lost a pawn!

| 1 | d4 | d5 |
| 2 | c4 | e6 |
| 3 | ⌱c3 | ⌱e7 |

To avoid the pin by 4 ⌱g5 if Black plays 3...⌱f6 first.

| 4 | cxd5 | exd5 |
| 5 | ⌱f4 | c6 |
| 6 | e3 | ⌱f5 |

At the time it was generally felt that, with the bishop on f5, Black had an equal game. However, it was later discovered that the bishop can become a target for the white pawns.

**7 h3**

Normally there are two ways to play this position: either just develop or fight for more space, for instance: 7 g4 ⌱g6 8 h4 and 9 h5 (if 8...⌱xh4 then 9 ⌱b3 b6 10 ⌱f3 with rapid development) or 7 ⌱e2 ⌱f6 8 ⌱g3 ⌱g6 and 9 ⌱d3. White prefers a third: he plays a waiting move to see what Black wants to do.

| 7 | ... | ⌱f6 |
| 8 | g4 | ⌱e6 |

Not 8...⌱g6 because of 9 ⌱ge2 followed by ⌱g3, g5 and h4.

| 9 | ⌱d3 | ⌱bd7 |
| 10 | ⌱f3 | ⌱b6 |
| 11 | ⌱c2 (D) | |

This position also occurred during the match between Botvinnik and Petrosian in 1963. White has more space and his bishops are better than Black's.

| 11 | ... | g6 |
| 12 | ⌱h6 | ⌱c4 |
| 13 | ⌱xc4 | dxc4 |
| 14 | e4 | ⌱a5 |
| 15 | a3 | 0-0-0 |
| 16 | 0-0-0 | ⌱e8 |

White has two strong centre pawns and is obviously looking for the right moment to march them forward. Black has no play

and can only wait. That explains the retreat of the knight.

| | | |
|---|---|---|
| 17 | ♗d2 | ♕a6 |
| 18 | ♗f4 | ♘c7 |

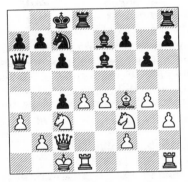

| | | |
|---|---|---|
| 19 | ♖he1 | ♗d6 |

If Black had played 19...♖he8 White could have tried to produce fireworks with 20 d5 cxd5 21 ♗xc7 ♔xc7 22 exd5 ♗c8 23 ♖xe7+ ♖xe7 24 d6+ ♖xd6 25 ♖xd6 ♔xd6 26 ♕d2+ ♔c7 27 ♘d5+ ♔d8 28 ♘b6+ ♔c7 29 ♕f4+ ♔xb6 30 ♕d6+ and mate next move. However Black has a defence. Instead of 28...♔c7 he can simply play 28...♗d7.

The search for such combinations is one of the main pleasures of playing chess and this is often the reason why we spend so much time on our clocks.

| | | |
|---|---|---|
| 20 | ♗g5 | ♖de8 |
| 21 | ♗f6 | ♖hg8 |
| 22 | ♘e5 | ♔b8 |
| 23 | f4 | ♗c8 |
| 24 | ♘e2 | ♖e6 |
| 25 | ♗h4 (D) | |

Of course it was better to play 25 g5 but White was expecting the move 25...b5, after which he intended to play 26 d5.

Black's reply was a surprise for me. At this stage of the game we had about three minutes each left on our clocks and it was no pleasure for me to have to play so fast in this important game, despite the fact that I nearly always get into time-trouble.

| | | |
|---|---|---|
| 25 | ... | ♗xa3 |

The first pawn.

| | | |
|---|---|---|
| 26 | bxa3 | ♕xa3+ |

Second pawn.

| | | |
|---|---|---|
| 27 | ♔d2 | ♘b5 |
| 28 | ♘xc4 | ♕xh3 |

Third pawn.

| | | |
|---|---|---|
| 29 | ♗g3 | f5 |
| 30 | e5 | ♘xd4 |

Fourth pawn.

| | | |
|---|---|---|
| 31 | ♕d3 | ♖d8 |
| 32 | ♘xd4 | c5 |
| 33 | ♗f2 | ♕h2 |
| 34 | ♖e2 | ♕xf4+ |

Fifth pawn.

| | | |
|---|---|---|
| 35 | ♗e3 | ♕xg4 |

Sixth pawn.

| | | |
|---|---|---|
| 36 | ♘d6 | ♖xe5 |

Seventh and last pawn!

Now it is easy for White to play as he no longer has to worry about his pawns!

It should also be mentioned that while Black was eating all of White's pawns he lost two pieces in the process. The black bishop which came out so early on move 6 is now back in its original position on c8.

With both flags about to fall, White's extra knights will now decide the game in his favour.

| 37 | ♘4b5 | a6 |
| 38 | ♕c3 | ♖d5+ |
| 39 | ♔c1 | ♕xe2 |
| 40 | ♖xd5 | axb5 |
| 41 | ♕xc5 | ♕a2 |

The adjourned position.

**42　♘xb5!**

It was not difficult to find and seal this move. It is too obvious to miss.

| 42 | ... | ♕a1+ |
| 43 | ♔d2 | ♖xd5+ |
| 44 | ♕xd5 | ♕a5+ |
| 45 | ♔e2 | |

**Black resigns**

## (35) Bronstein,D – Nikolayevsky,V

35th USSR Championship, Tbilisi, 1967

*[B06] Pirc Defence*

Besides being a good combinative player, my much younger opponent from Kiev was also an excellent wrestler with fast reflexes. So I was forewarned!

This game was proclaimed the best game of the tournament. Unfortunately I failed to qualify for the next Interzonal Tournament. The qualification itself was not of great significance for me but a good result was always important for the Dynamo Sports Club who paid my salary as a teacher of chess.

| 1 | e4 | d6 |
| 2 | d4 | g6 |
| 3 | c3 | |

A typical Morphy and Steinitz move!

| 3 | ... | ♗g7 |
| 4 | f4 | ♘f6 |
| 5 | e5 | |

Stopping Black from playing ...e5 and limiting the power of the bishop on g7. Now Black should have played 5...♘fd7 and ...c5 as soon as possible.

| 5 | ... | dxe5 |
| 6 | fxe5 | ♘d5 |
| 7 | ♘f3 | 0-0 |
| 8 | ♗c4 | |

The bishop is ideally placed here, looking at f7. The pawn will not go to c4 anyway and Black cannot play 8...c5 because after 9 dxc5 the knight is attacked twice.

| 8 | ... | ♗g4 |
| 9 | 0-0 | e6 |

Now ...c5 has become possible, therefore...

**10　♕b3**

The queen gets out of the pin.

| 10 | ... | ♗xf3 |
| 11 | ♖xf3 | ♘b6 |
| 12 | ♗e2 | ♕d5 |
| 13 | ♗e3 | ♕xb3 |
| 14 | axb3 | c5 |
| 15 | dxc5 | ♘d5 (D) |

If 15...♘6d7 then 16 ♘a3 ♘xe5 17 ♖ff1 and the white knight goes to d6.

**16　♗b5!!**

This prevents the development of the other knight. If 16...♞c6, then 17 ♗xc6 and ♖a6.

| 16 | ... | ♗xe5 |
| 17 | ♞d2! | ♞c7 |

Not 17...♞xe3 18 ♖xe3 ♗f4 19 ♖d3 ♗xd2 20 ♖xd2 and White has a superior position. His pawns are more mobile than Black's.

| 18 | ♗a4! | ♗g7 |
| 19 | ♞c4! | ♞ba6 |
| 20 | ♞d6! | |

It is easy to see the difference between the pawn structures. The black pawns on the kingside are totally passive but the white pawns on the queenside are ready to start an attack. However, this has to be prepared carefully.

| 20 | ... | ♖ab8 |
| 21 | b4 | b6 |
| 22 | ♗c6 | ♖bd8 |
| 23 | ♞b7 | ♖c8 |
| 24 | ♞d6 | ♖cd8 |
| 25 | ♗b7 | bxc5 |
| 26 | bxc5 | ♞b8 |
| 27 | ♖xa7 | |

The first move of this rook and one with great force. White did not 'waste' any time trying to develop the rook earlier. Now the path for the white pawns has been cleared.

| 27 | ... | ♖d7 |
| 28 | ♗c8 | ♖e7 |
| 29 | ♗g5 | f6 |
| 30 | ♗e3 | ♞c6 |
| 31 | ♖b7 | h6 |
| 32 | b4 | f5 |
| 33 | b5 | ♞d8 |
| 34 | c6 | e5 |
| 35 | ♗b6 | e4 |

Black finally manages to activate his pawns but it is too late.

| 36 | ♖xc7 | ♖xc7 |
| 37 | ♗xc7 | exf3 |
| 38 | ♗xd8 | ♗xc3 |
| 39 | ♗e7 | ♗d4+ |
| 40 | ♔f1 | |

**Black resigns**

A great demonstration of how effective a pair of bishops can be!

## (36) Bronstein,D – Zaitsev,A

100th Birthday Dr Emanuel Lasker
Tournament, Berlin, 1968
*[B30] Sicilian Defence*

This game was played in the first round. Amongst the guests of honour was the famous German grandmaster Lothar Schmid, a personal friend of Bobby Fischer and a well-known chess collector who has one of the best and largest chess libraries in the world. He told me afterwards that this game is a piece of art and will be his favourite for many years to come. I guess he said this because I played it in renaissance style.

| 1 | e4 | c5 |
| 2 | ♞c3 | e6 |
| 3 | ♞f3 | ♞c6 |
| 4 | ♗b5 | ♞d4 |
| 5 | ♗d3 | |

With the permission of the bishop on c1.

| 5 | ... | ♞xf3+ |
| 6 | ♕xf3 | ♗d6 (D) |

With the permission of the bishop on c8.

| 7 | ♕e3 | |

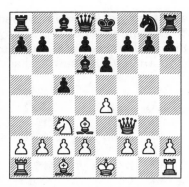

An unusual move which stops 7...♘e7 because of 8 ♘b5.

|     | 7  | ... | e5 |

This was too optimistic. Correct would have been careful play such as 7...b6 8 f4! ♗e7! 9 e5 d5.

|     | 8  | ♘b5 | ♕e7 |

If 8...♗e7, then 9 ♕g3 a6 10 ♕xg7 ♗f6 11 ♘d6+ ♔e7 12 ♘f5+. This is an example of a grandmaster calculating four moves ahead but this variation is easy to see as there is only one way to play. During real complications looking two moves ahead is already an accomplishment!

|     | 9  | b4! | |

Starting an attack on the queenside using the classical method of the 18th and 19th century.

|     | 9  | ... | cxb4 |
|     | 10 | ♕g3 | ♗b8 |
|     | 11 | ♕xg7 | ♕f6 |
|     | 12 | ♕xf6 | ♘xf6 |

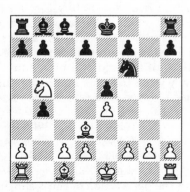

|     | 13 | a3! | d5 |
|     | 14 | f3 | ♖g8 |
|     | 15 | g3 | ♗h3 (D) |
|     | 16 | exd5 | ♗g2 |

|     | 17 | ♖g1 | ♗xf3 |

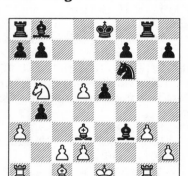

|     | 18 | d6 | |

Putting the bishop on b8 out of play.

|     | 18 | ... | bxa3 |
|     | 19 | ♖f1 | e4 |
|     | 20 | ♗e2 | ♖g5 |
|     | 21 | c4 | |

It was of course possible to play 21 ♗xa3 but why give up the strong position of the knight so easily?

|     | 21 | ... | a6 |
|     | 22 | ♖xa3 | ♗xe2 |
|     | 23 | ♔xe2 | ♘d7 |

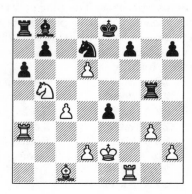

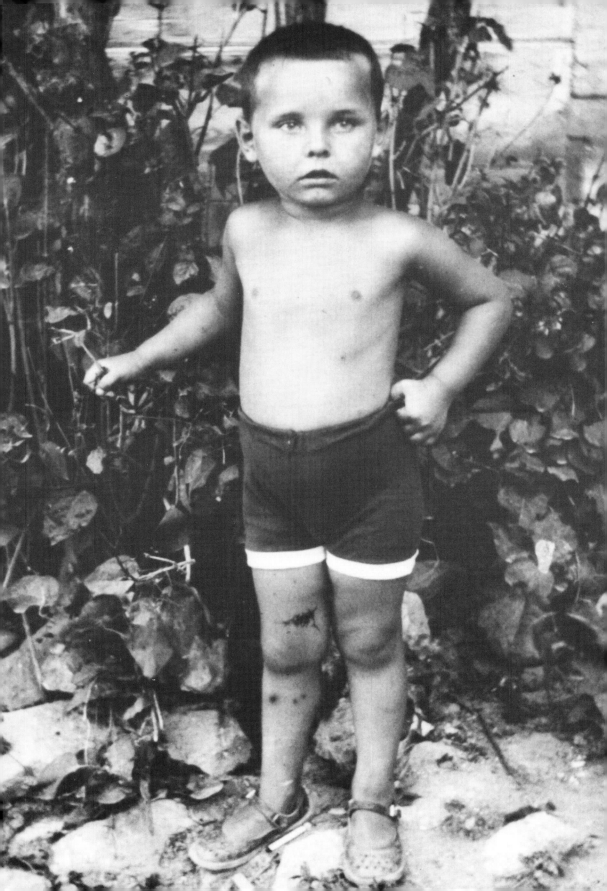

*Top left:* With his parents, 4½ months old, Smiela 1924.

*Top right:* His 3rd birthday. This rocking horse was a present for his 3rd birthday, but it did not last very long. After a few months, David took it apart as he wanted to find out how it could survive without eating! Berdyansk 17.2.1927.

*Previous page:* David, age five.

*Bottom left:* David, almost 4 years old, Berdyansk 16.12.1927

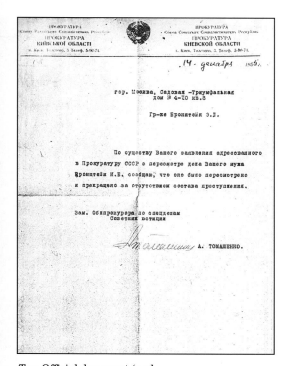

*Top:* Official document (and translation) relating to the charges against David's father.

Ministry of Justice
Prosecutor of the Kiev district

14th December 1955

Moscow
Sadovaya Triumphanaya
Dom 4-10 KV 8

Citizen Bronstein
Esther-Molka Duwid

Concerning the contents of your request which was addressed to the Office of the Prosecutor of the USSR to revise the file of your husband Bronstein I. B., we inform you that it has now been revised and stopped because of the absence of any evidence that a crime had been committed.

Deputy regional office of the prosecutor concerning special cases, advisor to the Justice Dept.

A. Tomaschenko

*Bottom:* Official document (and translation) relating to the imprisonment of David's father.

Ministry of Internal Affairs
of the USSR
Postbox AA 274/14
YCHTA Komi ASSR

8th June 1960

Ref. nr. 14/776

Citizen Bronstein

CONFIRMATION

It is given that Bronstein, Iohohon Berkovich, born 1895, was kept as a prisoner in a closed place of the Ministry of Internal Affairs, from 31.12.1937 until 12.2.1944 according to a decision of a special meeting ot the Council of the NKVD of the USSR, held on the 9th October 1938. This confirmation was passed on to the department of social welfare.

Head of the Branch,
Postbox 274.

Pomeranzov

Moscow, 25 June 1960.
The First Moscow State Notary Public Office confirms herewith that this photocopy is identical to the original document.
Taken: 2 Rubels State Tax.
Register 5F. No. 2306

*Top row from left to right:* Tunik Ginzburg (cousin of David's mother), Sarra Ginzburg (a close friend of David's mother, the wife of Mutsia Ginzburg), Ester Aptaker-Bronstein (David's mother), *1st row:* Mutsia Ginzburg (cousin of David's mother, husband of Sarra Guizburg), Israel Aptaker (the brother of David's mother), David himself, David's father Johonon Bronstein.

*Standing from left to right:* Bajnik, many times champion of Ukraine, Litnizky, Nabatnikov, R. Gorenstein. *Seated from left to right:* Hannan Muchnik, Morgulis, Kovalova, Simeon Jacovlevic Natov, Ljuba Kagan (in love with David) and David, Kiev 1939.

Final of the Championship for children of the Kiev Chess Club, seated in foreground and playing white (with a lot of hair) David, Palace of Pioneers, Kiev 1941.

15th birthday, photograph taken by his father's brother, manager of a photoshop, Kiev 19.2.1939.

David with his parents. When looking at this photograph and earlier ones one can see that mother Bronstein has aged 'normally'. Father Bronstein had just been released from seven years Gulag and what that has done to him can clearly be seen, Moscow 1948.

Opening Ceremony of the Match for the World Championship, Moscow 1951.
*From left to right:* V. Ragozin, M. Botvinnik, D. Postnikov (Deputy Minister of Sport) Folke Rogaard, Karl Opocensky, Bronstein, Gideon Stahlberg.
All good communists on the right of Folke Rogaard!

*Right:* Match with Boleslavsky, playing the decisive game nr. 14, Moscow 1950.

The joint winners of the
Candidates' Tournament
in Budapest 1950,
arriving home at Vnukovo
Airport, greeted by a large
crowd, Moscow 1950.

Olympiad.
*From left to right:* Keres
playing-Minev and David
playing Bobotsov of
Bulgaria, Apollo Hall,
Amsterdam 1954.

With Tal, playing the King's Gambit, Riga 1968.

Both authors discussing a just finished game, Oviedo, December 1993.

Bronstein, Furman, Karpov, 1973.

**24 d4**

This move changes the mind of the bishop (see the comment on move 5).

| | | |
|---|---|---|
| 24 | ... | **exd3+** |
| 25 | **♔xd3** | **♖c5** |
| 26 | **♗f4** | **f6** |

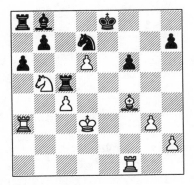

**27 ♔d4**

Another example of how right Steinitz was to say that the king is a strong piece in every part of the game. It takes part in the attack on equal terms with all the other pieces.

| | | |
|---|---|---|
| 27 | ... | **b6** |
| 28 | **♖e1+** | **♔d8** |
| 29 | **♖e6** | **♘e5** |

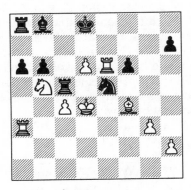

**30 ♗xe5**

Breaking the last line of Black's defences.

| | | |
|---|---|---|
| 30 | ... | **fxe5+** |
| 31 | **♖xe5** | **♖xc4+** |
| 32 | **♔d5** *(D)* | |
| 32 | ... | **♖c5+** |
| 33 | **♔e6** | **♖xe5+** |
| 34 | **♔xe5** | **♔d7** |
| 35 | **♔d5** | **a5** |

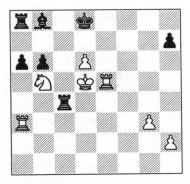

**36 ♖a4**

The finishing touch to a picturesque game! White's main achievement was that the rook on a8 was not able to play a part in the game at all.

| | | |
|---|---|---|
| 36 | ... | **h5** |

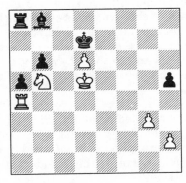

**37 ♖f4**
**Black resigns**

# (37) Bronstein,D – Zamikhovsky,A

Tournament for Veterans,
Leningrad, 1970
*[B17] Caro-Kann Defence*

At the start of 1970 I received a letter from Victor Korchnoi with the pleasant invitation to come as a guest to Leningrad to discuss various aspects of chess and to play a short training match with him. I arrived in June, receiving a warm welcome, and we spent a productive time together. As I was preparing to return to Moscow I received another invitation from a group of older chess players to join them in a friendly tournament. Of course I gratefully accepted.

The possibility to play this game was a pleasant surprise for Dr Alexander Zamikhovsky and myself. Although we have known each other for a long time – we are both from Kiev – we had never had a chance to play against each other. He was a physician and also one of the strongest players in the Ukraine. I don't know why he did not play in the 1939 and 1940 Ukraine and Kiev Championships just when I took my first steps in the real world of chess. After 22 June 1941 when Germany started the war against the Soviet Union Dr Zamikhovsky did his patriotic duty and served as a surgeon in an army field hospital, often situated close to the battlefield. He saved hundreds of lives but at the cost of his own health.

We should not forget the heroic feats of all Soviet citizens who, often in extreme conditions and in their own way, contributed to the final victory over the Nazi invaders.

Dr Zamikhovsky was very kind to me when he recalled how I had created a sensation in the Kiev Championship Semi-Final and Final playing a wild and unusual sort of chess against the sound strategy of adult players.

Again, the numbers in brackets indicate the time used for each move in minutes as recorded by myself during the game.

| 1 | e4 (5)    | c6 (1)    |
|---|-----------|-----------|
| 2 | d4 (1)    | d5 (0)    |
| 3 | ♘c3 (0)   | dxe4 (0)  |
| 4 | ♘xe4 (0)  | ♘d7 (1)   |
| 5 | c3 (1)    |           |

The idea of this move is to protect the pawn on d4 against future attacks and create a safe place on c2 to retreat the bishop to after it has gone to d3 first. White is not worried about the possibility of 5...e5 because after 6 ♘f3 exd4 7 ♘xd4 the knights in the centre are very strong.

| 5 | ...       | ♘gf6 (1)  |
|---|-----------|-----------|
| 6 | ♘g3 (0)   |           |

This retreat rarely seen today but in my opinion it is unwise to exchange knights on f6 and free the bishop on c8.

| 6  | ...       | e6 (4)    |
|----|-----------|-----------|
| 7  | ♘f3 (3)   | ♗e7 (0)   |
| 8  | ♗d3 (3)   | c5 (6)    |
| 9  | 0-0 (1)   | 0-0 (0)   |
| 10 | ♘e5 (2)   |           |

Now that the pawn on d4 has extra protection (see the comment on move 5), the knight can go to e5 without any fear. If 10...♕b6, White can play 11 ♗c2.

| 10 | ...       | ♕c7 (6)   |
|----|-----------|-----------|
| 11 | ♕e2 (14)  |           |

The obvious question is why I thought 14 minutes before making this natural move.

The answer is that there are more natural moves, for instance 11 ♗f4, 11 ♖e1 or 11 f4. Each of them has advantages and disadvantages. Probably the most logical one is 11 f4 to create the threat of f4-f5 but I was a little worried about the reply 11...♖d8. The other plausible explanation is that I was already preparing the combination which follows.

| 11 | ...       | b6 (6)    |
|----|-----------|-----------|
| 12 | f4 (0)    | ♖e8 (21)  |

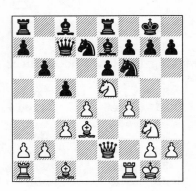

To have the f8 square for the knight if White plays f4-f5.

**13 ⊘e4! (7)**

With the threat 14 ⊘xf7 or 14 ⊘g5. Black can't play 13...⊘xe5 as White plays 14 ⊘xf6+. But Black should have exchanged knights on e4 because after 14 ♗xe4 ♗b7 15 ♗xh7+ ♔xh7 16 ♕h5+ White has no more than perpetual check and after 14 ♕xe4 ⊘f6 15 ♕xa8 ♗b7 16 ♕xe8+ ⊘xe8 17 ♗e3 Black has nothing to fear.

However, after a long think, Black rejected this idea and with his next move he puts the wind in my sails.

**13 ... h6 (16)**

**14 ⊘g5! (8) ♖f8 (22)**

Taking the knight on g5 is too dangerous and besides, Black had to protect f7. But White has another surprise.

**15 ⊘g6! (35) ♖e8 (8)**

Now Black should have taken the knight on g6, regardless of what happens after 16 ♕xe6+ ♔h8 17 ♕xe7 or 16 ⊘xe6 ♕d6 17 f5 g5 18 h4. However, Black did not see White's next move.

**16 ⊘xe6! (1) ♕d6 (1)**

**17 f5!! (5)**

Now White has the f4-square for his bishop. His attack is becoming irresistible.

| | | |
|---|---|---|
| 17 | ... | fxg6 (11) |
| 18 | ♗f4 (1) | ♕c6 (1) |
| 19 | ♗b5 (4) | ♕e4 (15) |
| 20 | ♕xe4 (3) | ⊘xe4 (0) |
| 21 | fxg6 (6) | ⊘df6 (7) |
| 22 | ⊘c7 (1) | ♗d7 (1) |
| 23 | ♗xd7 (1) | ⊘xd7 (0) |

The last white piece comes into action. The rest is simple.

| | | |
|---|---|---|
| 24 | ♖ae1 (3) | ⊘7f6 (0) |
| 25 | ⊘xa8 (9) | ♖xa8 (0) |
| 26 | ♖xe4 (0) | ⊘xe4 (0) |
| 27 | ♖e1 (0) | ♗d6 (4) |
| 28 | ♖xe4 (1) | ♗xf4 (0) |
| 29 | ♖xf4 (0) | ♖e8 (0) |
| 30 | dxc5 (1) | bxc5 (0) |
| 31 | ♖f7 (0) | ♖e6 (0) |
| 32 | ♖xa7 (1) | ♖xg6 (0) |
| 33 | ♖c7 (0) | ♖d6 (0) |
| 34 | b3 (1) | ♖d2 (0) |
| 35 | ♖xc5 (1) | |

**Black resigns**

Total time used:
White: 1.59 Black: 2.12
(See Time Graph on the next page)

## (38) Bronstein,D – Lein,A

41st USSR Championship,
Leningrad, 1971
*[B89] Sicilian Defence*

The move 6 ♗c4 was made popular by Bobby Fischer but it was Karl Schlechter

## Time Graph Bronstein,D-Zamikhovsky,A

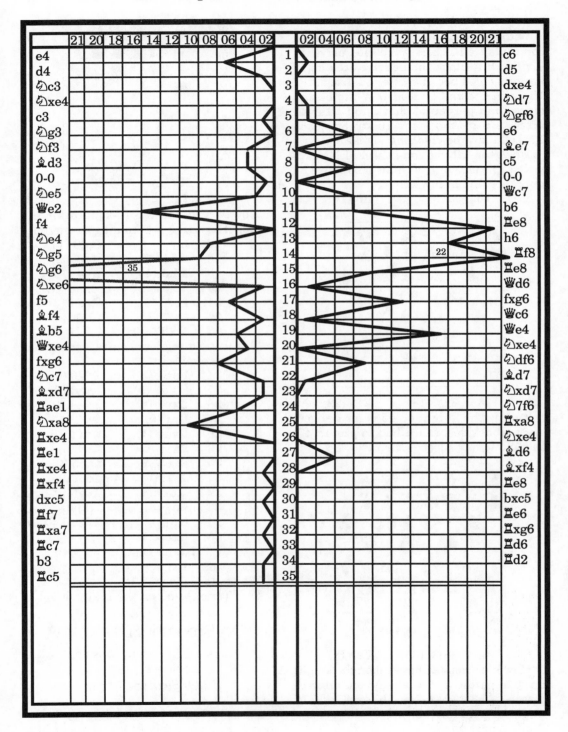

| 13 | g5 | ♞c5 |

This position is well-known in chess theory. My next move is a novelty which I found over the board but will never play again. Of course I understood that it was very risky but it is my style to take my opponent and myself onto unknown grounds. A game of chess is not an examination of knowledge, it is a battle of nerves.

| 14 | e5 | dxe5 |

The best way to refute the gambit style of play is to accept the sacrifice. However, equally good was 14...d5 15 f4 b5 and it is far from clear whether White will have sufficient means to organise an attack.

| 15 | ♖h4 | g6 |
| 16 | ♖h6 | |

Preparing the advance of the h-pawn to connect the rooks.

This original way of leading the attack attracted the attention of Leonid Stein, himself a brilliant attacking player. He violated the strict rule of no talking between participants during the games and told me how much he liked my idea of conducting this game. I sensed a bit of jealousy that he was not playing with the white pieces himself!

It would have been easy for him to continue the attack from this position because, being a great combinative grandmaster, Stein produced hundreds of masterpieces during his short chess career. His untimely death was a severe blow not only to his family and close friends but also to millions of chess fans.

| 16 | ... | f5 |
| 17 | h4 | ♞xb3+ |

---

who played it first against Dr Emanuel Lasker in their World Championship match in 1910. Later it was also often played by the Soviet master Veniamin Sozin.

This move was pulled out of the old hat by Isaac Boleslavsky in 1947 when he won a brilliant game against Lev Aronin in the 15th USSR Championship in Leningrad. Before the game Boleslavsky told me that he was going to use this Italian style move and even explained how he was going to push his pawns forward and on which square he intended to sacrifice his knight, and this is exactly what happened...!

I can heartily recommend to you the reprint of Boleslavsky's book *Selected Games* (named the best book of the year by the British Chess Federation in 1990).

| 1 | e4 | c5 |
| 2 | ♞f3 | d6 |
| 3 | d4 | cxd4 |
| 4 | ♞xd4 | ♞f6 |
| 5 | ♞c3 | ♞c6 |
| 6 | ♗c4 | |

| 6 | ... | e6 |
| 7 | ♗b3 | ♗e7 |
| 8 | ♗e3 | 0-0 |
| 9 | ♕e2 | a6 |
| 10 | 0-0-0 | ♕c7 |
| 11 | g4 | |

Also 11 ♖hg1 first and then 12 g4 has been played.

| 11 | ... | ♞xd4 |
| 12 | ♖xd4 | ♞d7 |

If Black plays 12...e5, then 13 ♖c4 ♕d8 14 ♖xc8 ♖xc8 15 g5 ♞d7 and 16 h4 with a dangerous attack. White controls the centre.

**18    axb3**

According to the rule of taking towards the centre. At this moment it was difficult to see that the open a-file would become useful for Black.

**18    ...          f4**

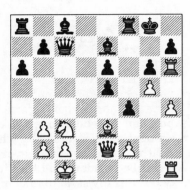

**19    ♘e4**

This is very courageous but not correct: 19 ♗d2 would have been a more promising choice.

**19    ...          fxe3**
**20    h5          ♖xf2!**
**21    ♕d3         ♗f8?**

Missing a chance to turn the wheel of fortune by 21...♕a5 22 ♔b1 e2 23 c3 ♕d5 24 ♕xd5 ♖f1+.

**22    ♘xf2**

Perhaps 22 ♘f6+ was possible. For instance 22...♖xf6 23 gxf6 ♗xh6 24 hxg6 e2+ 25 ♔b1 or 23...g5 24 ♖g6+ ♔h8 25 ♕e4 ♕c6 26 f7 ♗g7 27 h6 hxg6 28 hxg7++ ♔xg7 29 ♕xe5+.

**22    ...          exf2**
**23    hxg6         ♗xh6**
**24    gxh6**

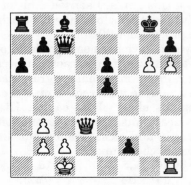

24 ♖xh6 is too dangerous for White as he should not leave the first rank, for instance 24...♕a5 threatening mate in two or loss of the white queen.

**24    ...          ♕e7**

Very logical but losing (because it gives up the guard of e5). However, the reply 24...♗d7, totally illogical (cutting off the queen), would have been winning, e.g. 25 gxh7+ ♔h8 26 ♕g6 ♗b5 27 c4 ♖f8, etc. Both sides were already in time-trouble.

**25    gxh7+        ♕xh7**

Also 25...♔h8 is not sufficient: 26 ♕g6 ♗d7 27 ♖f1 ♖f8 28 ♖xf2 ♗e8 29 ♕g7+ ♕xg7 30 hxg7+ ♔xg7 31 ♖xf8 ♔xf8 32 h8♕+. Or if 27...♕xh7, then 28 ♕f6+ ♔g8 29 ♖xf2 ♗c6 30 ♕g5+ ♔h8 31 ♕xe5+ ♔g8 32 ♕xe6+ ♔h8 33 ♕f6+ ♔g8 34 ♖f5 and then ♖g5+ is deadly.

**26    ♕g3+         ♔f7**
**27    ♕xf2+        ♔e8**
**28    ♕f6          ♕f7**
**29    ♕h8+         ♔d7**
**30    h7           ♔c6**
**31    ♕g8          ♕f4+**
**32    ♔b1**

**Black resigns**

This game was played before an audience of more than a thousand people in a large theatre. Although it was full of mistakes from both sides, there was prolonged applause when Black resigned!

## (39) Bronstein,D – Ljubojević,L

Interzonal Tournament,
Petropolis, 1973
*[B03] Alekhine's Defence*

(This is one of the most complex and fascinating games ever played. A game between two players who are renowned in the chess world for their original ideas and daring style of play.

It has been analysed by the best grandmasters, over and over again, but to keep matters comprehensible only some of their findings will be shown below.

After ten rounds, Ljubojević was leading by just half a point with 7½ points. Under the circumstances one might have expected conservative play from Ljubojević in round eleven, especially with the black pieces. However, to the surprise and delight of the chess world, Ljubojević chose an extremely risky and sharp variation of Alekhine's Defence, following his prepared variation up to at least move fifteen.

Towards the end Bronstein was extremely short of time whereas the nearly imperturbable Ljubojević had consumed less than an hour for the whole game! The result was a hair-raising sacrificial struggle for which Bronstein was awarded the first brilliancy prize.

Paul Keres annotated this game for *Chess Life & Review* of December 1973, number 12, Vol. 28, pages 708-10 and we have the editor's kind permission to reproduce his comments here, T.F.)

### 'Another Bronstein idea'
*by Paul Keres*

If I were asked to name that modern grandmaster who develops the most ideas, I would not mention Fischer, Spassky, Petrosian, Larsen but... Bronstein! The question does not concern only new ideas and variations on the chessboard but also many other aspects of the game. Of the many Bronstein suggestions to make the game more lively and interesting, we would mention the recording of time used for every move (see pages 144, 164 and 237 T.F.), giving both opponents half an hour to finish the game after the first control, limiting the time for the entire game to about an hour, providing national cup competitions in the form of short matches (the USSR Cup was first held in 1970 and it was won by Bronstein!) and many other ideas.

The latest Bronstein idea concerns World Championship contests. We already have the World Junior Championship, the Student Team World Championship, the men's and women's individual titles, the men's and women's team titles... But why not the Senior World Championship, asks Bronstein. His idea is to invite to such a tournament all grandmasters over the age

of fifty who have participated in at least one Candidates' Tournament or Match. The proposal has its logic and perhaps one of the forthcoming FIDE congresses will deal with this question.

But the most interesting and valuable ideas to come from Bronstein are still produced on the chessboard. I had the pleasure of following his games at the Petropolis Interzonal Tournament and of his magnificent fights I would especially mention the brilliant game against Ljubojević. The rook sacrifice on move sixteen in this game is really surprising and while I was watching the game it took me quite a lot of time to find the point of it. It is no wonder that this game was considered the most beautiful of the tournament.

Inspiration or Perspiration?

During the progress of the Bronstein-Ljubojević game, I was not quite certain whether Bronstein's rook sacrifice was an improvisation or a product of careful home preparation. And still I do not know the answer to that question. Up until move 14 the game between Ljubojević and Honfi from the 1971 Čačak tournament was repeated, ending in a short victory for Ljubojević (White). Here Ljubojević plays the variation with Black! He had an improvement in mind on the fourteenth move leading to that wonderful rook sacrifice on move sixteen.

Did Bronstein find all this in home analysis? We can only guess. (It was all conceived during the game! T.F.) Anyway, here I must recall the famous Bronstein-Tal game (page 66, T.F.) from the Riga 1968 tournament, where Bronstein explained his most surprising rook sacrifice by saying that he 'could not miss the opportunity' to make such a sacrifice; he said he might never have another chance to play such a move against Tal! Because we know Bronstein we may guess that he also decided on the rook sacrifice during this game – to make it more interesting, more complicated, more distinct from the other games.

Whatever the cause, the result is a wonderful fighting game and one of the most interesting games between leading grand-masters in recent years.

| 1 | e4 | ♘f6 |

**Keres:** Ljubojević usually chooses the Sicilian Defence. His choice of the Alek-hine Defence in this game is probably due to a prepared improvement in a compli-cated variation which is very hard to meet in over-the-board play. However it is not so easy to take Bronstein by surprise in complicated positions.

| 2 | e5 | ♘d5 |
| 3 | d4 | d6 |
| 4 | c4 | ♘b6 |
| 5 | f4 | |

Generally considered risky and there-fore 5 exd6 is seen more often, though without much danger for Black.

**Keres:** The Four Pawns Attack! Is this a clever choice against Ljubojević, whose main strength lies in complicated posi-tions? In most modern tournament games with this defence we see here 5 ♘f3.

| 5 | ... | dxe5 |
| 6 | fxe5 | |

The most vigorous variation against the Alekhine Defence – the Four Pawns At-tack. Seven successive moves with pawns. By this time in other openings White has managed to develop three minor pieces and has castled.

Here he has two far-advanced pawns, two open files and one knight in support. Today the positional continuation 4 ♘f3 ♗g4 5 ♗e2 is more fashionable.

| 6 | ... | c5 |

Extremely risky but not new. It was played in the 1920's with some success by the Soviet master Argunov. Ljubojević has had some success with it but now it is pro-nounced unsound.

**Keres:** Ljubojević was probably afraid of some prepared variation in the main line with 6...♗f5 when he chose this theo-retically inferior continuation. Anyhow, he was quite at home with the finesses in this variation as we will see.

| 7 | d5 | |

7 dxc5 is too materialistic as White has little chance of holding the pawn.

| 7 | ... | e6 |

Preparing threats with ...♕h4+

| 8 | ♘c3! | |

The attractive 8 d6 does not work as White falls just short of getting organ-ised to win the black queen, for example 8...♕h4+ 9 g3 ♕e4+ 10 ♕e2 ♕xh1 11 ♘f3 ♘c6 (11...♘xc4 12 ♘bd2! ♘xd2 13 ♔xd2 g6 14 ♔c2 – also 14 ♗g2 is strong – 14...♘c6 15 ♗g2 ♘b4+ 16 ♔b3 is better for White) 12 ♘bd2 ♘d7! 13 ♔f2 ♘dxe5! 14 ♘xe5 ♕xh2+ 15 ♗g2 ♘d4 16 ♕d1 ♗xd6 17 ♘f1 ♕xg2+ 18 ♔xg2 ♗xe5 is good for Black.

| 8 | ... | exd5 |

Of course not 8...♘xc4? 9 ♕a4+ (9 ♗xc4? ♕h4+) winning the knight. Also possible but less to the point is 8...♕h4+ 9 g3 ♕d4 when 10 ♕e2 or the speculative 10 ♗d2!? leads to good play for White.

**Keres:** Here 8...♕h4+ 9 g3 ♕d4 does not look quite logical. First, White can win the exchange with 10 ♕e2 exd5 11 ♘b5 and second, Boleslavsky's recommenda-tion 10 ♗f4! appears to be even stronger. If Black then takes the pawn with 10...g5 11 ♗d2 ♕xe5+, his position will remain hopelessly exposed after 12 ♗e2, etc.

| 9 | cxd5 | c4 |

This is the crux of the entire variation and it is rather annoying for White. It clears the f8-a3 diagonal for a possible ...♗c5 to keep the white king in the centre, or ...♗b4 while at the same time keeping the white bishop away from b5. 9...♕h4+ 10 g3 ♕d4 11 ♗f4!? is better for White, and 11 ♗b5+ ♗d7 12 ♕e2 ♘xd5 13 e6! gives White a strong attack. If White has-tens to occupy this diagonal by 10 ♗e3 then after 10...♗b4 he begins to have trouble with his breakaway d-pawn. In this situation White takes a crucial decision – he goes for forcing play, relying on his strong pawn centre and open lines.

**Keres**: A recommendation by Mikenas and probably Black's best chance. Again the manoeuvre 9...♕h4+ 10 g3 ♕d4 looks unnatural and leaves White with a good attacking game after 11 ♗b5+ (also 11 ♗f4 g5 12 ♗xg5 ♕xe5+ 13 ♕e2 is good for White) 11...♗d7 12 ♕e2 ♘xd5 13 e6! fxe6 14 ♕xe6+ ♘e7 15 ♘f3, etc. (Balashov-Grigorian, Riga 1967).

**10    ♘f3**

White threatens to take the pawn on c4.

**Keres**: This natural developing move looks best but also 10 d6 ♘c6 (11 ♘b5!? ♕h4+) has to be considered.

**Bronstein**: Brilliant intuition by the great Estonian player! Almost 22 years later the British international master Philip Morris (Charlton Chess Club) made a fantastic discovery in his game against T. Hinks-Edwards (Richmond Chess Club), which was played for the British National Team Championship, on 28 January 1995: after 10 d6! ♘c6 11 ♘b5 ♕h4+ 12 g3 ♕e4+ 13 ♕e2 ♕xh1 14 ♗g5!! White's attack becomes irresistible. The game continued 14...♗f5 15 0-0-0 ♔d7 (15...f6 16 ♘c7+ ♔f7 17 e6+ ♔g6 18 g4 ♗e4 19 ♗e3) 16 ♗g2 ♕xg2 17 ♕xg2 h6 18 ♗e3 g5 19 ♕f2 and Black resigned.

The move 10 d6 was also recommended by Boris Vainstein in his famous book *David Bronstein: Chess Improviser*.

**10    ...    ♗g4**

If 10...♗b4 then 11 ♗g5!, or 11 ♗xc4 ♘xc4 12 ♕a4+ ♘c6 13 dxc6 and Black is in serious difficulties.

**Keres**: The other possibility 10...♗b4 enables White to play 11 ♗xc4, for instance 11...♗xc3+ (good for White is 11...♘xc4 12 ♕a4+ ♘c6 13 dxc6 ♗xc3+ 14 bxc3 b5 15 ♕b4! a5 16 ♕c5 ♕d3 17 ♗g5 according to Boleslavsky) 12 bxc3 ♘xc4 13 ♕a4+ ♘d7 14 ♕xc4 ♘b6 15 ♕b5+ ♕d7 (Boleslavsky) and now White remains, at worst, with an extra pawn after 16 ♕xd7+ ♔xd7 17 d6.

**11    ♕d4!** *(D)*

Leads to almost unfathomable complications, right up Bronstein's alley!

**Keres**: Black would get a reasonable position after 11 ♗xc4 ♘xc4 12 ♕a4+ ♘d7 13 ♕xc4 ♗xf3 14 gxf3 ♘xe5 (15 ♕e4 ♕h4+!) although after 15 ♕e2! ♕h4+ there are still many problems to solve. The text move looks stronger.

**11    ...    ♗xf3**
**12    gxf3    ♗b4**

Quick development for an attack. The threat is now against White's pawn on d5. 12...♘c6 13 ♕e4 ♗b4 14 e6 benefits White.

**Keres**: 12...♘c6 13 ♕e4 ♗b4 leads to nothing after 14 e6!, etc. By sacrificing a pawn, Black will complete his development hoping to get attacking counter-chances against the white centre pawns. The position is now getting very exciting.

**13    ♗xc4**

Almost forced since the d-pawn is inadequately defended. If for instance 13 ♕g4 then 13...♘xd5 14 ♕xg7 ♖f8 and Black has nothing to fear. Black hastens to castle so as to begin an attack on the exposed white king, for which he is ready to sacrifice a pawn. If White should begin thinking about the safety of his king his extended centre will begin to creak. In fact 13...♕xd5 was already threatened and in some cases ...♘c6.

**13    ...    0-0**

White has won a pawn but his king is not yet in a safe position. He now comes up with a beautiful combination.

**14    ♖g1** *(D)*

14 ♗h6 is also interesting. If for instance: 14...gxh6 15 e6 f6 then 16 d6. But after 14...♘8d7 15 e6 ♘e5 or 15 ♖g1 g6 16

e6 ♘e5 17 ♗e2 ♗c5 Black starts the attack first, taking advantage of the fact that White's queenside is frozen.

**14 ... g6**

**Keres:** This is the improvement Ljubojević had prepared at home. The position was not unfamiliar to him since he had played it with White against Honfi two years earlier (Tchachak 1971). In that game Honfi chose a weak defence with 14...♕c7? and was rapidly mated after 15 e6! f6 16 ♗h6! ♕xc4 17 ♖xg7+ ♔h8 18 ♖g8+!, and so on.

The position now appears to be critical for White because of the very unpleasant threat 15...♘c6. After 15 ♗e3 Black may play 15...♘8d7 with triple threats 16...♘xc4, 16...♘xe5 and 16...♗c5. In this extremely complicated situation, Bronstein finds a wonderful way out.

**15 ♗g5!**

The first surprise. If now 15...♗e7 then White may simply exchange bishops with 16 ♗xe7 ♕xe7 and transform the game into a favourable endgame after 17 ♗b3 ♘bd7 18 f4 ♕h4+ 19 ♕f2 ♕xf2+ 20 ♔xf2.

Certainly not 15 ♗h6? because of the reply 15...♘c6! 16 ♕e4 ♘xe5!! 17 ♗xf8 ♕xf8 18 ♗b3 ♕c5 19 0-0-0 ♗xc3 20 bxc3 ♕xc3+ 21 ♕c2 ♕a1+ 22 ♔d2 (22 ♕b1 ♖c8+) 22...♘xf3+ 23 ♔e3 ♕f6 24 ♖gf1 ♖e8+.

**15 ... ♕c7**

Ljubojević threatens both ...♕xc4 and ...♗c5 pinning the queen and rook. These threats can be parried only by the awkward 16 ♖g4. If 15...♕c8 16 ♗b3 ♗c5 17 ♕h4 ♗xg1 (17...♘8d7 18 ♘e4 is better for White) 18 ♕h6 and mate can only be averted by 18...♗e3.

**16 ♗b3!!!?** (Reuben Fine)

Sacrificing a full rook without an immediate follow-up. Subsequent analysis has cast some doubt on the soundness of the sacrifice but in over-the-board play it remains a marvellous conception.

**Keres:** This most amazing move fully deserves at least two exclamation marks. White gives up a whole rook and, at first sight, one cannot see what he hopes to gain by it. But the further course of the game will make this clear.

Besides the text move, White could have tried here 16 ♗e2 ♗c5 17 ♕f4 as the rook could not be taken because of 17...♗xg1 18 ♗f6! with the unavoidable threat of 19 ♕h6. But by playing 17...f6! Black would have avoided all the mating threats with a good game.

**16 ... ♗c5** (D)

Black has to go for the rook because his own bishop is threatened. The continuation 16...♖e8 17 ♕xb4 ♕xe5+ 18 ♔f2 leads to nothing.

**17    ♕f4**

This simple move has three objectives: It prepares the move with the queen to h6, it leaves the square e4 free for the knight and it of course protects the pawn on e5.

**17    ...        ♗xg1**

**Keres**: The Russian language chess newspaper *64* has suggested a better line here to try to refute the rook sacrifice but in my opinion their conclusions are not convincing. The first line 17...♘8d7 18 d6 ♕c6 19 0-0-0 ♗xg1 20 ♖xg1 ♕c5 21 ♖e1 ♖ae8 would allow the very strong continuation 22 e6! for instance 22...fxe6 23 ♖xe6! ♖xf4 24 ♖xe8+ or 23...♖xe6 24 ♗xe6+ ♔h8 25 ♕xf8+! with mate to follow in both cases.

The other suggestion 17...♖e8 18 ♗f6 ♘8d7 19 d6 ♘xe5 20 ♔f1 ♗xd6 21 ♘b5 ♕c6 22 ♘xd6 ♕xd6 23 ♖d1 ♕c6 24 ♗xe5 ♕b5+ does not satisfy either after 25 ♔g2 ♕xe5 27 ♕xf7+ ♔h8 27 ♖ge1 ♕xb2+ 28 ♔h1 and White clearly has the better of it. Also 18 ♖g2 ♖xe5+ (18...♕xe5+ 19 ♖e2!) 19 ♘e4 has to be considered with many threats.

Let us now consider after 17... ♗xg1 what White has for his rook. His pieces are excellently developed, the centre pawns are very strong and the weakened position of the enemy king is almost without defence. But a whole rook is missing and what 'hard' value does White have for it?

Direct play for mating threats does not lead to anything as 18 ♗f6 is sufficiently met by either 18...♘8d7 for if 19 ♕h6 then 19...♘xf6 20 exf6 ♕e5+ or by 18...♕c5 threatening 19...♕e3+. Also, 18 ♘e4 will not do because of 18...♘8d7.

(**Bronstein**: This is probably a printing error as 20...♕e5+ is met by 21 ♘e4 and Black is mated! The correct play for Black is: 18 ♗f6 ♕c5! – instead of 18...♘8d7 – and if now 19 ♕h6 then 19...♕e3+).

Therefore White has to look for a combination of various methods of attack, making use of Black's backward development and the unfortunate position of the bishop on g1.

First, it must be mentioned that White gets the upper hand if he succeeds in capturing the bishop on g1, thus remaining only an exchange behind. Second, White can allow himself to develop the attack relatively slowly as Black has no way to get quick counterplay. But the character of the position makes exhaustive analysis extremely difficult and I hope that the reader will understand if some 'hole' may be found in the following explanations. A position like this must be **played**, not exhausted by extensive home analysis!

**18    d6**

This move prevents any action by Black on the f-file by opening up the diagonal for the bishop on b3. If 18 ♔e2? then 18...♕c5! It turns out that although a rook up Black's game hangs by a thread. If for example 18...♕c6 then 19 e6 fxe6 20 ♗xe6+ and 21 ♗h6+. On 18...♕c5 White intended 19 ♘e4! ♕e3+ 20 ♕xe3 ♗xe3 21 ♗xe3 ♘c6 22 f4 and Black's position is hopeless.

**Bronstein**: In this line Black should not play 19...♕e3+ but 19...♕d4 with an unclear position.

**Keres**: A normal move to release the pressure against e5 and to open the way for the bishop on b3. Black must now take care of the threat e6 which would be very strong if, for instance 18...♕c6 19 e6 ♘8d7, and now 20 exf7+ ♔g7 21 0-0-0! will lead to a position similar to our later analysis.

Of course bad would be 18...♕c5 19 ♘e4 ♕b4+ 20 ♔f1 allowing White to gain valuable tempi. If 20...♕d4 then 21 ♖d1 (21 e6 ♘8d7) 21...♕xb2 22 ♖d2 ♕c1+ 23 ♔e2.

**18    ...        ♕c8 (D)**
**19    ♔e2**

This move is universally condemned by the annotators, giving 19 0-0-0 as much stronger, for example 19...♗c5 20 e6! fxe6 21 ♕e5 ♖e8 22 ♗h6 ♕d7 23 ♘e4 or 19...♕c5 20 e6 ♘8d7 21 exf7+ ♔g7 22 ♔b1 ♕e5 23 ♖xg1.

Up to move 19 Ljubojević had played very quickly with the aim of creating a psychological superiority and also of forcing his opponent to spend much time on his own clock in calculating the complicated variations which he had already analysed beforehand.

**Keres**: This looks very good, but it actually exposes White's king too much giving Black good chances for a successful defence. In later analysis both players came to the conclusion that 19 0-0-0! was the proper move here. Since then 20 ♖xg1 is a threat Black would have only two main lines to consider:

a) 19...♗c5 20 e6! ♘8b7! (the only move, as 20...fxe6 21 ♕e5! ♖e8 22 ♗e7, or 21...♖f7 22 ♗xe6 ♘8d7 23 ♗xf7+ ♔xf7 24 ♕e7+ ♔g8 25 ♗h6 would lead to immediate loss) 21 e7, and White wins his material back with a decisive attack.

b)  19...♕c5! 20 e6 (20 ♔b1 ♘8d7 would be too slow) 20...♘8d7 (Black's best *practical* chance would probably be 20...♗e3+ 21 ♕xe3 ♕xe3+ 22 ♗xe3 fxe6 although the ending is clearly in White's favour) 21 exf7+ (21 e7 wins the rook but gives Black enough play after 21...♗xh2!) 21...♔g7 22 ♔b1! and although a rook ahead Black seems helpless against the threat 23 ♘e4.

Black could also have chosen here the variation 19 0-0-0 ♘8d7 20 ♖xg1 ♕c5 mentioned in the analysis after Black's 17th move, leading to a terrific attack after 21 ♖e1 ♖ae8 22 e6!

Another curious idea was 19 ♔f1!? (19...♕c5 20 ♘c4) and if 19...♗c5 then 20 e6 fxe6 (or 20...♘8d7 21 exf7+ ♔g7 22 ♖d1 threatening 23 ♘e4) 21 ♕e5 ♖xf3+ 22 ♔e2 but an analysis of all these possibilities would definitely lead us too far.

**19     ...     ♗c5**

In the heat of the battle Ljubojević had grown so used to the blitz rhythm that he instantaneously played this move just when a thorough consideration of the situation was required. He rejected 19...♕c5 assuming that 20 ♘e4 would lead to a loss for Black.

But now with the white king on e2 Ljubojević has the possibility of playing 20...♕b5+. With 19...♕c5 Black threatens ...♕f2+. If then 20 e6 ♘8d7 21 exf7+ ♔g7 22 ♗h6+ ♔h8 Black already has many counter-threats and White's king is almost as exposed as Black's. With 19...♕c5 he might even have won; after the text he is definitely lost. However it must have been hard to see how White was going to win from this position without any direct mating continuations available and with a whole rook down.

**Bronstein**: Black's move 20...♘8d7 in the variation with 19...♕c5 can also be played in the variation starting with 19...♗c5. White can then play 21 e7 and recover his rook while continuing the attack.

**Keres**: This definitely loses. Black had to try 19...♕c5 which would have given him excellent chances to repulse the attack. White would then have had the following choices:

a) 20 ♘e4 ♕b5+ 21 ♔e1 (or 21 ♔d2 ♘c4+ 22 ♗xc4 ♕xb2+!, etc.) 21...♘8d7 and Black seems to have adequate defensive possibilities for instance 22 ♘f6+ ♘xf6 23 ♗xf6 ♘d7, or 22 ♗f6 ♘xf6 23 ♘xf6+ ♔h8, etc.

b) 20 e6 ♘8d7 (the threat was 21 exf7+ mating and 20...fxe6 21 ♗xe6+ also leads to mate; worth considering was first 20...♕f2+ and if White plays 21 ♔d1 then 21...♕d4+ 22 ♕xd4 ♗xd4 is sufficient or

21 ♔d3 ♘8d7 is even stronger threatening 22...♘c5 mate) 21 exf7+ (on 21 e7 or 21 exd7 the answer 21...♕f2+ and 22...♗xh2 is strong and 21 ♘e4 is met by 21...♕b5+ and 22...fxe6 and a promising way to continue the attack is not to be seen) 21...♔g7 and Black will refute the attack.

Perhaps I am too pessimistic in estimating White's attacking possibilities after 19...♕c5! but it is clear that Black had to choose this defence. If it was as easy to find the correct defence during the game as it is in later analysis we would certainly see only very few attacking games!

**20 ♘e4! ♘8d7**

20...♘6d7 would have offered more resistance: 21 ♖c1 b6 22 ♗f6 ♘xf6 23 ♘xf6+ ♔g7 24 ♕h4 h6 (24...♖h8 25 ♘h5+ ♔g8 26 ♗xf7+!) 25 ♘h5+ ♔h7 (25...gxh5 26 ♕f6+ ♔g8 27 ♕g6+ ♔h8 28 ♕xh6+ ♔g8 29 ♗c2 f5 30 ♗b3+) 26 ♕f6 ♖g8 27 ♕xf7+ ♔h8 28 ♕f6+ ♔h7 29 ♗xg8+ ♕xg8 30 ♕e7+ ♔h8 31 ♘f6 and White wins: Black has no check on c4.

**Bronstein**: With a rook still in the corner on a8 and a knight still on b8 *de facto* White has a piece more, not a rook less and I cannot see any other move but to bring the knight into play as quickly as possible. However, there are some exceptions. Richard Réti once said: 'I am not interested in correct play and judgement, I am always looking for exceptions.' Probably this position can be called an exception. Black has a rook more so he may violate some common-sense rules and probably the move 20...♘6d7 is not so passive as it looks. Black's intentions are

clear: the knight on b8 is preparing to make a long journey via c6, d4 to f5!

This is why, with some imagination, Black should have tried 20...♘6d7 21 ♖c1 ♘c6 (22 ♖xc5 ♘d4+ 23 ♔d1 ♘xc5 24 ♘f6+ ♔h8 25 ♕h4 h5 26 ♘xh5 ♗xf3 and Black wins) 22 ♘xc5 ♘dxe5 hoping to play eventually ...♕h3 and ...♖ae8. In this variation Black sacrifices his bishop but activates both knights, queen and both rooks, eliminating one of White's strong pawns in the centre. In my opinion this is the most logical way to conduct this position. What the final result would have been is of less importance right now. Ljubojević started a sharp game and should have continued along this way with 21...♘c6 and not played a defensive move here. However, White can also use his imagination and play differently. Instead of losing time with 21 ♖c1 after 20...♘6d7 he can play 21 ♗f6 immediately and if now 21...♘c6 then White increases the pressure on the position of the black king by 22 e6.

This move has two goals: first, to attack the pawn on f7 and second, to open the diagonal for the bishop on f6 to defend the d4 square. If Ljubojević had chosen this line of defence then the game would have taken another turn, for example: 22...♘d4+ (if 22...♘xf6 then 23 ♘xf6+ ♔g7 24 ♘h5+ gxh5 25 ♕g5+ ♔h8 26 ♕f6+ ♔g8 27 exf7+, and if 22...fxe6 then 23 ♗xe6+ ♖f7 24 ♗xf7+ ♔xf7 25 ♘g5+ ♔e8 26 ♕e4+) 23 ♗xd4 ♗xd4 24 ♖c1 ♕e8 (if 24...♘c5 then 25 ♖xc5 ♗xc5 26 ♘f6+) 25 e7 and White can get his rook back with a dangerous attack. All White's pieces are ideally placed to launch a second wave of attack. For instance White's surviving rook is now looking forward to coming to c7.

All this looks perfect but in chess, as it is played today, the attack and defence are well balanced. The promising variation 20..♘6d7 21 ♗f6 has a drawish line: 21..♘xf6 22 ♘xf6+ ♔g7 23 ♕h4 h6 24 ♘h5+ ♔h7 25 ♕f6 ♖g8 26 ♕xf7+ ♔h8 27 ♕f6+ ♔h7 28 ♕e7+ ♔h8 29 ♗xg8 ♕xg8 30 ♘f6 ♕c4+ with perpetual check.

The reader could ask me of course if this is the final truth.

Oh, I don't know; the human mind has its limits. But you may well try 29 ♖c1! instead of 29 ♗xg8 and then ... who knows ...

**21 ♖c1!**

**Keres**: This quiet move now decides as Black has no defence against the following sacrifice. A really curious position!

**21 ... ♛c6**

The white pieces are swarming over the king's refuge and it only requires one further determined effort to break triumphantly into the fortress, especially since a yawning breach has already been made in the wall.

**22 ♖xc5!!** (Reuben Fine)

The amazing denouement now unfolds. By sacrificing the exchange on c5, White removes a key defender of f6.

**Bronstein**: What is better – to castle or to leave the king in the centre? In his book *My Match with Capablanca* (1921) Dr Emanuel Lasker wrote that he was a little sad that the Italians introduced castling in chess as the king could now flee into hiding very quickly and it would be more difficult to attack him.

From experience chess players know quite well that if there are open files in the centre it is better for the king to castle but if pawns block the centre there is no hurry to do so.

In this game White did the latter. The king abandoned the right to castle to give his rook free play on the first rank. If White had castled queenside the king would have blocked c1 and his rook would not have had access to this important square.

By the way, the strongest and most important chess piece became restricted in his movements. Many years ago the queen suddenly increased her steps to an unlimited number of squares. Before she had equal rights with the king.

Has, with the 21st century, the time not come to allow the king an extra step in all directions? I think it would be fair. It could bring a breath of fresh air to our noble game. After all, the king already moves more than one square when castling.

**Keres**: Bronstein still has something left to sacrifice! Now the black king comes under a devastating mating attack.

**22 ... ♘xc5**
**23 ♘f6+ ♔h8**

No better is 23...♔g7 24 ♛h4.

**Keres**: On 23...♔g7 the answer 24 ♛h4! is even stronger than in the game.

**24 ♛h4**

Now Black can only avoid mate by wholesale abandonment of his pieces. He still has a few spite checks.

**Keres**: White has not many pieces left but the few that remain create a mating net around the black king. There is no defence.

**24 ... ♛b5+**

A desperate sortie by the main forces, timed to coincide with White's time-trouble. White had less than one minute per move left on his clock whereas Black had used only 30 minutes for his 24 moves.

There follows a spurt forward by the white king, going personally into the attack. Note that Black is now not only a rook up but also the exchange.

**Bronstein:** When Ljubojević made his 20th move ...♘8d7 he calculated this long variation and was of the opinion that he had found a draw by repetition of moves. After the game was over he told me: 'You were lucky to find 25 ♔e3,' but I answered without hesitation: 'No, it was you who were lucky that in this position only this move wins. The white attack is so strong that normally there should be more than one possibility to win. You played too risky for a serious tournament game.'

I never talk like this during friendly analysis after a game but Ljubojević should have known that attacking with sacrifices, of which nobody can calculate exactly all the consequences, is my hobby-horse and this is how I made my name.

**25 &e3!!**

If 25 &f2? (25 &e1? **♛b4+** forces the exchange of queens) 25...♘d3+ 26 &g1 (26 &g2 ♘e1+) 26...♛c5+ 27 &h1 h5 28 ♘xh5 ♛f2! 29 ♘g3+ &g8 30 &f6 and Black has perpetual check with 30... ♛xf3+.

**25 ... h5**

After 25...♛d3+ 26 &f2 there are no more checks. Black is without resource but played on as White was in severe time-trouble.

**Keres**: There are no more checks after 25...♛d3+ 26 &f2, etc.

**26 ♘xh5 ♛xb3+**

Desperation. If instead 26...♛d3+ 27 &f2 gxh5 28 &f6+ and mate in a few moves. And if 26...♘d5+ then 27 &xd5.

**Bronstein**: Ljubojević told me that he had calculated the move 28 ♛xh5+ and did not see the check with the bishop on f6.

**Keres**: Desperation but there is no defence. On 26...♛d3+ 27 &f2 gxh5 28 &f6+ mates and 26...♘d5+ 27 &xd5 ♛d3+ 28 &f2 ♛c2+ 29 &g3 means only a short period of relief. A little more play for Black was offered by 26...♛d3+ 27 &f2 ♘e4+ 28 fxe4 ♛d4+ but this also leads to a loss after 29 &g2 ♛xb2+ 30 ♘g3+ and 31 &f6.

**27 axb3 ♘d5+**
**28 &d4!**

White continues aggressively. Black was hoping for 28 &f2 gxh5 29 ♛xh5+ &g8 30

&f6 ♘xf6 31 exf6 ♘e6 and now Black escapes.

**Bronstein**: Normally, when the king comes to the middle of the board, the battle is over. In this case it is the opposite: the king attacks both Black's knights in the very centre of the battlefield. With this action he supports the attack of the white queen.

**Keres**: Black was hoping for 28 &f2 gxh5 29 ♛xh5+ &g8 30 &f6 ♘xf6 31 exf6 ♘e6, etc.

**28 ... ♘e6+**
**29 &xd5 ♘xg5**

**Keres**: Now 29...gxh5 30 &f6+ &g8 31 &e4 leads to mate.

**30 ♘f6+ &g7**
**31 ♛xg5**

With queen and knight for the two rooks and Black still being in a mating net, the rest is simple.

**Keres**: The game is finished. Ljubojević played on in the hope of taking advantage of his opponent's severe time-trouble but it is already too simple.

**31 ... ♖fc8**

Here the curtain could have been lowered. A worthy conclusion to the game would have been 33 ♘g4 &h8 34 ♛h6+ &g8 35 ♘f6 mate.

**32 e6 fxe6+**
**33 &xe6**

A most enterprising king!

**33 ... ♖f8**
**34 d7 a5**
**35 ♘g4 ♖a6+**

The first move in the game for this rook.

**36 &e5 ♖f5+**
**37 ♛xf5 gxf5**
**38 d8♛ fxg4**
**39 ♛d7+ &h6**
**40 ♛xb7 ♖g6**
**41 f4**

**Black resigns**

**Bronstein**: After the game the American chess *maecenas* Isidor Turover gave me his own brilliancy prize in the form of two magnum bottles of the finest French champagne. It took us only two hours to finish them! While we were 'celebrating' he repeated several times, in Russian, that he did not send someone but 'I went into a shop on my old legs to buy them!'

**Keres**: A wonderful game!

## (40) Palatnik,S – Bronstein,D

USSR Championship 1st League,
Tbilisi, 1973

*[A13] English Opening*

This was the first year that the Soviet Championship was divided into two groups: a Super League and a First League. As I had participated in the Interzonal Tournament in Petropolis I should have played in the Super League. The Soviet Chess Federation however had, once again, something else in mind for me. They decided to penalise me because six months earlier I had refused to play in the Semi-Finals.

What could I do? Refuse again? That was not really an option. I accepted their decision and went to Tbilisi where I had spent so much time earlier in my life and where I had many friends. So in fact it was not a penalty but a favour!

Why had I refused earlier to play in the Semi-Finals? It was just not possible physically as the Interzonal Tournament in Leningrad was held at the same time and I preferred to go there as a reporter for *Izvestia*. I felt that I had an obligation to my readers.

As it turned out my name was on the list as a reserve player but I only found out years later. No one had ever bothered to tell me that at the time!

This Interzonal Tournament was remarkable for two reasons: (1) It was the beginning of the rivalry between Korchnoi and Karpov and (2) I got the idea for my electronic chess clock and published an article in *Izvestia* about it when I saw how Korchnoi had lost a game in a terrible time-scramble.

| 1 | c4 | e6 |
|---|-----|-----|
| 2 | ♘f3 | d5 |
| 3 | g3 | d4 |

Attempting to delay the development of White's 'lazy knight' on b1. Also Black has

prevented White from playing d4 himself and controlling the squares c5 and e5.

| 4 | d3 | ♘c6 |
|---|-----|-----|

It is not logical to play 4...c5 as this would weaken the diagonal h1-a8 making the task of the bishop on g2 much easier. Also the move b2-b4 will be stronger with the black pawn on c5.

| 5 | ♗g2 | ♘f6 |
|---|-----|-----|
| 6 | 0-0 | |

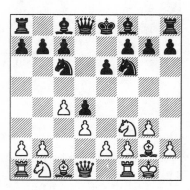

| 6 | ... | ♗e7 |
|---|-----|-----|

Another possibility was 6...e5. It would then have been natural to continue with 7 b4 ♗xb4 8 ♘xe5 ♘xe5 9 ♕a4+. Is that good for White of for Black? After 9...♗d7 10 ♕xb4 b6 11 ♗xa8 c5 12 ♕a3 ♕xa8 the position is very sharp. Despite having won the exchange, White should be very careful because Black's bishops are very strong. Also there is the possibility for Black to open the h-file with ...h7-h5-h4. However, after 13 f3 it is difficult to see how Black can make any progress. The white pawns are passive but in good defensive positions.

| 7 | e3 | |
|---|-----|-----|

Better is 7 e4 because after 7...dxe3 8 fxe3 e5 9 d4 the white pawn centre is very active. That is why 6...e5 would have been more precise. If then 7 e4 Black can play 7...dxe3 8 fxe3 e4 destroying White's pawn chain.

Does this mean that the opening has been in White's favour? Yes and no! The privilege of making the first move gives White a slight edge. If you want to fight you need to take some risk. For instance, after 7 e4 Black could try 7...dxe3 8 fxe3 e5

9 d4 ♝g4 10 h3 ♝xf3 11 ♝xf3 exd4 12
♝xc6+ bxc6 13 exd4 ♛d7 to break White's
pawn centre and the white king is not well
protected.

| 7 | ... | 0-0 |
| 8 | exd4 | ♞xd4 |
| 9 | ♞xd4 | ♛xd4 |

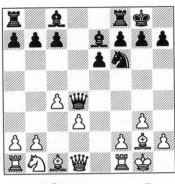

| 10 | ♞c3 | e5 |
| 11 | ♝e3 | ♛d8 |
| 12 | h3 | c6 |
| 13 | d4 | exd4 |
| 14 | ♛xd4 | ♝e6 |

The game was played in the last round
of the tournament and I was convinced
that White would exchange queens to en-
ter into a slightly better endgame. That
was why I proposed to call the game a
draw at this stage but my opponent said,
apologetically, that he would have a slight
chance to qualify to play in the first divi-
sion of next year's Soviet Championship. I
acknowledged that I understood his motivation to play on.

| 15 | b3 | ♛a5 |
| 16 | ♞a4 | ♜fd8 |

| 17 | ♛c3 | |

Now it was my opponent who offered a
peaceful conclusion to this game but with
the black queen looking forward to the
journey from a5 to h5, I was suddenly full
of chess energy and politely expressed my
wish to continue to play a game of chess.

| 17 | ... | ♝b4 |
| 18 | ♛b2 | |

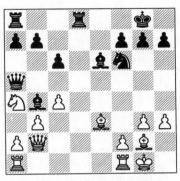

| 18 | ... | ♛h5 |

I remember that I spent about half an
hour before changing the position of my
queen. The problem was not how to react
to White's brave pawn move 19 g4 but
how to answer if White decided to play
safe with 19 h4. I could not find an active
plan and was ready to propose a draw once
again. But my opponent, still in search of
complications, hoping to get lucky, played
the g-pawn without hesitation.

| 19 | g4 | ♝xg4 |

The bishop took the pawn with the
same speed as it had appeared on g4. Certainly, it is clear that Black will get a
strong attack, but will it be enough to
win? And how should Black play to get the
best practical chances?

This was the main problem I had to
solve and I am proud to say that it seems I
found my way along a super-highway to
my destination.

| 20 | hxg4 | ♞xg4 |
| 21 | ♝f4 | |

The best defence against the threat of
...♛h2 mate. If 21 ♜fe1 then Black could
try the beautiful variation 21...♝xe1 22
♜xe1 ♛h2+ 23 ♔f1 ♞e3+ 24 ♜xe3 (if 24
fxe3 then 24...♜d6) 24...♜d1+ 25 ♔e2 ♛xg2

26 ♔xd1 ♖d8+ 27 ♔e2 ♕g4+ 28 ♔f1 ♖d1+ 29 ♖e1 ♕h3+ 30 ♔e2 ♕d3 mate.

After the text it seems that the Black attack has ground to a halt. If now 21...♖d2 then 22 ♕c1 and if 21...♗d2 then 22 ♗g3.

**21    ...        ♗d6**

Simple and strong. The white bishop on f4 is White's only active piece. In such cases it is recommended that one should try to reduce the power of such a piece. By exchanging bishops on d6 White loses control over the diagonal h2-b8 but if 22 ♕d2 or 22 ♕d4 then 22...♕h2+ 23 ♗xh2 ♗xh2+ 24 ♔h1 ♖xd2 (or 24... ♖xd4) 25 f3 ♗e3 and the endgame is in Black's favour thanks to the advantage of three connected pawns on the kingside against one lone isolated white pawn. Also the black rooks are much stronger in this type of open position than White's knight and bishop. Furthermore, if White plays 22 ♕c1 then Black's g-pawn can join into the attack. The main line is 22...g5 23 ♗xd6 ♖xd6 24 ♖e1 ♕h2+ 25 ♔f1 ♘xf2 26 ♕xg5+ ♖g6 27 ♕xg6+ fxg6 28 ♔xf2 and a black rook on a8 will announce the decisive check 28...♖f8+.

By the way, as far as I have observed from thousands of games, if both white and black rooks are still in quiet positions on a1 and a8 the rook that centralises first usually helps to decide the battle. We shall see this later.

**22    ♗xd6        ♖xd6**
**23    ♖fe1        ♖g6** (D)

While the black rook on a8 is still awaiting orders to march to a more active position, the rook on g6 is looking for subtle

combinations like 24 ♕e2 (if 24 ♖e4 then 24...♕h2+ 25 ♔f1 ♘f6 and if 24 ♖e7 then Black continues 24...♕h2+ 25 ♔f1 ♕h4 26 ♖ae1 h5) 24...♕h2+ 25 ♔f1 ♕h1+ 26 ♗xh1 ♘h2 mate or 24 ♖e2 ♖d8 25 ♘c3 (if 25 ♕d4 then 25...♕h2+ 26 ♔f1 ♕xg2+ ♔xg2 ♘f6+) 25...♕h2+ 26 ♔f1 ♕h1+ 27 ♗xh1 ♘h2+ 28 ♔e1 ♖g1 mate.

That is why White is in a hurry to bring the knight, gone astray on a4, closer to his king. If Black loses the momentum of the attack then, after ♘c3-e4-g3, the knight could become very useful in the defence of the white king.

**24    ♘c3        ♕h2+**
**25    ♔f1        ♘f6**
**26    ♗e4**

It is easy to understand my opponent's desire to play actively in this game. Of course, if White had realised that he could no longer win would he be able to make a draw by playing passively, in spite of his extra piece? I don't think so. After 26 f3 his bishop would have become merely another pawn and Black would have had the choice whether to play 26...♘h5 and ...♘f4 or just to push his h-pawn forward to ...h5-h4-h3.

Looking back after more than 20 years I can now see that Black has created a winning attack but during the game I was not so certain. After all, I was thinking all the time, I was tired, I was respecting my opponent and I was expecting unusual moves from all sides. Besides, I took risks and was looking for the most economical way to play, not only for myself but also for the chess army of my king.

I was very pleased and grateful to Dr Max Euwe when I read in one of his books: 'David Bronstein often takes a long time to think before making even obvious moves. The explanation of this is that he likes not only to win the game but wants to do it in the most beautiful way.'

Do I need to add that in many complicated chess games the most beautiful way to win a game is not necessarily like the Niagara Falls but could resemble also a little country stream as in this game.

| | 26 | ... | ♕h3+ |
|---|---|---|---|
| | 27 | ♔e2 | ♘xe4 |
| | 28 | ♘xe4 | ♖e6 |
| | 29 | ♔d2 | ♖d8+ |

The rook has been waiting in his corner for a very long time to give this simple but decisive check. Now Black's rooks are co-operating. If 30 ♔c2 or 30 ♔c1 then simply 30...♖xe4 and after 31 ♖xe4 the queen gives check on d3 or h1 and takes the rook on e4. Therefore...

**White resigns**

# (41) Kaplan,J – Bronstein,D

International Tournament,
Hastings, 1975/76
*[C11] French Defence*

This was my first game at Hastings for 22 years. It was in 1953/54 that I had lost an historic game to C.H.O'D. Alexander in 120 moves (page 275, T.F.). As I started to play my main aim was to try to forget how old I was.

I was glad to find myself paired in the first round against a very pleasant young

man (as he still is), who had won the World Junior Championship in 1967.

Mark Taimanov and I recalled how we had visited Liverpool in the Spring of 1952, invited by the International Union of Students, to take part in the first Students World Championship. The next championship was played as a team event and another such individual championship was never held again. So presumably Taimanov and I, as we tied for first place, are still Co-World Student Champions! That thought made me feel a lot younger!

In 1974 I proposed to Dr Max Euwe, President of FIDE, that a new World Championship should be instituted for grandmasters over 50, limited to players who had qualified for at least two Candidates' Tournaments or match sequences. He replied: 'What a nice idea! I might compete myself.' It made **him** feel younger.

Facing Julio Kaplan the idea came to me that there must be about 15 World Junior Champions, past or present. Why not bring them all together in one tournament? After that there could be a match between them and fifteen of the over fifties...

| | 1 | e4 | e6 |
|---|---|---|---|
| | 2 | d4 | d5 |
| | 3 | ♘c3 | ♘f6 |
| | 4 | ♗g5 | dxe4 |
| | 5 | ♘xe4 | ♗e7 |
| | 6 | ♗xf6 | gxf6 |

Some may find this variation too committal but I like such situations, with the black pawns on e6 and f6 controlling the centre, the open g-file for my rook and maybe, if the game opens up, as this game amply proves, a promising future for my light-squared bishop.

| | 7 | ♘f3 | ♘d7 |
|---|---|---|---|

Usually, 7...b6 is played here.

| | 8 | ♕d2 | c5 |
|---|---|---|---|

As Kaplan had shown no great eagerness to play 8 d5 I deliberately provoked him to do so! I was slightly nervous about playing this but it had to be done.

| | 9 | d5 | |
|---|---|---|---|

Instead 9 0-0-0 first would have been better and then not 9...cxd4 10 ♕xd4 0-0 with a restrained position for Black but

9...f5 followed by 10 ♘g3 cxd4 11 ♕xd4 ♗f6 and 12 ♕d2 0-0.

| 9 | ... | f5 |
|---|-----|-----|
| 10 | dxe6 | |

Played after long thought.

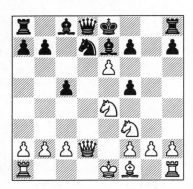

| 10 | ... | fxe4 |
|----|-----|------|
| 11 | exd7+ | |

White rejected 11 exf7+ because he liked his position after his next move.

| 13 | ... | ♕xd7 |
|----|-----|------|
| 12 | ♕c3 | |

Kaplan can hardly be blamed for feeling that he now had an excellent position. Black's queenside is underdeveloped.

Also, compare White's neat compact pawns to Black's.

| 12 | ... | 0-0 |
|----|-----|-----|
| 13 | ♘d2 | ♕f5 |
| 14 | 0-0-0 | ♕xf2 |
| 15 | ♘xe4? | |

Now White made, to my mind, the losing move. White ties himself up regaining an unimportant pawn. Better would have been 15 ♗c4.

| 15 | ... | ♕f4+! |
|----|-----|-------|
| 16 | ♘d2 | ♗g4 |
| 17 | ♖e1 | ♗g5 |
| 18 | ♗d3 | |

To block any attack by Black's rook along the d-file. If 18 h3 then 18...♖ae8.

Now it is possible for Black to activate his rooks by putting one of them in the centre. But which one, and where should it move? This is one of the most difficult decisions to make during a chess game.

There seems to be nothing wrong if Black plays his king's rook to e8 and then his queen's rook to d8 but what for instance

if a white rook comes to f1? Then f7 will be very weak.

| 18 | ... | ♖ae8 |
|----|-----|------|

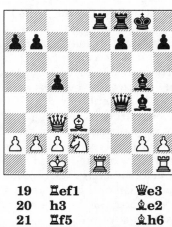

| 19 | ♖ef1 | ♕e3 |
|----|------|------|
| 20 | h3 | ♗e2 |
| 21 | ♖f5 | ♗h6 |

Such a lovely bishop! If there had been a few even safer squares further back along the diagonal, I would have retreated him still further!

| 22 | ♗xe2 | |
|----|------|---|

If 22 ♖e1 then 22...♕g3 23 ♖xe2 ♕e1+ but now came a little surprise for White.

| 22 | ... | ♕xc3 |
|----|-----|------|

I had half an hour left for 18 moves, Kaplan had a minute. I think he saw what was coming but wanted it demonstrated.

| 23 | bxc3 | ♖xe2 |
|----|------|------|
| 24 | ♖d5 | |

Protecting the knight and preventing 24...♖d8. This looks good but...

| 24 | ... | ♖xd2 |
|----|-----|------|
| 25 | ♖xd2 | ♖d8 |
| 26 | ♖hd1 | c4 |

**White resigns**

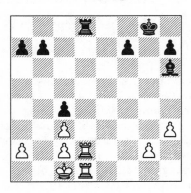

A beautiful finish. When White runs out of pawn moves he will have to move his king and lose a piece.

My old friend Baruch Wood, owner and publisher of *Chess* asked me immediately after the game to dictate my comments to him. Already the very next morning I received the printed page of my imaginative work and it was published in *Chess* in February 1976.

## (42) Bronstein,D – Petrosian,T

USSR Team Championship,
Ordzhonikidze, 1978

*[C15] French Defence*

When the German Nazi troops crossed the border and started the war against the Soviet Union on Sunday 22 June 1941, I only had one point in my favour; I had just finished my studies. I was 17 and, as other youngsters of my age, was to be drafted as a soldier. I therefore had to follow the instructions of the recruitment office to leave Kiev immediately. First I found myself in southern Ukraine, then I went to Ordzhonikidze, the capital of North Ossetia.

The House of the Red Army gave me a place to sleep and a temporary job which consisted in visiting wounded soldiers in various military hospitals where I played chess with them. I stayed there for a year and even played a tournament with local players, taking first place and receiving the title of champion of Ordzhonikidze!

In the Spring of 1942, at the age of 18, I was called by the officials to join the army. When I reported for duty they sent me to the doctors for a thorough medical examination. It was then that I learned that my eyesight was very bad (-5.0) and that I was not fit for military duty. I received permission to leave.

In August 1942, I hitchhiked my way to Tbilisi on military trucks. I stayed there for about a year making a living by doing exactly the same work in the hospitals of Georgia as I did in North Ossetia.

Then, in the Winter of 1942/3, the Red Army achieved a great victory over the Germans at Stalingrad in a famous battle. A couple of months later I was sent by army officials, together with some Georgian youngsters, to Stalingrad to help with the reconstruction of a large steel factory called Red October.

At the end of May 1945 I came to Moscow where I have lived ever since.

When I met Tigran Petrosian in Ordzhonikidze to play this game I remembered that I had met him for the first time in Tbilisi in November 1942. He was recommended to me as a young, promising chess talent by the famous chess player Varvara Stepanovna Zargarjan, long time women champion of Georgia and chief manager of the Tbilisi Chess Club.

In the thirties there used to be a championship of the Caucasus for all three Soviet republics of Armenia, Georgia and Azerbaidjan and, besides being a highly intelligent and attractive woman, she also won this women's champion title.

So when I played this game my mind was far away from the chessboard.

| | | |
|---|---|---|
| 1 | e4 | e6 |
| 2 | d4 | d5 |
| 3 | ♘c3 | ♗b4 |
| 4 | ♘ge2 | dxe4 |

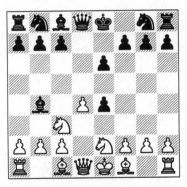

| | | |
|---|---|---|
| 5 | a3 | ♗e7 |
| 6 | ♘xe4 | ♘f6 |
| 7 | ♘2g3 | 0-0 |
| 8 | ♗e2 | ♘bd7 |
| 9 | 0-0 | b6 |

Too simple; better was 9...♘xe4 10 ♘xe4 ♘f6.

| | | |
|---|---|---|
| 10 | ♗f3 | ♘xe4 |
| 11 | ♗xe4 | ♖b8 |

| 12 | c4 | ♘f6 |
|----|----|-----|
| 13 | ♗f3 | |

Not 13 ♗c2 as White must keep the diagonal h1-a8.

| 13 | ... | ♗b7 |
|----|-----|-----|
| 14 | ♗xb7 | ♖xb7 |

| 15 | ♕f3 | c6 |
|----|-----|-----|
| 16 | ♘e2! | |

Protecting d4 and looking for better squares.

| 16 | ... | ♕c8 |
|----|-----|-----|
| 17 | b4 | ♖d8 |
| 18 | ♗f4 | |

Here the bishop is more active than on b2.

| 18 | ... | ♖bd7 |
|----|-----|-----|
| 19 | ♖fc1 | h6 |
| 20 | h3 | c5 |

Too early; it would have been better to play 20...♕b7 and ...b5 to fight for the square d5.

| 21 | dxc5 | ♖d3 |
|----|------|-----|
| 22 | ♗e3 | bxc5 |
| 23 | b5 | ♕c7 |
| 24 | a4! | |

Forcing Black to use the queen to block the a-pawn but she is out of play there.

| 24 | ... | ♕a5 |
|----|-----|-----|
| 25 | ♕c6 | ♘d7 |
| 26 | ♗f4 | e5 |

This weakens the d5-square.

| 27 | ♕e4 | ♖d6 |
|----|-----|-----|
| 28 | ♗e3 | ♗f8 |
| 29 | ♘c3 (D) | |
| 29 | ... | ♖d4 |
| 30 | ♗xd4 | cxd4 |
| 31 | ♘d5 | ♖e8 |
| 32 | ♕g4 | ♖e6 |

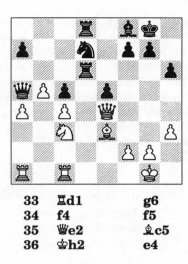

| 33 | ♖d1 | g6 |
|----|-----|-----|
| 34 | f4 | f5 |
| 35 | ♕e2 | ♗c5 |
| 36 | ♔h2 | e4 |

Black has achieved what he wanted. It is hard to believe that he will resign after only four more moves!

| 37 | g4 | ♕d8 |
|----|-----|-----|
| 38 | gxf5 | gxf5 |
| 39 | ♕h5 | ♕f8 |
| 40 | ♖a2 | d3 |
| 41 | ♖g2+ | |

**Black resigns**

# (43) Bronstein,D – Vaganian,R

Friendly simultaneous match
Erevan, 1978
*[C15] French Defence*

In 1978 I played a tournament in Armenia and afterwards stayed in Erevan for another fortnight, giving lectures and simultaneous exhibitions. One day I suggested to the young grandmaster Rafael Vaganian that we play a mini-match of eight games to be played simultaneously at the speed of 40 moves in two hours on every board. We agreed eventually to play four games. The match ended in a draw (+1 −1=2) and was even shown on the main news on national television the next day. After the match he told me that my idea was most interesting but very tiring. Who says that chess should be easy? Nevertheless, recently Vaganian told me that he still likes my idea. Later I played several such matches.

This is my winning game.

| | | |
|---|---|---|
| 1 | e4 | e6 |
| 2 | d4 | d5 |
| 3 | ♘c3 | ♗b4 |
| 4 | ♘ge2 | |

The French Defence is one of my favourite openings. I have played several hundred games with it as White and Black. In this variation the common line is 4 e5 c5 5 a3 ♗xc3+ 6 bxc3 etc., but sometimes it is better to deviate. I saw this quiet move with the knight for the first time in the game Alekhine-Nimzowitsch, played in Bled in 1931.

When I started to read chess columns as a boy I saw another game with the same move Lasker-Capablanca in Moscow 1935 played perfectly by the old master.

| | | |
|---|---|---|
| 4 | ... | dxe4 |
| 5 | a3 | ♗e7 |

Capablanca also played this move. Nimzowitsch however played 5...♗xc3+ 6 ♘xc3 f5 but lost very quickly after 7 f3 exf3 8 ♕xf3.

| | | |
|---|---|---|
| 6 | ♘xe4 | ♘f6 |
| 7 | ♕d3 | ♘c6 |

The knight blocks the c-pawn which can become a target.

| | | |
|---|---|---|
| 8 | ♗f4 | b6 |
| 9 | ♘xf6+ | ♗xf6 |
| 10 | ♕g3 | ♕e7 |
| 11 | 0-0-0 | |

King safety first! If White plays 11 ♗xc7 then 11...e5.

| | | |
|---|---|---|
| 11 | ... | e5! |
| 12 | dxe5 | ♗xe5 |
| 13 | ♘c3 | 0-0 |
| 14 | ♗c4 | |

This threatens 15 ♖he1. If White had played 14 ♘d5 then 14...♕d6 15 ♗xe5 ♘xe5 16 ♘xb6 ♕xb6 17 ♕xe5 ♕xf2 and if White now takes the c-pawn 18 ♕xc7? then Black wins after 18...♗g4!

| | | |
|---|---|---|
| 14 | ... | ♗xf4+ |
| 15 | ♕xf4 | ♕e5 |

| | | |
|---|---|---|
| 16 | ♗xf7+! | ♔h8 |
| 17 | ♕xe5 | ♘xe5 |
| 18 | ♗b3 | ♘g4 |
| 19 | ♖d2 | ♗b7 |

If 19...♘xf2 then 20 ♖e1 ♗b7 21 ♖e7 ♗xg2 22 ♖dd7.

| 20 | f3 | ♘f6 |
|----|------|------|
| 21 | ♘b5 | ♖fc8 |
| 22 | ♗e6 | |

**Black resigns**

## (44) Bronstein,D – Zlotnik,B

Moscow Championship, 1978
*[C07] French Defence*

My opponent in this game is an experienced chess teacher who has had many good students who have received the master title. He had his own system of education but in our game, he experimented a little too much in the opening.

Zlotnik had also written and published a monograph about the French Defence. Therefore this game was a not only a contest about moves but on a wider scale – the understanding of the French Defence itself with all its finesses.

| 1 | e4 | e6 |
|---|-----|-----|
| 2 | d4 | d5 |
| 3 | ♘d2 | a6 |

To prevent a check on b5.

| 4 | ♘gf3 | c5 |
|---|------|-----|
| 5 | dxc5 | ♗xc5 |
| 6 | ♗d3 | ♘c6 |
| 7 | 0-0 | ♘b4 |

This move is not as simple as it looks. Black wants to avoid variations with ♗xh7!+.

| 8 | ♗e2 | ♘e7 |
|---|------|------|

Also 8...dxe4 9 ♘xe4 ♕xd1 10 ♖xd1 ♘xc2 was possible.

| 9 | a3 | ♘bc6 |
|----|-----|------|
| 10 | b4 | ♗b6 |

| 11 | c4 | 0-0 |
|----|-----|------|
| 12 | ♗b2 | ♗c7 |
| 13 | ♕c2 | ♘g6 |

Looking to go to f4. White is better: two of his pawns are attacking in the centre and his bishops are good, especially the one on b2. Black has only one good bishop.

| 14 | ♖fd1 | |
|----|------|--|

Increasing the pressure on d5 and making space for the bishop on e2.

| 14 | ... | dxc4 |
|----|-----|------|
| 15 | ♘xc4 | ♕e7 |
| 16 | e5 | |

This closes the diagonal for the bishop on c7 and aims to put a knight on d6 while creating a transit square on e4.

| 16 | ... | ♖d8 |
|----|------|------|
| 17 | ♖xd8+ | ♗xd8 |
| 18 | ♕e4 | |

Preventing the liberating ...b5.

| 18 | ... | ♗d7 |
|----|------|------|
| 19 | ♖d1 | ♖b8 |

| 20 | h4 | |
|----|-----|--|

With the knight on g6 this is a strong move. The pawn wants to go to h6.

| 20 | ... | ♘f8 |
|----|-----|------|
| 21 | h5 | h6 |

This stops White from playing h6 but now this pawn will become a target for the knight.

| 22 | ♘h2 | ♕h4 |
|----|------|----------|
| 23 | ♘g4 | ♔h8 *(D)* |
| 24 | ♘d6 | ♕e7 |
| 25 | ♕f3 | ♗c7 |

If 25...♗e8 then 26 ♘f6 gxf6 27 exf6 ♕d7 28 ♕g3.

| 26 | ♘xf7+ | ♔g8 |
|----|-------|------|
| 27 | ♘f6+ | gxf6 |

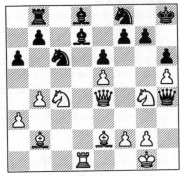

| 28 | ♘xh6+ | ♔h8 |
| 29 | exf6 | ♕h7 |
| 30 | ♕e3 | e5 |
| 31 | ♗d3 | ♗b6 |
| 32 | ♕c1 | ♗e6 |
| 33 | ♗xh7 | ♘xh7 |
| 34 | ♖d6 | ♗a2 |
| 35 | ♖xc6 | bxc6 |
| 36 | ♗xe5 | ♖e8 |
| 37 | ♕xc6 | |

**Black resigns**

## (45) Bronstein,D – Lukin,A

50th USSR Championship, Semi-Final,
Yaroslavl, 1982

*[D20] Queen's Gambit Accepted*

This was one of my last Semi-Finals in the USSR Championship after 40 years! The reception I received from the local chess fans was very kind. I tried to play my best, using a lot of energy, and I won 8 games but still failed, once again by the narrowest of margins, to qualify for the Final.

It was important for me to continue playing in order not to lose my salary as, according to the regulations, I had two more years to go to be able to claim my pension at the age of 60. In reality I only received my pension in 1988 from the Moscow Council as a reward for my contribution over the years to Moscow's chess culture.

| 1 | d4 | d5 |
| 2 | c4 | dxc4 |

The Queen's Gambit has many variations but if one is trying to play for a draw the best answer is to accept the pawn sacrifice. White's next move is the latest

fashion. In the last century 3 e3 was very popular and in the first half of this century it was 3 ♘f3. By pushing the king's pawn to the equator White makes the position very sharp.

| 3 | e4 | ♘f6 |

It is not yet clear whether this move is better than 3...c5 or 3...e5.

| 4 | e5 | ♘d5 |
| 5 | ♗xc4 | ♘b6 |
| 6 | ♗b3 | ♘c6 |
| 7 | ♗e3 | ♗f5 |

| 8 | e6 |

It is difficult to resist the temptation to delay the development of the black bishop on f8 by blocking the pawn on e7 but White's pawn is strong enough on e5 and there was no need to give it away. After such natural moves as 8 ♘c3 or 8 ♘ge2 White is better.

| 8 | ... | ♗xe6 |
| 9 | ♗xe6 | fxe6 |
| 10 | ♘c3 | ♕d7 |
| 11 | ♘f3 | 0-0-0 |
| 12 | 0-0 | h6? |

The idea of this move is to play ...g7-g5-g4 but Black loses time. Better was 12...g6 13 ♘g5 ♗g7 14 ♘f7 ♘xd4 15 ♘xh8 ♗xh8 with an unclear position. Black has enough compensation for the exchange with two pawns more and a strong knight in the centre.

|    | 13 | b4! | ♘d5 |

If 13...♘xb4 then 14 ♘e5 ♕e8 15 ♕b3 with a strong attack.

|    | 14 | ♘e4 | e5 |

The attempt to free the bishop on f8 comes too late.

|    | 15 | b5 | ♘xd4 |
|    | 16 | ♘xe5 |  |

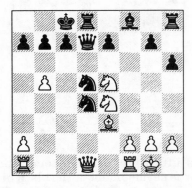

All knights in the centre. However the white ones are more effective.

|    | 16 | ... | ♘xe3 |
|    | 17 | fxe3 | ♕d5 |
|    | 18 | ♕xd4 |  |

**Black resigns**

## (46) Bronstein,D – Browne,W

International Open Tournament,
Reykjavik, 1990

*[B92] Sicilian Defence*

This was my second tournament in Iceland and I hope to play many more since I will never forget the cordial hospitality I experienced during my stay in 1974.

To postpone a round in a tournament for one day in order to celebrate my 50th birthday can only happen in a real chess community!

Many years ago Fridrik Olafsson told me that in Iceland chess forms part of the

National Heritage but probably he was being somewhat modest. I think in Iceland it is part of everyday culture!

There are two methods to play a game of chess from the initial position. You may either follow book recommendations and wait for some new move prepared at home by your opponent, or you yourself may discover a novelty.

I prefer the second way, making new moves myself, not necessarily found by deep calculation but mostly by intuition.

I try to deviate from routine positions, even if they are not very promising. I think that it is necessary to use one's imagination to find new ways and to bring life into a chess struggle.

However, this game is just the opposite. I was playing a well-known line because during my home preparation I convinced myself that it was perfectly playable.

|    | 1 | e4 | c5 |
|    | 2 | ♘f3 | d6 |
|    | 3 | d4 | cxd4 |
|    | 4 | ♘xd4 | ♘f6 |
|    | 5 | ♘c3 | a6 |
|    | 6 | ♗g5 | e6 |
|    | 7 | f4 | ♘bd7 |
|    | 8 | ♕f3 | ♕c7 |
|    | 9 | 0-0-0 | ♗e7 |
|    | 10 | g4 | b5 |

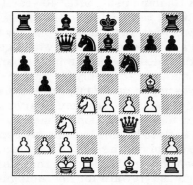

A favourite variation of Walter Browne who has achieved many successes with it.

|    | 11 | ♗xf6 | ♘xf6 |
|    | 12 | g5 | ♘d7 |
|    | 13 | f5 | ♗xg5+ |
|    | 14 | ♔b1 | ♘e5 |
|    | 15 | ♕h5 | ♕d8 *(D)* |

A new move, introduced successfully by Browne in one of his latest games. I was not surprised because several days earlier Browne had given me a copy of his magazine in which this latest game was printed. I played through it and found that White could have played better. Up to now he had always played 15...♕e7.

**16 ♖g1 h6**

This is Browne's prepared improvement on the old line, but it seems that White can find a flaw in this variation.

**17 fxe6 g6**

**18 exf7+ ♚xf7**
**19 ♕e2 ♚g7**

In subsequent games Browne played 19...♖f8.

**20 h4 ♗xh4**
**21 ♘f5+ ♚h7**

A surprising move. During my preparations for this game I had only considered 21...♗xf5 when after 22 exf5 White has a strong attack. Now I had to find a refutation.

**22 ♖xd6 ♕f8** (D)
**23 ♕h2!!**

This is the refutation I was looking for. If 23...♘f3 then White continues 24 ♖dxg6 ♘xh2 (if 24...♖a7 then 25 ♕b8 ♘xg1 26 ♖xh6+ ♚g8 27 ♖g6+ ♚h7 28 ♖xg1 ♖f7 29 ♕h2) 25 ♖g7+ and if 23...♗f6 then 24 ♖xf6 ♕xf6 25 ♘d5 ♕f8 26 ♕xe5.

**23 ... ♗xf5**
**24 ♕xe5**

**24 ... ♕e7**
**25 ♕xe7+ ♗xe7**
**26 ♖c6!**

An accurate move, provoking Black's reply and thereby taking away the c8 square from the bishop.

**26 ... ♖hc8**
**27 ♖b6 ♖xc3**

This is necessary because after 27...♗d7 White wins a piece with 28 ♖b7.

**28 exf5 ♖e3**
**29 ♗d3 ♗c5**
**30 ♖bxg6 ♖ae8**
**31 a4 bxa4**
**32 f6 ♖xd3**
**33 ♖g7+ ♚h8**
**34 ♖h1**
**Black resigns**

Life can also be very human. I was very pleased and grateful when Walter Browne thanked me for the game and added that, in his opinion, all my moves were the best.

## (47) Bronstein,D – Rebel 90

AEGON Human v Computer
Tournament, The Hague, 1990
*[D42] Caro-Kann Defence*

The AEGON Insurance Company staged their 10th Human vs. Computer tournament this year (1995). To me it is obvious that such events will become a fact of life in the chess world in the 21st century. They will be spectacular and form major attractions to a wide audience, possibly pushing matches and tournaments between humans somewhat into the background.

Mr C. de Gorter always organises these tournaments perfectly and each time I wonder if it is still possible to improve next year. The answer is yes, he can and he does!

It is held in the best playing hall one can imagine, perfect food and drinks, nice accommodation, generous compensation and prize money. The tournament gets good publicity in the Dutch press – several chess playing journalists are amongst the participants – games and scores can be seen on television's teletext, and a daily bulletin with all the games is available. What more can one wish for?

Yes, I have one wish: to meet old friends and make new ones!

What makes the AEGON tournament so interesting? Can human intellect be victorious over pure computing power? The answer is yes – **for the time being** – but equally pressing is the question: for how much longer? That machine will conquer man in chess is a fact. In many other fields the computer can perform many times better than man and there is absolutely no reason to believe that chess will be any different.

I myself became interested in artificial intelligence when I received my first lessons in computer chess many years ago

from the famous mathematician Professor A. Kronrod. He was the first to say that chess computers are the drosophilae of artificial intellect.

He and my friend Professor A. Brudno gave me a lot of valuable knowledge about the mathematical problems in connection with writing chess programs.

As a grandmaster with a great interest in the subject I was asked to be an advisor to the Moscow Institute of Mathematics when they played their famous match against Stanford University about 30 years ago.

It was then that I played my first two games against computers (see page 278). Now of course I have more experience and understand much better the strong and weak points of chess playing programs and of course ... my own weaknesses against computers.

Of course, humans don't find chess moves in the same way computers do. They are stuffed with millions of opening moves, which is of course impossible to do with humans.

Then they calculate their chips into oblivion in order to find a move. Grandmasters calculate much less but use their experience, understanding, knowledge and imagination.

It is exactly this different approach that makes these tournaments so interesting and exciting.

In 1992 I was invited to visit the Hewlett Packard Laboratories in Palo Alto, California to give a couple of lectures and play some games against Deep Thought. It seems that they were pleased with my work as the last day of my stay I was awarded the, for this occasion specially created, title of 'Honorary Doctor of Chess Science of HP Laboratories' with all rights and privileges!

Their motivation to award me this title was: 'We know that you did not study at university but we, people of science, recognise and respect your knowledge.'

| 1 | d4 | c6 |
| 2 | e4 | d5 |
| 3 | exd5 | cxd5 |

| 4 | c4 | ♘f6 |
|---|----|-----|
| 5 | ♘c3 | ♘c6 |
| 6 | ♘f3 | ♗g4 |
| 7 | ♗e3 | e6 |
| 8 | ♕b3 | ♗xf3 |

Against a human being I would now probably have played 9 ♕xb7 ♘b4 10 c5 but not against a computer. It could have continued with 10...♖b8, for instance 11 ♗b5+ ♘d7 12 ♗xd7+ ♔e7.

This was my first game in an AEGON Tournament. Now, after having played many games against computers, I know that this line is not as dangerous for White as I thought at the time: 13 ♕xa7 ♖a8 14 ♕b6 etc.

However, when playing against an electronic monster you don't want to compete in calculating power!

| 9 | gxf3 | ♗b4 |
|---|------|-----|
| 10 | 0-0-0 | 0-0 |

If I had been playing Black in this position, I would have preferred 10...♗xc3 11 ♕xc3 dxc4 12 ♗xc4 ♘d5 assuming that one cannot lose with a knight on d5, well protected by the pawn on e6.

| 11 | ♔b1 | ♕a5 |
|----|-----|-----|
| 12 | cxd5 | ♘xd5 |
| 13 | ♘xd5 | ♕xd5 |

What to do now? My next move is probably the best of the game. After 14 ♗c4 I was afraid of 14...♕xf3 15 d5 ♘e5.

| 14 | ♕c2! | |
|----|------|--|

In order to meet 14...♖ac8 by 15 ♕e4. 14...♕xf3 poses no problems for White because the disappearance of the f-pawn makes more space available for his pieces.

| 14 | ... | ♕xf3 |
|----|-----|------|
| 15 | ♗d3 | ♕h5 |

Better would have been 15...h6.

| 16 | f4 | ♖ac8 |
|----|----|------|
| 17 | ♕g2 | ♖fd8 |
| 18 | ♗e4 | a6 |

This is not necessary. Better is 18...♘e7 because 19 ♗xb7 does not fit in White's plan.

| 19 | ♖hg1 | g6 (D) |
|----|------|--------|

A human would have played 19...♗f8 here, but not a computer. Its program tells it that the bishop is 'developed' on b4 and bad on f8.

| 20 | f5 | |
|----|----|--|

A cunning move. After 20...exf5 21 ♗f3 ♕h4 22 ♗g5 the black queen is trapped.

| 20 | ... | ♗d6 |
|----|-----|-----|
| 21 | h3 | ♗e7 |

Now planning ...♘b4 and ...♘d5 and Black's problems are solved.

| 22 | fxe6 | fxe6 |
|----|------|------|
| 23 | d5 | ♘b4 |

This move surprised me. I was expecting 23...exd5 24 ♗xd5+ ♔g7. I have the pair of bishops and a good position.

| 24 | d6! | ♖xd6 |
|----|-----|------|
| 25 | ♖xd6! | ♗xd6 |
| 26 | ♗g5 | |

Threatening to win the queen with ♗f3.

| 26 | ... | ♖f8 |
|----|-----|-----|

White could have won a pawn with 27 ♗xb7 but why should he waste time?

| 27 | h4 | |
|----|----|--|

To free the queen and rook.

| 27 | ... | ♗c5 |
|----|-----|-----|
| 28 | ♖c1 | b6 |

Now after 29 a3 ♘d5 30 ♗xd5 exd5 31 ♕xd5+ ♔g7 32 ♕e5+ ♔g8 33 ♕e6+ ♔g7 34 b4 h6 35 ♗d2 (35...♗d4 36 ♕d7+ or 35...♗f2 36 ♗c3+) White might have won at once but my attention was completely concentrated on the weak black pawn on e6.

| 29 | ♕h3 | ♖f7 |
|----|-----|-----|
| 30 | ♕xe6 | ♕e2 (D) |

Here I thought: 'Why did I not play a3 earlier?'

| 31 | ♗f5 | |
|----|-----|--|

I didn't see a forced continuation but thought: 'There must be something.' There was of course something but I missed it. Immediately after I had made my move I saw it: I should have played 31 ♗f6.

| 31 | ... | ♛f2 |

It was now clear to me that there is no immediate win.

| 32 | ♛e8+ | ♜f8 |
| 33 | ♛e6+ | ♜f7 |

I did not want a draw, therefore...

| 34 | ♝e4 | ♛d4 |

If Black plays 34...♝d4 then 35 ♜c8+ ♚g7 36 ♝c1 and 37 h5 or 37 ♛e8.

But why not 34...♛e2 again? Probably because of the move which I had missed earlier: 35 ♝f6 as 35...♞d3 is losing as 36 ♛c8+ ♝f8 37 ♛xf8+ ♚xf8 38 ♜c8 is mate or 37...♜xf8 38 ♝d5+ ♜f7 39 ♜c8+ ♛e8 40 ♜xe8 is mate.

If White had played 35 ♝f5 again Rebel 90 could have played 35...♛b5 because after, say 36 ♛c8+ ♚g7 37 h5!? ♜xf5 38 h6+ ♚f7 39 ♛c7+ ♚e6 40 ♜e1+ ♚d5 41 ♛d8+ ♝d6 42 ♛a8+ ♞c6 43 ♛g8+ ♚d4 White has nothing. The black king is quite safe in the centre protected by his own army.

After the text White has an easy win thanks to the possibility of 35 ♜f1 ♛d7 (g7) 36 ♛xf7+! ♛xf7 37 ♜xf7 ♚xf7 38 a3 and the black knight is lost.

| 35 | ♜f1 | ♛xe4+ |
| 36 | ♛xe4 | ♜xf1+ |
| 37 | ♝c1 | ♜f5 |
| 38 | ♛c4+ | ♚g7 |
| 39 | a3 | ♞d5 |
| 40 | ♛xa6 | ♞f4 |
| 41 | b4 | ♝f2 |
| 42 | ♛b7+ | ♜f7 |
| 43 | ♝b2+ | ♚f8 |
| 44 | ♛b8+ | ♚e7 |
| 45 | ♝e5 | ♞h5 |
| 46 | ♝c7 | |

**Black resigns**

Who would have thought that one day I would give comments to one of my own games against a computer!

## (48) Bronstein,D – Fidelity Elite 10

AEGON Human v Computer
Tournament, The Hague, 1991
*[C35] King's Gambit Accepted*

(I was very honoured when I was asked to operate the computer for this game with David Bronstein.

I knew this particular computer very well because I had operated it for Anatoly Karpov's team during the World Championship's match between Karpov and Kasparov in 1990 in New York and Lyon.

Because of my earlier experience with this monster, I was well aware of its strength (and weaknesses) and was therefore very curious to see how David would cope. After all, he knows perfectly well how to play with computers.

However, David violated all the rules of how to play against computers, especially against strong ones and won in a most spectacular fashion. It is probably the most remarkable game ever played against a computer by a human being.

That David takes computers very seriously is clear from his book *Chess in the Eighties* (1978), chapter 'On the way to the electronic grandmaster.' We are not there yet but there are few people who do not believe that it will happen one day. David Bronstein is the only grandmaster who considers playing against computers as an experiment and does not care if he loses. On the contrary, if a lost game gives an answer to the right or wrong of his experimental moves, then he is satisfied.

Before this tournament he had decided to play three rounds as 'Bronstein' and the other three as 'a normal player'.

Fortunately, this round he played as 'Bronstein'. He asked me if I had any preference regarding the type of opening he should play. I suggested the King's

Gambit: after all he was playing this round as 'Bronstein'!

Suddenly David Bronstein realised that, in making such a 'deal' he was maybe violating the rules of the tournament. After all he is 'Mr Fairplay' himself but I reassured him.

So the King's Gambit it was! T.F.)

| 1 | e4 | e5 |
|---|----|----|
| 2 | f4 |    |

| 2 | ... | exf4 |
|---|-----|------|
| 3 | ♘f3 | ♗e7 |
| 4 | ♗c4 | ♘f6 |
| 5 | ♘c3 | ♘xe4 |
| 6 | ♘e5 | ♘g5 |

As recommended by modern opening books.

| 7 | d4 | d6 |
|---|-----|------|
| 8 | ♘d3 | f3 |
| 9 | ♗e3 | ♗g4 |

Here David Bronstein asked me: 'What kind of a game would you like to see?' I still do not regret my reply: 'Make it as spectacular as you can.'

| 10 | ♔d2 | fxg2 |
|----|-----|------|

| 11 | ♕xg4 | gxh1♕ |
|----|------|-------|
| 12 | ♖xh1 | c6 |

Meanwhile David Bronstein started to think out loud and I took notes: 'It can't be bad to play the rook to e1 now.'

| 13 | ♖e1 | h6 |
|----|-----|------|
| 14 | d5 | ♕d7 |

'If I had seen 14...♕d7 I would of course not have played 14 d5.'

| 15 | ♕g3 | ♕f5 |
|----|-----|------|
| 16 | ♘f4 |      |

'Some extra support for d5 and it does not spoil anything.'

| 16 | ... | cxd5 |
|----|-----|------|
| 17 | ♗xd5 |     |

'I originally intended to take back with the knight on f4 but now I believe that taking back with the bishop is somewhat better.

If I had taken with the other knight then he plays 17...♘e4! of course and he is better.'

| 17 | ... | ♘c6 |
|----|-----|------|
| 18 | ♕g2 | ♖c8 |
| 19 | ♖f1 | ♘b4 |

'I completely missed that move. 20 ♗b3 is now forced but I believe there are no serious problems yet.'

| 20 | ♗b3 | ♕d7 |
|----|-----|------|

'It is time to chase away the knight.'

| 21 | a3 | d5 |
|----|-----|------|

'Now what?!? I missed that move also.'

| 22 | ♗d4 | ♘c6 |
|----|-----|------|

'I want to keep this bishop. Therefore...'

| 23 | ♗g1 | d4 |
|----|-----|------|
| 24 | ♘cd5 | d3 |

'Can I take that pawn on d3? Yes, I believe I can, so...'

| 25 | ♘xd3 | ♘a5 |
|----|------|------|

'It seems to me that the computer is improving its position somewhat. I have to watch out that c2 does not become weak.'

| 26 | ♗a2 | b6 |
|----|-----|------|

'Why does it play this move? There were better moves. Oh yes, I see, it does not want to lose the pawn on a7. Still, I believe it should have played 26...♘c4+.'

| 27 | h4 |    |
|----|-----|------|

'If it wants to lose time saving an unimportant pawn I think the time has come to start an attack.'

| 27 | ... | ♘e6 |
|----|-----|-----|
| 28 | ♘e5 | ♛a4 |

'Why did I miss that move too? Maybe I am now in some danger of losing this game.'

| 29 | ♔c1 | ♛xh4 |
|----|-----|------|

'Well, let's go for broke! It's now or never!'

| 30 | ♘xf7 | 0-0 |
|----|------|-----|
| 31 | ♛g6 |     |

'Maybe I can scare it with this kind of move. But it is a computer, so probably not. Hopefully it is not a genius and will not play 31...♛g5+ now.'

| 31 | ... | ♗g5+ |
|----|-----|------|
| 32 | ♔b1 | ♛h3 |
| 33 | ♖f6 |     |

'I don't expect it to take the rook now but it looks nice.'

| 33 | ... | ♖ce8 |
|----|-----|------|

'Now the knight must go because I want to play my bishop to c4.'

| 34 | b4 | ♛h1 |
|----|----|-----|

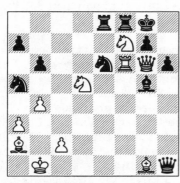

| 35 | ♖f1 | ♘c6 |
|----|-----|-----|
| 36 | ♗c4 | ♛h3 |

| 37 | ♗d3 | ♛xf1+ |
|----|-----|-------|
| 38 | ♗xf1 | ♖xf7 |
| 39 | ♗d3 | ♘f8 |
| 40 | ♛xc6 | ♖e1+ |
| 41 | ♔a2 | ♖xg1 |
| 42 | ♘c3 |     |

'I need my knight in the attack.'

| 42 | ... | ♔h8 |
|----|-----|-----|

(Because of mutual time-trouble the game was blitzed until after the time control and then I resigned this exciting and complicated game on behalf of the computer. T.F.)

| 43 | ♛e8 | ♖f2 |
|----|-----|-----|
| 44 | ♘e4 | ♖f3 |
| 45 | ♘d6 | ♖f6 |
| 46 | ♘f7+ | ♔g8 |
| 47 | ♗c4 | b5 |
| 48 | ♛xb5 | ♖xf7 |
| 49 | ♛f5 | ♗f6 |
| 50 | ♛d5 | ♔h7 |
| 51 | ♛xf7 |     |

**Black resigns**

(I have never been able to catch David actually calculating variations. I really believe that most of his moves were made by intuition and of course, based on a wealth of experience. T.F.)

## (49) Bronstein,D – Deep Thought II

Played by modem between HP Laboratories, Palo Alto (Bronstein) and IBM Headquarters (Deep Thought II), 1992, 30 minutes each
*[D21] Queen's Gambit Accepted*

In brackets the thinking times per moves in minutes and seconds as recorded by Deep Thought II.

| 1 | d4 (1.14) | d5 (0.00) |
|---|-----------|-----------|
| 2 | c4 (0.15) | dxc4 (0.01) |
| 3 | ♘f3 (1.04) |          |

Why did I think over a minute about this move? I was wondering whether to take a risk by playing the slightly inferior move 3 e4.

In the AEGON tournament in 1991 I lost a game with this move against Hitech, the program written by my good friend

Professor Hans Berliner, which continued 3...e5 4 ♘f3 exd4 5 ♗xc4 ♘c6 6 0-0 ♗e6 7 ♗xe6 fxe6 8 ♕b3 ♕d7 9 ♕xb7 ♖b8 10 ♕a6 ♘f6 11 ♘bd2 ♗b4 12 a3? ♗xd2! 13 ♘xd2 0-0 14 ♕d3 ♘e5 15 ♕g3?? ♘h5!! etc., resulting in a disastrous position for White.

In a 'normal' chess game I would think longer. It is part of a game – to be able to choose a move.

By the way, in the international tournament at Hastings 1994/95, I decided to play Hitech's recommendation. My opponent, Sherbakov, being very surprised by the move 6...♗e6, thought for more than one hour and the game ended in a draw after only two new moves 12 e5 ♘g4 13 ♕e2 ♕d5. With this draw in the last round I managed, at the age of almost 71, to share first place!

Thank you Hitech!

| | | | |
|---|---|---|---|
| **3** | **...** | **a6** | (0.02) |
| **4** | **e4** (0.11) | **b5** | (0.00) |
| **5** | **b3** (0.14) | | |

This was the second game with this variation. In the first one I had played 5 a4 trying to recover the sacrificed pawn. However, a fresh idea came to my mind: if one sacrifices a pawn, why try to get it back? Then it was easy to make the most logical move with the intention to open as many lines as possible for my queen and rooks.

| | | | |
|---|---|---|---|
| **5** | **...** | **cxb3** | (0.39) |
| **6** | **♕xb3** (0.18) | **e6** | (0.52) |
| **7** | **a4** (1.23) | **b4** | (0.52) |

This is a typical computer solution: his evaluation tells him that this pawn takes away the squares a3 and c3 from the white pieces and that it has become a passed pawn. However, that this pawn is now blocking a path for a black rook and bishop has apparently not yet been programmed.

A human player would certainly have chosen to play 7...bxa4 in order to prepare the move ...c5 as soon as possible. But then the 'brain' of a chess computer works quite differently from a human brain!

| | | | |
|---|---|---|---|
| **8** | **♗c4** (0.39) | **♘c6** | (0.51) |

An active move with the clear intention of exchanging this knight for the bishop on c4.

| | | | |
|---|---|---|---|
| **9** | **♕e3** (2.04) | | |

It was a shame to lose a tempo like this but my sympathy for the power of bishops got the better of me!

Also good was 9 ♘d2.

| | | | |
|---|---|---|---|
| **9** | **...** | **♘f6** | (1.01) |
| **10** | **♗b2** (0.23) | **♘a5** | (0.50) |
| **11** | **♗e2** (2.41) | **♗e7** | (1.14) |
| **12** | **♘bd2** (0.13) | **0-0** | (0.34) |
| **13** | **0-0** (0.43) | **♗b7** | (0.03) |

| | | |
|---|---|---|
| **14** | **♖fd1** (2.02) | |

I am very proud of this move. Why? It is a routine decision of course but I made a bet with myself that the black queen would not like the X-rays on the d-file.

| | | | |
|---|---|---|---|
| **14** | **...** | **♕b8** | (1.03) |

So probably the computer is nearer to us than we often think. However, I will leave that judgement to the people of science...

| | | | |
|---|---|---|---|
| **15** | **♘e5** (0.56) | **♖d8** | (0.46) |
| **16** | **♖ac1** (2.07) | **♕a7** | (1.02) |

When my second for the occasion, scientist Bob English, executed this move on the board, I asked him to check with New

York if there had been a mistake. But two seconds later I changed my mind. 'No, don't call,' I said, 'I now see that I am playing against a genius!' I realised that Deep Thought was proposing an exchange of pieces after 17 ♖xc7 ♗d6 18 ♖cc1 ♗xe5 19 dxe5 ♕xe3 20 fxe3 in order to get itself into a favourable endgame.

I looked on the screen with great admiration! 'How interesting it would be,' I thought 'to see what computers can achieve in, let's not go too far ahead, 100 years from now!'

Then I realised that I also had to make a move. To take the pawn did not seem to me the thing to do but what if I could find 'something'? For instance, to play 17 ♘xf7 first. No, I could not see anything.

Then suddenly it dawned on me: I had to attack and my memory gave me a large list of moves known from chess history to choose from. First of all the rook sacrifice of Dr Tartakower against Geza Maroczy, Teplitz Schönau in 1922 1 d4 e6 2 c4 f5 3 ♘c3 ♘f6 4 a3 ♗e7 5 e3 0-0 6 ♗d3 d5 7 ♘f3 c6 8 0-0 ♘e4 9 ♕c2 ♗d6 10 b3 ♘d7 11 ♗b2 ♖f6 12 ♖fe1 ♖h6 13 g3 ♕f6 14 ♗f1 g5 15 ♖ad1 g4 16 ♘xe4 fxe4 17 ♘d2 ♖xh2 18 ♔xh2 ♕xf2+ 19 ♔h1 ♘f6 20 ♖e2 ♕xg3 21 ♘b1 ♘h5 22 ♕d2 ♗d7 23 ♖f2 ♕h4+ 24 ♔g1 ♗g3 25 ♗c3 ♗xf2+ 26 ♕xf2 g3 27 ♕g2 ♖f8 28 ♗e1 ♖xf1+ 29 ♔xf1 e5 30 ♔g1 ♗g4 31 ♗xg3 ♘xg3 32 ♖e1 ♘f5 33 ♕f2 ♕g5 34 dxe5 ♗f3+ 35 ♔f1 ♘g3+ White resigns.

If I was successful I might even be awarded a brilliancy prize.

Dr Tartakower only received the third brilliancy prize as the jury concluded that no human mind could calculate such a deep combination.

Then the brilliant book of Rudolf Spielmann about intuitive sacrifices came to my mind. I personally think that people should trust their own intuition more and that is exactly what I did!

| 17 | ♖xc7 (2.31) | ♗d6 (1.42) |
| 18 | ♖xf7 (0.55) | ♗xe5 (0.42) |
| 19 | ♖xg7+ (0.13) | ♔xg7 (0.41) |
| 20 | ♕g5+ (0.12) | ♔f7 (0.28) |
| 21 | dxe5 (0.27) | ♘g8 (0.13) *(D)* |

Voila! The result of intuition. The black king is in an unsafe position but is there a way to make the attack more effective? There is some hope as the black queen, rooks, bishop and knight on a5 cannot come to their king's assistance all in one move.

But also White cannot attack only with the queen. After 22 ♗h5+ ♔f8 I could play 23 ♖e1 and then on to e3 and f3. Yes, one can play like this against humans but a computer will play 23...♖d3. Really? Well, let's try!

| 22 | ♖e1 (1.43) | |

This move has the advantage that it unpins the knight on d2.

| 22 | ... | ♔f8! (2.34) |

A brilliant reply! The computer guessed my intention and on 23 ♗h5 had prepared 23...♖d3.

| 23 | ♘f3 (0.53) | ♗c6 (2.49) |
| 24 | ♗c1 (0.28) | ♘b3 (0.34) |
| 25 | ♗e3 (0.11) | |

Looking for a new diagonal.

| 25 | ... | ♕f7 (0.33) |
| 26 | ♗c4 (0.21) | ♗xa4 (0.32) |
| 27 | ♕g4 (0.49) | h5 (0.43) |
| 28 | ♕h3 (0.47) | ♕g6 (0.36) |

Up to now I am satisfied that my intuition created an interesting fight.

| 29 | ♘g5 (0.43) | ♘d4 (0.38) |
| 30 | f4 (1.45) | ♖dc8 (0.55) |
| 31 | f5 (0.32) | exf5 (1.26) |
| 32 | exf5 (0.16) | ♕e8 (0.01) *(D)* |

We have arrived at the crucial point. Now 33 f6 would win immediately but I decided to make a simple move which I thought was equally strong. I was so naïve that I thought that Deep Thought II would resign here!

| 33 | ♗d5 (0.59) | ♕xe5 (1.05) |
|----|-----------|-------------|
| 34 | ♘e6+ (0.16) | ♘xe6 1.09) |
| 35 | ♗h6+ (0.11) | |

It seemed obvious to give this check and I made this move almost without thinking, but I did not take the pawn on h5 into account. Better was 35 ♗c5+.

| 35 | ... | ♘xh6 (0.27) |
|----|-----|-------------|
| 36 | ♖xe5 (0.05) | ♖c1+ (0.24) |

Even now I wonder how Black's passive rook managed to give a check.

| 37 | ♔f2 (0.18) | ♘g4+ (0.08) |
|----|-----------|-------------|
| 38 | ♔g3 (0.08) | ♖c3+ (0.27) |
| 39 | ♗f3 (0.11) | ♘xe5 (0.01) |
| 40 | fxe6 (0.17) | ♘xf3 (0.09) |
| 41 | ♕f5+ (0.13) | ♔e7 (0.27) |
| 42 | ♕f7+ (0.07) | ♔d6 (0.19) |
| 43 | gxf3 (0.05) | ♗c6 (0.02) |
| 44 | ♕f4+ (0.21) | ♔xe6 (0.05) |
| 45 | ♕xb4 (0.17) | ♖xf3+ (0.10) |

Of course my position is now hopeless and I could have resigned here. Suddenly it dawned on me that a loss can also be beautiful and I wanted to give the computer an opportunity to create a nice finish to this game.

I think together we managed to do just that!

| 46 | ♔h4 (0.07) | ♗d5 (0.01) |
|----|-----------|-------------|
| 47 | h3!! (0.19) | ♖c8 (0.28) |
| 48 | ♕b6+ (0.41) | ♔e5 (0.35) |
| 49 | ♕xa6 (0.27) | ♖f4+ (0.29) |
| 50 | ♔xh5 (0.23) | ♗f7+ (0.28) |
| 51 | ♔g5 (0.28) | ♖g8+ (0.01) |
| 52 | ♔h6 (0.26) | ♖h4 (0.02) **mate** |

# (50) Bronstein,D – Gurevich,M

3rd ABN-AMRO Active Chess
Tournament, Brussels, 1993
*[C02] French Defence*

The game of chess is part of human culture. It has a long history, tradition, specialised literature and is well-known all over the world. One single practical game of chess is, in my opinion, only a psychological contest between two people. It is a competition in fantasy, logic, imagination, creativity and some calculation. Of course, in one game you can use a very limited part of your ability and knowledge but nevertheless you need to do it perfectly. This is why it is so difficult to play just one game. When I started to play chess I always liked to look for quick decisions on the basis of my knowledge and imagination. This is why I always liked to play five-minute chess games. If somebody asked me what was my best result in chess, I would name without any hesitation the three times I played in the five-minute Championships of Moscow in 1948, 1952 and 1953, each time taking the title against very strong opposition. Later

I became champion several times more and on many occasions I was amongst the top three. Whenever I was in Moscow during the championship, I played.

Needless to say I played in many other five-minute competitions with both pleasure and success. For instance in December 1949 I won a very strong five-minute tournament dedicated to the 70th birthday of Stalin.

My father was very pleased when I gave him my valuable prize, an engraved, high quality watch. He accepted this 'Stalinist' prize because he could not believe that one man could be so guilty of violating the socialist system.

Further, I came first in the strong five-minute tournament in Zagreb 1965 which was held immediately after the United Nations Peace tournament. In 1975 in Tallinn and in 1978 in Jurmala I also came first, leaving not only many good players behind me but also Mikhail Tal! He did not play in the regular tournaments but only turned up to snatch first prize in the subsequent five-minute tournaments.

The evening before the 1948 Interzonal Tournament in Saltsjöbaden started, I played many blitz games in front of a large audience with Miguel Najdorf who was then regarded by many as the five-minute champion of the West.

Even today, at the age of 84, he is still a very good Active (Rapid) Chess player, but then he was virtually unbeatable.

I am proud to say that I defended the East very well and I managed to win a 'match' of many games. The audience thanked us both with a big round of applause for the show.

More than 20 years ago I started to promote my idea of Active Chess. It is a form of competition where you need to play economically, making the best moves in a very limited time.

My first supporters were the chess players of Estonia. Since then I have played many times in Tallinn and I am proud to say that I have won every type of Active Chess tournament, be it 5, 10, 15, 20, 25 or 30 minutes per game.

Even one minute per game can be enough and to illustrate that, let me reproduce a short game. It was played during an interval at a meeting of the USSR Chess Federation.

**Bronstein,D – Spassky,B, 1 minute each, Moscow 1961, [A82] Dutch Defence**

1 d4 f5 2 e4 fxe4 3 ♘c3 ♘f6 4 f3 exf3 5 ♘xf3 d6 6 ♗f4 ♗g4 7 ♗c4 e6 8 0-0 ♘c6 9 h3 ♗xf3 10 ♕xf3 d5 11 ♗b5 ♗d6 12 ♖ae1 ♔d7(played with a smile) 13 ♗xd6 cxd6 14 ♖xe6 ♔xe6 15 ♘xd5 ♘xd4 16 ♕e3+ ♔xd5 17 ♖f5+ Black resigns (17...♘xf5 18 c4 and Black is checkmated).

A pure mate in the style of the Czech problemist school! And this with the players having a mere one to three seconds per move... This mini-burst of imagination gave us a lot of pleasure and Boris Spassky, the loser, enjoyed demonstrating the finale to friends.

(For further example of creative fast play, see pages 192, 241, 260, 277, 283, 284, 285 and 286, T.F.)

In my last tournament of this kind in Tallinn I came second, losing in the last round to my friend Walter Heuer, chess master, journalist and official biographer of Paul Keres. While playing the King's Gambit with White, I had a winning position at one stage.

As a member of the Anderlecht Chess Club of Brussels I was invited to participate in this tournament for the first time in 1991 and since then, as in Moscow, I have not missed a tournament. It is always a pleasure to play a tournament which lasts only two days, organised under beautiful conditions by amateurs who like chess and conduct it as a chess festival. I hope it will become a tradition for the Capital of Europe.

| 1 | e4 | e6 |
|---|----|----|
| 2 | d4 | d5 |
| 3 | e5 | |

The favourite move of Wilhelm Steinitz, which was later recommended by Aron Nimzowitsch. Nowadays Evgeny Sveshnikov plays this move regularly and wins almost every game with it. I myself also play it successfully.

The idea is to take away the square f6 from the black knight.

| 3 | ... | c5 |
| 4 | c3 | ♘c6 |
| 5 | ♘f3 | ♗d7 |

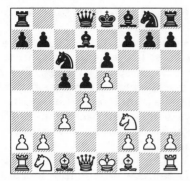

A clever waiting move. Now White needs to decide whether to play ♗e2 or ♗d3 or to go with the knight to a3 and then to c2. White has another idea, not better but rarely played: to attack the knight on c6.

| 6 | dxc5 | ♗xc5 |
| 7 | ♗d3 | ♘ge7 |
| 8 | b4 | |

This move can be called anti-positional but it helps to protect the e5 pawn. Probably better was 8 ♗f4 ♘g6 9 ♗g3 f6 10 exf6 ♕xf6 11 c4 0-0 12 ♘c3 with a sharp game and chances for both sides.

| 8 | ... | ♗b6 |
| 9 | b5 | ♘a5 |
| 10 | 0-0 | ♘g6 |
| 11 | a4 | |

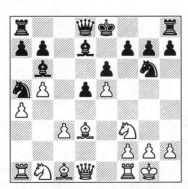

This advance creates space for the white pieces on the queenside and keeps the

black light-squared bishop out of play as long as possible.

| 11 | ... | ♖c8 |

A surprising move; 11...f6 seems more normal and White should then play 12 ♗a3.

| 12 | ♖a2 | |

This move looks too optimistic to be good. 12 ♗a3 would have been better but in Active Chess, when you should make fast decisions, it is best to take some risks.

| 12 | ... | ♘c4 |

Now Black has prevented this move.

| 13 | ♖e2 | |

White decides to keep the other rook on f1 to support a possible f4 later.

| 13 | ... | a6 |
| 14 | bxa6 | bxa6 |

| 15 | ♘a3 | |

Here 16 ♘bd2 looks better because after 16...♘f4 it is possible to play 17 ♗xc4 dxc4 18 ♖e4.

| 15 | ... | ♘xa3 |
| 16 | ♗xa3 | ♗c5 |

A very good positional move which stops all of White's expectations. Such moves one can never criticise but nevertheless, why not 16...♖xc3 instead? If then 17 ♗d6 Black can play 17...♘f4 (also 17...a5 immediately is possible) 18 ♖d2 ♖xd3 19 ♖xd3 ♘xd3 20 ♕xd3 a5 and Black has the pair of bishops and a pawn. White's only compensation is that Black cannot castle but that problem Black can solve with ...f6 and ...♔f7.

A better choice for White is the move 17 ♗b4 when Black can force a draw by means of 17...♖xd3 18 ♕xd3 ♘f4 19 ♕xa6

♗c8 20 ♕b5+ ♗d7, or play for a risky win with 17...♖c6 18 ♗xa6 ♗xf2+ 19 ♖exf2 ♖xa6.

| 17 | ♗xc5 | ♖xc5 |
|----|------|------|
| 18 | ♗xa6 | ♕a5 |
| 19 | ♗b5 | ♗xb5 |
| 20 | axb5 | ♕xb5 |

Black is entering the middlegame with some advantages. White's attack has been stopped and the pawn on c3 is weak. After the fall of this pawn the game is easily won for Black because of his passed pawn on d5. Therefore White must act immediately and he starts an attack to complicate matters.

| 21 | ♘d4 | ♕d7 |
|----|-----|-----|

This move looks all right but 21...♕a6 was probably better.

| 22 | f4 | 0-0 |
|----|----|-----|

Now Black can take again on c3 but after 22 f5 exf5 23 e6 fxe6 24 ♘xe6 the white knight is very strong. This is why Black puts the king to safety first. Nevertheless, probably 22...♘e7 would have been a better idea. After 23 f5 ♘xf5 24 ♘xf5 (if 24 ♖xf5?! then 24...exf5 25 e6 ♕a7!) 24...exf5 25 e6 fxe6 26 ♖xe6+ ♕xe6 27 ♖e1 White's initiative is over after 27...♕xe1+ 28 ♕xe1+ ♔f7 29 ♕e5 ♖hc8! 30 ♕xf5+ ♔g8 and it is Black who has excellent winning chances.

| 23 | f5 |
|----|----|

A classic way to attack and at first sight it looks sufficient for a draw. If Black is careful and plays 23...♘e7 then after the continuation 24 fxe6 fxe6 25 ♖xf8+ ♔xf8 26 ♖f2+ ♔g8 27 ♕g4 ♘f5 28 ♘xf5 exf5 29 ♕xf5 ♕xf5 30 ♖xf5 ♖xc3 it looks as if the position is coming to a draw, but the game takes another turn.

| 23 | ... | exf5 |
|----|-----|------|
| 24 | e6 | |

This move is even stronger than it looks. Now it is easy to see why the black queen should have gone to a6 and not to d7.

| 24 | ... | ♕a7 |
|----|-----|-----|

As c3 is still weak, the X-rays from a7 to g1 give Black some chances. The black king is protected by three pawns and appears to be completely safe but this position is somewhat exceptional. White's manoeuvre ♖a1-a2-e2 now proves to be very useful.

| 25 | exf7+ |
|----|-------|

This capture is a simple but surprisingly strong move.

| 25 | ... | ♖xf7 |
|----|-----|------|
| 26 | ♖e8+ | |

Another powerful move. Now the best move for Black may be 26...♘f8 27 ♔h1 g6 but after 28 ♖fe1 White has strong pressure, or 26...♘f8 27 ♔h1 g6 28 ♘e6 ♖b5 29 c4 with a strong attack. In any case Black should not have proposed an exchange of rooks on f8.

| 26 | ... | ♖f8 |
|----|-----|------|
| 27 | ♖xf8+ | ♘xf8 |
| 28 | ♘xf5!! | |

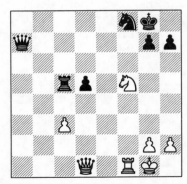

Black was so surprised at getting the opportunity for a discovered check that he thought for seven minutes about his next move. The pawns on c3 and d5 make the white queen safe and in Active Chess one needs to react fast.

| 28 | ... | ♘g6 |
|----|-----|------|

The knight is not well placed on this square. Black should have gone for a draw with 28...♖xc3+ 29 ♔h1 d4.

**29  ♔h1**

White is fine now. All his pieces are in the best possible position: the king is safe in the corner, the knight has a strong outpost and the rook is on the open file. Meanwhile, the h-pawn is ready to attack!

**29  ...  ♕d7**
**30  ♕g4  ♔h8**
**31  h4  ♖c4?**

Black loses a vital tempo: 31...♖c8! immediately was somewhat better but after 32 h5 ♘e5 33 ♕d4 ♖e8 White nevertheless plays 34 h6 and gets a strong initiative, e.g. 34...g6 35 ♘g7! or 34...gxh6 35 ♘xh6 with the threat of 36 ♘xf7+.

**32  ♕g5  ♖c8**

It appears that Black has finally organised a good defence. The 8th rank is protected, the g7-pawn is protected by the queen and the reduced number of pieces give the impression that after ...♖f8! Black is safe. As Fischer said in his famous book *My Sixty Memorable Games*: 'Chess is a matter of timing!'

**33  h5!**

This advance looks like a little too early because it helps the black knight to change a passive position on g6 for an active one on e6 but in reality this subtle move is the beginning of a pretty combination.

**33  ...  ♘f8**
**34  ♘e7!**

This not only attacks the rook but also opens the f-file for the white rook. It is a good example how to occupy the 7th rank with the rook. Why did White reject 34 h6 here? Because of 34...♘e6 35 hxg7+ ♕xg7! 36 ♕e3 ♕f6 but even in this line White

also has a promising attack because of the strong position of his knight on f5.

**34  ...  ♖e8**
**35  ♖f7**

It was possible to play 35 h6 ♘e6 36 hxg7+ ♘xg7 37 ♖f7 but from an artistic point of view, bringing the rook nearer to the black king is the perfect solution.

**35  ...  ♘e6**

**36  h6!**

The *coup de grâce!*

Now 36...♘xg5 fails because of 37 hxg7 mate and if 36...♖xe7 then 37 ♕xg7+! ♘xg7 38 ♖f8 mate.

**36  ...  ♖g8**

If 36...♘xg5 then 37 hxg7 mate.

**37  hxg7+**

Also possible was 37 ♕xg7+. It is mate after 37...♘xg7 (37...♖xg7 38 hxg7+ and mate) 38 hxg7+ ♖xg7 39 ♖f8+ ♖g8 40 ♖xg8+.

**37  ...  ♘xg7**
**38  ♕xg7+**

**Black resigns**

The mate is one move shorter after 38 ♘g6+ hxg6 39 ♕h6+ but then what is the rook on f7 doing?

I prefer a beautiful finish, not necessarily the shortest one.

# 60

The finest hour in David Bronstein's chess career must surely have been the 22nd game in his match with Mikhail Botvinnik in Moscow in 1951. Having attacked the black king relentlessly the pretender to the throne, aged 27, forced his formidable opponent to stop the clocks in resignation. This victorious attack permitted Bronstein to take the lead in this match only two games from the end: 11½-10½. He had to score just one more point out of the last two games in order to capture the title of World Champion. But he did not clear this decisive hurdle and Botvinnik managed to draw the match and hang on to his crown.

David Bronstein did not become World Champion but he has obtained the right to be named in the same breath as the most famous grandmasters. He played brilliantly in competitions at the highest level and his spiritual combinations and his paradoxical ideas gave him an unparalleled popularity in the world of chess.

But not only his results marked the path of Bronstein in the art of chess. We now offer Boris Vainstein the opportunity to describe the writing and creative talents of this remarkable Soviet grandmaster.

This article is extremely interesting as it is the opinion of a person who has been very close to David Bronstein during many years of friendship and creative co-operation. It is a pleasure for us to reiterate that the new edition of Bronstein's book *International Grandmaster Tournament* (Candidates' Tournament, Zürich/Neuhausen 1953, T.F.) original in its set-up and deep in content, was recognised as the best chess book of the year in 1983.

While we congratulate the grandmaster on his anniversary on behalf all the readers of our magazine *64* it is our wish that David Ionovich will remain the same person that his many, many admirers have come to know and appreciate: a true artist of Chess Art.

Editorial Board of *64*

So David Bronstein is 60! No, is time really flying so fast? We remember him as a boy in Kiev's House of Pioneers, as a young man in the reconstruction battalions in Stalingrad, as a very sociable and communicative young man and one who managed to stand up on equal terms with The Invincible (Botvinnik, T.F.). And now his anniversary!

There is so much one could say about the past 60 years in the life of this unique person, but why should we speak about the past? The past is a fact which you cannot change anymore regardless how much you try. Is it not better to look to the future based upon the treasure of our knowledge from the past?

In the year 2000 the value of sports achievements will be radically reduced as important tournaments will be held much more often all over the world. Of course Bronstein's performances in Prague, Stockholm, two Soviet Union Championships, his matches with Boleslavsky and Botvinnik, Hastings, Belgrade, Gothenburg, Gotha, six international team matches, best results in the FIDE Olympiads, all within a ten-year period, have been recorded in history and will be remembered by all. But in the 21st century it will be difficult to astonish someone by such things.

There is actually no chess theory in the sense of a scientifically formulated theory. However, towards the year 2000 a real theory will probably exist and then Bronstein's *Chess Self-Tutor* will be remembered in which the first shoots of chess theory became apparent. The players of the 21st century will say that in this manual a game of chess is explained, for the first time, as a system consisting of many elements, all interconnected. It is also mentioned that the basis of conflicts lies not only in the relations between the pieces but in those between the two opponents. Expressions such as 'lines of force', 'the equator', etc. were used for the first time in this chess book, so clear, so new.

Also new in this book is the idea that the ultimate goal – to checkmate your opponent's king – is only secondary but the aim is the strategy of how to use your forces to achieve this final result. 'You should move to your destination in stages,' says Bronstein, 'and because the system is conflicting you should take into consideration your opponent's plans all the time.' With the help of many examples the author demonstrates that the principles in chess, as in life, determine only a general approach and not a concrete move.

Yes, in the 21st century the theory might be different but even then, like the famous Icons of Rublev, the position from the game Zita-Bronstein will always be a famous landmark in the history of chess as an example of an active defence transforming into a counter-attack (page 33, T.F.)

In the second half of the 20th century there has been an explosive increase in the number of chess books. Once upon a time the publication of a chess book used to be an event we looked forward to but now we have hundreds of new books every year. Some authors even publish several books under their name which surely they could not have written all by themselves. Amongst those books are many reference books about openings, some about the lives of famous chess players, some with collections of games played in tournaments but very seldom will you find any books on the shelves about chess as an art.

David Bronstein wrote first of all about chess as an art. His book *International Grandmaster Tournament*, (Candidates' Tournament, Neuhausen/Zürich 1953, T.F.) of which more than 300,000 copies were sold in this country alone, is not a collection of chess games with commentaries but a real literary work.

The author has, in many respects, assumed the style of Arthur Haley. He is only one step away from becoming a professional novel writer and I wouldn't be astonished if this step is made before the end of the century.

The games played in this tournament have a certain connection as the grandmasters are learning from each other and trying out new ideas like a research symposium of the best chess brains and theoreticians of that time. It seems that the final result was of lesser importance. Instead of giving many variations Bronstein tries only to expose the general ideas. A reader can find a cognitive and aesthetic value in his commentaries and thoughts. In this consideration the book surpasses the traditional tournament collections.

Bronstein as an author possesses a very highly appreciated quality – the psychological compatibility with the reader. He never tries to put himself on a pedestal dominating the reader and giving him lessons. Instead he thinks with him, putting himself in his place as it were. He thinks it is strange and undesirable that there are authors (of chess books) who wish to show their superiority (over the reader).

When I read his annotations to the first game in this book about the weakness of the dark squares or the attack on the light squares, I thought for a long time that it concerned something quite incomprehensible for me. And a little further on he explains how one day he understood that the weakness of the dark squares is at the same time the weakness of the light squares. This thought now seems simple and self-evident enough but it was never declared as such, either by the theoreticians or by the champions. Maybe this will be part of the theory of chess when it is established one day.

Another highly original book by David Bronstein, which he wrote in collaboration with the doctor of philosophy G. Smolyan, is *A wonderful and furious World* (*Chess in the Eighties* is the title of the English translation, T.F.). Here the authors reveal the aesthetic and moral aspects of the game, worrying at the same time about the new trend in professional chess which turns it into a game where only points on the tournament chart are important, with all the negative consequences. There is no doubt that a struggle to defend the artistic side of Chess Art will take an important place in Bronstein's future.

Let's for a moment come back to David Bronstein's idea that chess is a system that is contradictory and dynamic at the same time. Such a system cannot be stable. Either it progresses and develops or it declines.

The role and place of chess in our social life now has progressive tendencies. Many young people are showing great interest in chess. But in which direction will chess develop when the younger generation brings new ideas to chess?

David Ionovich foresees a change in favour of artistic chess, favouring a tournament as a spectacle not only for professionals but also for amateurs. He not only suggests how to organise new types of tournaments but he has already organised them and taken part as a player.

Active (Rapid) Chess is the latest of his inventions, and it has been accepted with great pleasure and enthusiasm by millions of chess players and admirers.

'Who' he wonders, 'except a grandmaster, has the required stamina to play a "serious" game of chess taking five hours, with the possibility of an adjournment, after a normal working day? Who is willing to spend his vacation playing in a tournament that takes two or three weeks, sometimes even a month?' The rules for grandmasters that require them to make 40 moves in 2½ hours have existed for the last 100 years and they are still valid today.

Meanwhile the pace of life has changed and has become more hectic. Such developments are also taking place in sports. Just compare the records that were established this year to those of last year. But the speed of chess has not changed.

'Has the time not arrived to increase the speed of play?' asks Bronstein. It is a fact that the level of play of amateurs has increased and is coming close to that of masters in the past. The ability of being able to quickly assess a complicated situation, to find solutions to difficult problems in life, in business, in industry, in science is now a reality of our modern life. 'Why then' says Bronstein 'should the chess community be oblivious to these changes? Don't we, chess players, appear strange in the eyes of others? While mankind is now looking deep into outer space chess players still live in the trees!' Bronstein's remarks are very sharp but in reality not far from the truth. When you play faster you need to concentrate more but this is a prerequisite of our era. The time has come to give classification titles for competent players in tournaments with reduced time limits.

(In fact the FIDE congress held in Seville in 1987, accepted this idea and introduced a completely new type of chess competition, World Championships, titles, etc. This information was published in *Informator* nr. 44 and David Bronstein hailed this decision with great enthusiasm in his column in *Izvestia*. However, for unknown reasons it was never put into practice. T.F.)

All his life David Bronstein has often played in five-minute tournaments and now he accepts with pleasure invitations to participate in tournaments with reduced time limits. It is surprising to see that even in such tournaments the level of chess can be high, resulting in interesting and exciting games. The advantage of this system is that it is possible to play at least three rounds per day. Just recently a tournament, dedicated to the memory of Paul Keres, was organised in Tallinn this way with ten participants, amongst them two grandmasters and three international masters. The whole show took only three days in front of an enthusiastic audience.

Bronstein came first with 6½ points, and for his prize he could choose from five objects which were displayed on a table. There was a nice camera and other useful items. Without any hesitation, as a real champion of fast thinking, to my horror he chose a skateboard!

According to the instructions for use it was necessary to wear a motorcycle helmet and also knee and elbow protectors. I don't know if he is going to respect these safety rules but I can already imagine David Ionovich, grandmaster of chess, skateboarding into the 21st century! Well, I believe that he has the right to arrive there first!

To conclude I want to say a few words about the main reason why chess should not be regarded as a sport but as an art.

Now, in official chess the beauty of it is not being respected because it is not in any way being reflected in the rating system. This is how it is nowadays but real admirers of chess (and there are millions of them) are against the few but influential and powerful defendants of His Holiness The Rating.

There is no doubt that in the 21st century, maybe even earlier, we will see the renaissance of the cult for beauty in chess. Chess will develop into a kinder more humane game and, at the same time, the bad alien feelings and animosity between players will dissolve. And then David Bronstein's beautiful games will shine brightly like precious stones and will become a standard of the chess aesthetic. A perfect example is his game with grandmaster Paul Keres which was awarded the beauty prize in the Interzonal Tournament in Gothenburg in 1955 (page 50, T.F.)

Will you, dear reader, meet David Bronstein in the 21st century? If you are young, for sure. To the older people I wish this with all my heart.

And what about David Bronstein? A poet once said, with justification (supposedly grandmaster Ferzberi*):

On others the years weigh heavily
but you, you don't need to prove your cheerfulness, courageously
according to your passport you may be sixty
but if we measure the power of your vitality
you are only thirty

**Boris S. Vainstein.**
This article was published in *64* in February 1984.

* Queengrabber.

(Boris Vainstein himself, T.F.)

# 60 Games with Diagrams

## (1) Lipnitsky,I – Bronstein,D
Adult & Juniors tournament,
Kiev, 1938
*[D45] Queen's Gambit Declined*

**1 d4 d5 2 c4 e6 3 ♘c3 c6 4 e3 ♘f6 5 ♘f3
♗e7 6 ♕c2 ♘bd7 7 a3 0-0 8 b3 b6 9 ♗d3
♗b7 10 0-0 c5 11 cxd5 exd5 12 ♗b2 ♖c8**

**13 ♖ad1 ♗d6 14 dxc5 bxc5 15 ♗f5 ♗b8
16 ♘g5**

**16...h6 17 ♘h7 ♖e8 18 ♘xf6+ ♘xf6**

**19 ♗xc8 ♕xc8 20 h3 ♕c7 21 f4 ♖xe3
22 ♖d3 ♖xd3 23 ♕xd3 d4 24 ♘e2 ♕c6**

**25 ♖f2 ♘e4 26 ♖f3 ♗a6 27 ♘xd4 cxd4
28 ♕xd4**

**28...♕b6 29 ♖e3 ♕xd4 30 ♗xd4 f5**

**31 b4 ♗xf4 32 ♖f3 g5 33 a4 ♗e2 34
♖a3 a6 35 b5 axb5 36 a5 b4 37 a6** Draw
agreed.

## (2) Bronstein,D – Nazarevsky,V

Kiev Team Championship, 1939

*[B20] Sicilian Defence*

**1 e4 c5 2 ♘e2 d5 3 exd5 ♛xd5 4 ♘bc3 ♛d8 5 g3 ♗g4 6 ♗g2 ♘c6 7 0-0 ♘f6 8 h3 ♗h5 9 d3 e6 10 f4 ♗d6 11 ♗e3 0-0**

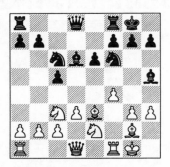

**12 g4 ♗g6 13 ♘g3 h6 14 ♛d2 ♗h7 15 ♖ad1 a6**

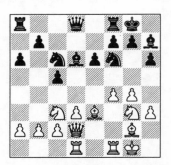

**16 ♘ce4 ♗xe4 17 dxe4 ♗e7 18 ♛f2 ♛a5 19 e5 ♘d5**

**20 ♖xd5 exd5 21 ♗xd5 ♗h4 22 ♛g2 ♗xg3 23 ♛xg3 ♖ac8 24 a3 c4 25 ♗e4 ♛b5** *(D)*

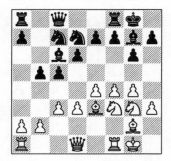

**26 g5 h5 27 g6 ♘e7 28 gxf7+ ♖xf7 29 f5 ♖cf8 30 f6 ♘d5 31 ♗h6 ♛b6+ 32 ♔h1 ♖d8 33 ♛g6** Black resigns.

## (3) Bronstein,D – Ratner,B

Ukrainian Championship,
Dnepropetrovsk, 1939

*[B16] Sicilian Defence*

**1 e4 c5 2 ♘e2 d6 3 g3 ♗g4 4 ♗g2 ♛c8 5 h3 ♗d7 6 d3 g6 7 ♗e3 ♗g7 8 c3 ♘f6 9 ♘d2 0-0 10 g4 ♗c6 11 0-0 ♘e8 12 ♘g3 ♘d7 13 f4 ♘c7 14 ♘f3 b5**

**15 d4 ♖b8 16 b4 cxb4 17 cxb4 ♘b6**

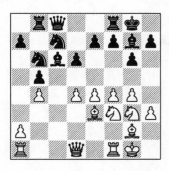

**18 d5 ♗xa1 19 ♛xa1 ♗d7** *(D)*

**20 f5 f6 21 ♗h6 ♖f7 22 fxg6 hxg6 23 ♘g5 ♘e8 24 ♘xf7 ♔xf7**

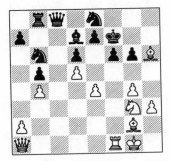

**25 e5 dxe5 26 ♘e4 ♘c4 27 ♘g5+ ♔g8**

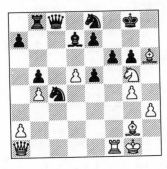

**28 ♕b1 f5 29 gxf5 gxf5 30 ♕d3 ♕d8**

**31 d6 ♘cxd6 32 ♗d5+ ♔h8**

**33 ♕g3 e6 34 ♘xe6 ♕e7 35 ♘f8 Black resigns.**

## (4) Bronstein,D – Zhukhovitsky,S
### Ukrainian Championship, Kiev, 1940
*[C98] Spanish Opening*

**1 e4 e5 2 ♘f3 ♘c6 3 ♗b5 a6 4 ♗a4 ♘f6 5 0-0 ♗e7 6 ♖e1 b5 7 ♗b3 d6 8 c3 0-0 9 h3 ♘a5 10 ♗c2 c5 11 d4 ♕c7**

**12 ♘bd2 ♘c6 13 dxc5 dxc5 14 ♘f1 ♖d8 15 ♕e2 ♗e6**

**16 ♘e3 h6 17 g4 ♗f8 18 g5 hxg5 19**

&xg5 &e7 20 &xe6 fxe6 21 &g4 &h7

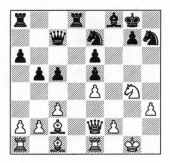

22 &h1 &h8 23 &g1 &g8 24 &g2 &e7

25 f4 exf4 26 e5 g5

27 &xf4 gxf4 28 &xh7 &h4 29 &e4 &g3 30 &xa8 &xa8 31 &f6 &f7 32 &h5+ Black resigns.

## (5) Lisitsin,G – Bronstein,D

### 13th USSR Championship, Moscow, 1944
*[E94] King's Indian Defence*

1 &f3 &f6 2 c4 d6 3 d4 &bd7 4 &c3 e5 5 e4 g6 6 &e2 &g7 7 0-0 0-0 8 d5 a5 9 &e1 &c5 10 &c2 b6 *(D)*

11 &g5 h6 12 &e3 &g4

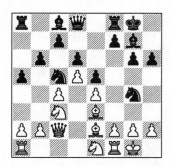

13 &xg4 &xg4 14 &d3 &d7 15 &ae1

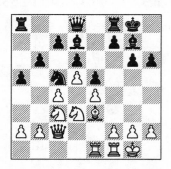

15...f5 16 &xc5 bxc5 17 f4 exf4 18 &xf4

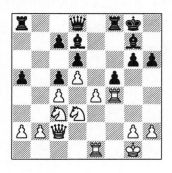

18...♗e5 19 ♘xe5 dxe5 20 ♖f2 f4 21 ♘e2 g5 22 ♕c3 ♕e7 23 ♘c1 g4

24 ♘d3 g3 25 hxg3 fxg3 26 ♖xf8+ ♖xf8 27 ♘xe5 ♕h4 28 ♘f3 ♖xf3 29 ♕xf3 h5

30 ♕e3 ♗g4 31 e5 ♗f5 32 ♖d1 ♕h2+ 33 ♔f1 ♕h1+ 34 ♕g1

34...♕h4 35 ♕xc5 ♕h1+ 36 ♕g1 ♕h4 37 ♖d4 ♗g4 38 ♖d2 ♕g5 39 ♕d4 *(D)*

39...♕f5+ 40 ♔e1 ♕b1+ 41 ♖d1 ♗xd1 42 ♕xd1 ♕xb2 43 ♕xh5 ♕f2+ 44 ♔d1 ♕d4+ 45 ♔e2 ♕e4+ 46 ♔d2 ♕d4+ Draw agreed.

## (6) Ravinsky,G – Bronstein,D
Moscow Championship, 1946
*[E61] King's Indian Defence*

1 d4 ♘f6 2 c4 d6 3 ♘f3 g6 4 ♘c3 ♗g7 5 ♗f4 ♘bd7 6 e3 0-0 7 ♕c2 c6

8 ♗e2 ♖e8 9 ♖d1 ♕a5 10 0-0 ♘h5 11 ♗g5 ♘f8 12 a3 h6 13 b4 ♕c7 14 ♗h4 ♗f5 15 ♕b3 g5 16 ♘d2 ♗g6 17 ♗g3 f5 18 c5+

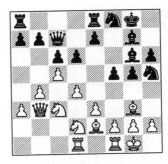

18...♔h8 19 ♗xh5 ♗xh5 20 ♖c1 ♕d7 21 ♘c4 ♗f7 22 ♖fd1 ♘g6 23 f3 ♖ad8 24 e4 f4 25 ♗f2 g4 26 ♘e2 ♖g8 27 d5 cxd5 28 exd5 dxc5 29 ♗xc5 gxf3 30 ♕xf3 *(D)*

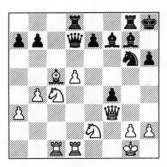

**30...♗xd5 31 ♘xf4 ♗xf3 32 ♘xg6+ ♔h7 33 ♖xd7 ♖xd7 34 ♘xe7**

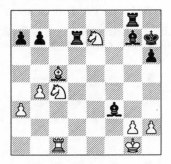

**34...♖xe7 35 ♗xe7 ♗d4+ 36 ♔f1 ♖xg2 37 ♔e1 ♖e2+ White resigns.**

## (7) Keres,P – Bronstein,D
Training game played in Hotel Moscow
the evening before the match
USSR-USA, Moscow, 1946
*[C81] Spanish Opening*

**1 e4 e5 2 ♘f3 ♘c6 3 ♗b5 a6 4 ♗a4 ♘f6 5 0-0 ♘xe4 6 d4 b5 7 ♗b3 d5 8 dxe5 ♗e6 9 ♕e2 ♗e7**

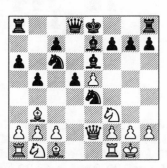

**10 c4 bxc4 11 ♗a4 ♗d7 12 e6 fxe6 13 ♗xc6 ♗xc6 14 ♘e5 ♗b7** *(D)*

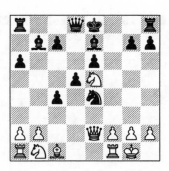

**15 ♕h5+ g6 16 ♘xg6 ♘f6 17 ♕h3 ♖g8 18 ♘e5 d4 19 f3 ♕d5 20 ♗f4**

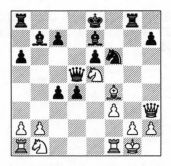

**20...♘d7 21 ♕h5+ ♖g6 22 ♕xh7 ♘xe5 23 ♗xe5**

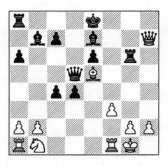

**23...♖xg2+ 24 ♔xg2 ♕xe5**

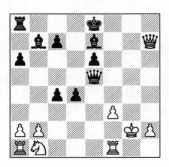

25 ♕g6+ ♔d7 26 ♘d2 ♕h8 27 ♔h1 ♖g8 28 ♕c2

28...♕h3 29 ♖f2 ♗d5 30 ♘e4 ♗h4 31 ♖ff1 d3 32 ♕d2 ♖g4 33 ♖f2 ♗xf2 34 ♕xf2

34...♕xf3+ 35 ♕xf3 ♗xe4 36 ♕xe4 ♖xe4 37 ♖d1 ♖e2 White resigns.

### (8) Averbakh,Y – Bronstein,D

15th USSR Championship,
Semi-Final, Leningrad, 1946
*[C11] French Defence*

1 e4 e6 2 d4 d5 3 ♘c3 ♘f6 4 ♗g5 dxe4 5 ♘xe4 ♘bd7 6 ♘f3 ♗e7 7 ♗xf6 gxf6

8 d5 ♘b6 9 ♗b5+ ♗d7 10 ♗xd7+ ♕xd7 11 dxe6 ♕xe6 12 ♕e2 0-0-0 13 0-0 f5 14 ♘g3 ♕xe2 15 ♘xe2 ♗f6 16 c3 ♖he8 17 ♖fe1

17...♘a4 18 ♖ab1 ♖d6 19 ♔f1 ♖b6 20 b3 ♘xc3 21 ♘xc3 ♖xe1+ 22 ♖xe1 ♗xc3 23 ♖e7 ♖f6 24 ♘g5

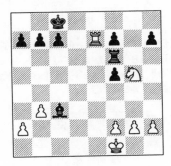

24...h6 25 ♘h7 ♖e6 26 ♖xe6 fxe6 27 ♘f8 e5 28 ♔e2 e4 29 f3 exf3+ 30 ♔xf3 ♗g7 31 ♘g6 ♔d7 32 h3 ♔d6 33 ♔f4 ♔c5 34 ♘e7 ♗f8 35 ♘g6 ♗g7 36 ♘e7

36...♔b4 37 ♘d5+ ♔a3 38 ♘xc7 ♔xa2 39 b4 ♗f8 40 ♘d5 ♔b3 41 ♔xf5 ♔c4 42 ♔e4 ♗xb4 White resigns.

## (9) Makogonov,V – Bronstein,D

15th USSR Championship,
Leningrad, 1947
*[A80] Dutch Defence*

1 d4 e6 2 ♘f3 f5 3 g3 d5 4 ♗g2 ♘d7 5
0-0 ♗d6 6 b3 ♕e7 7 c4 c6 8 ♕c2 ♕f6 9
♗g5 ♕g6 10 ♗f4 ♗xf4 11 gxf4 ♘h6 12
♘e5 ♕h5 13 ♕d3 ♘xe5 14 fxe5

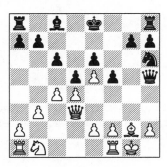

14...f4 15 ♕f3 ♕g5 16 ♘c3 ♘f5 17
♖ad1 0-0 18 ♔h1 ♗d7 19 ♖g1 ♗e8 20
♕h3 ♕h5 21 e4 fxe3 22 fxe3 ♕xh3 23
♗xh3 ♗h5 24 ♖df1

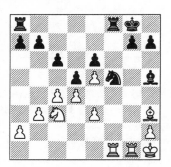

24...♘xe3 25 ♗xe6+ ♔h8 26 ♖xf8+
♖xf8 27 ♖c1 ♖f2 28 ♗h3 ♖f3 29 ♗e6
♖f2 30 ♗h3 g5 31 cxd5 cxd5 32 ♔g1
♖d2 33 e6 *(D)*

33...g4 34 ♗f1 ♘f5 35 ♘e2 ♔g7 36
♖c7+ ♔f6 37 ♖xh7 ♗g6 38 ♖xb7 ♘e3
39 e7 ♖xa2 40 ♘f4 ♖a1 41 ♔f2 ♖xf1+
42 ♔xe3 ♖f3+ 43 ♔d2 ♖xf4 44 ♔c3 ♖e4
45 ♖xa7 ♖xe7 46 ♖xe7 ♔xe7 47 ♔b4
♗c2 48 ♔c3 ♗d1 49 b4 ♗a4 50 ♔d3 ♔f6
White resigns.

## (10) Bronstein,D – Levenfish,G

15th USSR Championship,
Leningrad, 1947
*[D38] Nimzo-Indian Defence*

1 d4 ♘f6 2 c4 e6 3 ♘c3 ♗b4 4 ♘f3 0-0 5
♗g5 d5 6 e3 c5 7 cxd5 exd5 8 ♗e2 cxd4
9 ♘xd4 h6 10 ♗h4 ♗e6 11 0-0 ♘bd7

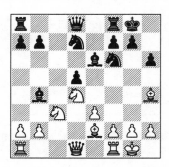

12 ♖c1 ♖c8 13 ♕a4 ♗xc3 14 bxc3 a6
15 ♕b4 ♘c5

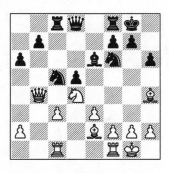

16 c4 dxc4 17 ♘xe6 ♘xe6 18 ♗xc4
b5 19 ♗b3 ♘g5 *(D)*
20 ♖xc8 ♕xc8 21 f3 ♕c7 22 ♖d1 ♖d8 23

☖xd8+ ♛xd8 24 ♗e1 ♛b6 25 ♗d2 ♘e6
26 ♔f2 ♘c5 27 ♗c2 ♛d6

## (11) Bronstein,D – Kan,I
Moscow Championship, 1947
*[C10] French Defence*

1 e4 e6 2 d4 d5 3 ♘d2 dxe4 4 ♘xe4 ♘d7
5 ♘f3 ♘gf6 6 ♘xf6+ ♘xf6 7 ♗d3 b6 8
♛e2 ♗b7 9 ♗g5 ♗e7 10 0-0-0 0-0 11 h4
♛d5 12 ♔b1 ☖fd8

28 ♛d4 ♛xd4 29 exd4 ♘e6 30 ♔e3
♔f8 31 ♗e4 ♘c7

13 c4 ♛d6 14 ☖he1 h6 15 ♗c1 ♗f8 16
♘e5 ♘d7

32 ♗b4+ ♔e8 33 ♗c6+ ♔d8 34 ♗a5
♔c8 35 ♔f4 ♘d7 36 h4 ♘e6+ 37 ♔e4
♘c7 38 g4 ♘b8 39 ♗d5 ♘xd5 40 ♔xd5
♔d7 41 ♔c5 ♘c6 42 ♗d2 ♘e7 43 d5
♘g6 44 h5 ♘h4 *(D)*

45 ♗c3 f6 46 ♔b6 ♘xf3 47 ♔xa6 b4
48 ♗xb4 ♘e5 49 ♔b7 ♘xg4 50 a4 ♘e3
51 a5 ♘xd5 52 ♗f8 f5 53 a6 f4 54 a7
♘c7 55 ♗xg7 f3 56 ♗d4 ♔d6 57 ♗f2
♔d7 58 ♗g3 Black resigns.

17 g4 ♘xe5 18 dxe5 ♛c6 19 g5 ♛f3
20 ♛c2 ♛h5 21 ☖g1 ♗h8 22 gxh6 gxh6
23 ☖g3 ♗c5 24 ♛d2 ♛xh4 25 ☖g4 ♛h5
26 ♛xh6+ ♛xh6 27 ♗xh6 ♗f3 *(D)*

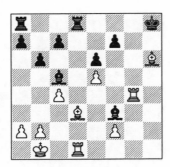

**28 ♗g7+ ♚g8 29 ♗f6+ ♚f8 30 ♖h4 ♚e8 31 ♖h8+ ♗f8 32 ♗xd8 ♖xd8 33 ♖g1 ♖xd3 34 ♖gg8 ♖d1+ 35 ♚c2 ♖e1 36 ♖xf8+ ♚e7 37 ♖e8+ ♚d7 38 ♖d8+ ♚c6 39 ♖df8 ♗e4+ 40 ♚d2 ♖b1 41 ♖xf7 ♖xb2+ 42 ♚e3** Black resigns.

## (12) Batuyev,A – Bronstein,D
16th USSR Championship, Semi-Final,
Leningrad, 1947
*[A48] London System*

**1 d4 ♘f6 2 ♘f3 g6 3 ♗f4 ♗g7 4 e3 0-0 5 h3 b6 6 ♘bd2 ♗b7 7 ♗d3 d6 8 0-0 ♘bd7 9 ♕e2 a6 10 e4 ♘h5 11 ♗h2 e5 12 c3 ♘f4 13 ♗xf4 exf4 14 g4**

**14...♖e8 15 ♖fe1 ♘f8 16 ♖ad1 ♕d7**

**17 ♕f1 ♘e6 18 ♕g2 ♖ad8 19 ♕h2 d5 20 e5 c5 21 ♘f1 ♗c6**

**22 ♗f5 gxf5 23 gxf5**

**23...♘xd4 24 ♘xd4 ♗xe5 25 ♖xe5 ♖xe5 26 ♕xf4 f6 27 ♘e6 ♖xe6 28 ♕g4+ ♚h8 29 fxe6 ♕d6 30 ♘g3 ♖g8 31 ♕e2 d4 32 c4 ♖xg3+ 33 fxg3 ♕xg3+ 34 ♚f1 ♗f3** White resigns.

## (13) Bronstein,D – Lundin,E
Interzonal Tournament,
Saltsjöbaden, 1948
*[A56] Benoni Defence*

**1 d4 ♘f6 2 c4 c5 3 d5 d6 4 ♘c3 g6 5 e4 b5 6 cxb5 ♗g7 7 ♗e2 a6 8 ♘f3 0-0 9 bxa6**

9...♗xa6 10 ♗xa6 ♘xa6 11 0-0 ♘d7
12 ♗g5 ♖b8 13 ♕d2 ♖e8 14 ♖ab1 ♕a5
15 ♖fc1 ♘c7 16 ♗h6 ♗f6 17 a3 ♖b3

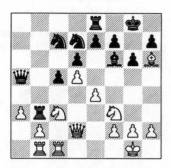

18 ♕c2 ♖eb8 19 ♘d2 ♖3b7 20 ♘c4
♕a6 21 ♕a4 ♕xa4 22 ♘xa4 ♘b5

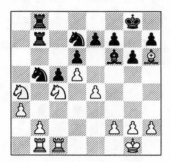

23 b4 ♘d4 24 ♔f1 ♗g7 25 ♗e3 ♖a8

26 bxc5 ♖xb1 27 ♖xb1 dxc5 28 ♘ab6
♖b8 (D)
29 a4 ♘xb6 30 ♖xb6 ♖xb6 31 ♘xb6
♘b3 32 ♔e2 ♗c3 33 ♔d3 ♗a5 34 ♔c4
Black resigns.

## (14) Taimanov,M – Bronstein,D
16th USSR Championship,
Moscow, 1948
*[B58] Sicilian Defence*

1 e4 c5 2 ♘f3 ♘c6 3 d4 cxd4 4 ♘xd4
♘f6 5 ♘c3 d6 6 ♗e2 e5 7 ♘f3 h6 8 0-0
♗e6 9 ♖e1 ♗e7 10 ♗f1 0-0 11 b3 ♖c8 12
♗b2 ♗g4 13 ♗e2 ♗xf3 14 ♗xf3 ♘d4 15
♕d3

15...♕a5 16 ♖ec1 ♖fd8 17 g3 d5 18
♘xd5 ♘xd5 19 exd5

**19...♗a3 20 ♗xd4 ♗xc1 21 c4 exd4 22 ♖xc1 ♕xa2 23 ♔g2 ♕a3 24 ♖d1 b5 25 ♕xd4 bxc4 26 bxc4 ♕c5 27 ♕a1 ♖d6**

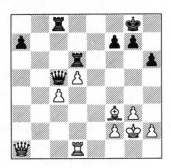

**28 ♖d4 ♖f6 29 ♖g4 ♕b6 30 h4 a6 31 h5 ♕d6 32 ♖e4 ♔f8 33 ♕e1 ♕c5 34 ♗d1 ♖d6 35 ♗a4 ♖dd8 36 ♕e2 a5 37 ♖f4 ♕a3 38 ♗c2 ♖d6 39 ♕e4**

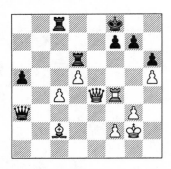

**39...♕c3 40 ♕h7 ♖xc4 41 ♖f3 ♕xc2 42 ♕h8+ ♔e7 43 ♕xg7 ♕e4 44 ♕xf7+**

**44...♔d8 45 ♔h2 ♖c1 46 ♕f8+ ♔c7 47 ♖f7+ ♖d7 48 d6+ ♔b6 49 ♖f3 ♔a7 50 ♕f6 ♕d5 51 ♕xh6 ♖e1** White resigns.

## (15) Bronstein,D – Ragozin,V

17th USSR Championship,
Moscow, 1949

*[B68] Sicilian Defence*

**1 e4 c5 2 ♘f3 ♘c6 3 d4 cxd4 4 ♘xd4 ♘f6 5 ♘c3 d6 6 ♗g5 e6 7 ♕d2 a6 8 0-0-0 ♗d7**

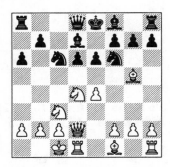

**9 f4 ♗e7 10 ♘xc6 ♗xc6 11 ♗d3 ♕d7 12 ♖he1 0-0-0**

**13 e5 ♘e8 14 ♗xe7 ♕xe7 15 ♗e4 d5 16 ♗d3 ♘c7**

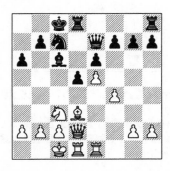

**17 ♕f2 ♔b8 18 ♘e2 f5 19 exf6 gxf6 20 ♘d4 ♗d7** *(D)*

**21 ♘f3 ♗c8 22 ♕d4 ♕g7 23 ♖d2 h5**

**24 ♕b6 ♕f8 25 g3 ♖d6 26 ♕b4 ♖d8 27 ♕xf8 ♖dxf8**

**28 c4 ♗d7 29 b3 ♗c6 30 ♘d4 ♖e8**

**31 ♗g6 ♖e7 32 c5 ♖g7 33 ♗d3 ♗d7 34 ♘f3 ♔c8 35 ♗f1 ♔d8**

**36 ♗h3 ♖e8 37 ♖de2 ♖ge7 38 ♔d2 ♗b5 39 ♖e3 ♗c6 40 ♘d4 ♗d7 41 ♘f3 ♖g8 42 a4 ♖ge8 43 ♗f1 ♖g7 44 ♗d3 ♖h8**

**45 ♗c2 ♘e8 46 b4 ♘c7 47 ♗d1 ♖hg8 48 ♖a3 ♖e8 49 ♗c2 ♖ge7**

**50 ♗g6 ♖h8 51 ♗d3 ♖he8 52 ♘h4 ♖g7 53 b5 axb5 54 axb5 ♗xb5 55 ♗xb5 ♘xb5 56 ♖a8+ ♔d7 57 ♖xe8 ♔xe8 58 ♖xe6+ ♖e7 59 ♖xf6 ♖c7 60 ♖e6+ ♔f7 61 ♖b6 ♘d4 62 ♔e3 ♘e6 63 f5 ♘xc5 64 ♘f3 ♘e4** (D)
  **65 ♔d4 ♖c2 66 ♘e5+ ♔f8 67 ♔xd5 ♘g5 68 ♖f6+ ♔e7 69 ♖g6 ♖d2+ 70 ♔c4**

Δe4 71 Ξe6+ &f8 72 Δg6+ Black resigns.

## (16) Bronstein,D – Szabo,L

Candidates' Tournament, 1st round,
Budapest, 1950

*[E27] Nimzo-Indian Defence*

**1 d4 Δf6 2 c4 e6 3 Δc3 &b4 4 a3 &xc3+ 5 bxc3 0-0**

**6 f3 Δh5 7 Δh3 f5**

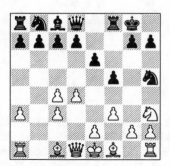

**8 e4 c5 9 e5 Δc6 10 f4 g6 11 &e2 b6 12 0-0 Δg7 13 &e3 cxd4 14 cxd4 &a6 15 Wa4 Wc8** *(D)*
**16 Ξfc1 Ξb8 17 Ξab1 Δa5 18 Δg5 Wc6**

**19 Wb4 Wc7 20 d5 Δb7 21 We1 Δc5 22 Wh4 h5 23 &f3 Ξbc8 24 d6 Wd8 25 Wg3 Δd3 26 Ξc3 &xc4**

**27 &b7 b5 28 &xc8 Wxc8 29 Δf3 &h7 30 Δh4 We8 31 &d4** Black resigns.

## (17) Bronstein,D – Flohr,S

Candidates' Tournament,
Budapest, 1950

*[B11] Caro-Kann Defence*

**1 e4 c6 2 Δc3 d5 3 Δf3 &g4 4 h3 &xf3 5 Wxf3 e6 6 g3 Δf6 7 d3 &e7 8 &g2 0-0 9 0-0 Δa6 10 We2 Δe8 11 e5 Δec7 12 Δd1 Δb8 13 h4**

**13...c5 14 h5 Δc6 15 c3 &h8 16 h6** *(D)*

**16...gxh6 17 ♘e3 ♘xe5 18 ♘xd5 ♘xd5 19 ♕xe5+ ♗f6 20 ♕h5 ♗g7 21 ♗xh6 ♗xh6 22 ♕xh6 ♕f6 23 ♕h5 ♕g6 24 ♕e5+ ♕g7 25 ♕h5 ♕g6 26 ♕e2 ♖ad8 27 ♖ad1 b5 28 c4 bxc4 29 dxc4 ♘b6 30 ♖xd8 ♖xd8**

**31 ♕e5+ ♕g7 32 ♕xc5 ♖d2 33 a4 ♖xb2 34 ♖d1 Black resigns.**

## (18) Bronstein,D – Boleslavsky,I
Candidates' Play-off
1st tie-break, Game 13,
Moscow, 1950
*[E68] King's Indian Defence*

**1 d4 ♘f6 2 c4 d6 3 ♘c3 e5 4 ♘f3 ♘bd7 5 g3 g6 6 ♗g2 ♗g7 7 0-0 0-0**

**8 e4 ♖e8 9 ♗e3 ♘g4 10 ♗g5 f6 11 ♗d2 ♘h6 12 h3 ♘f7 13 ♗e3 ♘f8 14 ♕d2 ♘e6 15 d5 ♘f8 16 ♖ae1 c5 17 a3 ♗d7 18 b4**

**18... ♕c8 19 bxc5 dxc5 20 ♔h2 ♘d6 21 ♕d3 ♕c7 22 ♘d2 f5 23 f4**

**23...h5 24 ♔h1 ♘h7 25 ♘b5 ♗xb5 26 cxb5 c4 27 ♕c2 c3 28 exf5 gxf5 29 ♘f3 e4 30 ♘d4 ♘f8 31 a4 ♖ac8 32 ♖c1 ♕f7 33 ♖fd1 ♗f6 34 ♕b3 ♔h8 35 ♗f1 ♖c7 36 ♗e2**

**36... ♕g6 37 ♖g1 ♖ec8 38 ♕d1 ♕f7 39 ♕b3 ♔g7 40 ♘c2 ♘c4 41 ♗xc4 ♖xc4 42 d6 (D)**
Adjourned position. **42...a5 43 ♗a7 ♕h7**

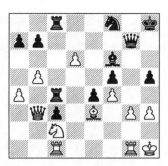

44 ♘e3 ♖b4 45 ♕d5 ♖xa4 46 ♖c2 ♖b4 47 ♘xf5 a4

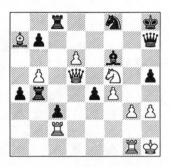

48 ♖d1 a3 49 ♗d4 ♗xd4 50 ♖xd4 a2

51 ♕e5+ ♔g8 52 ♖xb4 a1♕+

53 ♔h2 ♕d1 54 ♖g2 c2 55 ♘e7+

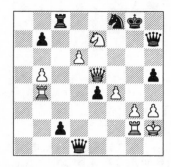

55...♕xe7 56 dxe7 c1♕

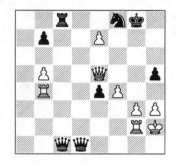

57 exf8♕+

57...♖xf8 58 ♕g5+ Draw agreed.

## (19) Cortlever,N – Bronstein,D
Olympiad, Helsinki, 1952
*[A98] Dutch Defence*

1 ♘f3 e6 2 g3 f5 3 ♗g2 ♘f6 4 d4 ♗e7 5 0-0 0-0 6 c4 d6 7 ♘c3 ♕e8 8 ♕c2 ♕h5 9 ♖e1 ♘c6 10 d5 ♘b4 11 ♕b3 ♘a6 12 dxe6 *(D)*

12...c6 13 e3 ♘g4 14 ♘e2 ♘c5 15 ♕c2 ♘xe6 16 ♘f4 ♕f7 17 b3 ♘c5 18 ♗b2 ♘e4

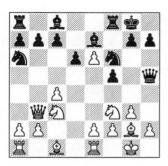

19 ♘d3 ♗d7 20 ♘d2 ♕h5 21 ♘f1 ♘gf6
22 ♘f4 ♕f7 23 f3 ♘c5 24 b4 ♘a6 25 ♘d3
♖ae8 26 a4 ♘c7 27 ♗d4 a6 28 ♖ac1 ♘e6
29 ♗b2 ♗c8 30 ♕d2 ♕h5 31 ♘f4 ♕h6 32
♘xe6 ♗xe6 33 e4

**33...fxe4 34 ♕xh6 gxh6 35 fxe4**

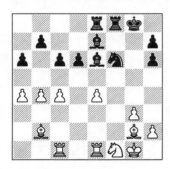

**35...♘g4 36 a5 ♘f2 37 e5 dxe5 38 ♖xe5
♗f6 39 ♖e2 ♗xb2 White resigns.**

## (20) Najdorf,M – Bronstein,D
Argentina vs. USSR Match, 1st board,
Buenos Aires, 1954
*[A55] Old Indian Defence*

1 d4 ♘f6 2 c4 d6 3 ♘c3 ♘bd7 4 ♘f3 c6
5 e4 e5 6 ♗e2 ♗e7 7 0-0 0-0 8 ♕c2 ♖e8

9 ♖d1 ♕c7 10 b3 ♘f8 11 h3 ♘g6 12 ♗e3
h6 13 ♗f1 ♘h7 14 ♘e2 ♘g5 15 ♘xg5
hxg5 16 ♘g3

16...c5 17 dxc5 dxc5 18 ♘e2 ♘f4 19
♘c3 ♕c6 20 ♘d5 ♗d8 21 ♗e2 ♘e6 22
♗g4 ♘d4 23 ♕d2 ♗xg4 24 hxg4 ♕h6 25
b4 b6 26 bxc5 bxc5 27 ♖ab1 ♖e6 28 f3

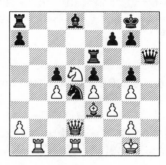

28...♕h4 29 ♕f2 ♕xf2+ 30 ♔xf2 ♖a6
31 ♖b2 ♖a4 32 ♖c1 ♘e6 33 ♔e2 ♖c8 34
♔d3 g6 35 ♖c3 ♔g7 36 ♖cb3 ♗a5 37
♖b7

37...♗b6 38 ♔c3 ♘d4 39 ♔d2 ♗a5+
40 ♔d1 ♖h8 41 ♗xd4 exd4 42 ♖xa7 d3
43 ♖xa5 ♖xa5 44 ♔d2 ♖h1 45 ♘c3 ♖a3
46 ♖b3 ♖xb3 47 axb3 ♔f6 48 ♘a4 ♔e5

49 ♔xd3 ♖d1+ 50 ♔e3 ♖e1+ 51 ♔f2 ♖b1 52 ♘xc5

52...♔d4 53 ♘b7 ♖xb3 54 ♘d6 f6 55 ♘e8 ♖b2+ 56 ♔g3 ♔e5 57 ♘c7 ♖c2 58 ♘d5 ♖xc4 59 ♔h2 ♖c1 60 ♘e3 ♔d4 61 ♘d5 f5 62 gxf5 gxf5 63 ♘e7 fxe4 64 ♘f5+ ♔e5 65 fxe4 ♖c3 66 ♘g3 ♖d3 67 ♘h1 g4 68 ♘g3 ♔f4 69 ♘h5+ ♔xe4 70 ♘g3+ ♔e5 71 ♘e2 ♖e3 72 ♘g3 ♔f4 White resigns.

## (21) Bernstein,O – Bronstein,D
France vs. USSR Match, 2nd board,
Paris, 1954
*[C01] French Defence*

1 e4 e6 2 d4 d5 3 ♘c3 ♗b4 4 exd5 exd5 5 ♗d3 ♘c6 6 ♘ge2 ♘ge7 7 0-0

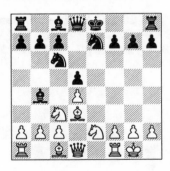

7...♗g4 8 h3 ♗h5 9 a3 ♗d6 10 ♘b5 0-0 11 c3 ♖e8 12 ♕c2 ♗g6 13 ♘xd6 ♕xd6 14 ♗f4 ♕d7 15 ♖ae1 ♘a5 16 ♗c1 ♗xd3 17 ♕xd3 ♘c4 18 ♘f4 *(D)*

18...♘g6 19 ♘xg6 hxg6 20 b3 ♘a5 21 ♕d1 ♕b5 22 b4 ♘c4 23 ♖xe8+ ♖xe8 24 ♖e1 ♔f8 25 ♖xe8+ ♕xe8 26 f3 a6 27 a4

♘b6 28 a5 ♘c4 29 ♗f4 ♕c6 30 ♕e1

30...b6 31 ♕h4 f6 32 ♕g3 bxa5 33 bxa5 ♘xa5 34 ♗xc7 ♘c4 35 ♗b8 ♕b6 36 ♔h2 g5 37 ♗c7 ♕c6 38 ♗b8 ♔f7 39 ♕e1 a5 40 f4 ♕b6 41 ♗e5 fxe5 42 fxe5 ♕g6 43 ♕d1 g4 44 hxg4 ♕h6+ 45 ♔g3 ♕e3+ 46 ♔h2 ♕f2 White resigns.

## (22) Denker,A – Bronstein,D
USA vs. USSR Match, 2nd board,
New York, 1954
*[A40] Queen's Pawn Opening*

1 d4 e6 2 g3 c5 3 dxc5 ♗xc5 4 ♗g2 ♘f6 5 ♘f3 ♘c6 6 c4

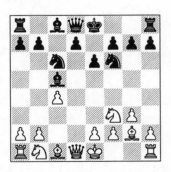

6...d5 7 cxd5 exd5 8 0-0 0-0 9 ♕c2 ♗b6 10 ♘c3 ♗e6 11 ♗g5 h6 12 ♗xf6 ♕xf6 13 ♖fd1 ♖ac8 14 ♖ac1 ♖fd8 15 ♘a4

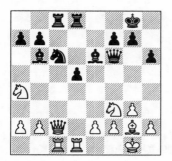

15...d4 16 ♘xb6 axb6 17 b3

17...d3 18 ♕d2 ♗g4 19 ♖c4 dxe2 20 ♕xe2 ♖e8 21 ♖e4

21...♘e5 22 ♖xe5 ♖xe5 23 ♕xe5 ♕xe5 24 ♘xe5 ♗xd1 25 ♗xb7 ♖c7 26 ♗e4 ♗c2 27 ♗d5 ♔f8 28 ♘c6 ♗b1 29 a3 ♗f5 30 ♔f1 ♗e6 31 ♗xe6 fxe6 32 ♘d4 ♖c1+ 33 ♔e2 ♔e7 34 ♔d3 ♖f1 35 f4 ♖f2 36 ♔c4 ♖xh2 37 ♔b5 ♖d2 38 ♘c6+ ♔d6 39 ♔xb6 ♖d3 40 b4 ♖xa3 41 g4 ♖f3 White resigns.

## (23) Golombek,H – Bronstein,D
Great Britain vs. USSR Match, 3rd board,
London, 1954
*[E97] King's Indian Defence*

1 c4 ♘f6 2 d4 g6 3 ♘c3 ♗g7 4 e4 d6 5 ♘f3 0-0 6 ♗e2 e5 7 0-0 ♘c6 8 d5 ♘e7 9 ♗g5 h6 10 ♗d2 ♘d7 11 ♕c1 ♔h7 12 ♘e1

12...f5 13 g3 fxe4 14 ♘xe4 ♘f5 15 ♘c2 c6 16 dxc6 bxc6 17 ♗b4 ♘f6 18 ♗f3 a5 19 ♗a3 ♕c7 20 ♕d2 ♖d8 21 ♖ac1 ♗e6 22 ♕e2 ♕f7 23 b3 ♘xe4 24 ♗xe4

24...d5 25 cxd5 cxd5 26 ♗g2 ♖ac8 27 ♕a6 e4 28 ♘e3 ♘d4

**29 Rxc8 Rxc8 30 Wxa5 Ne2+ 31 Kh1 d4 32 Nd1**

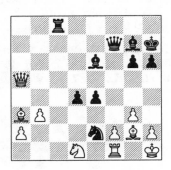

**32...Bg4 33 h3 Bf3 34 We1**

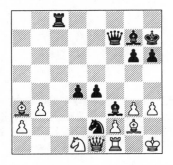

**34...Rc2 35 Kh2 Bxg2 36 Kxg2 Wf3+ 37 Kh2 Be5 38 Rg1 Nxg3 White resigns.**

## (24) Bronstein,D – Filip,M
Candidates' Tournament,
Amsterdam, 1956
*[D92] Grünfeld Defence*

**1 d4 Nf6 2 Nf3 g6 3 c4 Bg7 4 Nc3 d5 5 Bf4 0-0 6 Rc1 c5 7 dxc5 dxc4 8 Wxd8 Rxd8 9 e4 Na6 10 e5 Ng4 11 h3 Nh6 12 Bxc4 Nxc5**

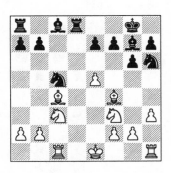

**13 Ke2 Be6 14 Nb5 Rac8 15 Nxa7 Ra8**

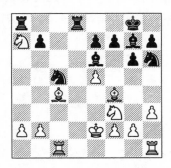

**16 Be3 Bxc4+ 17 Rxc4 Nd7 18 Nb5 Rxa2 19 Rb4 Nf5 20 Rd1 Raa8**

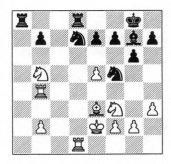

**21 e6 Nxe3 22 fxe3 Nc5 23 exf7+ Kxf7 24 Nbd4 Rd5 25 Rf1 Bf6 26 g4 Kg8 27 Rb5 Rad8 28 Ra1 Bxd4 29 Nxd4 R8d6 30 Ra8+ Kf7 31 Rb8 h5**

**32 b4 Ne6 33 Rxd5 Rxd5 34 Nxe6 Kxe6 35 Rxb7 hxg4 36 hxg4 Rg5 37 Kf3 Rd5 38 Rb6+ Kf7 39 Ke4 Rd1 40 g5 Rd2 41 Rb5 Ke6 42 Re5+ Kd6 43 Ra5 Rb2 44 Ra6+ Kd7 45 Rb6 Ke8 46 Kd4 Kf7 47 e4 Rd2+ 48 Kc3 Re2 49 Kd3 Rg2 50 Rb5 Ke6 51 Rd5 Rb2 52 Kc4 Re2 53 Kd4 Rd2+ 54 Kc5 Rc2+(D)**

**55 ♔b6 ♖e2 56 b5 ♖xe4 57 ♔c6 ♖b4 58 ♖c5** Black resigns.

Dr Euwe in *Schakend Nederland*: 'Best endgame of the month.'

## (25) Bronstein,D – Rojahn,E

Moscow Olympiad, 1956

*[C58] Two Knights Defence*

**1 e4 e5 2 ♘f3 ♘c6 3 ♗c4 ♘f6 4 ♘g5 d5 5 exd5 ♘a5**

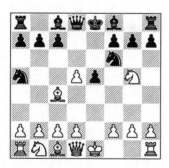

**6 d3 h6 7 ♘f3 e4**

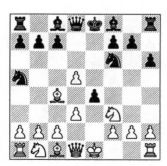

**8 dxe4 ♘xc4 9 ♕d4 ♘b6 10 c4 c5 11 ♕d3 ♗g4 12 ♘bd2 ♗e7 13 0-0 0-0 14 ♘e5 ♗h5 15 b3 ♘bd7 16 ♗b2 ♘xe5 17 ♗xe5 ♘d7 18 ♗c3 ♗f6 19 ♖ae1 ♗xc3**

**20 ♕xc3 ♕f6 21 e5 ♕f5 22 f4 ♗g6 23 ♘e4 ♖ab8 24 ♕f3 ♗h7**

**25 g4 ♕g6 26 f5 ♕b6 27 ♕g3 f6 28 e6 ♘e5 29 h4 ♔h8 30 g5 ♖bc8 31 ♔h1 ♕d8 32 g6 ♗xg6 33 fxg6 b5 34 d6 ♕b6 35 d7 ♘xd7 36 exd7 ♖cd8**

**37 ♘xf6 ♕c6+ 38 ♕g2** Black resigns.

## (26) Bronstein,D – Schmid,L

European Team Championship, Vienna, 1957

*[C17] French Defence*

**1 e4 e6 2 d4 d5 3 ♘c3 ♗b4 4 e5 c5 5 ♕g4 ♘e7 6 dxc5 ♘bc6**

7 ♗d2 0-0 8 ♘f3 f6

9 0-0-0 ♗xc5 10 exf6 ♖xf6 11 ♗g5 ♖f7 12 ♗d3 ♗d7 13 ♗e3 ♗xe3+ 14 fxe3 h6

15 e4 ♕c7 16 ♘b5 ♕f4+ 17 ♕xf4 ♖xf4 18 exd5 exd5 19 ♖he1 ♗g4 20 ♗e2 ♖d8 21 h3 ♗h5 22 c3 a6 23 ♘bd4 ♗xf3 24 ♘xf3 ♖e4

25 ♘d2 ♖e5 26 ♘b3 ♘f5 27 ♗f3 ♖xe1 28 ♖xe1 a5 29 ♖d1 ♘fe7 30 ♘c5 b6 31 ♘e6 ♖d6 32 ♘c7 ♔f7 33 a4 ♔g6 34 ♗xd5 ♔g5 35 g3 ♘f5 36 ♘e8 Black resigns.

## (27) Bronstein,D – Krogius,N

25th USSR Championship,
Riga, 1958

*[E80] King's Indian Defence*

1 d4 ♘f6 2 c4 g6 3 ♘c3 ♗g7 4 e4 d6 5 f3 e5 6 ♘ge2 ♘fd7 7 ♗e3 ♘h6 8 ♗f2 0-0

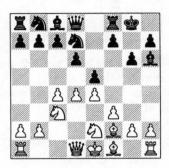

9 h4 c5 10 d5 ♖e8 11 g4 ♘a6 12 g5 ♗g7 13 ♘g3 ♘c7 14 ♗e3 ♘f8

15 ♕c2 ♖b8 16 a3 b6 17 b4 f5 18 gxf6 ♗xf6 19 ♕h2 h5

20 b5 ♘h7 21 ♖a2 ♔h8 22 ♖g2 ♕e7 23 ♗d3 ♗d7 24 ♔d2 ♖g8 25 ♘ge2 ♖be8 26 ♖hg1 ♕f7 *(D)*

27 &c2 &c8 28 ♘c1 ♖ef8 29 &e2 &d7
30 &d2 ♕e7 31 ♘d3 &e8

32 f4 &f7 33 fxe5 dxe5 34 ♘d1 a6 35
&c3 ♖e8 36 a4 ♖gf8 37 ♖f1 &g7

38 &xh5 axb5 39 axb5 ♘xb5 40 cxb5

40...c4 41 ♘b4 gxh5 42 ♖xg7 ☗xg7
43 ♘c6 ♕d6 44 ♘xe5 ♘f6

45 ♖xf6 ♕xf6 46 ♘d7 Black resigns.

## (28) Olafsson,F – Bronstein,D
Central Chess Club Tournament,
Moscow, 1959
*[E43] Nimzo-Indian Defence*

1 c4 e6 2 ♘c3 &b4 3 ♘f3 ♘f6 4 d4 b6 5
e3 ♘e4 6 ♕c2 &b7 7 &d3 f5

8 0-0 &xc3 9 bxc3 0-0 10 ♘e1 ♕h4

11 f3 ♘f6 12 &a3 d6 13 c5 dxc5 14
dxc5 ♖e8 15 c4 ♘bd7 16 ♕a4 *(D)*
16...♘e5 17 &b2 &c6 18 ♕c2 ♘ed7

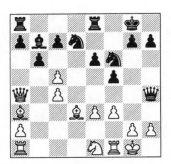

**19 cxb6 axb6 20 ♗e2**

**20...♕h6 21 ♕c1 e5 22 ♘c2 ♗b7 23 ♘a3 ♘c5 24 ♘b5 ♖ac8 25 ♗c3 ♖e6 26 ♗b4 ♘fd7**

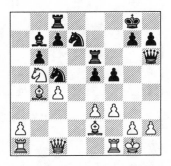

**27 ♕d2 c6 28 ♘a3 ♖d6 29 ♕c3**

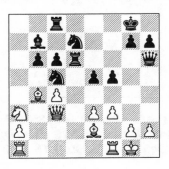

**29...♘d3 30 ♘c2 c5 31 ♗a3 e4 32 ♖ad1 ♘7e5 33 f4 ♖g6 34 ♘e1 ♕h3**

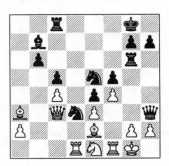

**35 ♗xd3 ♕xe3+ 36 ♔h1 ♘xd3 37 ♕d2 ♕d4 38 ♘c2 ♕f6 39 ♘e3 ♖d8 40 ♕e2 ♖a8 41 ♗c1 ♖h6**

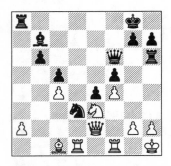

**42 g3 ♕f7 43 ♖g1 ♖d6 44 ♖df1 h5 45 ♖g2 ♗a6 46 ♕c2 ♘b4 47 ♕c3 ♖d3 48 ♕e5 ♗xc4 White resigns.**

## (29) Tolush,A – Bronstein,D
### Leningrad vs. Moscow, Moscow, 1960
*[E94] King's Indian Defence*

**1 d4 ♘f6 2 c4 g6 3 ♘c3 ♗g7 4 e4 d6 5 ♘f3 0-0 6 ♗e2 e5 7 d5 ♘bd7 8 ♗g5 h6 9 ♗h4 a5 10 ♘d2 ♘c5 11 0-0 c6 12 ♖b1**

**12....♗d7 13 b3 g5 14 ♗g3 cxd5 15 cxd5**

**15...b5 16 b4 axb4 17 ♖xb4 ♕a5 18 ♕b1 ♞a6 19 ♖b3 ♞c5 20 ♖b4 ♞a6 21 ♖b3 ♖fc8 22 ♕b2 b4 23 ♞cb1**

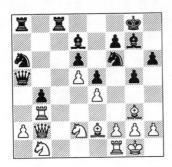

**23...♞c5 24 ♖xb4 ♕xa2 25 f3 ♞h5 26 ♕xa2 ♖xa2 27 ♖d1 ♞f4 28 ♗c4 ♞cd3 29 ♖b7**

**29...♖xc4 30 ♞xc4 ♖xg2+ 31 ♔h1** *(D)*
**31...♗h3 32 ♖d2 ♞e2 33 ♖xe2 ♖xe2 34 ♞bd2 h5 35 ♖b3 ♞f4 36 ♔g1 ♖g2+ 37 ♔h1 ♞e2 38 ♖b1 h4 39 ♗xe5 ♖f2** White resigns.

## (30) Bondarevsky,I – Bronstein,D
31st USSR Championship,
Leningrad, 1963
*[A48] London System*

**1 d4 ♞f6 2 ♞f3 g6 3 ♗f4 ♗g7 4 e3 0-0 5 ♞bd2 b6 6 c3 c5 7 h3 d6 8 ♗e2 ♗a6 9 ♗xa6 ♞xa6 10 0-0 ♕d7 11 ♕e2 ♞c7 12 dxc5 bxc5 13 e4 e5 14 ♗e3 ♖ab8 15 b3 ♕c6 16 ♕c4**

**16...♞d7 17 ♞h2 ♞b6 18 ♕d3 d5 19 f3 ♖bd8 20 ♕c2**

**20...f5 21 ♖ad1 ♞e6 22 exd5 ♞xd5 23 ♞c4 ♞ef4** *(D)*

**24 ♖f2 ♘xe3 25 ♘xe3 ♖xd1+ 26 ♕xd1**

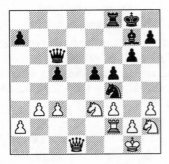

**26...e4 27 ♕c2 ♗h6 28 ♘hf1 ♘d3 29 ♖d2 c4 30 ♘xc4 ♕c5+ 31 ♔h2 ♗f4+ 32 g3 ♘e1** White resigns.
'Best game of the tournament.'

## (31) Bronstein,D – Korchnoi,V
20 years Liberation Tournament,
Belgrade, 1964
*[D87] Grünfeld Defence*

**1 d4 ♘f6 2 c4 g6 3 ♘c3 d5 4 cxd5 ♘xd5 5 e4 ♘xc3 6 bxc3 ♗g7 7 ♗c4 c5 8 ♘e2 0-0 9 0-0 ♘c6 10 ♗e3 ♘a5 11 ♗d3 b6 12 ♕a4 e5**

**13 ♖ad1 ♗d7 14 ♕a3 cxd4 15 cxd4 exd4 16 ♗xd4 ♗xd4 17 ♘xd4 ♗g4 18 ♗e2 ♗xe2 19 ♘xe2 ♕e8**

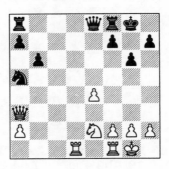

**20 ♘c3 f6 21 ♘d5 ♖f7 22 ♖fe1 ♕f8 23 ♕g3 ♘c6 24 h4 ♔h8 25 ♖c1 ♘b4 26 ♘c7 ♖c8 27 h5 ♘xa2**

**28 ♖c4 b5 29 ♘e6 ♕e8 30 ♖xc8 ♕xc8 31 hxg6 hxg6 32 ♕h4+ ♔g8 33 ♕g4 g5 34 ♕f5 ♕d7**

**35 e5 fxe5 36 ♕xg5+ ♔h8 37 ♕xe5+ ♔g8 38 ♕g5+ ♔h8 39 ♕h5+ ♖h7 40 ♕e5+ ♔g8 41 ♕g5+ ♔h8 42 ♕f6+** Black resigns.
'Best game of the tournament.'

## (32) Suetin,A – Bronstein,D
### 32nd USSR Championship,
### Kiev, 1964/65
*[B01] Scandinavian Defence*

1 e4 d5 2 exd5 ♘f6 3 ♗b5+ ♗d7 4 ♗c4
b5 5 ♗e2 ♘xd5 6 ♘f3 ♗c6 7 ♘e2 ♘f6 8
♗xc6+ ♘xc6 9 0-0 e6 10 d4 ♗e7 11 ♕d3
a6 12 a4

12...♘b4 13 ♕d1 0-0 14 ♘bc3 ♕d7 15
♗g5 ♘bd5 16 ♕d3 b4 17 ♘b1 c5 18
dxc5 ♕c7 19 ♕f3 ♕xc5 20 ♖c1

20...♘c3 21 ♘bxc3 ♕xg5 22 ♘e4 ♕e5
23 ♘d2 ♖ac8 24 c3 ♖fd8 25 ♘b3 bxc3
26 ♖xc3 ♘d5 27 ♖xc8 ♖xc8 28 ♘bd4
♗f6 29 ♖d1

29...♕b8 30 b3 ♕b6 31 g3 ♘e7 32
♖d3 ♘g6 33 ♖c3 ♖d8 34 ♖c6 ♕a7 35
♕e4

35...♗xd4 36 ♘xd4 ♕xd4 37 ♕xd4
♖xd4 38 ♖xa6 ♖b4 39 ♖a8+ ♘f8 40 a5
♖xb3 41 a6 ♖a3 White resigns.

## (33) Bronstein,D – Vasiukov,Y
### 32rd USSR Championship,
### Kiev, 1964/65
*[B17] Caro-Kann Defence*

1 e4 c6 2 d4 d5 3 ♘c3 dxe4 4 ♘xe4 ♘d7
5 ♗c4 ♘gf6 6 ♘g5 e6 7 ♘e2 h6 8 ♘f3
b5 9 ♗d3 ♗b7 10 c3 ♕b6

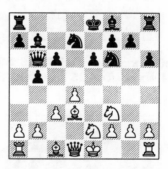

11 a4 a5 12 axb5 cxb5 13 ♘g3 ♗d6

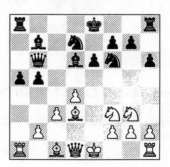

**14 ♕e2 0-0 15 ♘e5 ♖fd8 16 f4 b4 17 0-0 a4 18 ♗e3 a3**

**19 c4 axb2 20 ♖ad1 ♖a3 21 ♗f2 ♕c7 22 ♖fe1 ♘f8 23 h3 ♖da8 24 ♕xb2 ♘6h7 25 c5 ♗xe5 26 dxe5 b3 27 ♗b1 ♘g6 28 ♘h5 ♘hf8 29 ♖d6 ♘e7 30 ♖ed1 ♘f5**

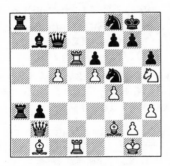

**31 c6 ♗xc6 32 ♕c3 ♖3a6 33 ♗xf5 exf5 34 ♕xb3 ♗e4 35 ♗b6 ♕b7 36 ♕g3 ♘g6**

**37 e6 ♖a2 38 ♗f2 ♔h7 39 ♖d7 ♕b2 40 ♖xf7 ♖g8** *(D)*

**41 ♘f6+ ♔h8 42 ♘xg8 ♔xg8 43 ♖d8+** Black resigns.

## (34) Bronstein,D – Padevsky,N
United Nations Peace Tournament,
Zagreb, 1965
*[B06] Bird's Opening*

**1 f4 g6 2 ♘f3 ♗g7 3 e4 c5 4 c3 d5 5 e5 ♘h6 6 ♗b5+ ♗d7 7 ♗xd7+ ♕xd7 8 d4 cxd4 9 cxd4 0-0 10 ♘c3 ♘c6**

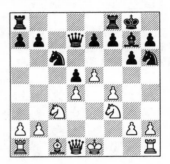

**11 h3 f6 12 ♕b3 fxe5 13 dxe5 e6**

**14 ♘e2 ♖ac8 15 ♗d2 ♘f5 16 g4 ♘fe7 17 ♕d3 d4 18 a3 ♕d5 19 0-0 ♖fd8 20 ♗e1 ♖d7** *(D)*

**21 ♖c1 a6 22 ♗f2 ♖cd8 23 ♘g5 h6 24**

♘e4 ♖f8 25 ♖c5 ♕a2 26 b4 g5 27 ♘c1 ♕a1

28 ♕b3 ♘d5 29 f5 ♘e3

30 ♖e1 ♘xe5 31 ♖xe5 ♗xe5

32 ♘d3 ♕xe1+ 33 ♗xe1 ♖d5 34 ♘ec5 ♗f6 35 ♗d2 ♖d6 36 ♘xe6 ♖f7 37 ♘dc5 ♘d5 38 ♘e4 ♖dd7 39 ♘6c5 ♖d8 40 ♘xb7

Black resigns.

## (35) Bertok,M – Bronstein,D
United Nations Peace Tournament,
Zagreb, 1965
*[A95] Dutch Defence*

**1 c4 e6 2 g3 f5 3 ♘f3 ♘f6 4 ♗g2 ♗e7 5 ♘c3 0-0 6 0-0 d5 7 d4 c6**

**8 b3 ♕e8 9 ♘e5 ♘bd7 10 ♘d3 ♘e4 11 ♗b2 ♗d6 12 c5 ♗c7 13 f4 b6 14 ♖c1 ♗b7**

**15 ♘xe4 dxe4 16 ♘e5 ♘f6 17 a4 ♘d5
18 ♕d2 b5 19 axb5 ♗xe5 20 dxe5 cxb5
21 b4 e3 22 ♕d4 a5 23 bxa5 ♖xa5 24
♖a1 ♖a4 25 ♖xa4 bxa4 26 ♗a3 ♗c6 27
♖b1 h6**

**28 ♗xd5 ♗xd5 29 ♕xe3 ♕a8 30 ♖b6
♗c6 31 ♕c1 ♖d8 32 ♔f2 ♔h7 33 ♕c4
♗h1**

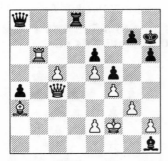

**34 c6 ♗d5 35 ♕c5 ♖c8 36 c7 ♕a7 37
♖c6 ♕b7 38 ♖b6 ♕xc7 39 ♕xc7 ♖xc7**

**40 ♖a6 ♗b3 41 ♗d6 ♖c2 42 ♖a7 ♗c4
43 ♖xa4 ♖xe2+ 44 ♔g1 ♗d5** *(D)*
**45 ♖a7 ♔g8 46 ♗c5 ♖g2+ 47 ♔f1 ♖xh2
48 ♗f2 ♖h1+ 49 ♔g1 ♖h3 50 ♔f2 g5 51**

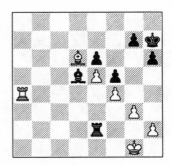

**fxg5 hxg5 52 ♖c7 ♖h1+ 53 ♔g1 g4**

**54 ♖a7 ♖h3 55 ♗f2 ♔f8 56 ♗c5+ ♔e8
57 ♔f2 ♖h2+ 58 ♔e3 ♖c2 59 ♗d4 ♔f8
60 ♖a3 ♔f7 61 ♖d3 ♔g6**

**62 ♔f4 ♖c4 63 ♖d2 ♖a4 64 ♖d1 ♗b3**

65 ♖d2 ♗c2 66 ♔e3 ♖a3+ 67 ♔e2 ♖xg3 68 ♖xc2 f4

69 ♖c3 ♖g2+ 70 ♔d3 ♔f5 71 ♖c8 ♖g3+ 72 ♔c4 ♖a3

73 ♗b2 ♖a2 74 ♗c3 ♔e4 75 ♔b3 ♖e2 76 ♖e8 f3 77 ♖xe6 g3 78 ♖f6 g2 79 ♖g6 f2

White resigns.

## (36) Barendregt,J – Bronstein,D
### European Team Championship, Hamburg, 1965
*[C00] French Defence*

(The time taken for each move is given in brackets)

1 e4 (0) e6 (2) 2 ♘f3 (2) d5 (3) 3 e5 (0) c5 (1) 4 b4 (3) cxb4 (9) 5 d4 (0) ♗d7 (1) 6 ♗d3 (5) ♘e7 (5) 7 a3 (3) ♘bc6 (1) 8 axb4 (4) ♘xb4 (1) 9 ♗e2 (1) ♘f5 (6) 10 c3 (1) ♘c6 (1)

11 h4 (3) a6 (3) 12 g4 (3) ♘fe7 (0) 13 h5 (1) h6 (4) 14 ♘h4 (5) ♘a7 (1) 15 f4 (8) ♘ec8 (7) 16 g5 (10) ♘b6 (2) 17 ♗d3 (12) ♗b5 (4) 18 ♗c2 (2) ♗e7 (1) 19 ♕g4 (1) ♕d7 (2) 20 f5 (3)

20...hxg5 (5) 21 fxe6 (3) ♕xe6 (1) 22 ♘f5 (23) ♔d7 (1) 23 ♗xg5 (0) f6 (3) 24 ♗h4 (3)

24...♗f8 (13) 25 ♘e3 (23) ♕xg4 (3) 26 ♘xg4 (0) ♖xh5 (7) 27 ♗g6 (3) ♖h8 (2) (D)

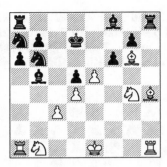

**28 exf6** (3) **gxf6** (1) **29 ♘xf6+** (3) **♔c7** (4) **30 ♘a3** (3) **♗c6** (5)

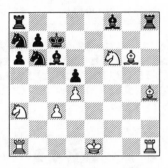

**31 c4** (5) **♗b4+** (2) **32 ♔f2** (2) **dxc4** (2) **33 d5** (1) **♗c5+** (1) **34 ♔e1** (0) **♘xd5** (3) **35 ♘e4** (5) **♗b4+** (1) **36 ♔f2** (0) **♖af8+** (1) **37 ♔g1** (0) **♘f4** (1) **38 ♗g3** (1)

**38...♖hg8** (5) White resigns.

**Total time used:**
White 2.25
Black 1.55
(see Time Graph on the next page)

## (37) Kavalek,L – Bronstein,D
Asztalos Memorial Tournament,
Szombathely, 1966
*[B16] Caro-Kann Defence*

**1 e4 c6 2 d4 d5 3 ♘c3 dxe4 4 ♘xe4 ♘f6 5 ♘xf6+ gxf6 6 ♗e2 ♗f5 7 ♘f3 ♘d7 8 0-0 e6 9 c4 ♗g6 10 d5 e5 11 ♘d2 ♕c7 12 ♘b3 ♗d6**

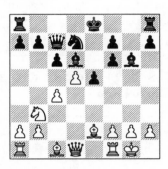

**13 ♗h6 c5 14 h4 f5 15 f4**

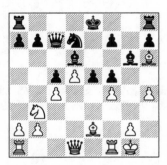

**15...e4 16 h5 f6 17 g3 0-0-0 18 ♖f2 ♗e8 19 ♗f1 ♖g8 20 ♔h2**

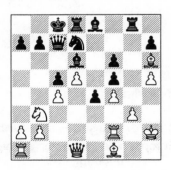

# Time Graph Barendregt,J-Bronstein,D

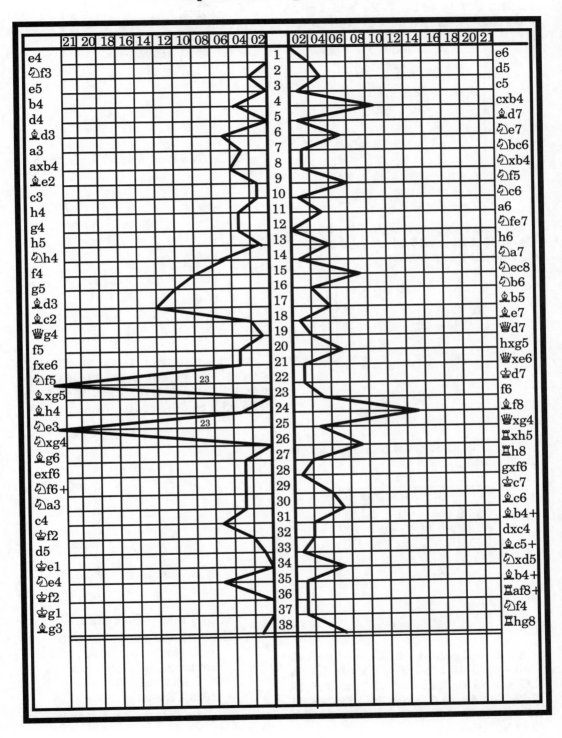

| White | Move | Black |
|-------|------|-------|
| e4 | 1 | e6 |
| ♘f3 | 2 | d5 |
| e5 | 3 | c5 |
| b4 | 4 | cxb4 |
| d4 | 5 | ♗d7 |
| ♗d3 | 6 | ♘e7 |
| a3 | 7 | ♘bc6 |
| axb4 | 8 | ♘xb4 |
| ♗e2 | 9 | ♘f5 |
| c3 | 10 | ♘c6 |
| h4 | 11 | a6 |
| g4 | 12 | ♘fe7 |
| h5 | 13 | h6 |
| ♘h4 | 14 | ♘a7 |
| f4 | 15 | ♘ec8 |
| g5 | 16 | ♘b6 |
| ♗d3 | 17 | ♗b5 |
| ♗c2 | 18 | ♗e7 |
| ♕g4 | 19 | ♕d7 |
| f5 | 20 | hxg5 |
| fxe6 | 21 | ♕xe6 |
| ♘f5 | 22 | ♔d7 |
| ♗xg5 | 23 | f6 |
| ♗h4 | 24 | ♗f8 |
| ♘e3 | 25 | ♕xg4 |
| ♘xg4 | 26 | ♖xh5 |
| ♗g6 | 27 | ♖h8 |
| exf6 | 28 | gxf6 |
| ♘f6+ | 29 | ♔c7 |
| ♘a3 | 30 | ♗c6 |
| c4 | 31 | ♗b4+ |
| ♔f2 | 32 | dxc4 |
| d5 | 33 | ♗c5+ |
| ♔e1 | 34 | ♘xd5 |
| ♘e4 | 35 | ♗b4+ |
| ♔f2 | 36 | ♖af8+ |
| ♔g1 | 37 | ♘f4 |
| ♗g3 | 38 | ♖hg8 |

20...♖g4 21 ♗e2 ♗xh5 22 ♔h1 ♘b6
23 ♖h2 ♕f7 24 ♕f1 ♘d7 25 ♕h3 ♗g6 26
♘d2 ♖e8 27 ♘f1 e3 28 ♖e1 ♕g8 29 ♗f3
♗f7

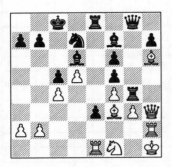

30 ♗xg4 fxg4 31 ♕g2 ♘b6 32 ♕c2
♘xc4 33 ♔g1 ♗xd5 34 b3 ♘b6 35 ♖xe3
♔c7 36 ♖d2 ♔c6 37 ♕f5

37...c4 38 bxc4 ♗xc4 39 ♕xf6 ♘d5 40
♖xd5 ♔xd5

Adjourned position. 41 ♖e5+ ♗xe5 42
♘e3+ ♔c5 43 fxe5 ♕e6 44 ♕f4 b5 45
♗f8+ ♔b6 46 ♗d6 ♔a6 47 ♘c2 ♕g6 48
♕d2 ♕e4 49 ♗c5 ♕xe5 50 ♗f2 ♖c8 51
a4 ♔b7 52 ♕a5 ♖a8 53 ♘d4 ♕c7 54 ♕e1
♕d7 55 axb5 (D)

55...♖e8 56 ♕a1 ♔a8 57 ♘c6 ♗xb5 58
♘xa7

58...♗a4 59 ♕c3 ♕d1+ 60 ♔h2 ♖f8
61 ♕c5 ♕f3 62 ♗g1 ♕e2+ 63 ♔h1 ♕e4+
64 ♔h2 ♕c2+ 65 ♕xc2 ♗xc2 66 ♘b5 ♗e4
67 ♘c3 ♗c6 68 ♘e2 ♖f1 White resigns.

## (38) Tal,M – Bronstein,D
Experimental game: 'Thinking
aloud for the audience',
Central House of Literature,
Moscow, 1966
*[B10] Caro-Kann Defence*

1 e4 c6 2 d3 e5 3 f4 d5 4 ♘f3 dxe4 5
♘xe5 (D)

**5...♕h4+ 6 g3 ♕e7 7 d4 ♘h6 8 ♗c4 ♗e6**

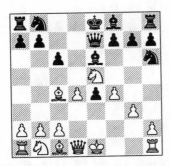

**9 d5 cxd5 10 ♗xd5 f6 11 ♘c4 ♘c6 12 ♘e3 ♖d8 13 c4 ♕f7 14 ♘c3 ♗c5**

**15 ♘xe4 ♗d4 16 f5 ♗xd5 17 ♘xd5**

♘xf5 18 ♕g4 ♘d6 19 ♘xd6+ ♖xd6 20 ♕c8+ ♖d8 21 ♘c7+ ♔e7 22 ♕xb7 ♕xc4 23 ♗f4 ♘e5 24 ♖c1

**24...♘d3+ 25 ♔d2 ♘xc1 26 ♘d5++**

**26...♔e6 27 ♕e7+ ♔xd5 28 ♖xc1**

**28...♗e3+ 29 ♗xe3 ♔c6+ 30 ♔e1 ♕xc1+ White resigns.**

## (39) Moiseyev,O – Bronstein,D
### Moscow Championship, 1968
*[A48] Torre Attack*

**1 d4 ♘f6 2 ♘f3 g6 3 ♗g5 ♗g7 4 ♘bd2 d6 5 e3 0-0 6 ♗d3 ♘bd7 7 0-0 h6 8 ♗h4 e5 9 c3 ♕e8 10 ♘e1 (D)**

**10...d5 11 ♘b3 a5 12 a4 ♘b6 13 ♘c5**

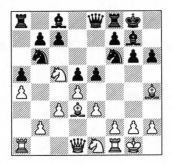

**13...♘fd7 14 ♕b3 ♘xc5 15 dxc5**

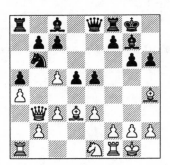

**15...♘c4 16 ♗xc4 dxc4 17 ♕xc4 ♗e6
18 ♕e2 ♕c6 19 e4 ♕xc5 20 ♘d3 ♕c6 21
♕e3 ♖fe8 22 ♘c5 ♗c8 23 ♘b3 b6**

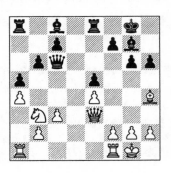

**24 ♘d2 ♗f8 25 b3 ♗b7 26 g4 g5 27
♗g3 ♖ad8 28 ♖fd1 ♕d7 29 h3 ♗c5 30
♕e1 ♕d3 31 ♘f1 ♕f3 White resigns.**

## (40) Bronstein,D – Benkö,P
International Tournament,
Monte Carlo, 1969
*[B09] Pirc Defence*

**1 e4 d6 2 d4 ♘f6 3 ♘c3 g6 4 f4 ♗g7 5 e5
dxe5 6 dxe5 ♕xd1+ 7 ♔xd1 ♘g4 8 ♔e1
c6**

**9 h3 ♘h6 10 g4 f6 11 exf6 exf6 12
♗c4 ♘f7 13 ♖h2 ♘d6 14 ♗b3 ♔d8**

**15 f5 ♖e8+ 16 ♔f1 g5**

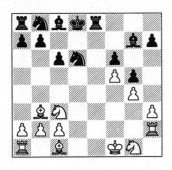

17 h4 h6 18 ♘f3 ♘d7 19 ♗d2 ♔c7 20
♖e1 b6 21 ♖xe8 ♘xe8 22 ♗e1 ♗a6+ 23
♔g1 ♗f8 24 ♗g3+ ♗d6 25 ♗xd6+ ♘xd6
26 hxg5 hxg5 27 ♖h7 ♖e8 28 ♗e6 ♗c8
29 ♘d4 a6 30 a4 ♖d8

31 ♗d5 ♖e8 32 ♗xc6 ♘c4 33 ♗d5
♘e3 34 ♗e6 ♘xg4 35 ♘e4 ♖d8 36 c4
♘ge5 37 ♘xf6 ♔d6 38 ♘e4+ ♔c7 39
♗d5 ♖e8 40 ♘e6+ ♔b8 41 ♘d6 ♖g8 42
b3 ♘f6 43 ♖c7 ♘xd5 44 cxd5 Black resigns.

## (41) Honfi,K – Bronstein,D
International Tournament,
Monte Carlo, 1969
*[C16] French Defence*

1 e4 e6 2 d4 d5 3 ♘c3 ♗b4 4 e5 b6 5
♕g4 ♗f8 6 ♗g5 ♕d7 7 ♗b5

7...♘c6 8 ♘f3 ♗b7 9 0-0-0 h6 10 ♗f4
a6 11 ♗e2 0-0-0 12 h4 h5 13 ♕h3 f6 14
g4 hxg4 15 ♕xg4 ♘h6 16 ♕h3 ♗b4 17
♘b1 ♕f7 18 exf6 gxf6 19 c3 ♗f8 20
♘bd2 ♖e8 21 ♕f1 *(D)*
21...e5 22 ♗xh6 ♗xh6 23 ♗xa6 e4 24
♘g1 ♖hg8 25 ♔b1 ♕g6 26 ♘b3 ♘b8 27
♕h3+ f5 28 ♗xb7+ ♔xb7 29 ♘e2 f4 30

♖dg1 ♕h5 31 ♘bc1 ♘c6 32 ♖f1 ♘e7 33
f3 ♘f5 34 fxe4 ♖xe4 35 ♖hg1 ♖xg1 36
♘xg1 ♘g3 37 ♖f2 ♖e3 38 ♕g2

38...♕f5+ 39 ♖c2 ♘e4 40 a3 f3 White
resigns.
(2nd brilliancy prize)

## (42) Fischer,R – Bronstein,D
Unofficial World Championship
5-minute blitz chess
Herceg Novi, 1970
*[C16] French Defence*

1 e4 e6 2 d4 d5 3 ♘c3 ♗b4 4 e5 b6 5 a3
♗f8 6 f4 ♘c6 7 ♘f3 ♘h6 8 ♗d3 ♘f5 9
♘e2 h5 10 g3 ♗b7 11 c3 ♕d7 12 ♕c2 0-0-0
13 b4 f6 14 ♗d2 ♔b8 15 0-0 ♘fe7 16 ♖fb1

**16...h4 17 ♘xh4 g5 18 fxg5 fxe5**

**19 ♖f1 exd4 20 cxd4 ♗g7 21 ♗c3 e5 22 ♖f7 exd4 23 ♖xg7 ♖xh4 24 gxh4 ♕g4+ 25 ♘g3 dxc3 26 ♕xc3 d4 27 ♕d2**

**27...♘e5 28 ♖f1 ♘d5 29 ♗f5 ♘f3+ 30 ♖xf3 ♕xf3**

**31 ♗e4 ♕xa3 32 ♕xd4 ♕c1+ 33 ♔f2 ♖f8+ 34 ♘f5 ♘c3 35 ♗xb7 ♖xf5+ 36 ♗f3 ♘d5 37 ♖g8+ ♔b7 38 ♕e4 ♕d2+ 39 ♔g3 c6 (D)**

**40 ♕xf5 ♕e1+ 41 ♔g4 ♘e3+ 42 ♔f4 ♘xf5 43 ♔xf5 ♕xb4 44 ♖g7+ ♔c8 45 ♗e4 ♕f8+ 46 ♔g6 ♕e8+ 47 ♔f5 ♕f8+ Draw agreed.**

## (43) Janosević,D – Bronstein,D
International Tournament,
Sarajevo, 1971
*[C09] French Defence*

**1 e4 e6 2 d4 d5 3 ♘d2 c5 4 exd5 exd5 5 ♘gf3 ♘c6 6 ♗b5 ♗d6 7 0-0 cxd4 8 ♘b3 ♘ge7 9 ♘bxd4 0-0 10 ♗e3 ♗g4 11 h3 ♗h5 12 ♗d3**

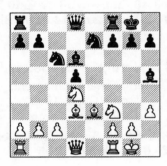

**12...♘xd4 13 ♗xd4 ♘c6 14 c3 ♘xd4 15 cxd4 ♕f6 16 g4 ♗g6 17 ♖e1**

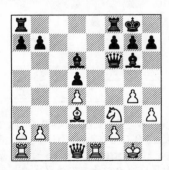

**17...♕f4 18 ♗xg6 fxg6 19 ♖e3 h5 20 ♕b3 hxg4 21 ♕xd5+ ♔h7 22 hxg4 ♕xg4+ 23 ♔f1 (D)**

**23...♗f4 24 ♘e5 ♕h5 25 ♖ae1 ♗xe3 26 ♖xe3**

**26...♖f4 27 ♕e6 ♖af8 28 ♖h3 ♖xf2+ 29 ♔g1 ♖f1+ 30 ♔g2 ♖8f2+ 31 ♔g3 ♖f3+ 32 ♘xf3 ♖xf3+ 33 ♔g2 ♕xh3+ 34 ♕xh3+ ♖xh3 35 ♔xh3 ♔g8** White resigns.

## (44) Bronstein,D – Gheorghiu,F
International Tournament,
Las Palmas, 1972
*[D94] Grünfeld Defence*

**1 d4 ♘f6 2 c4 g6 3 ♘c3 d5**

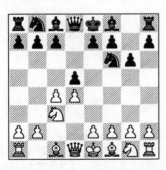

**4 ♘f3 ♗g7 5 e3 0-0 6 ♗d2 c6 7 ♖c1 ♗e6** (D)

**8 cxd5 ♘xd5 9 ♗e2 ♘d7 10 0-0 ♘7f6**

**11 ♘a4 ♘e4 12 ♗d3 ♘xd2 13 ♕xd2 ♗g4**

**14 ♘e5 ♗xe5 15 dxe5 ♕c7 16 h3 ♗e6 17 f4 ♖ad8**

**18 ♘c5 ♗c8 19 e4 b6**

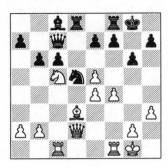

**20 ♘a6 ♗xa6 21 ♗xa6 ♘f6 22 ♕e3 ♘d7**

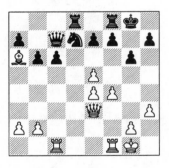

**23 b4 ♘b8 24 ♗c4 ♕d7 25 ♔h2 ♕d4 26 ♕e1 e6**

**27 ♗b3 ♘a6 28 a3 c5 29 ♕e2 ♕d3 30 ♗c4 ♕xe2 31 ♗xe2 ♘c7 32 bxc5 ♖d2 33 cxb6 axb6** *(D)*

**34 ♖fe1 ♖d7 35 ♖c6 ♖a8 36 ♖ec1 ♖a7 37 ♖d6 ♖e7 38 ♖xb6 ♖xa3 39 ♖b7 ♘d5 40 ♖b8+** Black resigns.

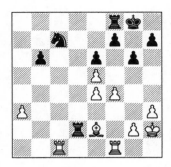

**(45) Bronstein,D – Kapengut,V**
40th USSR Championship,
Baku, 1972
*[E90] King's Indian Defence*

**1 c4 ♘f6 2 ♘f3 g6 3 ♘c3 ♗g7 4 e4 0-0 5 d4 d6 6 h3 e5 7 d5 ♘a6 8 ♗g5 h6 9 ♗e3 ♘c5 10 ♘d2 ♘h7 11 b4 ♘a6 12 a3 f5 13 ♘b3 ♘f6**

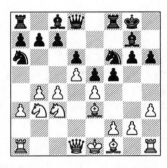

**14 c5 ♘xe4 15 ♘xe4 fxe4 16 ♗c4 ♕e8**

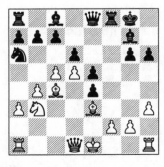

**17 c6 bxc6 18 dxc6+ ♗e6 19 ♗xe6+ ♕xe6 20 ♘a5 d5 21 ♕b3 ♖f6 22 0-0 ♖d8 23 ♘b7 ♖e8 24 b5 d4 25 ♕xe6+ ♖exe6**

**26 ♗d2 ♗f8**

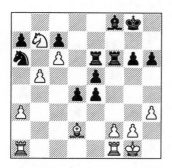

**27 ♖fc1 ♘b8 28 ♘c5 ♗xc5 29 ♖xc5 ♖f5 30 ♖e1 ♖ef6 31 ♖xe4 ♖xf2 32 ♗xh6 d3**

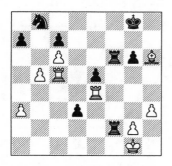

**33 ♖d5 ♖e2 34 ♖exe5 ♘xc6 35 bxc6 ♖xe5 36 ♖xe5 ♖xc6 37 ♗e3 ♖c3 38 ♔f2 ♔f7 39 a4 ♖c2+ 40 ♔f3 ♔f6 41 ♖d5** Black resigns.

## (46) Bronstein,D – Panno,O
Interzonal Tournament,
Petropolis, 1973
*[C65] Spanish Opening*

**1 e4 e5 2 ♘f3 ♘c6 3 ♗b5 ♘f6 4 ♕e2 ♗e7 5 c3 d6 6 d4 ♗d7 7 d5 ♘b8 8 ♗d3**

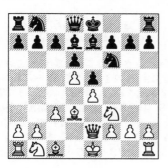

**8...c6 9 c4 ♘a6 10 ♘c3 0-0 11 h3 ♘c5 12 ♗c2 cxd5 13 cxd5 ♕c7 14 ♗d2 g6**

**15 b4 ♘a6 16 a3 ♘h5 17 g3 ♖ac8 18 ♗b3 ♔h8**

**19 0-0-0 b5 20 ♔b2 ♕b7 21 ♗h6 ♖fd8 22 ♕d2 ♘b8 23 g4 ♘f6 24 ♗g5 ♗e8 25 ♕e2 ♘bd7 26 ♕xb5 ♕c7 27 ♖c1 ♘b6 28 ♕a6 ♕d7 29 ♖he1 ♔g7 30 ♗e3 ♖b8 31 ♘d2**

**31...h5 32 g5 ♘h7 33 h4 f6 34 gxf6+♗xf6 35 ♖h1 ♕e7 36 ♘f3 ♖d7 37 ♘b5 ♖db7 38 ♘c3 ♗d7 39 ♔a2 ♗g4 40 ♘h2 ♗d7** *(D)*

Adjourned position. **41 ♘f3 ♗g4 42 ♘d2 ♗xh4 43 ♗c2 ♗g5 44 ♘b3 ♗xe3 45 fxe3**

**Rc7 46 Ld3 Lc8 47 Wa5 a6**

**48 Lxa6 Ra7 49 b5 Nc4 50 Wb4 Nxa3**
**51 Kxa3 Lxa6**

**52 b6 Raa8 53 Na4 Nf6 54 Na5 Rc8**
**55 Rc6 Kh6**

**56 Rxd6 Rc2 57 Rc6 Ra2+ 58 Kb3**
**Wxb4+ 59 Kxb4 Nxe4**

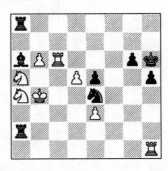

**60 Rg1 Ng5 61 Rc7 Rd8 62 Rd1 Le2**
**63 Rb1 Rxd5 64 Nc5 Ne6**

**65 b7 Rxa5 66 Kxa5 Nxc7 67 b8W**
**Rxc5+ 68 Kb6 Ne6**

**69 We8 Lg4 70 Rg1 Rd5 71 e4 Rd6+**
**72 Ka5 Ra6+ 73 Kb4 Rb6+ 74 Kc3 Kg5**
**75 We7+ Kf4 76 Wf6+ Kxe4 77 Re1+**
**Kd5 78 Rxe5+ Kd6 79 Ra5 Rc6+ 80**
**Kd2 Lf5 81 We5+ Kd7 82 Rd5+ Ke7**
**83 Ra5 Rd6+ 84 Ke1 Rd8** *(D)*
  **85 Ke2 Ld3+ 86 Ke3 Lf5 87 Ra3**

**97 ♔g3 ♖d8 98 ♕c7+ ♖d7 99 ♕c4+ ♗e6 100 ♕b4 ♖e7**

**101 ♔h4 ♖e8 102 ♔g5 ♗f5**

**103 ♔h6 ♖e7 104 ♕b3+ ♗e6 105 ♕b2**

Black resigns.

## (47) Bronstein,D – Reshevsky,S
### Interzonal Tournament, Petropolis, 1973
*[C50] Hungarian Defence*

1 e4 e5 2 ♘f3 ♘c6 3 ♗c4 d6 4 d4 ♗e7 5 dxe5 dxe5 6 ♗d5 ♗d6 7 ♘g5 ♘h6 8 c3 ♘e7 9 ♗b3 ♘g6 10 g3 ♕e7 11 h3 ♗d7 *(D)* 12 ♕e2 0-0-0 13 ♘f3 ♗c5 14 ♗e3 ♔b8

**♖d7 88 ♕h8 ♔f7**

**89 ♖a8 ♖c7 90 ♔f2 ♔e7 91 ♕e5 ♔f7 92 ♖h8 ♖c2+ 93 ♔e3 ♘f8**

**94 ♕d5+ ♘e6 95 ♕e5 ♘f8 96 ♔f4 ♖c8**

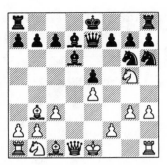

**15 ᐃbd2 ᵫxe3 16 ᐌxe3 f5 17 0-0-0 f4
18 ᐌe2 ᐃf7**

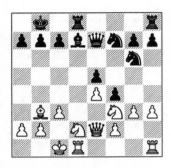

**19 h4 h5 20 ᐃh2 ᵫe6 21 ᐃc4 ᐌc5 22
ᖏxd8+ ᐃxd8 23 ᖏd1 ᐃf7 24 ᐃd2 ᐌc6**

**25 ᐃdf3 a6 26 ᐌc2 ᵫxb3 27 axb3 ᖏf8**

**28 ᐌe2 ᐌe6 29 ᐃd2 ᖏh8 30 ᐃc4 fxg3
31 fxg3 ᐃe7 32 ᐃf1 g6 33 ᐃfe3 ᖏd8**

**34 ᖏf1 ᐃd6 35 ᐃxd6 cxd6 36 ᐌc4
ᐌh3 37 ᖏf3 ᐌh1+ 38 ᐌf1 ᐌxf1+ 39
ᖏxf1 ᗄc8**

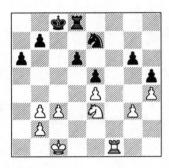

**40 ᖏf7 ᖏd7 41 ᐃc4 ᗄc7**

Adjourned position. **42 ᖏf6 ᖏd8 43 ᖏe6
ᖏd7 44 ᗄc2 ᐃc8 45 ᖏxg6 ᖏh7 46 b4 b5
47 ᐃe3 ᐃe7 48 ᖏg5 ᗄd7 49 b3 ᗄe6 50
c4 ᐃc6 51 ᗄc3 ᐃd4 52 ᐃf5 ᐃxf5 53
exf5+ ᗄf6 54 ᗄd3 bxc4+ 55 bxc4 ᖏb7
56 ᖏxh5 ᖏxb4 57 g4 d5** *(D)*
    **58 ᖏh6+ ᗄf7 59 g5 ᖏxc4 60 f6 ᖏd4+
61 ᗄc2 ᖏc4+ 62 ᗄb2 ᖏb4+ 63 ᗄa3 ᖏf4
64 ᖏh7+ ᗄe6 65 ᖏh6 ᗄf7 66 ᖏh7+ ᗄg6**

67 ♖h6+ ♔f7

12 ♗a3 ♘d4 13 0-0-0 e6 14 ♘e2 ♘b5
15 ♗e7 ♖d7

68 h5 e4 69 ♖h7+ ♔e6 70 h6 ♔f5 71
♖e7 ♔g5 72 h7 ♖f3+ 73 ♔b2 ♔xf6

16 ♗h4 exd5 17 ♘f4 ♘c7 18 ♘xd5
♘xd5 19 ♖xd5 ♖xd5 20 exd5 ♗b7

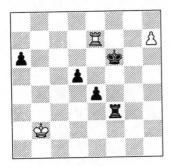

74 ♖e8 ♖h3 75 h8♕+ ♖xh8 76 ♖xh8
♔e5 77 ♔c3 d4+ 78 ♔c4 d3 79 ♔c3 a5
80 ♖e8+ ♔f4 81 ♔d2 a4 82 ♖f8+ ♔e5
83 ♔e3 ♔d5 84 ♖a8 Black resigns.

### (48) Bronstein,D – Dvoretsky,M
USSR Zonal Tournament, Vilnius 1975
*[E81] King's Indian Defence*

1 d4 ♘f6 2 c4 g6 3 ♘c3 ♗g7 4 e4 d6 5 f3
0-0 6 ♗e3 c5 7 dxc5 dxc5 8 ♕xd8 ♖xd8
9 ♗xc5 ♘c6 10 ♘d5 ♘xd5 11 cxd5 b6 *(D)*

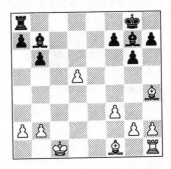

21 d6 ♗f8 22 d7 ♗h6+ 23 ♔b1 g5

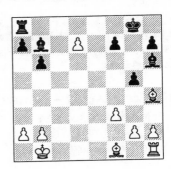

24 ♗f2 ♗c6 25 ♗e3 ♗xd7

26 ♗d3 ♖e8 27 ♗c1 ♖e6 28 ♗f5 ♖d6 29 ♗xd7 ♖xd7

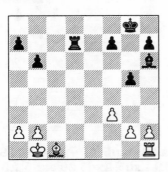

30 h4 ♖e7 31 hxg5 ♗f8 32 ♖d1 ♖e2 33 ♖d8 ♖xg2

34 ♗f4 ♔g7 35 ♗e5+ f6 36 ♗xf6+ ♔f7 37 f4 h5 38 gxh6 ♗xh6 39 ♗e5 ♖g4 40 ♖d6 ♖h4 41 ♔c2 ♔e7 42 f5 ♗f4 43 f6+ Black resigns.

## (49) Bronstein,D – Nowak,I
International Tournament,
Sandomierz, 1976
*[C00] Chigorin Attack*

1 e4 c5 2 ♘f3 e6 3 d3 ♘c6 4 g3 ♗e7 5 ♗g2 ♘f6 6 0-0 d5 7 ♕e2 b6 8 e5 ♘d7 9 c4 ♘db8 10 ♘c3 d4 11 ♘e4 h6

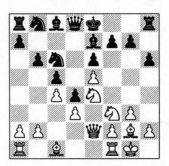

12 h4 ♗b7 13 ♗f4 ♘d7 14 h5 ♘f8 15 g4 ♘h7 16 ♗g3 ♕d7 17 ♘fd2 0-0

18 f4 f5 19 exf6 gxf6 20 f5 e5 21 ♘f3 ♘d8

22 g5 hxg5 23 ♘h2 ♘f7 24 h6 ♖ab8 25 ♕h5 ♘h8 26 ♘g4 ♗d6 27 ♖ae1 ♕d8 28 ♘exf6+ ♖xf6 29 ♗xe5 ♗xe5 30 ♖xe5 ♗xg2 *(D)*

31 ♖fe1 ♖f7 32 ♔xg2 ♔f8 33 ♔g1 ♕c7 34 ♕h2 ♖d8 35 ♖1e4 ♕c8 36 ♕h5 ♕c7 37 ♔g2 ♕c8 38 ♖e6 ♖xf5 39 ♖e7 ♘f6 40

**✎xf6 ♖xf6 41 ♕xg5**

Black resigns.

## (50) Ree,H – Bronstein,D
3rd Tungsram International
Tournament, Budapest, 1977
*[A92] Dutch Defence*

**1 d4 e6 2 c4 f5 3 g3 ✎f6 4 ♗g2 ♗e7 5 ✎f3 0-0 6 0-0 ✎e4 7 ✎bd2 ♗f6 8 ♕c2 d5 9 b3**

**9...c5 10 ♗b2 cxd4 11 ♗xd4 ✎c6 12 ♗xf6 ♕xf6 13 cxd5 exd5 14 a3 a5 15 ♕d3 ♗e6 16 e3 ♖ad8 17 ♖fd1** *(D)*

**17...♗f7 18 ✎d4 ✎e5 19 ✎xe4 fxe4 20 ♕b5 b6 21 ♖ac1 ✎d3 22 ♖c2 ♖c8 23**

**♖dd2 ♖c5 24 ♕a6 ♗e8 25 h3**

**25...♗d7 26 ♖xc5 bxc5 27 ♕xf6 ♖xf6 28 ✎c2 ♖b6 29 f3 ♗c6 30 fxe4 dxe4 31 ✎a1**

**31...a4 32 b4 cxb4 33 axb4 ♖xb4** White resigns.

## (51) Bronstein,D – Gufeld,E
3rd Paul Keres Memorial
Tournament, Tallinn, 1981
*[A48] Torre Attack*

**1 ✎f3 g6 2 d4 ✎f6 3 ♗g5 ♗g7 4 ✎bd2 d6 5 e4 h6 6 ♗h4 g5 7 ♗g3 ✎h5 8 c3 e6 9 ✎b3 ✎d7 10 ✎fd2 ✎xg3 11 hxg3 a5 12 a4 0-0 13 ♗d3 f5 14 ♕e2 ✎f6** *(D)*

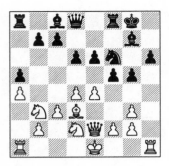

15 f4 gxf4 16 gxf4 ♗d7 17 e5 ♘d5 18
g3 ♕e8

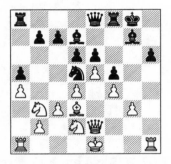

19 ♔f2 dxe5 20 dxe5 ♗xa4

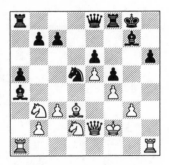

21 ♖xa4 ♕xa4 22 ♗b5 ♕a2 23 ♗d7
♖a6

24 ♖b1 ♘e7 25 ♕c4 a4 26 ♘c5 ♕xc4
27 ♘xc4 ♖a7 28 ♖d1 ♖fa8 29 ♗xe6+

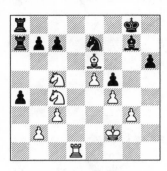

29...♔f8 30 g4 b5 31 ♘e3 fxg4 32 f5
g3+ 33 ♔g2 ♘c6 34 ♘d7+ ♔e8

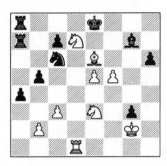

35 f6 ♗f8 36 ♘f5 ♘d8 37 f7+ ♘xf7

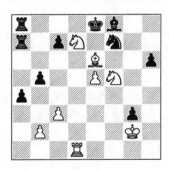

38 ♘f6 mate.

## (52) Bronstein,D – Yusupov,A
USSR Team Competition,
Veterans against Youngsters,
Moscow, 1981
*[C30] King's Gambit*

1 e4 e5 2 f4 ♘f6 3 ♘f3 ♘xe4 4 d3 ♘c5 5
fxe5 d5 6 d4 ♘e6 7 c4 ♗b4+ 8 ♗d2

&xd2+ 9 ♕xd2 c6 10 ♘c3 0-0 11 ♖c1
♘c7 12 cxd5 cxd5 13 &d3 &g4

14 ♘g5 f5 15 h3 &h5 16 0-0 &g6 17
♘b5 ♘ba6 18 ♘d6 h6 19 ♘f3 ♘e6 20
♔h1 ♖b8 21 ♘g1

21...♕g5 22 ♕f2 ♘b4 23 &b5 f4 24
♘f3 ♕e7 25 ♕d2 ♘a6 26 &d3 &h5 27
&c2 ♘ac7 28 ♕d3 g6 29 &b3 ♔h8 30
&a4 ♖g8 31 ♕d2 ♖g7 32 ♕f2 ♖f8 33 ♖c3
g5 34 ♖fc1 &g6

35 &c2 ♘e8 36 &xg6 ♖xg6 37 ♕c2
♖gg8 38 ♘c8 ♕f7 39 ♕b3 ♘6g7 40 ♘d6
♘xd6 41 exd6 ♕e6 42 ♕xb7 g4 43 hxg4
♕xg4 *(D)*
44 ♘e5 ♕g5 45 ♕e7 ♖f6 46 ♖c7 ♖e8

47 ♘f7+ ♖xf7 48 ♕xg5 Black resigns.

## (53) Bronstein,D – Psakhis,L
Moscow Open Championship, 1981
*[B20] Sicilian Defence*

1 e4 c5 2 ♘e2 d6 3 g3 ♘c6 4 &g2 g6 5 0-0
&g7 6 d3 e5

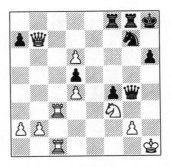

7 ♘a3 ♘ge7 8 f4 0-0 9 ♘c3 exf4 10
&xf4 &e6 11 ♕d2 d5

12 ♘ab5 d4 13 ♘d5 ♘e5 14 c4 ♘xd5
15 cxd5 &d7 16 ♘a3 b5 17 ♖ac1 ♕b6
18 h3 a5 19 g4 ♖ac8 20 ♔h1 a4 21 ♖cd1
f5 22 gxf5 gxf5 *(D)*
23 ♘c2 fxe4 24 &xe4 ♘g6 25 &g3
♖xf1+ 26 ♖xf1 &xh3 27 ♖f2 c4 28 ♕g5

**&d7 29 d6 ♕c5**

**30 &d5+ ♔h8 31 dxc4 bxc4 32 a3 h6 33 ♕h5 ♘e5 34 ♘b4 ♕xd6**

**35 ♖f7 ♖e8 36 &xc4 &c6+ 37 ♔h2 &d7 38 ♘d3 &g4 39 ♕h4 ♕g6**

**40 ♘xe5 ♖xe5 41 ♕d8+ ♔h7 42 &xe5** Black resigns.

## (54) Bronstein,D – Sokolov,A

Moscow Open Championship, dedicated to 60 years of the Soviet Union, 1982
*[A46] London System*

**1 d4 ♘f6 2 ♘f3 e6 3 c3 b6 4 &f4 &b7 5 ♘bd2 &e7 6 h3 0-0 7 e3 c5 8 &d3 cxd4 9 exd4 d6 10 0-0 ♘bd7**

**11 ♘c4 ♕c7 12 ♖e1 ♖fe8 13 &g3 ♘f8 14 ♘fd2 &c6 15 a4 ♘g6 16 ♘e3 ♕b7 17 b4 ♖ac8**

**18 c4 a5 19 b5 &d7 20 &e2 e5 21 ♘b3 ♕b8 22 ♖c1 ♘e4**

**23 ♗g4 ♗xg4 24 ♕xg4 ♘xg3 25 ♕xg3 ♗f8 26 ♕f3 ♖e6 27 ♖cd1 ♕a7 28 ♕g4 ♖ce8**

**29 d5 ♖f6 30 ♘d2 ♖f4 31 ♕e2 ♖d4 32 g3**

**32...♘f4 33 gxf4 exf4 34 ♕g4 h5 35 ♕h4 g6**

**36 ♘g4 ♖xe1+ 37 ♖xe1 hxg4 38 ♘e4 ♖xe4 39 ♖xe4 gxh3** *(D)*

**40 ♕d8 f5 41 ♖e8 ♕f7 42 ♖e6 ♔g7 43 ♔h2 f3 44 ♕g5 ♔h7 45 ♔xh3** Black resigns.

## (55) Bronstein,D − Kupreichik,V
51st USSR Championship, Semi-Final, Minsk, 1983
*[E90] King's Indian Defence*

**1 ♘f3 ♘f6 2 c4 d6 3 ♘c3 g6 4 d4 ♗g7 5 e4 0-0 6 h3 e5 7 d5 ♘a6 8 ♗g5 h6 9 ♗e3 ♕e8**

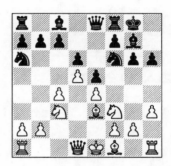

**10 g4 ♗d7 11 ♗d3 c6 12 ♘d2 ♘c5 13 ♗c2 a5 14 a3 cxd5 15 cxd5 ♖c8**

**16 a4 ♕d8 17 ♕e2 ♘e8 18 h4 f5 19 gxf5 gxf5 20 exf5 ♗xf5 21 ♗xf5 ♖xf5 22 ♗xc5 ♖xc5 23 ♘de4 ♖c8** *(D)*

**24 0-0-0 ♖f4 25 h5 ♘f6 26 ♔b1 ♕d7**

**27 f3 ♕f5 28 ♔a2**

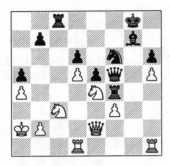

**28...♖xc3 29 ♘xc3 ♖b4**

**30 ♕d3 e4 31 fxe4 ♘xe4**

**32 ♘xe4 ♖xa4+ 33 ♔b1 ♖xe4 34 ♖hg1**

**♔h8 35 ♕c2 ♕e5 36 ♕c8+ ♕e8 37 ♖c1 b6 38 ♖c7 ♗f8**

**39 ♕f5 ♖e1+ 40 ♖xe1 ♕xe1+ 41 ♔a2**
Black resigns.

## (56) Conquest,S – Bronstein,D
### Young Masters Tournament,
### London, 1989
*[B14] Caro-Kann Defence*

**1 e4 c6 2 c4 d5 3 cxd5 cxd5 4 exd5 ♘f6
5 ♘c3 g6 6 ♗c4 ♗g7 7 ♘ge2 0-0 8 0-0
♘a6 9 d4 ♘c7 10 ♘f4 b6 11 a4 ♗b7 12
♕b3**

**12...♖b8 13 ♗e3 a6 14 ♖fc1**

**14...g5 15 ②fe2 h6 16 h4**

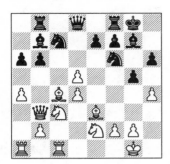

**16...b5 17 axb5 axb5 18 ②d3 b4 19 hxg5 hxg5 20 ②a4 ②cxd5 21 ②xg5 ♕d6 22 ②g3 ②g4 23 ②e2**

**23...②xf2 24 ♕f3 ②xd4 25 ②f5 ②g4+ 26 ♔f1 ②h2+ White resigns.**

### (57) Bronstein,D – Farago,I
International Tournament, Tåstrup 1990
*[C18] French Defence*

**1 e4 e6 2 d4 d5 3 ②c3 ②b4 4 e5 c5 5 a3 ②xc3+ 6 bxc3 ②e7 7 ♕g4 0-0**

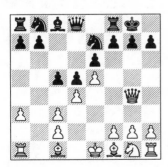

**8 ②d3 f5 9 exf6 ♖xf6** (D)

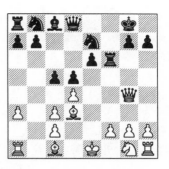

**10 ♕h5 h6 11 g4 c4**

**12 g5 g6 13 ♕d1 ♖f7**

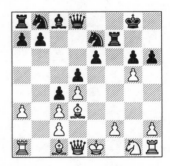

**14 ②xg6 ②xg6 15 ♕h5 ②h8**

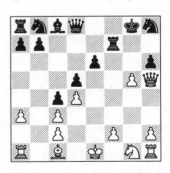

**16 ②h3 e5 17 ♖g1 ②xh3** (D)

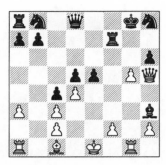

**18 gxh6+ ⌗f8 19 h7**

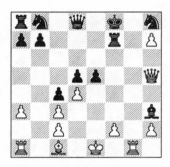

**19...♕c8 20 ♖g8+ ♚e7 21 ♖xc8 ♗xc8
22 ♕xe5+ ♗e6 23 ♕xh8**

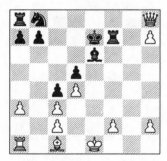

Black resigns.

## (58) Bronstein,D – Petursson,M

International Open Tournament,
Reykjavik, 1990
*[E12] Queen's Indian Defence*

**1 d4 ♘f6 2 c4 e6 3 ♘f3 b6 4 ♘c3 ♗b7 5
a3 d5 6 cxd5 ♘xd5 7 ♕c2 ♘xc3 8 bxc3
♗e7 9 e4 0-0 10 ♗d3 c5 11 0-0 ♕c8 12
♕e2 ♗a6 13 d5 ♗xd3 14 ♕xd3 c4 15
♕c2 exd5 16 exd5 ♗f6** *(D)*
**17 ♘g5 ♗xg5 18 ♗xg5 f6 19 ♗f4 ♘d7 20**

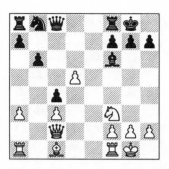

**♕a4 ♖d8 21 ♖ad1 a6 22 ♕b4 b5 23 ♕a5
♘c5**

**24 d6 ♖d7 25 ♗g3 ♕c6 26 ♖fe1 ♖ad8**

**27 a4 ♘xa4 28 ♖d4 ♕b6 29 ♕b4 ♕c5
30 ♕a5 ♕c8 31 h4 ♘c5**

**32 ♕a2 ♖e8 33 ♖xe8+ ♕xe8 34 ♖d5**

**34...♘a4 35 ♕d2 ♕e4 36 f3 ♕e6 37 ♖d4**

**37...♘c5 38 ♕a2 ♔f7 39 ♔h2 h5 40 ♕c2**

**40...g6 41 ♕a2 ♕e3 42 ♕c2 ♘e6 43 ♖d1**

**43...♘g7 44 ♕a2 ♘f5 45 ♕xa6 ♕c5 46 ♗f4 ♘xh4**

**47 ♕a8 ♘f5**

**48 ♕h8 g5 49 ♕xh5+ ♔g7**

**50 ♕e8 ♕c6 51 ♖e1 ♕b7 52 ♗xg5 ♘xd6 53 ♗xf6+ Black resigns.**

## (59) Bronstein,D – Gurevich,D
National Open Tournament,
Las Vegas, 1993
*[A70] Modern Benoni Defence*

**1 d4 ♘f6 2 c4 e6 3 ♘f3 c5 4 d5 exd5 5 cxd5 d6 6 ♘c3 g6 7 e4 ♗g7 8 h3 0-0 9 ♗d3 ♗d7 (D)**

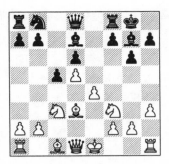

**10 ♗f4 ♖e8 11 ♘d2 b5 12 0-0 c4 13 ♗c2 b4**

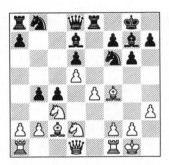

**14 ♘e2 c3 15 bxc3 bxc3 16 ♘c4 ♘xe4**

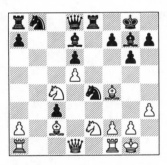

**17 ♘g3 ♕h4 18 ♘xe4 ♕xf4 19 g3 ♕h6 20 h4 ♘a6 21 ♘cxd6 ♖f8**

**22 ♗b3 ♘b4 23 ♖c1 ♖ad8 24 a3 ♗h3 25 axb4 ♗xf1**

**26 ♘xf7 ♖xf7 27 d6 ♗e2 28 ♗xf7+ ♔h8 29 ♕e1 ♗d4 30 ♘g5 ♕h5**

**31 ♖c2 ♕g4 32 ♔h2 ♗a6 33 ♗e6 ♕h5 34 ♘f7+ ♔g7 35 ♘xd8 ♕f3 36 ♗h3 ♗d3 37 ♘e6+ Black resigns.**

**(60) de Firmian,N – Bronstein,D**
3rd Oviedo Open Active Chess
Tournament (45 minutes each), 1993
*[C16] French Defence*

**1 e4 e6 2 d4 d5 3 ♘c3 ♗b4**

**4 e5 b6 5 a3 ♗f8 6 ♗b5+ ♗d7 7 ♗d3**

c5 8 ♘f3 ♘c6 9 0-0 ♘ge7

10 ♘b5 ♘g6 11 c3 c4 12 ♗xg6 hxg6

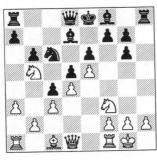

13 ♗g5 f6 14 exf6 gxf6 15 ♗f4 ♖c8

16 ♘d6+ ♗xd6 17 ♗xd6

17...♔f7 18 ♖e1 g5 19 h3 ♘e7 20 ♗h2 ♘f5 21 g4

21...♖xh3 22 gxf5 exf5 23 ♕e2 f4 24 ♘d2 ♗f5 25 f3

25...♕h8 26 ♕e7+ ♔g6 27 ♖e2 ♕h4 28 ♖g2

28...♖h8 29 ♕e2 ♖g3 30 ♘f1 ♗d3 31 ♘xg3 ♗xe2 32 ♘xe2 ♔f7 33 ♖f1 ♖e8 34 ♔h1 ♖e3 35 ♘g1 ♕h7 36 ♖d2 ♔e6 37 ♔g2 ♔d7 38 ♖ff2 f5 39 ♖de2 ♕h4 40 ♔f1 ♕h5 41 ♔e1 b5 42 ♔d2 ♖d3+ ♔c2 ♕h4 44 ♖g2 ♖e3 45 ♔d2 ♖xe2+ 46 ♘xe2

♕h3 47 ♖f2

♖f1 fxe2 53 ♖e1 f4 54 ♗f2 f3 55 ♖g1

47...a5 48 ♗g1 ♕h1 49 ♔c2

55...♕f4+ 56 ♔c2 ♕h2

49...g4 50 fxg4 ♕e4+ 51 ♔c1 f3 52

**White resigns.**

# 70

On the 19th of February 1994 David Bronstein celebrated his 70th birthday with his dear friends in Iceland. A milestone? By most standards, yes! By his standards, no! He will have an 80th birthday and then a 90th. In fact he will live for ever! He will live on through thousands and thousands of beautiful chess games. In the centuries to come his name will be pronounced with all the respect it deserves, just as we today respectfully mention players like Philidor, Morphy, Anderssen, Lasker, Capablanca and Alekhine, etc. (see footnote on page 272).

In the next century people will realise that Bronstein's way of creating chess is an art form of spiritual beauty. His games will be acknowledged as an integral feature in the life of modern chess society and he will be accepted as one of the most important leaders of chess and the most important bearer of chess culture. David Bronstein, a brilliant, diverse and unique chess artist ...

David's parents, Esther-Molka Duwid Aptaker and Iohonon Boruch Bronstein, both born in 1895, married in 1921. It must have taken them some time to adjust to their new way of life as David, who was to be their only child, was born three years later, exactly 29 days after Lenin died, on the 19th of February 1924 in a little town in the Ukraine called Byelaya Tserkov.

By the way, let's answer a question that arises quite often right here and now: Is the Bronstein family related to Lev Davidovich Trotsky (his communist name), whose 'non-Russian' name was also Bronstein? The answer is: NO ..., unless proven to the contrary! When David was in South America in 1974 a man walked up to David and introduced himself as a nephew of Lev Davidovich, wanting to know if they were related. However, they were unable to establish a link to one another.

From 1915 to 1918 Iohonon Bronstein was a soldier in the frontline of the Russian army where he was subjected to mustard gas when the Germans used this forbidden weapon. It had lasting effects on him and contributed to his frail health. In 1919 he abandoned his Zionist views, joined the Ukrainian Communist Party and helped create the very system that later put him in jail.

Bronstein's father was the manager of a flour mill and, at the age of 8, already a local draughts champion. Father and mother Bronstein occasionally played draughts together but, as soon as Mrs Bronstein knew that she was pregnant, she and her husband started playing draughts every day after work, sometimes deep into the night. Mother Bronstein's theory was that she could influence her unborn child. Of course she was way ahead of her time as only in the last 20 years or so has this theory been proven correct! It was obvious to David's parents that he was a bright child because they arranged for private tuition. That is why David could already read and write at the age of 3!

At that age he was also a very inquisitive child. Once, when his father telephoned home from the factory, David spoke to him and when the conversation was finished he started taking the telephone apart to see where his father was!

When he was 6 years old his grandfather taught him the game of chess and for a while he played draughts and chess until he had nearly achieved master strength at both! Luckily for us, David decided to concentrate on chess as this was being played worldwide and had a long history and tradition.

After having lived a few years in Berdyansk the family moved to Kiev in 1930 where young David started school. He was a good pupil but showed more interest in the school's clubs and tried practically everything including radio engineering and model aircraft construction until he took chess more seriously. However, he has kept an interest in many other things besides chess to this day.

After taking second place in a school tournament when he was about 12 David joined the Kiev Junior Draughts and Chess Club. He made rapid progress and very soon he had won the schoolboy championship of Kiev. At the age of 16 he was selected as a reserve candidate for the Ukrainian Championship and the indisposition of one of the regular competitors gave him his chance. Most of the experienced players thought that this boy would be easy prey but he won game after game and finished second to Boleslavsky with a score of 11½ out of 17. Because of this achievement he became the youngest Soviet player to be awarded the national master title and gained the right to play in the USSR Championship Semi-Final in Rostov. However, the tournament was stopped after six rounds as World War II had come to the Soviet Union.

For three years David did not play serious chess, but then in February 1944 he was invited to play in the Semi-Final of the USSR Championship in Baku. Without any practice he nevertheless managed to qualify for the Final to be held in June that year. He attracted the attention of the outside chess world when he beat several of the leading players of that time – Botvinnik, Lilienthal, Ragozin, Tolush – and drew with Smyslov, Boleslavsky, Makogonov, while playing an unusual style of chess that became his trademark.

The head of the Soviet Chess Federation, Boris Vainstein, who was also Chairman of the Dynamo Moscow Chess Club, recognised the enormous talent and personal qualities of this modest young boy. He obtained permission from the Ministry of Industry to have David transferred from Stalingrad – where he worked on the reconstruction of a steel factory – to Moscow. In June 1945 David became a member of the Dynamo Chess Club for whom he played for almost half a century! To stay physically fit David often spent his free time training with the Dynamo football and ice-hockey teams. His best friend during that period was Lev Yashin, the world-famous goalkeeper.

When David arrived in Moscow after the war in May 1945 it was Boris Vainstein who gave him a room in his own flat and David stayed with him, on and off, for many years, an arrangement that suited both of them.

His rise into the chess elite was meteoric: first place in USSR Championship Semi-Final in 1945; third place in the 14th USSR Championship, behind Botvinnik and Boleslavsky but ahead of Smyslov, Kotov and Bondarevsky; in the next two championships he did even better, finishing equal first with Kotov and Smyslov respectively; he won both his games against Anthony Santasiere in the radio match against the USA; first place in the Moscow Championship 1946, ahead of such established grandmasters as Bondarevsky, Kotov, Lilienthal and Smyslov.

Bronstein played brilliantly in the Prague vs. Moscow Match, scoring 10½ out of 12, winning all five games with Black playing King's Indian Defence and making this opening very popular.

Despite this he was not selected by the Soviet Chess Federation to participate in the first FIDE Interzonal Tournament but owed his place to the votes of foreign chess federations. This tremendously strong tournament was held in July 1948 in Saltsjöbaden, Sweden and David took first place, securing him a place in the first Candidates' Tournament. He was awarded the title of International Grandmaster in 1949 at the FIDE congress in Paris when this title was introduced internationally.

In the double-round Candidates' Tournament in Budapest 1950, the winner of which would be Botvinnik's ordained challenger, David seemed out of form in the first half and lost two games, but in the second he played with extraordinary energy, showing great determination to win, and thanks to a remarkable last-minute victory over Paul Keres finished equal with his old rival and close friend Isaac Boleslavsky. He went on to win the play-off in Moscow, August 1950 and obtained the right to challenge Botvinnik for the title of World Champion.

The match was held in March, April and May 1951 and David surprised everybody, except himself, by more than holding his own against the considered 'unplayable' Botvinnik.

Botvinnik, the cool, hardworking, totally concentrated player who saw the opponent as the enemy to be overcome in the subsequent struggle.

Bronstein, utterly in love with the game, Chess Artist, romantic at heart, always looking for brilliant combinations and fantastic positions.

With the uncanny talent of being able to judge a position within a split-second David did not always need to calculate as much and as deeply as other grandmasters but usually intuitively found the right move in a specific position. During his match with Botvinnik the first thing he did in the morning was to go out and buy a newspaper to see all the variations he was supposed to have seen! Often he bluffed, in similar fashion to Tal, but contrary to Tal's combinations, David's were usually correct, as subsequent analysis proved.

Many years later David wrote about this match: 'I can never agree with the idea of fostering a hostile attitude to your opponent on the grounds that this will help you beat him. Of course, I, like any other player, strive to win and I am very happy if I succeed in overcoming my opponent by logic, fantasy, ingenuity, knowledge or sometimes even deep calculation. 'But to make yourself hate the opponent, to sacrifice peace of mind for the sake of a point in the tournament table, this is an impoverishment of chess.' There is little doubt at whom these remarks were pointed...

David prepared well for this match and surprised Botvinnik by playing the very openings Botvinnik himself liked to play! Tension during the match was high and became almost unbearable towards the end. With only two of the scheduled 24 games remaining David was leading by one point. It was then that he was summoned to the KGB's private room at the theatre where the match was held. There has been a lot of speculation about what was said but David maintains to this day that General Victor Abakumov, head of the KGB and also a member of the Dynamo Sports Club, only introduced David to his wife and congratulated him with his beautiful win in the 22nd game (page 45). It was obvious that the majority of the chess fans wanted David to win the match because they all admired his beautiful and creative new style of chess.

The next morning David went, as had been his routine for every day of the match, for a walk with Lydia Bogdanova, whom he had met some time before through a wonderful trick. He had bought two tickets to the Bolshoi theatre, and on the evening of the performance, which was always sold out, he searched amongst the people who had no tickets but wanted to go until he found a beautiful girl to go with him. He fell in love almost instantly! During their walk he indicated to her that it seemed that he was now very close to becoming the next World Champion. Would she like that? He was completely unnerved by her answer: 'I really don't care.' It shocked him and in that state of mind he came to play the 23rd game. During that game David may well have been pre-occupied by what Lydia had told him. What did she mean? Did she really not care? It was hard to believe but yet that is what she had said. David lost the game.

Probably this was Lydia Bogdanova's first mistake which brought into question their intended marriage. Of course she wanted very much to be the wife of a famous chess player, yes, even the new World Champion. The second mistake she made a year later when she became a member of the Communist Party. She did not do this for ideological reasons but for purely opportunistic ones – to be able to obtain promotion. David told her that he did not like it at all and this betrayal put a shadow on their relationship and marked the beginning of the end.

After the game Lydia Bogdanova, probably realising what she had brought on, confessed to David that she really did not mean what she had said during their walk; in reality she very much wanted him to have the title...

However, the last game was a draw. The score was level and David became 'Co-World Champion', as Dr Euwe put it. He was awarded the title of Honoured Master of Sport of the Soviet Union for this result.

David played for the USSR in the Chess Olympiads of 1952, 1954, 1956 and 1958. He played in five Interzonal Tournaments, three Candidates' Tournaments, more than twenty Soviet Championships, was a member of the Moscow team for more than 30 years and played in the Moscow Championship on every occasion, both five-minute and conventional chess. His achievements are endless, and he has made almost 100 grandmaster norms in the process!

As a player he is a great strategist and his formidable tactical abilities are based on his thorough knowledge of the classical chess heritage.

With this knowledge, enhanced by his outstanding fantasy and imagination combined with pure logic, he is able to infuse life into the dullest-looking position, making something out of nothing. His grasp of combinative possibilities is amazing. Despite the opinion of some of his colleagues he is a very good endgame player and the reader can find ample proof of that in this book.

No dogmas are sacred to him. He delights in upsetting the analysts and sometimes flagrantly breaks the long established tenets of positional play.

David also shows a great understanding of psychology, which has on many occasions served him in good stead. A classic example was the fourteenth game of his play-off with Boleslavsky. He played a move in the French Defence condemned by all the analysts. Boleslavsky, taken by surprise, failed to find the right reply and David emerged triumphant.

His courage is enormous and he is never afraid to make almost incalculable sacrifices. A fantastic example of this can be found in his game with Spassky on page 128. David is most likely the only player who would dare to make such a sacrifice in a Candidates' Tournament when there is so much at stake!

His approach to a game of chess: 'I cannot say what feelings an artist experiences in front of an empty canvas but whenever I have to start a game I cannot stop thinking that today, right now, I have the very fortunate possibility of playing the most beautiful, the most fighting and the most profound game. It is now more than 50 years that I have been coming regularly to the Sacred Hall of Chess Creativity and have reverently sent a white pawn forward with a prayer to heroic feats. I am tormented, given no rest and am cut to pieces by that eternal sword of Damocles known to generations of chess players: the question of how to begin the attack...'

In search of fresh paths he regards each contest as a creative challenge but sometimes his results suffer from excessive experimentation when he pursues beauty first and the result of a game becomes secondary.

He can even be disappointed after winning a game in a tournament because his opponent failed to put up the best defence!

David also achieved recognition as an author when he published his first book in 1956 about the Candidates' Tournament in Neuhausen/Zürich 1953 (which, by the way, the Soviet officials had determined that Smyslov should win). 'I started,' he wrote 'from the premise that every full-bodied game of chess is an artistic endeavour arising out of the battle of chess ideas,' and added that he wished to display the richness and limitless extent of these ideas. The book has no extensive variations showing what might have been. He wrote that 'the moves played in each game serve to annotate the author's ideas', a complete reversal of the normal practice.

What also makes the book unique is that a grandmaster of World Champion level discloses many nuances of chess secrets, giving a clear guidance how to conduct the most complicated part of a chess game, the middlegame.

It was written with very great respect not only to the grandmasters but also to the reader.

Contrary to other books, when reading this one you do not feel inferior to the author; you get a feeling that you too can play at this level!

The format is that of a literary work. It became so popular in the USSR that further editions followed in 1960 and 1983. It was translated into English, French, Spanish, German and even Icelandic. Some people call it the Chess Bible. The book has become a classic, the best of all tournament books. It is still being reprinted today!

David has made many contributions to opening theory. In particular he and Isaac Boleslavsky introduced new strategic ideas in the King's Indian Defence as a consequence of which this opening became fashionable for many years and forms part of the repertoire of many grandmasters of this day and age! He is also largely responsible for the revival of the King's Gambit, long obsolete in master play, and has scored many notable victories with it.

Tigran Petrosian told the students of his chess school: 'David Bronstein revived and improved old openings and made many of them modern.' Gideon Barcza once said: 'Without Bronstein neither Tal nor Fischer would have played such an important role in the history of chess.'

David himself explained many times that he doesn't play openings – he just starts to create an attack... from the first move! It seems he knows some secrets about the initial position and has found a 'simple algorithm' how to change the opening strategy, avoiding routine paths of established theory. Playing White or Black does not make any difference to David; his positions are always flexible and active. This is why he does not have a specific opening repertoire. He just plays everything!

On occasion, out of respect, he plays the French Defence if his opponent is French or the Dutch Defence if he is Dutch or the English Defence if he is an Englishman. It is typical Bronstein to surprise his opponent by playing opening lines they themselves often play, challenging them on their own ground. Svetozar Gligorić, the strong Yugoslavian grandmaster, well-known for his meticulous preparation, was once asked during a tournament why he wasn't preparing for the next round. The reply was simple: he had to play Bronstein and any preparation would be futile!

Let's also shed some light on David Bronstein, the man.

He married at an early age in 1948. His first wife, Olga Ignatieva was also a chess player who won the Leningrad Women's championship in 1941 (she achived her greatest success when she shared 2nd and 3rd place with Fenny Heemskerk in the Women's Candidates' Tournament in Moscow 1952). They had one son, born 12 December 1947 in Leningrad. They separated in 1949 but were officially divorced only in 1959.

He lived alone for a long time, staying mostly in rented rooms and sometimes even in hotels. Eventually he found a two-room apartment in the House of KGB. One room he officially registered in the name of his parents, a very courageous thing to do, and his parents moved into the apartment with him.

He met his second wife Marina Mikhailova in 1957. She was a student of history and a secretary of the Anti Fascist Committee of Soviet Youth. They married in 1961 when they were able to rent a nice flat. In 1980 she died untimely at the age of 48.

Since 1984 he has been married to Tatiana Boleslavskaya, professor of musical history and the daughter of Isaac Boleslavsky, one of his three best friends (the others being Paul Keres and Boris Vainstein).

His father and mother died in Moscow in 1952 and 1967 respectively.

He does not have much respect for today's money-hungry grandmasters nor for the system that tries to put a number on one's brain (the Elo rating). All the more does he respect players like Philidor, Morphy, Anderssen, Staunton, Steinitz, Chigorin, Dr Tarrasch, Rubinstein, Dr Emanuel Lasker, Capablanca, Dr Tartakower, Dr Euwe, just to name a dozen.

David is an excellent teacher and trainer as he has the uncanny ability to pass on his knowledge.

He successfully prepared Nona Gaprindashvili for her ascent to the World Championship title and gave lessons five hours a day to WGM Maya Chiburdanidze while she was World Champion. He was also asked to give classes for 60 masters over a fortnight in Tbilisi. Two further examples of this I have witnessed myself:

A couple of years ago David gave a lecture for the first team of the Chess Club Anderlecht in Belgium to prepare them for their forthcoming match. He must have done an excellent job as Anderlecht crushed their opponents the next day by the widest possible margin, 8-0; a feat never seen before in the Belgian Team Championships.

In November 1993 David suggested that I participate in the Active Chess tournament in Oviedo. At first I refused as I did not want to make a fool of myself. However, he promised to prepare me for each round. Every day David took the time and trouble to sit with me for an hour or so. The result was that I finished only half a point behind the great man himself, albeit that he had faced much stronger opposition. I even managed to achieve a winning position against someone with 400 Elo more, just by following some basic rules which David had taught me!

Being a kind, modest and unselfish person, he is eager to teach people to play better chess, sometimes even for little or no money and some people, regrettably, take advantage of him. Also some of his fellow grandmasters think that he thus 'spoils the market' for them.

Quite recently he was asked to hold a lecture for promising Belgian youngsters. Afterwards he felt he had been overpaid and suggested that his next lecture would be free of charge!

The basic trait of David's character is undoubtedly his sociable and friendly attitude. He simply likes people. He can get carried away in conversations with normal mortals who have no idea what the game of chess is about. It is probably these people he respects most of all!

A few years ago we drove from Holland to Belgium and stopped at a road-side restaurant. When we returned to the car all his luggage had been stolen from it. Of course he was sad having lost a considerable amount of money that he had packed with his luggage; of course he was sad having lost his personal belongings; but what he was really upset about very much until this day is the fact that he had lost all the visiting cards he had collected from friends and admirers over many years. He felt that he had betrayed them by not being more careful!

Amongst his friends are people from the most varied circles; mathematicians, writers, football players and builders, each of whom he questions with genuine interest and often with a knowledge of the subject.

In psychological clashes he is extremely vulnerable. A breaking of ethics can put him in a state of shock and he cannot bear rudeness. The tension created by Botvinnik, on and off the board, before, during and after their match for the World Championship in 1951 was more than he could bear.

Nowadays he maintains that he just wanted to prove that Botvinnik was no god. Winning was not so important – but rather, it was important to prove that his was not the only way to play chess. David gives several other reasons why he didn't (want to) become world champion. They seem mere justifications after the fact and, surely, if it is repeated often enough, one might eventually start to believe it but if true, with hindsight, he surely must have made the biggest mistake of his life.

But then we must also ask ourselves this question: *If* he had become World Champion, would David Bronstein have been the same person we know today?

David is a man of principles. During his school years he avoided having to become a member of the Communist Youth Party (Komsomol) and of course he declined all offers (and pressure) to become a member of the regular Communist Party, even when it seemed beneficial to do so. This was mainly due to an 'education' at an early age, not by his parents or at school, but to the reality of everyday life:

His father was expelled from the Communist Party in 1935 because he tried to defend peasants in some region outside Kiev who were put under pressure by corrupt officials.

He was witness to his father's arrest by soldiers of the N.K.V.D. on the 31st of December 1937 in the middle of the night and his sentencing to eight years hard labour in various camps of the Gulag network in Russia, north of the Arctic Circle. His father was released in February 1944 due to very bad health but was 'banned' and had to live in Kazakhstan. However, he violated the rules, visiting Moscow regularly and eventually found a job in the Singer factory, 40 kilometres from the centre but still within the city limits! In order to accomplish this he went to the head of the local police in his native town which he knew very well from childhood. He gave him a sack of 100 kgs of flour as a friendly gift and in return the police chief destroyed his passport and issued a new one without the stamp that he had been a political prisoner.

Most Soviet grandmasters were members of the Union of Writers of the USSR, which gave them many privileges, but David refused to join. He also rejected an invitation to become a member of the Union of Journalists of the USSR.

David was of course very happy that his parents were reunited and that they were able to watch when he was playing tournaments in Moscow. Especially during his match with Botvinnik, when David's father and mother were present every game in the first row of spectators. This helped David to keep his spirits high but, as his father had no permission to be in Moscow, he glanced regularly into the audience in order to reassure himself that his father was still there.

Only in December 1955 did David's mother receive a formal letter from the Ministry of Justice in Kiev that the case against her husband was closed and that no crime was ever committed by him against the State. Iohonan Bronstein was fully rehabilitated three years after his death.

In 1945 David refused to sign a letter to Stalin which was prepared by Botvinnik's friend Ragozin, asking the Soviet government to permit Botvinnik to challenge Alekhine for the title of World Champion.

He was also one of the very few Soviet grandmasters (the others were Gulko, Spassky and Botvinnik – although Botvinnik's only reason not to sign was because he would not sign 'collective letters') who did not sign a letter from the Soviet Chess Federation condemning Korchnoi for defecting to the West.

He had helped Korchnoi before and during his first match with Karpov and, because of this 'independent' behaviour, David received less tournaments than other grandmasters and there was a total ban on his going to countries where prizes were in hard currencies. But never in his life did he beg the Soviet Sport Committee, the Soviet Chess Federation or his club, Dynamo, to 'do him a favour' and give him tournaments abroad (like so many other grandmasters did).

This boycott lasted for almost 14 years. During this period he made a living as a chess correspondent for the government newspaper *Izvestia*, holding lecture, giving simultaneous exhibitions and playing in the Moscow championships. His last tournament outside the Iron Curtain was Hastings 1975/76 where he shared first place.

David received private invitations to come as a 'tourist' to Sandomierz in Poland in 1976 and to Budapest in 1977. What a 'coincidence'; in both cities two strong tournaments were just about to start when David arrived there! In addition to sightseeing, he played in and won both tournaments. He then accepted an invitation from the Latvian Chess Federation to play in the first Jurmala tournament in 1978 and again took the first prize.

In the same year the Soviet Chess Federation organised a Zonal Tournament but they removed David from the list of participants at the very last moment. This was done in a very strange way. When an official asked, in the presence of some of the participants: 'Who is the oldest player who will participate in this tournament?' Smyslov answered 'I am.' This official, who thought that Bronstein was the oldest, realised his mistake and tried to save face: 'Well, we cannot throw you out. Who is the next oldest?' 'Bronstein,' someone replied and as Bronstein was not present he said 'OK, he's out.' Their decision was 'justified' by the necessity to give his place to a younger player. Obviously they still did not forgive him for helping Korchnoi and for not siding with Karpov. The Moscow Sport Committee protested against this decision but it was in vain. In 1989 the boycott finally came to an end when David was allowed to participate in the Lloyds Bank tournament in London.

David is constantly putting forward new ideas, sometimes impractical, sometimes provocative, sometimes brilliant.

It was he who thought up the idea of recording the times in tournament games and then making graphs, which are so meaningful in determining the degree of tension and at what stage during a game. Three such graphs are given in this book, see pages 144, 164, and 237.

Already 25 years ago he suggested the idea of Active Chess. He believes that grandmasters, with their knowledge and experience, don't need five hours for 40 moves. They could play much faster and he is a strong advocate of the idea of playing mini-matches instead of one serious game. Exactly as in tennis. Why not play four or six sets (games) of Active Chess (with tie-break games with reduced time as only recently were introduced)? Or play several games simultaneously against the same opponent?

Chess will definitely become much more attractive like this for the players, the public and for the sponsors. He dreams about a mixed media chess show – flashing great chess combinations to the accompaniment of music and ballet!

Long before Fischer, David Bronstein wanted to abolish the adjournment of games altogether. He believes it is not fair to analyse all night the given position, moving pieces in all directions, taking them back, starting again, writing the moves on paper and memorising them.

Then some players come to the board pretending that they are so clever. They want people to believe that they have created something fresh while they have found the way how to play in their study or hotel room, alone or maybe with assistance or even with the help of a computer.

Already back in 1965 David suggested introducing time controls which would eliminate adjournments altogether. The Soviet Chess Federation accepted his idea and started to organise tournaments where 40 moves had to be played in two hours and all the remaining moves in 30 minutes.

In 1973 David played a game with Oscar Panno in the Interzonal Tournament in Petropolis. After 40 moves, the game was adjourned in a very complicated position and when it seemed that the best way to play was to make a repetition of moves, David decided not go for a draw but to create even more complications. When the game was resumed the next day, David sacrificed a pawn and started a very sharp attack. Then there came the moment to adjourn the game for a second time. At that moment, while Panno was thinking, David asked the chief arbiter for permission to play the game to the end without any adjournment. The arbiter agreed and then David proposed this to Panno and he also agreed. David's main reason to suggest this was because the endgame should be winning for him with a queen and a rook against Panno's rook, bishop, knight and two pawns but Panno had created a fortress and it was not evident how to win (page 245). David was ashamed to seal a move and then to analyse all night. Instead he preferred to find the win over the board. This game took 104 moves and lasted a total of 13 hours! Please take courage and play through all the moves and enjoy this heroic struggle; it's worth it!

David also created a new rule which is still in force today. During the long and tiring negotiations with Botvinnik before the match in 1951, Botvinnik had complained that often young players would interrupt his thoughts by asking him several times for a draw during a game. Therefore, David suggested that one could only offer a draw after having executed a move on the board but before pushing the clock. If the draw was refused the right to offer a draw a second time was forfeited.

This rule was included in the Laws of Chess by FIDE and also accepted by Botvinnik but already in game three of the match he violated it when he fell into a trap, in an equal position and feared the possibility of losing the game. Instead of making a move he leaned over the board and said nervously: 'I propose a draw.' David accepted without hesitation but was very upset when Botvinnik sank back in his chair, relieved and said: 'I think you accepted the draw too early.' At that moment David felt an overwhelming urge to punch someone on the nose. However, our gentleman controlled himself, shook hands and left.

He proposed a revolutionary idea for an electronic chess clock in...1973 and published details about it in *Izvestia* (where he had a chess column for nearly a quarter of a century until 1988). Who knows, maybe Bobby Fischer got his ideas for his clock from that article? After all, he was known to read all Soviet chess publications and books.

Bronstein thinks that his way of time-keeping is more correct than Fischer's method. Anyway, the Bronstein clock is at last commercially available but the manufacturer is neither paying Fischer nor Bronstein any royalties for the use of their names!

The 1995 AEGON-tournament, where humans play against computers, was the first tournament in which the Bronstein clock was used for time-keeping.

And what about his latest brain child? New rules to make chess even more interesting! He suggests that pawns should be able to move backwards but should not be able to 'stab other pieces in the back' (not be able to take backwards) and that pieces should also be able to take pawns 'en passant'! Figure this: a white bishop on d2 should be able to take the black pawn on h6 if it moves from h7 to h5. And why not? It makes perfect sense! In a real battle the infantry can also retreat and why should the privilege of taking 'en passant' be limited to pawns? Surely this is at least as interesting as 'shuffle' chess or 'FischeRandom' which is now being suggested by Bobby Fischer. Already more than 20 years ago David himself suggested this, albeit in a slightly different form (see also page 118).

By the way, can you imagine what this would mean to computer chess?!

Furthermore he strongly supports Dr Emanuel Lasker's and Dr Max Euwe's ideas of scoring game results in such a way that a win is not automatically noted as 1, a loss as 0 and a draw as ½, but all would depend on the material balance at the end of a game.

'Everyone thinks I'm crazy,' he says with a twinkle in his eye, 'but I have one big advantage over other people who are also crazy: at least I know it but they don't!' When he met Bill Hartston in the bar after he had lost a brilliant game to David in Hastings 1975/76 (page 281) Hartston said to him: 'David, when I listen to you speaking about modern chess you sound like a madman but chess you play quite normally!' Yes, being a genius has its price!

David has so much to talk about that he constantly 'harasses' organisers, sponsors, arbiters and players with his ideas, even to the point of annoying them. This is why organisers occasionally do not want him in their tournaments and people sometimes do not take him seriously.

Where and what is David today? Well, after having survived a serious operation five years ago, he seems to be in better spirits than ever, especially after the free elections in Russia. It seems that he has a country again.

David has been travelling extensively for the last few years. His passport probably shows a larger variety of visas than the passport of any other former Soviet citizen!

He speaks English and Spanish fluently, has a good knowledge of German and can make himself understood in French. Now he is studying Dutch and the Scandinavian languages, not to forget Icelandic!

He received the distinguished degree of Honorary Doctor of Chess Science in 1992 when he was invited to Hewlett Packard Laboratories, Palo Alto, USA and toured the United States extensively in 1992 and 1993.

He plays in many tournaments both with humans and computers, gives lectures and simuls, displays his immense gift for teaching the art of chess. For the last four years he has been the coach of the British Junior Team during the annual tournament at Hastings.

He prepares them for their next round on days that he has to play himself. Either this man has a surplus of energy or is just a little mad (probably both!). Obviously time passes him by and he does not feel his age.

He plays the Team Championships of Belgium (as a member of the Chess Club Anderlecht), of Asturias (in the team of the University of Oviedo, Spain – he has Spanish residence and a work permit!), of France (as a member of Paris Echecs XV) and of Iceland (as a member of the Reykjavik Chess Club) where he also has a residence and work permit.

Besides the above mentioned clubs is also a member of the Oslo Chess Club in Norway, Charlton Chess Club in London, DD in The Hague, Holland and since 1975 a member of the Bois Gentil Chess Club in Geneva, Switzerland. Who knows how many more clubs will offer him membership!

He has signed contracts for his books *200 Closed Games*, *Understanding the King's Indian* and *The Chess Self-Tutor*, for publication in 1995 and 1996. Even if they are only half as good as his previous books, the chess world can be grateful again!

In short, David is more active than ever before!

**We wish him a very long, fruitful and healthy life!**

**Tom Fürstenberg**

---

* In stark contrast to a Dutch journalist who showed no respect whatsoever for the older players participating in the Donner Memorial Tournament in Amsterdam 1994. He had the nerve to call their group the 'Old Geezers' group thereby, disrespectfully, totally ignoring the achievements of the older generation of grandmasters.

# 70 Picturesque Games

## (1) Bronstein,D – Zaslavsky,I
Adults & Juniors Tournament,
Kiev, 1938
*[C43] Petroff's Defence*

1 e4 e5 2 ♘f3 ♘f6 3 d4 ♘xe4 4 ♗d3 d5 5
dxe5 ♘c6 6 ♕e2 ♘c5 7 0-0 ♘xd3 8 cxd3
♗g4 9 ♗e3 d4 10 ♗f4 ♗e7 11 ♘bd2 0-0 12
♘e4 ♕d7 13 h3 ♗e6 14 ♘g3 ♖ae8 15 ♖fe1
h6 16 a3 f5 17 exf6 ♗xf6 18 ♘c5 ♕c8 19
♘xe6 ♘d8 20 ♘xf8 ♖xe2 21 ♖xe2 ♔xf8 22
♖ae1 c6 23 ♗d6+ ♔f7 24 ♘e5+ ♗xe5 25
♖xe5 Black resigns.

## (2) Makogonov,V – Bronstein,D
Bolshevik Sports Society Championship,
Kiev, 1944
*[E90] King's Indian Defence*

1 d4 ♘f6 2 c4 g6 3 ♘f3 ♗g7 4 ♘c3 d6 5 e4
0-0 6 h3 c6 7 ♗d3 e5 8 d5 cxd5 9 cxd5 ♘h5
10 g3 ♘d7 11 ♗e3 a6 12 ♗e2 b5 13 ♘d2
♘hf6 14 a3 ♘b6 15 g4 ♘fd7 16 h4 f5 17
gxf5 gxf5 18 exf5 ♘f6 19 h5 h6 20 ♖g1
♔h8 21 ♘f1 ♗xf5 22 ♕d2 ♘g8 23 ♘g3
♗h7 24 ♗d3 ♘c4 25 ♗xc4 bxc4 26 0-0-0
♖b8 27 ♘ge4 ♖f7 28 ♖g3 ♘f6 29 ♘xf6
♕xf6 30 ♖dg1 ♕f5 31 f3 ♖b3 32 ♘e4 c3 33
bxc3 ♖fb7 34 ♕c2 ♖xa3 35 ♖xg7 ♕xf3 36
♖xb7 ♕xe3+ 37 ♔b2 ♗xe4 38 ♕c1 ♖xc3
39 ♕xc3 ♕xg1 40 ♕c8+ ♕g8 41 ♕c7 ♕g2+
42 ♔a3 Black resigns.

## (3) Smyslov,V – Bronstein,D
13th USSR Championship,
Moscow, 1944
*[C61] Spanish Opening*

1 e4 e5 2 ♘f3 ♘c6 3 ♗b5 ♘d4 4 ♘xd4 exd4
5 0-0 ♘e7 6 ♖e1 g6 7 c3 ♘c6 8 b3 ♗g7 9
♗b2 0-0 10 ♘a3 d5 11 ♗xc6 bxc6 12 cxd4
dxe4 13 ♕c2 ♗xd4 14 ♖xe4 ♗xb2 15 ♕xb2
♗e6 16 ♖ae1 a5 17 h4 a4 18 h5 ♕g5 19
♖e5 ♕h6 20 ♖1e3 axb3 21 axb3 ♖ad8 22
♕c3 ♘d5 23 hxg6 hxg6 24 ♘c4 ♖fd8 25

♖xd5 cxd5 26 ♕d4 ♖a8 27 ♘e5 c5 28 ♕b2
d4 29 ♖e1 ♖b8 30 ♕c2 Draw agreed.

## (4) Botvinnik,M – Bronstein,D
14th USSR Championship,
Moscow, 1945
*[E68] King's Indian Defence*

1 ♘f3 ♘f6 2 d4 d6 3 c4 ♘bd7 4 g3 g6 5 ♗g2
♗g7 6 ♘c3 e5 7 0-0 0-0 8 e4 c6 9 d5 cxd5
10 cxd5 ♘c5 11 ♕c2 a5 12 ♘d2 b6 13 ♘b3
♗a6 14 ♖d1 ♘cd7 15 a4 ♖c8 16 ♗h3 ♖c7
17 ♗e3 h5 18 ♗g5 ♕e8 19 f3 ♘h7 20 ♗e3
♕e7 21 ♗f1 ♗xf1 22 ♖xf1 f5 23 ♕e2 f4 24
♘b5 ♖cc8 25 gxf4 exf4 26 ♗d4 ♘hf6 27
♘a7 ♖ce8 28 ♕g2 ♔h7 29 ♖ac1 ♘c5 30
♘c6 ♕d7 31 ♘xc5 bxc5 32 ♗c3 ♗h6 33
♖cd1 ♕f7 34 ♖fe1 ♗g7 35 ♗xa5 ♘d7 36
♗c3 g5 37 ♗xg7 ♕xg7 38 ♔h1 ♘e5 39 ♖g1
♔h6 40 ♘xe5 ♕xe5 41 ♕h3 (sealed move)
♖f6 42 ♖g2 ♖g8 43 ♖dg1 ♕d4 44 ♖e1 ♖fg6
45 ♕f5 ♕d3 46 ♖f2 ♕d4 47 ♖g2 ♖f6 48
♖d2 ♖xf5 49 ♖xd4 ♖e5 50 ♖d3 ♖b8 51 b3
g4 52 ♔g2 ♔g5 53 a5 ♖a8 54 ♖a1 ♖e7 55
♖a3 ♖ea7 56 e5 dxe5 57 d6 ♔f5 58 ♖d5
♖d8 59 ♖a2 ♔e6 60 ♖xc5 ♖xd6 61 ♖ac2
♖d5 62 ♖xd5 ♔xd5 63 b4 ♖a8 64 ♔f2 ♖b8
Draw agreed.

## (5) Bronstein,D – Rudakovsky,I
14th USSR Championship,
Moscow, 1945
*[B03] Alekhine's Defence*

1 e4 ♘f6 2 e5 ♘d5 3 d4 d6 4 c4 ♘b6 5 f4
dxe5 6 fxe5 ♘c6 7 ♗e3 ♗f5 8 ♘c3 e6 9 ♗e2
♗e7 10 ♘f3 0-0 11 0-0 f6 12 exf6 ♗xf6 13
♕d2 ♕e7 14 ♖ad1 ♖ad8 15 ♕c1 ♗g6 16
♔h1 ♖d7 17 d5 ♘b4 18 a3 ♘a6 19 b4 ♖fd8
20 ♗d4 c5 21 ♗xf6 gxf6 22 ♘h4 exd5 23
♗g4 cxb4 24 axb4 ♖c7 25 c5 ♘xc5 26 bxc5
♕xc5 27 ♘xg6 ♕xc3 28 ♕h6 ♕c6 29 ♖de1
f5 30 ♗xf5 ♖f7 31 ♘e7+ ♖xe7 32 ♕g5+
Black resigns.

### (6) Chekhover,V – Bronstein,D
14th USSR Championship,
Moscow, 1945

*[A53] Old Indian Defence*

1 ♘f3 ♘f6 2 c4 d6 3 d4 ♘bd7 4 g3 e5 5 ♗g2
c6 6 0-0 e4 7 ♘e1 d5 8 ♘c3 ♗d6 9 ♕b3 dxc4
10 ♕c2 ♕e7 11 ♘xe4 ♘xe4 12 ♗xe4 h5 13
♗g2 ♘b6 14 ♘f3 ♗g4 15 a4 a5 16 b3 cxb3
17 ♕xb3 ♘d5 18 e4 ♘b4 19 d5 ♗xf3 20
♗xf3 ♗e5 21 ♗b2 h4 22 ♗xe5 ♕xe5 23
dxc6 bxc6 24 ♖ad1 0-0 25 ♗g2 ♖ab8 26 ♕c4
♖fd8 27 ♕e2 c5 28 ♖xd8+ ♖xd8 29 ♕b5
♕d4 30 ♕xa5 ♘d3 31 e5 ♘xe5 32 ♕c7 ♖d7
33 ♕c8+ ♖d8 34 ♕c7 ♖d7 35 ♕c8+ ♔h7 36
a5 c4 37 a6 g6 38 ♗b7 h3 39 ♕b8 ♖xb7 40
♕xb7 ♕d3 41 f4 ♕d4+ Draw agreed.

### (7) Bronstein,D – Furman,S
15th USSR Championship, Semi-Final,
Leningrad, 1946

*[C09] French Defence*

1 e4 e6 2 d4 d5 3 ♘d2 c5 4 ♘gf3 ♘c6 5 exd5
exd5 6 ♗b5 ♗d6 7 0-0 ♘ge7 8 dxc5 ♗xc5 9
♘b3 ♗d6 10 ♗g5 0-0 11 ♗h4 ♗g4 12 ♖e1
♕c7 13 ♗g3 ♖ad8 14 c3 ♗xg3 15 hxg3 ♖d6
16 ♕d3 ♘g6 17 ♗xc6 bxc6 18 ♘c5 ♗xf3 19
♕xf3 ♖dd8 20 ♕e3 ♕b8 21 b3 ♖fe8 22 ♕d4
♘f8 23 ♕b4 ♘e6 24 ♕xb8 ♖xb8 25 ♘d3 c5
26 ♖ad1 ♖ed8 27 ♘f4 ♘xf4 28 gxf4 ♖d7 29
♖e5 ♖bd8 30 c4 f6 31 ♖exd5 ♖xd5 32 cxd5
♔f7 33 g3 ♖d7 34 ♖c1 ♖xd5 35 ♖c4 ♔e7 36
♖a4 ♖d7 37 ♖a6 ♖c7 38 ♔f1 ♔d8 39 ♔e2
♔c8 40 ♔d3 ♖d7+ 41 ♔c4 ♔b7 42 ♖e6 ♖d2
43 ♔xc5 ♖xf2 44 ♖e7+ ♔b8 45 ♖xg7 h5 46
a4 ♖c2+ 47 ♔b5 ♖g2 48 ♔a6 h4 49 ♖b7+
♔c8 50 gxh4 ♖g4 51 h5 ♖h4 52 ♖xa7 ♖xh5
53 b4 ♖f5 54 b5 ♖xf4 55 a5 ♖f5 56 a6 ♖e5
57 b6 Black resigns.

### (8) Bronstein,D – Levenfish,G
15th USSR Championship, Semi-Final,
Leningrad, 1946

*[D48] Semi-Slav Defence*

1 d4 d5 2 ♘f3 ♘f6 3 c4 c6 4 e3 e6 5 ♗d3
dxc4 6 ♗xc4 ♘bd7 7 ♘c3 b5 8 ♗d3 a6 9 e4
c5 10 e5 cxd4 11 ♘e4 ♘d5 12 0-0 ♗b7 13
♗g5 ♕b8 14 a4 ♘xe5 15 ♘xe5 ♕xe5 16
axb5 a5 17 f4 ♕b8 18 f5 ♕e5 19 b6 ♗d6 20

♘xd6+ ♕xd6 21 fxe6 f6 22 ♕h5+ ♔d8 23
♗h4 ♕xe6 24 ♖ae1 ♘e3 25 ♕c5 ♕d5 26
♕c7+ ♔e8 27 ♕xg7 ♖f8 28 ♗b5+ ♗c6 29
♗xc6+ ♕xc6 30 ♗xf6 ♖f7 31 ♕g8+ ♖f8 32
♕g5 ♔d7 33 ♖f2 ♕xb6 34 ♕g7+ ♔c6 35
♗xd4 ♖xf2 36 ♗xe3 ♕xb2 37 ♖c1+ ♔b5
38 ♕b7+ ♔a4 39 ♖c4+ ♔a3 40 ♗c1 Black
resigns.

### (9) Abrahams,G – Bronstein,D
Match Great Britain vs. USSR,
London, 1947

*[E94] King's Indian Defence*

1 ♘f3 ♘f6 2 c4 g6 3 ♘c3 ♗g7 4 e4 d6 5 d4
0-0 6 ♗e2 ♘bd7 7 0-0 e5 8 ♗g5 h6 9 ♗e3
c6 10 h3 ♖e8 11 d5 c5 12 ♕d2 ♔h7 13 g4
♘g8 14 ♔h2 ♘f8 15 ♗d3 ♗h8 16 ♖g1 ♘h7
17 ♖g2 ♗d7 18 ♘e2 ♕f6 19 ♔g3 ♖f8 20 h4
♕e7 21 ♕c2 ♘hf6 22 ♘h2 ♘xg4 23 ♘xg4
f5 24 ♘xe5 dxe5 25 f4 ♘f6 26 ♖h1 fxe4 27
♗xe4 ♘xe4+ 28 ♕xe4 exf4+ 29 ♔f3 ♕xe4+
30 ♔xe4 ♖ae8+ 31 ♔d3 ♗f5+ 32 ♔d2
fxe3+ White resigns.

### (10) Keres,P – Bronstein,D
15th USSR Championship,
Leningrad, 1947

*[C07] French Defence*

1 e4 e6 2 d4 d5 3 ♘d2 c5 4 ♘gf3 ♘f6 5
exd5 ♘xd5 6 ♘e4 cxd4 7 ♘xd4 ♗e7 8 ♗e2
0-0 9 0-0 e5 10 ♘b5 ♘c6 11 c4 ♘db4 12 a3
♕xd1 13 ♗xd1 ♘d3 14 ♘c7 ♖b8 15 ♘d5
♗d8 16 ♘d6 ♗e6 17 b4 ♘d4 18 ♗e3 b5 19
f4 bxc4 20 fxe5 ♗xd5 21 ♗xd4 ♗b6 22
♗xb6 axb6 23 ♘f5 ♖fe8 24 ♘e3 ♖xe5 25
♘xd5 ♖xd5 26 ♗c2 g6 27 ♗xd3 ♖xd3 28 a4
♖b3 29 ♖fb1 ♖xb1+ 30 ♖xb1 ♔g7 31 ♖c1
♖c8 32 a5 b5 33 a6 ♔f6 34 ♔f2 ♔e5 35 ♔e3
♔d5 36 g4 ♖e8+ 37 ♔d2 ♔d4 38 ♖f1 ♖e6
39 ♖f4+ ♔e5 40 a7 ♖a6 41 ♖xf7 ♖a2+ 42
♔c3 ♖a3+ 43 ♔b2 Draw agreed.

### (11) Bronstein,D – Najdorf,M
Candidates' Tournament,
Budapest, 1950

*[E29] Nimzo-Indian Defence*

1 d4 ♘f6 2 c4 e6 3 ♘c3 ♗b4 4 a3 ♗xc3+ 5
bxc3 c5 6 e3 ♘c6 7 ♗d3 0-0 8 ♘e2 d6 9 e4

⚘e8 10 0-0 b6 11 f4 ♗a6 12 f5 e5 13 f6 ♔h8 14 d5 ⚘a5 15 ⚘g3 gxf6 16 ⚘f5 ♗c8 17 ♕h5 ♗xf5 18 exf5 ♖g8 19 ♖f3 ♖g7 20 ♗h6 ♖g8 21 ♖h3 Black resigns.

## (12) Botvinnik,M – Bronstein,D
### World Championship Match, 21st game, Moscow, 1951
*[E69] King's Indian Defence*

1 d4 ⚘f6 2 c4 d6 3 ⚘c3 e5 4 ⚘f3 ⚘bd7 5 g3 g6 6 ♗g2 ♗g7 7 0-0 0-0 8 e4 c6 9 h3 ⚘h5 10 ♗e3 ♕e7 11 ⚘h2 ♔h8 12 ♖e1 a6 13 a3 ♖b8 14 ♗f1 ⚘hf6 15 ♕d2 b5 16 cxb5 axb5 17 ♖ad1 ⚘b6 18 ♗h6 ♗xh6 19 ♕xh6 ♗e6 20 ⚘f3 ♗b3 21 ♖d2 ⚘fd7 22 ♕e3 ♗c4 23 ♗g2 f6 24 ♖c2 ♗b3 25 ♖ce2 ⚘c4 26 ♕d3 ⚘a5 27 ♖d2 ⚘b6 28 ♕b1 ⚘bc4 29 ♖de2 b4 30 axb4 ♖xb4 31 h4 ⚘b6 32 ⚘a2 ♗xa2 33 ♕xa2 ⚘bc4 34 h5 ♖fb8 35 hxg6 hxg6 36 ♕b1 ♔g7 37 dxe5 fxe5 38 ♕c1 ⚘xb2 39 ♕c3 ⚘a4 40 ♕c1 ♖c4 41 ♕g5 ♕xg5 42 ⚘xg5 ♖b3 43 f4 ⚘d4 44 ♖a2 ♖b2 45 ♖xb2 ⚘xb2 46 ♔h2 ⚘d3 47 ♖e3 ♖c3 48 ♗f1 ♖c2+ 49 ♔h3 ⚘f2+ 50 ♔h4 ♖c1 51 ♗g2 ♖g1 52 ♗h3 ♖h1 53 fxe5 dxe5 54 ♖a3 ♔f6 55 ⚘h7+ ♔e7 56 ⚘g5 ♔d6 57 ⚘f7+ ♔e7 58 ♔g5 ♔xf7 59 ♖a7+ ♔e8 60 ♗d7+ ♔d8 61 ♔xg6 ⚘xe4 62 g4 ♖f1 63 ♗f5 ⚘xf5 64 gxf5 ♔e8 White resigns.

## (13) Bronstein,D – Geller,E
### 19th USSR Championship, Moscow, 1951
*[C99] Spanish Opening*

1 e4 e5 2 ⚘f3 ⚘c6 3 ♗b5 a6 4 ♗a4 ⚘f6 5 0-0 ♗e7 6 ♖e1 b5 7 ♗b3 d6 8 c3 0-0 9 h3 ⚘a5 10 ♗c2 c5 11 d4 ♕c7 12 ⚘bd2 cxd4 13 cxd4 ♗b7 14 d5 ♗c8 15 ♖b1 ♗d7 16 ♗d3 ♖fc8 17 ⚘f1 ♗d8 18 ⚘g3 ♕a7 19 ♖f1 ⚘e8 20 ♔h1 ⚘b7 21 b4 a5 22 a3 axb4 23 axb4 ♗e7 24 ⚘e2 ♗d8 25 ♗d2 ♗b6 26 ⚘c3 ♗xf2 27 ⚘xb5 ♕b6 28 ♕e2 ♗g3 29 ♗e3 ♕d8 30 ⚘a7 ♖c3 31 ♕d2 ♖a3 32 ⚘c6 ♕f6 33 ⚘fxe5 ♗xe5 34 ♖xf6 ♗xf6 35 ♗c4 ♖c3 36 e5 ♖xc4 37 exf6 ⚘xf6 38 ♗d4 ♗xc6 39 dxc6 ♖xc6 40 ♕g5 d5 41 ♖f1 h6 42 ♕g3 ⚘e8 43 ♕e5 ♖d8 44 ♕h5 ⚘f6 45 ♗xf6 ♖xf6 46 ♖xf6 gxf6 47 ♕f3 ♖d6 48 ♕g4+ ♔h7 49 ♕c8 ♖b6 50 ♕c7 Black resigns.

## (14) Bronstein,D – Horne,D
### International Tournament, Hastings, 1953/54
*[E50] Nimzo-Indian Defence*

1 d4 ⚘f6 2 c4 e6 3 ⚘c3 ♗b4 4 e3 c5 5 ⚘f3 0-0 6 ♗e2 ⚘c6 7 ♕c2 b6 8 0-0 ♗xc3 9 ♕xc3 ♗b7 10 dxc5 ⚘e4 11 ♕c2 ⚘xc5 12 a3 f5 13 b4 ⚘e4 14 ♗b2 d6 15 ♖ad1 ♕e7 16 ⚘e1 ♖ac8 17 ♕b3 ♖c7 18 ⚘d3 ♖fc8 19 f3 ⚘f6 20 ⚘f4 ⚘d8 21 ♗xf6 gxf6 22 e4 b5 23 cxb5 ♖c3 24 ♕b1 ♖xa3 25 ♗d3 e5 26 ⚘e2 ♕f7 27 ⚘g3 f4 28 ⚘f5 ♕c7 29 ⚘xd6 ♕b6+ 30 ♔h1 ♖cc3 31 ⚘c4 Black resigns.

## (15) Bronstein,D – Alexander,C.H.O'D
### International Tournament, Hastings, 1953/54
*[A82] Dutch Defence*

1 d4 f5 2 e4 fxe4 3 ⚘c3 ⚘f6 4 f3 exf3 5 ⚘xf3 g6 6 ♗f4 ♗g7 7 ♕d2 0-0 8 ♗h6 d5 9 ♗xg7 ♔xg7 10 0-0-0 ♗f5 11 ♗d3 ♗xd3 12 ♕xd3 ⚘c6 13 ♖de1 ♕d6 14 ⚘b1 a6 15 ♖e2 ♖ae8 16 ♖he1 e6 17 ⚘e5 ⚘d7 18 ⚘f3 ♖f5 19 ♖e3 e5 20 dxe5 ⚘dxe5 21 ⚘xe5 ♖fxe5 22 ♖xe5 ♖xe5 23 ♖xe5 ♕xe5 24 ♕xd5 ♕xh2 25 ♕d7+ ♔h6 26 a3 ♕d6 27 ♕c8 ⚘d8 28 g4 ♔g7 29 b3 c6 30 g5 ♕e7 31 ♕g4 ⚘f7 32 ⚘e4 ♕xa3 33 ♕e6 ♕a5 34 ⚘d6 ⚘xd6 35 ♕f6+ ♔g8 36 ♕xd6 ♕e1+ 37 ♔a2 ♕e8 38 ♕c7 b5 39 ♔b1 ♕e1+ 40 ♔b2 ♕e6 41 b4 ♕e4 42 ♕d8+ ♔f7 43 ♕f6+ ♔e8 44 ♕d6 ♕d5 45 ♕f6 ♔d7 46 ♕g7+ ♔d6 47 ♕f6+ ♔c7 48 ♕g7+ ♔d7 49 ♕e5+ ♔d6 50 ♕g7+ ♔b6 51 ♕c3 ♕e7 52 ♕d4+ ♔b7 53 c3 ♕c7 54 ♕h8 ♔b6 55 ♕d4+ ♔b7 56 ♕h8 ♕d7 57 ♔a3 ♕e7 58 ♕f6 ♕c7 59 ♔b2 a5 60 bxa5 ♕xa5 61 ♕e6 ♕c7 62 ♔b3 ♕f4 63 ♕d7+ ♔b6 64 ♕d8+ ♔c5 65 ♕e7+ ♔b6 66 ♕d8+ ♔c5 67 ♕e7+ ♔d5 68 ♕d7+ ♕d6 69 ♕g4 ♕c5 70 ♕d7+ ♔e5 71 ♕xh7 ♔f5 72 ♕d7+ ♔xg5 73 ♕d2+ ♔f6 74 ♕d8+ ♔f7 75 ♕c7+ ♕e7 76 ♕f4+ ♔g7 77 ♕d4+ ♕f6 78 ♕e4 ♔f7 79 ♔b2 ♕d6 80 ♕f3+ ♕f6 81 ♕e4 g5 82 ♕h7+ ♔e6 83 ♕e4+ ♔d6 84 ♕d3+ ♔c7 85 ♕h7+ ♔b6 86 ♔c2 ♕f4 87 ♕e7 ♕f2+ 88 ♔b3 ♕d2 89 ♕e8 ♕d5+ 90 ♔b2 ♕d6 91 ♕e3+ ♔c5 92

♕e8 ♕f2+ 93 ♔b3 ♕f6 94 ♕d7 ♔c5 95 ♔c2 ♕e5 96 ♕d8 ♕e4+ 97 ♔b2 g4 98 ♕d7 ♔c4 99 ♕d1 ♕g2+ 100 ♔a1 c5 101 ♕c2 ♕f1+ 102 ♔b2 ♔d5 103 ♕d2+ ♔e4 104 ♕g5 ♕f5 105 ♕h4 ♔f3 106 ♕h1+ ♔e2 107 ♕g2+ ♔e1 108 c4 b4 109 ♕g1+ ♔e2 110 ♕g2+ ♔e3 111 ♔b3 ♕d3+ 112 ♔a4 ♕xc4 113 ♕g3+ ♔d2 114 ♕f2+ ♔c3 115 ♕e3+ ♔b2 116 ♕e5+ ♔c3 117 ♕g5 g3 118 ♕g4 g2 119 ♕g5 ♕c1 120 ♕xc5 ♕c2+ White resigns.

## (16) Bronstein,D – Teschner,R
International Tournament,
Hastings, 1953/54
*[C77] Spanish Opening*

1 e4 e5 2 ♘f3 ♘c6 3 ♗b5 a6 4 ♗a4 ♘f6 5 d3 d6 6 c3 ♗e7 7 0-0 0-0 8 ♕e2 ♘d7 9 d4 ♗f6 10 ♗e3 b5 11 ♗c2 ♘b6 12 ♘bd2 ♗g4 13 d5 ♘e7 14 ♖fd1 ♘g6 15 h3 ♗d7 16 ♘f1 ♘h4 17 ♘1d2 ♖b8 18 b3 ♘g6 19 ♕d3 ♗e7 20 a4 bxa4 21 bxa4 a5 22 c4 f5 23 c5 dxc5 24 ♕c3 ♔h8 25 ♗xc5 ♗d6 26 ♗e3 fxe4 27 ♗xe4 ♘xa4 28 ♕c2 ♖b2 29 ♕c1 ♘f4 30 ♖e1 ♖b4 31 ♘c4 ♗b5 32 ♘cd2 ♘b2 33 ♕c2 ♗d3 34 ♗xd3 ♘bxd3 35 ♖eb1 ♖xb1+ 36 ♖xb1 ♘b4 37 ♕c4 ♘bxd5 38 ♘e4 h6 39 g3 ♘xe3 40 fxe3 ♘g6 41 ♖f1 ♕d7 42 ♔h2 a4 43 h4 ♖b8 44 h5 ♖b2+ 45 ♘fd2 ♘f8 46 ♔g1 ♘e6 47 ♘f3 ♖b4 48 ♕d5 ♖b5 49 ♕a8+ ♕d8 50 ♕xa4 ♖b4 51 ♕c2 ♕a8 52 ♘xd6 cxd6 53 ♘h4 ♖e4 54 ♘g6+ ♔h7 55 ♕b1 d5 56 ♕b6 ♘g5 57 ♘f8+ ♔g8 58 ♘g6 ♖g4 59 ♕a7 ♖xg3+ 60 ♔h2 ♖h3+ 61 ♔g2 ♕e8 62 ♖b1 ♘f7 63 ♖b8 ♘d8 64 ♔xh3 ♕e6+ 65 ♔g3 ♕d6 66 ♕e7 ♕xe7 67 ♘xe7+ ♔f7 68 ♖xd8 Black resigns.

## (17) Bronstein,D – Gligorić,S
10 years Liberation Tournament,
Belgrade, 1954
*[E53] Nimzo-Indian Defence*

1 d4 ♘f6 2 c4 e6 3 ♘c3 ♗b4 4 e3 0-0 5 ♘f3 c5 6 ♗d3 d5 7 0-0 ♘bd7 8 cxd5 exd5 9 ♗d2 ♖e8 10 a3 ♗xc3 11 ♗xc3 c4 12 ♗e2 ♘e4 13 ♗e1 ♘b6 14 b3 ♗g4 15 h3 ♗h5 16 g4 ♗g6 17 ♘e5 ♖c8 18 bxc4 ♘xc4 19 ♗xc4 dxc4 20 f3 ♘d6 21 e4 f6 22 ♘xg6 hxg6 23 a4 ♘f7

24 ♗c3 ♘g5 25 ♔g2 ♘e6 26 ♕d2 g5 27 ♖h1 ♘f4+ 28 ♔f1 ♘d3 29 ♖b1 ♖c7 30 h4 ♖d7 31 hxg5 fxg5 32 ♕h2 ♕f6 33 ♕h7+ ♔f7 34 ♕f5 ♕xf5 35 gxf5 b6 36 ♖h5 ♘f4 37 ♖h2 ♖dd8 38 ♔f2 g4 39 ♔g3 ♘d5 40 exd5 ♖e3 41 ♗d2 ♖xf3+ 42 ♔xg4 ♖d3 43 ♗f4 ♖xd4 44 a5 ♖8xd5 45 axb6 axb6 46 ♖xb6 ♖d1 47 ♖b7+ ♔g8 48 ♖b8+ ♔f7 49 ♖b7+ ♔g8 50 ♖g2 ♖f1 51 ♔g5 ♖a1 52 ♖e7 c3 53 ♔g6 ♖a6+ 54 ♖e6 ♖xe6+ 55 fxe6 ♔f8 56 ♗g5 ♖d6 57 ♔f5 ♖c6 58 ♖a2 ♖c8 59 ♖a7 c2 60 ♗c1 ♖c5+ 61 ♔e4 Black resigns.

## (18) Porreca,G – Bronstein,D
10 years Liberation Tournament,
Belgrade, 1954
*[B18] Caro-Kann Defence*

1 e4 c6 2 d4 d5 3 ♘c3 dxe4 4 ♘xe4 ♗f5 5 ♘g3 ♗g6 6 h4 h6 7 ♘h3 ♗h7 8 ♗c4 ♘f6 9 ♘f4 ♘bd7 10 0-0 ♕c7 11 ♖e1Bg8 12 ♘d3 e6 13 ♗f4 ♗d6 14 ♗xd6 ♕xd6 15 ♘f5 ♕f8 16 ♕f3 0-0-0 17 ♘g3 ♗h7 18 a4 ♗xd3 19 ♗xd3 ♕d6 20 a5 a6 21 ♖a3 g5 22 h5 ♕f4 23 ♕e2 ♔c7 24 c3 ♖he8 25 ♘e4 ♘xe4 26 ♕xe4 ♕xe4 27 ♗xe4 ♘f6 28 ♗f3 g4 29 ♗d1 ♖g8 30 ♖e5 ♖d5 31 ♖a4 ♖g5 32 ♗b3 ♖dxe5 33 dxe5 ♘d7 34 ♗d1 ♘xe5 35 ♖e4 ♖xh5 36 ♗xg4 ♘xg4 37 ♖xg4 ♖xa5 38 ♖g7 ♖f5 39 g4 ♖f6 40 ♔g2 ♔d6 41 ♔g3 e5 42 ♖g8 ♔d5 White resigns.

## (19) Spassky,B – Bronstein,D
24th USSR Championship,
Moscow, 1957
*[C17] French Defence*

1 d4 e6 2 e4 d5 3 ♘c3 ♗b4 4 e5 c5 5 ♗d2 ♘e7 6 ♘b5 ♗xd2+ 7 ♕xd2 0-0 8 dxc5 ♘bc6 9 ♘f3 b6 10 cxb6 ♕xb6 11 0-0-0 ♖b8 12 b3 ♕c5 13 ♘bd4 a5 14 ♔b2 a4 15 ♗d3 h6 16 ♖he1 ♖b6 17 ♗f1 ♗a6 18 ♗xa6 ♖xa6 19 ♖e2 ♖b8 20 ♘xc6 ♘xc6 21 ♘d4 ♘a5 22 f4 ♖a7 23 ♕c1 ♘c4+ 24 ♔a1 ♘a3 25 ♕b2 ♘b5 26 ♘xb5 ♕xb5 27 ♖e3 ♖c7 28 ♖ed3 ♕c5 29 ♖3d2 ♖bc8 30 ♔b1 ♕a7 31 g3 ♖c3 32 ♖e1 a3 33 ♕c1 ♕c5 34 ♕d1 ♔h7 35 ♖ee2 g6 36 ♖d4 ♖f3 37 ♖d3 ♖xd3 38 cxd3 ♕d4 39 ♕d2 ♖c3 40 ♕e3 ♕b4 41 ♖d2 h5 42 h3 ♕b7 43 ♕f2 ♔g7 Draw agreed.

## (20) Gurgenidze,B – Bronstein,D

25th USSR Championship,
Riga 1958

*[B66] Sicilian Defence*

1 e4 c5 2 ♘f3 ♘c6 3 d4 cxd4 4 ♘xd4 ♘f6 5
♘c3 d6 6 ♗g5 e6 7 ♕d2 a6 8 ♗e2 ♗d7 9
0-0 ♖c8 10 ♖ad1 ♗e7 11 ♘b3 0-0 12 ♗xf6
gxf6 13 ♕h6 ♔h8 14 ♕h5 ♖g8 15 f4 ♖g6
16 ♔h1 ♕b6 17 a3 ♖cg8 18 ♗f3 ♗f8 19
♘e2 f5 20 exf5 ♖h6 21 ♕xf7 ♕d8 22 fxe6
♗xe6 23 ♕xb7 ♕h4 24 ♔g1 ♘e7 25 ♘bd4
♗c8 26 ♕b4 ♗g7 27 ♕e1 ♕xh2+ 28 ♔f2
♗f6 29 ♘e3 ♘f5+ 30 ♘xf5 ♗xf5 31 ♖h1
♕xh1 32 ♕xh1 ♖xh1 33 ♖xh1 ♗xb2 34
♔d2 ♗xa3 35 ♖a1 ♗c5 36 ♖xa6 ♖e8 37
♖a8 ♗e3+ 38 ♔d1 ♖xa8 39 ♗xa8 ♗g4
Draw agreed.

## (21) Bisguier,A – Bronstein,D

Maroczy Memorial Tournament,
Budapest, 1961

*[A54] Old Indian Defence*

1 d4 ♘f6 2 c4 d6 3 ♘c3 e5 4 ♘f3 e4 5 ♘g1
h6 6 ♗f4 g5 7 ♗d2 ♗g7 8 e3 ♗f5 9 ♘ge2
♗g6 10 ♕b3 b6 11 ♘g3 0-0 12 ♗e2 c5 13
dxc5 bxc5 14 f3 d5 15 cxd5 exf3 16 gxf3
♘bd7 17 e4 ♖b8 18 ♕a3 ♖e8 19 0-0-0 g4 20
♖hg1 ♖b4 21 ♕xa7 gxf3 22 ♗xf3 ♘e5 23
♗e2 ♖e7 24 ♕xc5 ♖eb7 25 b3 ♕a8 26 ♔c2
♖xe4 27 ♘gxe4 ♘xe4 28 ♖xg6 ♘xc5 29 ♖g2
♖a7 30 a4 ♘g6 31 ♗c4 ♕c8 32 ♖f1 ♕h3 33
♖ff2 ♘e5 34 ♗f1 ♕h4 35 ♖f4 ♕d8 36 ♖b4
♔h7 37 ♘b5 ♖d7 38 d6 ♕f6 39 ♖f4 ♕e6 40
♘d4 ♕d5 41 ♗c3 ♘g6 White resigns.

## (22) Bronstein,D – Donner,J

Maroczy Memorial Tournament,
Budapest, 1961

*[B12] Caro-Kann Defence*

1 e4 c6 2 d4 d5 3 e5 ♗f5 4 h4 h6 5 g4 ♗d7
6 ♗e3 c5 7 c3 ♘c6 8 a3 a5 9 b3 e6 10 h5 b5
11 ♘f3 ♕b8 12 ♗g2 c4 13 bxc4 bxc4 14
♕c2 a4 15 ♘bd2 ♘a5 16 0-0 ♘b3 17 ♖a2
♘e7 18 ♘h4 ♘c6 19 f4 ♘xd2 20 ♕xd2 ♗e7
21 ♗f2 ♘a7 22 f5 ♗g5 23 ♕d1 ♕b3 24 ♕a1
♖b8 25 ♘f3 exf5 26 e6 ♗xe6 27 gxf5 ♗d7
28 ♖e2+ ♔f8 29 ♗g3 ♖b5 30 ♘e5 ♗c6 31
♕e1 ♔g8 32 ♘xc6 Black resigns.

## (23) Bronstein,D – Muchnik,H

5-minute blitz chess,
Moscow, 1962

*[C99] Spanish Opening*

1 e4 e5 2 ♘f3 ♘c6 3 ♗b5 a6 4 ♗a4 ♘f6 5
0-0 ♗e7 6 ♖e1 b5 7 ♗b3 d6 8 c3 0-0 9 h3
♘a5 10 ♗c2 c5 11 d4 ♕c7 12 ♘bd2 cxd4 13
cxd4 ♗b7 14 ♘f1 ♖ac8 15 ♗b1 ♖fd8 16 d5
♘c4 17 b3 ♘b6 18 ♗b2 ♘fd7 19 ♘e3 ♗f8
20 ♕d2 ♘c5 21 ♗d3 ♘xd3 22 ♕xd3 ♘d7
23 ♕d2 ♘c5 24 ♘f5 a5 25 ♖ac1 b4 26 ♕g5
♕d7 27 ♗xe5 ♘xe4 28 ♘h6+ ♔h8 29 ♖xe4
♖xc1+ 30 ♕xc1 ♗xd5 31 ♖d4 ♗xf3 32
♖xd6 ♗xd6 33 ♗xg7+ ♔xg7 34 ♕g5+ ♔f8
35 ♕g8+ ♔e7 36 ♕xf7 mate.

## (24) Stein,L – Bronstein,D

USSR Team Championship,
Ukraine vs. Moscow, 1st board,
Leningrad, 1962

*[B97] Sicilian Defence*

1 e4 c5 2 ♘f3 d6 3 d4 cxd4 4 ♘xd4 ♘f6 5
♘c3 a6 6 ♗g5 e6 7 f4 ♕b6 8 ♕d2 ♕xb2 9
♖b1 ♕a3 10 ♗xf6 gxf6 11 ♗e2 ♗g7 12 f5
0-0 13 ♖b3 ♕a5 14 0-0 ♘c6 15 ♘xc6 bxc6
16 ♕xd6 exf5 17 ♗c4 f4 18 ♕xc6 ♖a7 19
♘d5 ♗e6 20 ♔h1 f5 21 exf5 ♗xf5 22 ♕d6
♗xc2 23 ♖b8 ♖a8 24 ♖xa8 ♖xa8 25 ♘xf4
♕e5 26 ♗xf7+ ♔h8 27 ♕d2 ♗e4 28 ♘e6
♗d5 29 ♘xg7 ♕f8 30 ♘e8 ♖xf7 31 ♖e1 ♕f4
32 ♕xf4 ♖xf4 33 ♘c7 ♗xa2 34 ♘xa6 ♗c4
35 ♘c5 ♖f1+ 36 ♖xf1 ♗xf1 37 ♔g1 ♗b5 38
♔f2 ♗g7 39 ♔e3 ♔f6 40 ♔f4 h6 41 ♘e4+
♔g6 42 g4 Draw agreed.

## (25) Bronstein,D – O'Kelly,A

Hoogovens Tournament,
Beverwijk, 1963

*[A08] King's Indian Attack*

1 g3 ♘f6 2 ♗g2 d5 3 ♘f3 e6 4 0-0 ♗e7 5 d3
c5 6 ♘bd2 ♘c6 7 e4 0-0 8 ♖e1 ♕c7 9 e5
♘d7 10 ♕e2 b5 11 h4 a5 12 ♘f1 ♗a6 13
♘1h2 b4 14 h5 ♖fc8 15 h6 g6 16 ♗f4 ♕d8
17 ♘g4 a4 18 ♕d2 c4 19 dxc4 ♗xc4 20 ♗g5
a3 21 b3 ♗a6 22 ♖ac1 ♘a7 23 ♗xe7 ♕xe7
24 ♘g5 ♘b5 25 ♗xd5 ♖d8 26 ♗xa8 ♘xe5
27 ♕xd8+ ♕xd8 28 ♖xe5 ♘c3 29 ♗f3 f5
30 ♘xe6 Black resigns.

## (26) Bronstein,D – M20 Computer
### Institute of Mathematics, Moscow 1963
*[C34] King's Gambit Accepted*

1 e4 e5 2 f4 exf4 3 Nf3 Nf6 4 e5 Ng4 5 d4 g5 6 Nc3 Ne3 7 Qe2 Nxf1 8 Ne4 Ne3 9 Nf6+ Ke7 10 Bd2 Nxc2+ 11 Kf2 Nxa1 12 Nd5+ Ke6 13 Qc4 b5 14 Nxg5+ Qxg5 15 Nxc7++ Ke7 16 Nd5+ Ke6 17 Nxf4++ Ke7 18 Nd5+ Ke8 19 Qxc8+ Qd8 20 Nc7+ Ke7 21 Bb4+ d6 22 Bxd6+ Qxd6 23 Qe8 mate.

## (27) Bronstein,D – Dely,P
### Asztalos Memorial Tournament, Miskolcz, 1963
*[A27] English Opening*

1 c4 e5 2 Nc3 Nc6 3 Nf3 f5 4 d4 e4 5 Bg5 Be7 6 Bxe7 Qxe7 7 Nd5 Qd6 8 Nd2 Nge7 9 Nxe7 Nxe7 10 e3 0-0 11 g4 c5 12 Nb3 cxd4 13 c5 Qg6 14 Qxd4 Qxg4 15 Be2 Qg6 16 0-0-0 b6 17 f4 exf3 18 Bxf3 bxc5 19 Nxc5 Nc6 20 Qf4 Qe8 21 Kb1 Qe7 22 Qd6 Qxd6 23 Rxd6 Rb8 24 Nxd7 Bxd7 25 Rxd7 Ne5 26 Bd5+ Kh8 27 Rxa7 Rfd8 28 Rb7 Rxb7 29 Bxb7 Nc4 30 Rc1 Nxe3 31 a4 g5 32 a5 Black resigns.

## (28) Bronstein,D – Korchnoi,V
### USSR Zonal Tournament, Moscow, 1964
*[D24] Queen's Gambit Accepted*

1 d4 d5 2 c4 dxc4 3 Nf3 Nf6 4 Nc3 a6 5 e4 b5 6 e5 Nd5 7 a4 Nxc3 8 bxc3 Qd5 9 g3 Bb7 10 Bg2 Qd7 11 Ba3 e6 12 Bxf8 Kxf8 13 0-0 g6 14 Nh4 c6 15 f4 Qe7 16 Qd2 Kg7 17 f5 exf5 18 Rxf5 Bc8 19 Rf6 Ra7 20 Raf1 Be6 21 Qg5 Qe8 22 Be4 Rg8 23 Ng2 Kh8 24 Nf4 Re7 25 axb5 axb5 26 Qh6 Nd7 27 Bxc6 b4 28 d5 Bg4 29 e6 Qf8 30 Qxf8 Nxf8 31 h3 g5 32 d6 Rxe6 33 Nxe6 Bxe6 34 cxb4 Kg7 35 Be8 c3 36 Bxf7 Black resigns.

## (29) Bronstein,D – Korchnoi,V
### Match Moscow vs. Leningrad by telephone, 1st board, 1964
*[B81] Sicilian Defence*

1 e4 c5 2 Nf3 e6 3 d4 cxd4 4 Nxd4 Nf6 5 Nc3 d6 6 g4 a6 7 g5 Nfd7 8 Bc4 Ne5 9 Be2 b5 10 a3 Bb7 11 f4 Nc4 12 f5 e5 13 Nf3 Nd7 14 Bxc4 bxc4 15 Be3 g6 16 fxg6 hxg6 17 Qe2 Qc7 18 0-0-0 Be7 19 h4 Nf8 20 Nd2 Rc8 21 Rdf1 Bd8 22 Rh2 Rh7 23 Kb1 Rh5 24 Rhf2 Rh7 25 Rf3 Ne6 26 Qf2 Qe7 27 Nd5 Bxd5 28 exd5 Nc7 29 Nxc4 Nb5 30 Nb6 Bxb6 31 Bxb6 Rc4 32 h5 gxh5 33 Rf6 Rg7 34 Qf5 Black resigns.

## (30) Bronstein,D – Uhlmann,W
### United Nations Peace Tournament, Zagreb, 1965
*[C18] French Defence*

1 e4 e6 2 d4 d5 3 Nc3 Bb4 4 e5 Ne7 5 a3 Bxc3+ 6 bxc3 c5 7 Qg4 Qc7 8 Qxg7 Rg8 9 Qxh7 cxd4 10 Kd1 Nd7 11 Nf3 Nxe5 12 Bf4 Qxc3 13 Nxe5 Qxa1+ 14 Bc1 d3 15 Qxf7+ Kd8 16 Qf6 dxc2+ 17 Kd2 Qd4+ 18 Bd3 Ke8 19 Ke2 Bd7 20 Be3 Qb2 21 Rc1 Rc8 22 Nxd7 d4 23 Bd2 Bxd7 24 Bb4 Rge8 25 Bb5+ Rc6 26 Kd2 Nd5 27 Qf7+ Re7 28 Bxe7 Qc3+ 29 Ke2 d3+ 30 Bxd3 Nxe7 31 Rxc2 Qe5+ 32 Kd1 Qa1+ 33 Kd2 Qxa3 34 Rxc6 bxc6 35 Bc4 Qb4+ 36 Kd3 Qb1+ 37 Kc3 Qc1+ 38 Kd3 Qb1+ Draw agreed.

## (31) Polugayevsky,L – Bronstein,D
### 35th USSR Championship, Tbilisi, 1967
*[D34] Tarrasch Defence*

1 c4 Nf6 2 Nc3 e6 3 Nf3 c5 4 g3 d5 5 cxd5 exd5 6 d4 Nc6 7 Bg2 Be7 8 0-0 0-0 9 Bg5 cxd4 10 Nxd4 h6 11 Bf4 Qb6 12 Nxc6 bxc6 13 Qc2 Bg4 14 Be3 Qa6 15 Bd4 Rfd8 16 h3 Be6 17 Rfd1 Rac8 18 Rac1 Nd7 19 e4 dxe4 20 Qxe4 c5 21 Be3 Bf6 22

♗f1 c4 23 ♖c2 ♖e8 24 ♖cd2 ♗xh3 25 ♖d6
♘b6 26 ♗xh3 ♖xe4 27 ♗xc8 ♕xc8 28
♘xe4 ♗e7 29 ♖6d2 ♕e6 30 ♘c3 ♗b4 31
♗d4 ♕g4 32 a3 ♗a5 33 ♗e3 ♘h7 34 ♖d4
♕g6 35 ♖c1 ♕e6 36 ♘e2 ♕e5 37 ♘f4 ♕b5
38 ♖c2 ♕b3 39 ♖e2 ♘a4 40 ♖d5 ♗c7 41
♖d7 ♗e5 (sealed move) 42 ♗xa7 ♗f6 43
♔h2 ♘xb2 44 ♖xf7 ♘d3 45 ♘d5 ♔g6 46
♖d7 ♘e5 47 ♖c7 ♕xa3 48 ♘xf6 gxf6 49
♗e3 ♕d3 50 ♖a2 ♕f1 51 g4 ♘xg4+ 52 ♔g3
♘e5 53 ♔h2 ♘f3+ 54 ♔g3 ♘e1 55 ♔f4
♕g2 White resigns.

## (32) Fuchs,R – Bronstein,D
100th Birthday Dr Lasker Tournament,
Berlin, 1968
*[B14] Caro-Kann Defence*

1 e4 c6 2 d4 d5 3 exd5 cxd5 4 c4 ♘f6 5 ♘c3
g6 6 ♕b3 ♗g7 7 cxd5 0-0 8 ♘ge2 ♘bd7 9
g3 ♘b6 10 ♗g2 ♗f5 11 0-0 ♕d7 12 ♖e1 h6
13 a4 ♖ad8 14 d6 ♕xd6 15 ♘b5 ♕d7 16
♘xa7 ♘bd5 17 ♘b5 ♗e4 18 ♘f4 ♗xg2 19
♔xg2 b6 20 ♕f3 ♘b4 21 ♖e2 ♖fe8 22 ♗e3
g5 23 ♘h5 g4 24 ♘xf6+ exf6 25 ♕f4 ♘d5
White resigns.

## (33) Jongsma,L – Bronstein,D
IBM Tournament,
Amsterdam, 1968
*[B10] Caro-Kann Defence*

1 e4 c6 2 d3 e5 3 f4 exf4 4 ♗xf4 d5 5 ♘d2
♕f6 6 ♗g3 ♕xb2 7 ♘gf3 ♘f6 8 ♗e5 ♕a3 9
♗xf6 gxf6 10 ♗e2 dxe4 11 ♘xe4 ♗g7 12
0-0 f5 13 ♘g3 f4 14 ♘e4 0-0 15 d4 ♗f5 16
♘f2 c5 17 ♖b1 ♘c6 18 ♖b3 ♕xa2 19 ♖xb7
♖ad8 20 ♗d3 ♗g6 21 dxc5 a5 22 ♕b1
♕xb1 23 ♖fxb1 a4 24 ♖1b6 a3 25 ♖xc6 a2
26 ♖a6 ♖a8 27 ♖ba7 a1♕+ 28 ♖xa1 ♗xa1
29 ♖xa8 ♖xa8 30 ♘h3 ♖c8 31 ♘xf4 ♖xc5
32 ♘xg6 hxg6 33 ♔f2 f5 34 ♔e3 ♗g7 35 h3
♔f6 36 g4 ♗c3 37 gxf5 gxf5 38 ♘h4 ♖e5+
39 ♔f3 ♔g5 40 ♘xf5 ♖xf5+ 41 ♗xf5 ♔xf5
Draw agreed.

## (34) Shamkovich,L – Bronstein,D
39th USSR Championship,
Leningrad, 1971
*[E80] King's Indian Defence*

1 c4 g6 2 d4 ♘f6 3 ♘c3 ♗g7 4 e4 d6 5 f3 b6
6 ♗d3 ♗b7 7 ♘ge2 c5 8 d5 ♘bd7 9 0-0 ♘e5
10 ♗b1 a6 11 ♕b3 b5 12 a4 b4 13 ♘d1 a5
14 ♗g5 h6 15 ♗h4 g5 16 ♗g3 ♘h5 17 ♘e3
e6 18 ♗c2 ♕e7 19 ♖ad1 0-0-0 20 ♗b1 ♘g6
21 ♕c2 ♘hf4 22 ♕d2 h5 23 b3 ♗h6 24 ♔h1
h4 25 ♗xf4 gxf4 26 ♘g4 h3 27 gxh3 ♗g5
28 ♘g1 e5 29 ♖f2 ♔c7 30 ♗d3 ♘h4 31 ♖g2
♗c8 32 ♘e2 ♖h5 33 ♘g1 ♖dh8 34 ♕e2
♗g5 35 ♕c2 ♗h6 36 ♖f1 ♗g7 37 ♖e2 ♘h4
38 ♖ef2 f5 39 exf5 ♘xf5 40 ♕d2 ♗h6 41
♗xf5 ♗xf5 42 ♖e2 ♖g8 43 ♖fe1 ♗d7 44
♖g2 ♗g5 45 ♘f2 ♖gh8 46 ♘e4 ♗h4 47 ♖d1
♖5h6 48 ♕e2 ♗f5 49 ♖d2 ♔b6 50 ♕d3 ♕d7
51 ♖de2 ♗g3 52 ♕d2 ♗xh3 53 ♘xh3 ♕xh3
54 ♘f2 ♕xh2+ 55 ♖xh2 ♖xh2+ 56 ♔g1
♗xf2+ White resigns.

## (35) Bronstein,D – Parma,B
Alekhine Memorial Tournament,
Moscow, 1971
*[B79] Sicilian Defence*

1 e4 c5 2 ♘f3 d6 3 d4 cxd4 4 ♘xd4 ♘f6 5
♘c3 g6 6 ♗e3 ♗g7 7 f3 ♘c6 8 ♕d2 0-0 9
♗c4 ♗d7 10 ♗b3 ♕a5 11 0-0-0 ♖fc8 12 h4
♘e5 13 h5 ♘xh5 14 ♘d5 ♕xd2+ 15 ♖xd2
♔f8 16 g4 ♗xg4 17 fxg4 ♘xg4 18 ♗g5 ♘gf6
19 ♘xf6 ♗xf6 20 ♘f3 ♔g7 21 ♗xf6+ ♘xf6
22 e5 dxe5 23 ♘xe5 ♘e4 24 ♖dh2 h5 25
♘xf7 ♖c7 26 ♖g2 ♖f8 27 ♗d5 ♘c5 28 ♘e5
♖f5 29 ♖xg6+ ♔h7 30 ♗g8+ Black resigns.

## (36) Bronstein,D – Hug,W
Interzonal Tournament,
Petropolis, 1973
*[C05] French Defence*

1 e4 e6 2 d4 d5 3 ♘d2 ♘f6 4 e5 ♘fd7 5 f4
c5 6 c3 ♘c6 7 ♘df3 cxd4 8 cxd4 ♘b6 9 ♘e2

h5 10 ♘c3 ♗d7 11 ♗e2 ♖c8 12 0-0 g6 13 ♔h1 a6 14 b3 ♘e7 15 ♕d2 ♘f5 16 ♗b2 ♗b4 17 a3 ♗e7 18 ♘a2 ♔f8 19 ♗c3 ♘a8 20 ♗a5 ♕e8 21 a4 ♔g7 22 ♗d3 ♘h6 23 ♕e2 ♗d8 24 ♗d2 ♗e7 25 ♕e1 ♖c7 26 ♘c3 ♗c6 27 ♘e2 ♘f5 28 g3 ♕c8 29 ♘c1 b6 30 ♔g1 a5 31 ♘a2 ♗b7 32 ♘c3 ♖c6 33 ♘b5 ♕b8 34 ♕e2 ♘c7 35 ♗e1 ♘a6 36 ♖d1 ♘b4 37 ♗b1 ♗a6 38 h3 ♖h6 39 ♕d2 ♖c8 40 ♔g2 ♘c2 41 ♗f2 ♗xb5 42 axb5 ♘a3 43 ♗d3 ♗b4 44 ♕e2 ♖c3 45 g4 ♘e7 46 ♗h4 ♖xb3 47 ♗g5 ♖h7 48 f5 gxf5 49 gxf5 ♘xf5 50 ♘h4 ♘xh4+ 51 ♗xh4 ♕g8 52 ♔h2 ♗f8 53 ♗f6 ♗c3 54 ♖g1 ♖h8 55 ♖xg8+ ♖xg8 56 ♕xh5 Black resigns.

## (37) Bronstein,D – Gheorghiu,F
Interzonal Tournament,
Petropolis 1973
*[B96] Sicilian Defence*

1 e4 c5 2 ♘f3 d6 3 d4 cxd4 4 ♘xd4 ♘f6 5 ♘c3 a6 6 ♗g5 e6 7 f4 ♘bd7 8 ♕e2 ♕c7 9 0-0-0 b5 10 a3 ♖b8 11 ♘d5 exd5 12 exd5+ ♗e7 13 ♘c6 ♘b6 14 ♗xf6 gxf6 15 g3 ♗b7 16 ♘xb8 ♕xb8 17 ♗g2 ♕d8 18 ♖he1 f5 19 ♖d3 ♔d7 20 ♕h5 ♕c8 21 ♕xf5+ ♔b8 22 ♕xf7 ♗f6 23 ♖de3 ♗xb2+ 24 ♔xb2 ♘c4+ 25 ♔a2 ♘xe3 26 ♖xe3 ♕b6 27 ♖e8+ ♖xe8 28 ♕xe8+ ♔a7 29 ♕e4 ♕f2 30 ♕b2 a5 31 f5 ♔b6 32 g4 h6 33 ♗f3 ♕xh2 34 f6 ♕h4 35 ♕d4+ ♔c7 36 f7 Black resigns.

## (38) Bronstein,D – Saidy,A
International Tournament,
Tallinn 1973
*[B10] Caro-Kann Defence*

1 e4 c6 2 d3 d5 3 ♘d2 g6 4 g3 ♗g7 5 ♗g2 e5 6 ♘gf3 ♘e7 7 0-0 0-0 8 b4 ♘d7 9 ♗b2 b6 10 ♖e1 d4 11 c3 dxc3 12 ♗xc3 ♗a6 13 ♘b3 ♕c7 14 d4 ♖ad8 15 ♕c1 exd4 16 ♗xd4 ♘e5 17 ♗xe5 ♗xe5 18 ♘xe5 ♕xe5 19 ♕a3 ♗c4 20 f4 ♕c7 21 ♕b2 c5 22 ♘d2 ♗a6 23 ♖ac1 ♕d6 24 ♘f3 cxb4 25 e5 ♕b8 26 ♕xb4 ♘f5 27 ♘g5 ♗g7 28 e6 fxe6 29 ♘xe6 ♘xe6 30 ♖xe6 ♖f7 31 ♕b3 ♖c8 32 ♖xc8+ ♕xc8 33 ♗c6 ♕c7 34 ♕c3 ♖f8 35 ♖xg6+ hxg6 36 ♗d5+ ♕f7 37 ♗xf7+ ♖xf7 38 ♕c2 ♔g7 39 ♕a4 ♗c8 40 ♕d4+ ♔h7 41 ♕c4 Black resigns.

## (39) Bronstein,D – Beliavsky,A
USSR Super League Championship,
Erevan, 1975
*[B18] Caro-Kann Defence*

1 e4 c6 2 d4 d5 3 ♘c3 dxe4 4 ♘xe4 ♗f5 5 ♘c5 ♕b6 6 g4 ♗g6 7 f4 e6 8 ♕e2 ♗e7 9 h4 h5 10 f5 exf5 11 g5 ♘d7 12 ♘b3 ♕c7 13 ♘h3 0-0-0 14 ♗f4 ♗d6 15 ♕h2 ♘f8 16 0-0-0 ♘e6 17 ♗xd6 ♖xd6 18 ♗c4 ♘e7 19 ♘f4 ♘xf4 20 ♕xf4 ♖dd8 21 ♕xc7+ ♔xc7 22 c3 ♖he8 23 ♘c5 ♖c8 24 ♘d3 ♗d6 25 ♗b3 ♖e3 26 ♘f4 ♖de8 27 ♖hg1 ♖8e7 28 ♖df1 ♘e4 29 ♗d1 ♔d6 30 ♗f3 c5 31 dxc5+ ♔xc5 32 ♘g2 ♖d3 33 ♘f4 ♖d8 34 ♖d1 ♖ed7 35 ♖xd7 ♖xd7 36 ♖d1 ♖xd1+ 37 ♔xd1 ♘d6 38 ♔c2 a5 39 a4 ♔b6 40 ♔d3 ♔c7 41 ♔d4 ♘c8 42 b4 axb4 43 cxb4 ♘e7 44 a5 f6 45 gxf6 gxf6 46 ♔c5 ♗f7 47 b5 ♔c8 48 b6 Black resigns.

## (40) Bronstein,D – Romanishin,O
USSR Super League Championship,
Erevan, 1975
*[B27] Sicilian Defence*

1 e4 c5 2 ♘f3 g6 3 d4 ♗g7 4 c3 ♕a5 5 ♘bd2 cxd4 6 b4 ♕b6 7 cxd4 d5 8 exd5 ♘f6 9 ♗c4 ♕xb4 10 a4 0-0 11 ♗a3 ♕a5 12 ♘b3 ♘e4 13 ♗b4 ♘xd2 14 ♗xd2 ♕b6 15 ♕xb6 axb6 16 0-0 ♗f5 17 ♖fe1 ♗f6 18 ♗b4 ♖c8 19 ♗b5 ♘a6 20 ♗xe7 ♗xe7 21 ♖xe7 ♘c7 22 ♖ae1 ♘xd5 23 ♖xb7 ♘c3 24 ♘g5 ♘xb5 25 axb5 ♖ab8 26 ♖be7 ♖f8 27 ♖1e3 ♖bd8 28 ♘f3 ♗g4 29 h3 ♗xf3 30 ♖xf3 ♖d5 31 ♖e5 ♖fd8 32 ♖f6 ♖xe5 33 dxe5 ♖d5 34 ♖xb6 ♖xe5 35 ♔f1 ♔g7 36 g3 h5 37 h4 ♔h7 38 ♔g2 ♖f5 39 ♖b7 ♔g7 40 b6 ♖b5 41 ♔f3 ♖b2 42 ♔e4 (sealed move) ♖xf2 43 ♖c7 ♖b2 44 b7 ♔f6 45 ♔d5 ♖f5 46 ♖xf7+ ♔g4 47 ♖g7 ♔xg3 48 ♖xg6+ ♔xh4 49 ♔c6 ♔h3 50 ♖g5 ♖xb7 51 ♔xb7 h4 52 ♔c6 ♔h2 53 ♔d5 h3 54 ♔e4 Black resigns.

## (41) Bronstein,D – Tal,M
USSR Super League Championship,
Erevan, 1975
*[B44] Sicilian Defence*

1 e4 c5 2 ♘f3 e6 3 d4 cxd4 4 ♘xd4 ♘c6 5 ♘b5 d6 6 c4 ♘f6 7 ♘5c3 ♗e7 8 ♗e2 0-0 9

0-0 b6 10 ♗f4 ♗b7 11 ♘d2 ♘d7 12 ♖c1
♖c8 13 ♗g3 a6 14 ♔h1 ♘d4 15 ♗d3 ♘e5
16 ♗b1 ♗h4 17 ♗f4 ♘xc4 18 ♘xc4 ♖xc4
19 ♕d3 ♖c5 20 ♗e3 e5 21 ♖cd1 ♖e8 22 a3
b5 23 ♗a2 ♗f6 24 ♗d5 ♗c8 25 f4 ♕e7 26
f5 ♗d7 27 ♖fe1 ♖ec8 28 ♗a2 ♗c6 29 b4
♖xc3 30 ♕xc3 ♘xf5 31 ♖c1 ♘xe3 32 ♖xe3
♗g5 33 ♖f3 ♗xc1 34 ♖xf7 ♕xf7 35 ♗xf7+
♔xf7 36 ♕xc1 ♗b7 37 ♕e3 ♗xe4 38 ♔g1
♗d5 39 ♕d3 ♖c1+ 40 ♔f2 ♔e6 41 ♕h3+
♔f6 42 ♕h4+ ♔g6 43 ♕g3+ ♔f6 44 ♕d3
♗e6 45 ♕xd6 ♖c2+ 46 ♔e1 ♖xg2 47 h4
♖a2 48 ♕xa6 ♔f5 49 ♕xb5 ♖a1+ 50 ♔d2
♖a2+ 51 ♔c1 ♖a1+ 52 ♔b2 ♖a2+ 53 ♔b1
♖xa3 54 ♕c5 ♖d3 55 b5 ♗d5 56 ♕c8+ ♔f4
57 ♕f8+ ♔e3 58 ♕c5+ ♔f4 59 ♔c1 ♗e4 60
♕c7 ♖d5 61 ♕f7+ ♔e3 62 ♕a7+ ♔d3 63
♕f2 ♖d4 64 ♕c2+ ♔e3 65 ♕c7 ♖d5 66
♕a7+ ♔e2 67 ♕a2+ ♔e3 68 ♕a3+ ♔e2 69
♕b2+ ♔e3 70 ♕c3+ ♔e2 71 ♕c4+ ♔e3 72
♕b3+ ♖d3 73 ♕e6 ♖d5 74 ♕c6 ♔e2 75
♕c4+ ♔e3 76 b6 ♖d7 77 ♕e6 ♖d5 78
♕h3+ ♗f3 79 ♕h2 ♖d1+ 80 ♔c2 ♖d5 81
♕g1+ ♔e2 82 ♕h2+ ♔e3 83 ♔c3 g6 84
♕g1+ ♔f4 85 ♕g5+ ♔e4 86 ♕f6 ♔e3 87
♔b4 ♗e4 88 ♔c4 ♖d4+ 89 ♔c5 ♖d5+ 90
♔b4 ♖d4+ 91 ♔a5 ♖d1 92 ♔a6 ♖a1+ 93
♔b5 ♖b1+ 94 ♔a4 ♖a1+ 95 ♔b3 ♖b1+ 96
♔a3 ♖a1+ 97 ♔b2 ♖b1+ 98 ♔a2 ♖b5 99
♕f1 ♗d5+ 100 ♔a3 ♖b3+ 101 ♔a4 ♔d4
102 ♕f2+ ♔c4 103 ♕c2+ ♖c3 104 ♕e2+
♖d3 105 ♕c2+ ♖c3 106 ♕a2+ ♔c5 107
♕f2+ ♔c4 108 ♕e2+ ♖d3 109 ♕a2+ ♔c3
110 ♕a3+ ♔c2 111 ♕c5+ ♔d1 112 ♕g1+
♔e2 113 ♕h2+ ♔f3 114 ♕xe5 ♗e4 115
♕f6+ ♔g4 116 ♕e6+ ♔f4 117 ♕f7+ ♔g3
118 ♕c7+ ♔h3 119 ♕f4 ♗g2 120 b7 ♗c6+
121 ♔b4 Black resigns.

### (42) Bronstein,D – Korchnoi,V
International Tournament,
Hastings, 1975/76
*[B74] Sicilian Defence*

1 e4 c5 2 ♘f3 d6 3 d4 cxd4 4 ♘xd4 ♘f6 5
♘c3 g6 6 ♗e2 ♗g7 7 ♗e3 0-0 8 ♘b3 ♘c6 9
0-0 ♗e6 10 f4 ♕c8 11 ♔h1 ♖d8 12 ♗g1 b6
13 ♕e1 ♘b4 14 ♖c1 ♗c4 15 ♗xc4 ♕xc4 16
♘d2 ♕c8 17 a3 ♘c6 18 ♘f3 ♖b8 19 ♘d5 e6
20 ♘xf6+ ♗xf6 21 c3 ♖b7 22 ♗f2 ♕c7 23
♖d1 ♖e8 24 ♗g3 ♗g7 25 ♕f2 f5 26 ♖fe1

♗f8 27 h3 ♕c8 28 ♗h4 fxe4 29 ♖xe4 d5 30
♖e2 ♗d6 31 ♘g5 ♗e7 32 ♖xe6 ♗xg5 33
♖xe8+ ♕xe8 34 ♗xg5 ♕f7 35 ♕f3 ♖d7 36
♖e1 ♖d6 37 ♕g4 ♕d7 38 ♕e2 ♔f7 39 ♖d1
♕f5 40 ♗h4 d4 41 cxd4 ♕e6 42 ♕f2 ♕e4
43 d5 ♖xd5 44 ♖e1 ♕d3 45 ♔h2 ♖d6 46
♖e3 ♕d5 47 ♕c2 ♖d7 48 ♕e2 ♕d1 49 ♕a6
♕d4 50 ♕e2 ♕d1 51 ♕c4+ ♕d5 52 ♕c3
♘d4 53 ♖d3 ♕e4 54 ♗g3 b5 55 ♔h1 ♖d5
56 ♗f2 ♘e6 57 ♖xd5 ♕xd5 58 ♗xa7 ♕d6
59 ♗e3 ♕d5 60 ♔g1 h5 61 ♕c2 ♘g7 62
♕c7+ ♔g8 63 ♕b8+ ♔f7 64 ♕c7+ ♔g8 65
♕e5 ♕c6 66 ♗f2 ♔f7 67 ♕c5 ♕xc5 68
♗xc5 ♔e6 69 ♗f8 ♘f5 70 ♔f2 ♔d5 71 g4
♘d4 72 f5 gxf5 73 gxh5 ♘e6 74 ♗g7 ♔g5
75 h4 ♘e4+ 76 ♔e3 ♔e6 77 ♗d4 ♔f7 78
♔f4 Black resigns.

### (43) Bronstein,D – Hartston,W
International Tournament,
Hastings, 1975/76
*[B22] Sicilian Defence*

1 e4 c5 2 ♘f3 e6 3 c3 ♘f6 4 e5 ♘d5 5 d4
cxd4 6 cxd4 d6 7 a3 ♗e7 8 ♗d3 ♘c6 9 0-0
♗d7 10 ♖e1 dxe5 11 dxe5 ♖c8 12 ♗e4 0-0
13 ♕d3 h6 14 ♗d2 ♕b6 15 ♗xd5 exd5 16
♘c3 ♗e6 17 ♘xd5 ♖cd8 18 ♘xe7+ ♘xe7
19 ♕e3 ♕xe3 20 ♗xe3 ♘c6 21 h3 ♖d5 22
♗d2 ♖fd8 23 ♗c3 a5 24 ♖ac1 b5 25 ♗d2
♖c8 26 ♖e3 b4 27 axb4 axb4 28 ♖e4 b3 29
♖ec4 ♘e7 30 ♖xc8+ ♘xc8 31 ♗e3 ♘e7 32
♘d4 ♖xe5 33 ♘xe6 fxe6 34 ♖c3 ♖b5 35
♔f1 ♘d5 36 ♖c8+ ♔f7 37 ♗d2 g5 38 g3
♘f6 39 ♔e2 h5 40 ♗e3 g4 41 h4 ♘d5 42
♗d4 e5 43 ♗e3 e4 44 ♗d2 ♔e6 45 ♖e8+
♔f5 46 ♖h8 ♔g6 47 ♖h6+ ♔f7 48 ♖c6 ♖b6
49 ♖c4 ♖e6 50 ♖c5 ♖e5 51 ♖a5 ♔e6 52 ♖a3
e3 53 fxe3 ♘e7 54 ♗c3 ♖f5 55 ♖xb3 ♖f3 56
♖b6+ ♔d5 57 e4+ ♔c5 58 ♖f6 ♖xg3 59
♗e1 ♖b3 60 ♗c3 ♔c4 61 ♖e6 ♖b7 62 ♔e3
♖c7 63 ♗e5 ♖d7 64 ♔f4 ♔d3 65 ♖d6+
♖xd6 66 ♗xd6 Black resigns.

### (44) Sax,G – Bronstein,D
3rd Tungsram International Tournament,
Budapest, 1977
*[C16] French Defence*

1 e4 e6 2 d4 d5 3 ♘c3 ♗b4 4 e5 b6 5 ♕g4
♗f8 6 ♘f3 ♕d7 7 ♗d3 ♘c6 8 a3 ♗b7 9 ♗g5

h6 10 ♗e3 0-0-0 11 h4 h5 12 ♕g3 f6 13 0-0-0 ♘h6 14 ♖he1 ♘g4 15 ♗f4 a6 16 ♖e2 f5 17 ♗g5 ♖e8 18 ♔b1 ♔b8 19 ♖ed2 ♘a7 20 ♘e2 ♕a4 21 ♖c1 ♘b5 22 ♗xb5 axb5 23 ♘f4 b4 24 axb4 ♗a6 25 b3 ♕xb4 26 ♘g6 ♔b7 27 ♘e1 ♗c4 28 ♘d3 ♕a5 29 bxc4 ♖a8 30 c3 ♕a1+ 31 ♔c2 ♕a4+ Draw agreed.

## (45) Tal,M – Bronstein,D
Simultaneous play on 8 boards
against each other,
Tbilisi, 1982

*[E12] Queen's Indian Defence*

1 d4 ♘f6 2 c4 e6 3 ♘f3 b6 4 a3 ♗e7 5 ♘c3 d5 6 cxd5 exd5 7 ♗f4 0-0 8 e3 c5 9 ♘e5 ♗b7 10 ♗d3 ♘bd7 11 ♕f3 ♖e8 12 0-0 a6 13 ♕h3 ♘f8 14 ♗g5 cxd4 15 exd4 ♘e4 16 ♘xe4 dxe4 17 ♗c4 ♗d5 18 ♕b3 ♗xc4 19 ♕xc4 ♘e6 20 ♘c6 b5 21 ♕a2 ♕d7 22 ♘xe7+ ♔h8 23 ♗h4 g5 24 ♘d5 gxh4 25 ♘b6 ♕b7 26 ♘xa8 ♘f4 27 b4 ♖g8 28 d5 ♖xg2+ 29 ♔h1 ♕d7 30 ♕b2+ ♔g8 31 ♕b3 ♘d3 32 ♖g1 ♖g4 33 ♕c2 ♔f8 34 f3 ♖xg1+ 35 ♖xg1 ♕f5 36 ♖f1 e3 37 ♘b6 h3 38 d6 ♘f2+ 39 ♖xf2 exf2 40 ♕xf2 ♕d3 41 ♘d7+ ♔e8 42 ♘f6+ ♔f8 43 ♘d7+ ♔e8 44 ♘e5 ♕xd6 45 ♕e2 ♕e6 46 ♕e4 Black resigns.

## (46) Rashkovsky,N – Bronstein,D
Moscow Open Championship,
dedicated to 60 years existence of the
Soviet Union, 1982

*[E21] Nimzo-Indian Defence*

1 d4 ♘f6 2 c4 e6 3 ♘c3 ♗b4 4 ♘f3 d6 5 ♗g5 h6 6 ♗h4 ♕e7 7 e3 ♘bd7 8 ♗e2 ♗xc3+ 9 bxc3 b6 10 ♘d2 ♗b7 11 ♗f3 ♗xf3 12 ♕xf3 0-0 13 ♕c6 ♖ac8 14 0-0 ♕e8 15 f4 ♘h7 16 a4 ♘b8 17 ♕b5 ♘c6 18 ♘b3 a6 19 ♕xa6 ♖a8 20 ♕b5 ♘a5 21 ♘d2 f5 22 ♕xe8 ♖fxe8 23 c5 bxc5 24 dxc5 dxc5 25 ♖fb1 ♘f8 26 ♘b3 ♘d7 27 ♘xa5 ♖xa5 28 ♖b7 Draw agreed.

## (47) Bronstein,D – Hodgson,J
Young Masters Tournament,
London, 1989

*[D98] Grünfeld Defence*

1 d4 ♘f6 2 ♘f3 g6 3 c4 ♗g7 4 ♘c3 d5 5 ♕b3 dxc4 6 ♕xc4 0-0 7 e4 ♗g4 8 ♗e2 ♘fd7

9 d5 ♘b6 10 ♕b3 c6 11 0-0 cxd5 12 exd5 ♘8d7 13 ♖d1 ♕b8 14 ♗g5 ♘c8 15 ♖ac1 h6 16 ♗e3 ♗xf3 17 ♗xf3 ♘e5 18 ♗e2 ♘d6 19 ♘b5 ♘xb5 20 ♕xb5 ♖d8 21 ♗c5 ♗f8 22 ♕b4 ♖e8 23 ♗b5 a5 24 ♕e4 f5 25 ♕e2 ♖c8 26 a4 ♔h7 27 h3 b6 28 ♗d4 ♖xc1 29 ♖xc1 ♘f7 30 ♖c6 ♕f4 31 ♗xb6 ♘d6 32 ♗c7 ♖a7 33 g3 ♕d4 34 ♗b6 Black resigns.

## (48) Bronstein,D – Rexchess
AEGON Tournament,
The Hague, 1991

*[A01] Nimzowitsch-Larsen Attack*

1 b3 d5 2 ♗b2 ♗g4 3 h3 ♗h5 4 g4 ♗g6 5 ♘f3 e6 6 e3 ♘f6 7 d3 ♗e7 8 ♘bd2 0-0 9 ♘e5 ♘bd7 10 ♘xg6 fxg6 11 g5 ♘h5 12 h4 ♗d6 13 ♗h3 ♕e7 14 ♕e2 c6 15 0-0-0 a5 16 f4 ♘g3 17 ♕g4 ♘xh1 18 ♕xe6+ ♖f7 19 ♖xh1 a4 20 ♘f3 ♕f8 21 h5 ♖e8 22 hxg6 ♖xe6 23 ♗xe6 hxg6 24 ♘h4 ♔h7 25 f5 gxf5 26 ♗xf7 ♕xf7 27 g6+ ♕xg6 28 ♘xg6+ ♔xg6 29 ♖g1+ ♔f7 30 ♖xg7+ ♔e6 31 bxa4 Black resigns.

## (49) Welling,G – Bronstein,D
B.S.G. Weekend Tournament,
Bussum, 1991

*[C12] French Defence*

1 e4 e6 2 d4 d5 3 ♘c3 ♘f6 4 ♗g5 ♗b4 5 e5 h6 6 exf6 hxg5 7 fxg7 ♖g8 8 h4 gxh4 9 ♕h5 ♕f6 10 ♘f3 a6 11 ♖xh4 ♘c6 12 0-0-0 ♕xg7 13 ♗d3 ♗d7 14 g3 ♗e7 15 ♖h2 0-0-0 16 ♖dh1 ♘xd4 17 ♘xd4 ♕xd4 18 ♕xf7 ♗g5+ 19 ♔b1 ♖df8 20 ♕h7 ♗f6 21 ♘d1 ♖h8 22 ♕g6 ♖xh2 23 ♖xh2 ♗e8 White resigns.

## (50) Bronstein,D – Perez Garcia,H
Paul Keres Chess Club Tournament,
Utrecht, 1991

*[A81] Dutch Defence*

1 d4 f5 2 g3 ♘f6 3 ♗g2 g6 4 ♘h3 ♗g7 5 ♘f4 d6 6 d5 c6 7 ♘c3 0-0 8 h4 ♕e8 9 h5 ♘a6 10 hxg6 hxg6 11 e4 e5 12 dxe6 ♗xe6 13 0-0 fxe4 14 ♘xe4 d5 15 ♘xe6 ♕xe6 16 ♘g5 ♕g4 17 ♕xg4 ♘xg4 18 ♗h3 ♘h6 19 ♗e6+ ♔h8 20 ♔g2 ♖ae8 21 ♖h1 ♖e7 22 ♗e3 d4 23 ♖xh6+ Black resigns.

## (51) Bronstein,D – Finegold,B

Hoogovens Tournament,
Wijk aan Zee, 1992
*[D19] Slav Defence*

1 d4 d5 2 c4 c6 3 ♘f3 ♘f6 4 ♘c3 dxc4 5 a4
♗f5 6 e3 e6 7 ♗xc4 ♗b4 8 0-0 ♘bd7 9 ♕e2
♗g6 10 e4 0-0 11 ♗d3 ♗h5 12 ♗f4 e5 13
dxe5 ♘g4 14 ♕c2 ♖e8 15 ♗e2 ♗g6 16 ♖ad1
♕c8 17 e6 fxe6 18 ♘h4 ♘ge5 19 ♗xe5 ♘xe5
20 f4 ♘d7 21 ♘xg6 hxg6 22 ♗c4 ♘b6 23
♗a2 ♕c7 24 f5 ♗xc3 25 bxc3 gxf5 26 exf5
♘d5 27 fxe6 ♖xe6 28 ♕f5 ♖h6 29 h3 ♔h8 30
♗b1 ♖g8 31 ♕f3 ♕b6+ 32 ♖d4 ♕c5 33 ♔h1
♘xc3 34 ♖d7 ♘xb1 35 ♖xb1 b5 36 axb5
cxb5 37 ♖e1 a6 38 ♖ee7 ♕c6 39 ♕g4 ♕f6
40 ♖f7 ♕a1+ 41 ♖d1 ♕e5 42 ♖fd7 ♕e6 43
♕g3 ♕g6 44 ♕a3 ♖e8 45 ♔g2 ♕f6 46 ♕d3
♖g6 47 ♖d5 ♖g5 48 ♖d4 ♕f2 49 ♖g1 ♖f8 50
♔h1 a5 51 ♕c3 a4 52 ♕b4 ♖f6 53 ♖d8+
♔h7 54 ♕e4+ ♕f5 55 ♕a8 ♕e6 56 ♖c1 ♕e3
57 ♖cd1 ♖g3 58 ♖h8+ ♔g6 59 ♕d5 ♖g5 60
♕g8 ♖h5 61 ♖xh5 ♔xh5 62 ♕xg7 ♕e5 63
♕h7+ ♔g5 64 h4+ ♔g4 65 ♕g8+ ♔xh4 66
g3+ ♕xg3 67 ♕h8+ ♔g4 68 ♕xf6 ♕h3+
69 ♔g1 ♕g3+ 70 ♔f1 ♕h3+ 71 ♔e2 ♕g2+
72 ♔d3 ♕g3+ 73 ♔d4 Black resigns

## (52) Bronstein,D – Deep Thought II

Played by modem between HP
Laboratories, Palo Alto (Bronstein) and
IBM Headquarters (Deep Thought II),
1992, 20 minutes each
*[B20] Sicilian Defence*

1 e4 c5 2 b4 cxb4 3 a3 d5 4 exd5 ♕xd5 5
♘f3 ♗g4 6 axb4 ♕e4+ 7 ♗e2 ♗xf3 8 gxf3
♕xb4 9 ♘a3 ♕a5 10 ♗b2 ♘c6 11 c4 ♕g5
12 ♕b3 0-0-0 13 d4 ♕g2 14 0-0-0 ♕xf2 15
d5 ♘a5 16 ♕b5 ♕e3+ 17 ♔b1 ♕xe2 18
♕xa5 a6 19 ♖he1 ♕f2 20 c5 ♘f6 21 ♗e5
♘xd5 22 ♘c4 ♕xe1 23 ♖xe1 f6 24 ♘b6+
♘xb6 25 ♕xb6 Black resigns.

## (53) Bronstein,D – Deep Thought II

Played by modem between
HP Laboratories, Palo Alto (Bronstein)
and IBM Headquarters (Deep Thought II),
1992, 15 minutes each
*[B20] Sicilian Defence*

1 e4 c5 2 b4 cxb4 3 a3 d5 4 exd5 ♕xd5 5
♘f3 e5 6 axb4 ♗xb4 7 ♖a3 ♗xa3 8 ♘xa3
♗g4 9 ♘b5 ♘a6 10 ♗a3 0-0-0 11 c4 ♕e4+
12 ♗e2 ♗xf3 13 gxf3 ♕g6 14 ♘xa7+ ♔b8
15 ♘b5 ♘h6 16 c5 ♘c7 17 ♘d6 ♕g2 18 ♖f1
♘e8 19 ♘xb7 ♖d7 20 c6 ♖xb7 21 cxb7 ♕g6
22 ♕b3 ♕c6 23 ♗c4 ♕xb7 24 ♕d3 e4 25
fxe4 f5 26 f3 ♘c7 27 ♔e2 ♕c6 28 ♖b1+
♔c8 29 e5 ♖d8 30 ♗d6 g6 31 ♕d4 f4 32
♖c1 ♘f5 33 ♗e6+ ♔b7 34 ♕b2+ ♕b5+ 35
♕xb5+ ♘xb5 36 ♗xf5 ♘d4+ 37 ♔f2 ♘xf5
38 ♗b4 ♖d5 39 ♖e1 ♔c7 40 e6 ♔d8 41 h4
♘d6 42 e7+ ♔e8 43 ♖e6 ♘f5 44 h5 gxh5
45 ♔g2 ♖d4 46 ♗c3 ♖d3 47 ♖e5 ♘h4+ 48
♔f2 ♖xf3+ 49 ♔e2 ♖h3 50 ♗d4 ♘f3 51
♖e4 ♘xd4+ 52 ♖xd4 f3+ 53 ♔f2 ♔xe7 54
♖f4 ♖h2+ 55 ♔xf3 ♖xd2 56 ♔g3 ♖d5 57
♖a4 ♔f6 58 ♖a8 ♔g5 59 ♖g8+ ♔h6 60 ♔g2
♖g5+ Draw agreed.

## (54) Deep Thought II – Bronstein,D

Played by modem between
HP Laboratories, Palo Alto (Bronstein)
and IBM Headquarters (Deep Thought II),
1992, 20 minutes each
*[A69] King's Indian Defence*

1 d4 ♘f6 2 c4 g6 3 ♘c3 ♗g7 4 e4 d6 5 f4 0-0
6 ♘f3 c5 7 d5 e6 8 ♗e2 exd5 9 cxd5 ♖e8 10
e5 dxe5 11 fxe5 ♘g4 12 ♗g5 ♕b6 13 0-0
♘xe5 14 ♘xe5 ♖xe5 15 ♕d2 ♗f5 16 ♗c4
♘d7 17 ♖ac1 ♖ae8 18 ♗f4 a6 19 ♗xe5
♘xe5 20 ♖fe1 ♕d8 21 ♗f1 ♕h4 22 ♖a1
♖d8 23 h3 ♘g4 24 hxg4 ♗d4+ 25 ♖e3
♗xg4 26 ♕f2 ♕xf2+ 27 ♔xf2 ♖e8 28 ♔g3
♖xe3+ 29 ♔xg4 f5+ 30 ♔f4 ♔f7 31 d6
♔e6 32 ♖d1 h6 33 ♗c4+ ♔xd6 34 ♗f7 g5+
35 ♔xf5 b5 36 ♘e4+ ♔e7 37 ♗d5 ♖e2 38
b4 ♖xg2 39 bxc5 ♗e3 40 ♖e1 ♗d4 41
♘xg5+ ♔d7 42 c6+ ♔d6 43 ♗xg2 hxg5 44
♖d1 Black resigns.

## (55) Bronstein,D – Martens,M

Belgian Team Competition,
Ghent, 1992
*[A00] Sokolsky's Opening*

1 b4 e5 2 ♗b2 ♗xb4 3 ♗xe5 ♘f6 4 ♘f3 0-0
5 e3 ♖e8 6 ♗e2 d5 7 0-0 c5 8 d3 ♘c6 9 ♗g3
♘e7 10 ♘fd2 ♘f5 11 ♗f4 ♗a5 12 g4 ♘h4
13 ♘b3 ♘g6 14 ♗g3 ♗b6 15 g5 ♘d7 16

♘c3 ♘df8 17 h4 ♘e6 18 ♗f3 d4 19 ♘b5 dxe3 20 fxe3 c4 21 dxc4 ♗xe3+ 22 ♔h1 ♕b6 23 ♕d6 ♗f4 24 ♕xb6 axb6 25 ♗f2 ♖a4 26 ♗d5 ♗d7 27 ♖xb6 ♗c6 28 ♘a5 ♗e5 29 ♖ad1 ♗xb5 30 cxb5 ♖xh4+ 31 ♔g1 ♖g4+ 32 ♔h1 ♖h4+ 33 ♔g1 ♘xg5 34 ♗xb7 ♘f4 35 ♖fe1 f6 36 ♘c6 ♘fh3+ 37 ♔f1 ♖f4+ 38 ♔g2 ♖g4+ 39 ♔f1 h5 40 ♘xe5 fxe5 41 ♖d8 ♖xd8 42 ♗xd8 ♖f4+ 43 ♔g2 ♖f2+ 44 ♔g3 ♖xc2 45 ♗xg5 ♘xg5 46 ♖xe5 ♘h7 47 ♗d5+ ♔f8 48 b6 ♘f6 49 b7 ♘d7 50 ♖f5+ ♔e8 51 ♖f7 ♖b2 52 ♖xg7 ♖b6 53 ♗c6 Black resigns.

## (56) Berkmortel v.d.,T – Bronstein,D

Belgian Team Competition,
Brussels, 1993
*[A69] King's Indian Defence*

1 d4 ♘f6 2 c4 g6 3 ♘c3 ♗g7 4 e4 d6 5 f4 0-0 6 ♘f3 c5 7 d5 e6 8 ♗e2 exd5 9 cxd5 ♖e8 10 e5 dxe5 11 fxe5 ♘g4 12 ♗g5 ♕b6 13 ♕d2 ♘xe5 14 0-0-0 ♘a6 15 d6 ♗e6 16 ♘xe5 ♗xe5 17 ♗xa6 bxa6 18 ♖he1 ♗d4 19 d7 ♖eb8 20 ♖e2 ♕c6 21 d8♕+ ♖xd8 22 ♗xd8 ♖xd8 23 ♕g5 ♖b8 24 ♖de1 ♗f5 25 g4 ♗d3 26 ♕f4 ♖f8 27 ♖e7 ♗f6 28 ♖7e3 c4 29 g5 ♕g2 White resigns.

## (57) José Antonio Nuñez – Bronstein,D

Team Competition of Asturias,
Oviedo, 1993
*[C47] Scotch Opening*

1 e4 e5 2 ♘f3 ♘c6 3 d4 exd4 4 ♘xd4 ♘f6 5 ♘c3 ♗b4 6 ♘xc6 bxc6 7 ♗d3 d5 8 exd5 cxd5 9 0-0 0-0 10 ♗g5 c6 11 ♘e2 h6 12 ♗h4 ♗d6 13 ♗g3 c5 14 ♗xd6 ♕xd6 15 ♘g3 ♕f4 16 ♘h5 ♘xh5 17 ♕xh5 ♗e6 18 ♖fe1 c4 19 ♗f1 ♖ab8 20 b3 ♖fc8 21 bxc4 dxc4 22 ♕a5 ♖b2 23 ♕c3 ♕f6 24 ♕xf6 gxf6 25 c3 ♖d8 26 ♖e4 ♖dd2 27 ♗xc4 f5 28 ♖xe6 fxe6 29 ♗xe6+ ♔f8 30 ♖f1 f4 31 g3 ♔e7 32 ♗b3 f3 33 h3 ♔d6 34 h4 a5 35 ♗d1 ♖xa2 36 ♗xf3 a4 37 g4 ♔e5 38 ♔g2 ♔f4 39

g5 hxg5 40 hxg5 a3 41 g6 ♖d6 42 ♗h5 ♖d5 43 ♗d1 ♖g5+ 44 ♔h2 ♖d2 White resigns.

## (58) Escalona Cuevas,L – Bronstein,D

3rd Oviedo Open
Active Chess Tournament, 1993
45 minutes each,
*[C15] French Defence*

1 e4 e6 2 d4 d5 3 ♘c3 ♗b4 4 ♗d2 dxe4 5 ♕g4 ♘f6 6 ♕xg7 ♖g8 7 ♕h6 ♕xd4 8 0-0-0 ♗f8 9 ♕h4 ♖g4 10 ♕h3 ♕xf2 11 ♗e2 ♖h4 12 ♕xh4 ♕xh4 13 g3 ♕h6 14 ♗xh6 ♗xh6+ 15 ♔b1 e5 16 h3 c6 17 ♗g4 ♘bd7 18 ♗f5 ♘c5 19 ♗xc8 ♖xc8 20 ♘ge2 ♔e7 21 ♖hf1 a5 22 ♖f5 ♔e6 23 ♖df1 ♗g7 24 g4 h6 25 ♘g3 ♖d8 26 a3 a4 27 ♘h5 ♘xh5 28 ♖xh5 ♖d2 29 ♖hf5 f6 30 ♖e1 ♖d4 31 ♖f2 h5 32 ♘e2 ♖d2! 33 ♖f5 hxg4 34 hxg4 ♗h6 35 ♘g3 e3 36 ♘h5 ♘e4 37 ♖f3 ♖g2 38 ♖h3 ♘f2 39 ♖f3 ♘xg4 40 ♖g3 ♖xg3 41 ♘xg3 f5 White resigns.

## (59) Bronstein,D – Plaskett,J

3rd Oviedo Open
Active Chess Tournament, 1993
45 minutes each
*[C00] Chigorin Attack*

1 e4 c5 2 ♘f3 e6 3 d3 ♘c6 4 g3 d5 5 ♕e2 ♘f6 6 ♗g2 ♗e7 7 0-0 0-0 8 e5 ♘d7 9 c4 ♖e8 10 ♖e1 ♘f8 11 h4 b6 12 ♘c3 ♗b7 13 b3 ♕d7 14 ♗b2 ♖ad8 15 ♖ad1 a6 16 d4 ♘a5 17 dxc5 bxc5 18 ♘g5 d4 19 ♘ce4 h6 20 ♕h5 hxg5 21 hxg5 g6 22 ♕h4 ♗xe4 23 ♗xe4 ♘h7 24 f4 ♗f8 25 ♔g2 ♗g7 26 ♖h1 ♘f8 27 ♕g4 ♘c6 28 ♖h4 ♘e7 29 ♗c1 ♘f5 30 ♖h3 ♕c7 31 ♖dh1 d3 32 ♗d2 ♖d4 33 ♕f3 ♖ed8 34 g4 ♘e7 35 ♖h4 ♖xe4 36 ♕xe4 ♕c6 37 ♔f3 ♕xe4+ 38 ♔xe4 ♖d4+ 39 ♔e3 ♘c6 40 ♗c3 ♖d7 41 ♖d1 a5 42 ♖xd3 ♖xd3+ 43 ♔xd3 ♘d7 44 ♔e4 ♔f8 45 ♖h1 ♔e8 46 ♗d2 ♗f8 47 a3 ♗e7 48 ♗c3 ♗f8 49 f5 exf5+ 50 gxf5 gxf5+ 51 ♔xf5 ♘e7+ 52 ♔e4 ♘c6 53 g6 fxg6 54 e6 ♘b6 55 ♗f6 a4 56 bxa4 ♘xc4 57 ♔d5 ♘4a5 58 ♖h8 c4 59 ♗g7 ♘e7+ 60 ♔e4 ♘f5 61 ♗xf8 Black resigns.

## (60) Bronstein,D – Spangenberg,H
### International Tournament, Hastings, 1993/94

*[B31] Sicilian Defence*

1 e4 c5 2 ♘f3 ♘c6 3 ♗b5 g6 4 c3 ♗g7 5 d4 ♕b6 6 a4 cxd4 7 0-0 ♘f6 8 e5 ♘d5 9 cxd4 0-0 10 ♘c3 ♘xc3 11 bxc3 d6 12 exd6 exd6 13 ♗f4 a6 14 ♗e2 ♘a5 15 ♖b1 ♕c6 16 d5 ♕c7 17 c4 ♖e8 18 ♗d3 ♗g4 19 h3 ♗xf3 20 ♕xf3 ♕c5 21 ♖fd1 ♖ac8 22 ♗d2 ♘xc4 23 ♗xc4 ♕xc4 24 ♖xb7 ♖c7 25 ♖xc7 ♕xc7 26 ♕d3 ♗e5 27 ♖c1 ♕b6 28 ♗e3 ♕a5 29 ♕c4 h5 30 ♖b1 ♖a8 31 ♕c6 ♕d8 32 a5 ♖c8 33 ♕xa6 ♖a8 34 ♕b6 ♕c8 35 f4 ♗f6 36 ♕xd6 ♕c3 37 ♗f2 ♗d4 38 ♗xd4 ♕xd4+ 39 ♔h1 ♔h7 40 a6 ♕d3 41 ♖b7 Black resigns.

## (61) M-Chess Pro – Bronstein,D
### AEGON Tournament, The Hague, 1994

*[B16] Caro-Kann Defence*

1 e4 c6 2 d4 d5 3 ♘d2 dxe4 4 ♘xe4 ♘f6 5 ♘xf6+ gxf6 6 ♘f3 ♗f5 7 c3 ♘d7 8 g3 ♕a5 9 ♘h4 ♗g6 10 ♗e3 0-0-0 11 ♕b3 e6 12 0-0-0 ♗h5 13 ♖e1 ♘b6 14 ♗g2 c5 15 ♔b1 ♖d7 16 h3 ♗g6+ 17 ♘xg6 hxg6 18 h4 c4 19 ♕c2 ♘d5 20 ♗c1 f5 21 ♗g5 ♖d6 22 ♖e5 ♗g7 23 ♖e2 ♖a6 24 a3 ♗f8 25 ♕c1 ♗d6 26 ♔a1 ♖b6 27 ♗f3 ♔d7 28 ♗xd5 ♕xd5 29 ♗f6 ♖c8 30 ♗e5 ♗e7 31 ♖he1 f6 32 ♗f4 ♖cc6 33 ♗b8 ♖a6 34 ♔a2 ♖cb6 35 ♗f4 ♖b3 36 ♖e3 ♗xa3 37 bxa3 ♕a5 White resigns.

## (62) Bronstein,D – Åstrup,K
### Arnold Eikrem Cup, Gausdal, 1994

*[C39] King's Gambit Accepted*

1 e4 e5 2 f4 exf4 3 ♘f3 g5 4 h4 g4 5 ♘e5 ♘f6 6 ♘xg4 ♘xe4 7 ♘c3 ♘g3 8 ♘d5 ♗g7 9 d4 0-0 10 ♗xf4 ♘xh1 11 ♘h6+ ♔h8 12 ♕h5 ♕e8+ 13 ♔d2 f5 14 ♕xe8 ♖xe8 15 ♗d3 ♘a6 16 ♖xh1 c6 17 ♘f7+ ♔g8 18 ♘d6 ♖e6 19 ♘e3 ♗h6 20 ♗xh6 ♖xd6 21 ♗c4+ ♔h8 22 ♘xf5 ♖xh6 23 ♘xh6 d5 24 ♗xa6 Black resigns.

## (63) Velimirović,D – Bronstein,D
### Donner Memorial Tournament, Amsterdam, 1994

*[B80] Sicilian Defence*

1 e4 c5 2 ♘f3 d6 3 d4 cxd4 4 ♘xd4 ♘f6 5 ♘c3 a6 6 ♗e3 e6 7 ♕d2 b5 8 f3 ♘bd7 9 g4 h6 10 0-0-0 ♗b7 11 h4 b4 12 ♘ce2 d5 13 ♗h3 dxe4 14 g5 hxg5 15 hxg5 exf3 16 ♘g3 ♘e5 17 gxf6 gxf6 18 ♔b1 ♕c7 19 ♗f4 ♗d5 20 ♕e3 ♗e7 21 ♗g2 ♖xh1 22 ♗xh1 0-0-0 23 ♘xf3 ♗xa2+ 24 ♔c1 ♖xd1+ 25 ♔xd1 ♘c4 26 ♕c1 e5 27 ♗h6 f5 28 b3 f4 29 ♘f1 ♕d6+ 30 ♔e2 ♗xh6 31 ♘3d2 ♕xh1 32 bxc4 e4 33 ♕a1 ♕h5+ 34 ♔f2 ♗c5+ 35 ♔g2 f3+ 36 ♔g3 ♗d6+ 37 ♔f2 ♕h4+ 38 ♔e3 ♗c5+ White resigns.

## (64) Bronstein,D – Hunt,H
### Vera Menchik Memorial, Maidstone, 1994

*[B12] Caro-Kann Defence*

1 e4 c6 2 d4 d5 3 f3 e6 4 ♘c3 ♗b4 5 ♘ge2 dxe4 6 fxe4 ♕h4+ 7 ♘g3 ♘f6 8 e5 ♘e4 9 ♕d3 ♘xg3 10 ♕xg3 ♕xd4 11 ♕xg7 ♗xc3+ 12 bxc3 ♕xc3+ 13 ♔f2 ♖f8 14 ♗h6 ♘d7 15 ♗d3 f6 16 ♖ae1 b6 17 ♕xh7 ♕d4+ 18 ♔g3 ♘xe5 19 ♖xe5 ♕xe5+ 20 ♗f4 ♕c3 21 ♔h4 f5 22 ♗e2 ♕f6+ 23 ♔h3 ♖f7 24 ♗h5 ♔e7 25 ♗xf7 ♕xf7 26 ♗d6+ ♔f6 27 ♕h6+ ♕g6 28 ♗e7+ Black resigns.

## (65) Bronstein,D – Chess Genius 2/486-33
### 10 minutes each, Lasne, 1994

*[B18] Caro-Kann Defence*

1 e4 c6 2 d4 d5 3 ♘c3 dxe4 4 ♘xe4 ♗f5 5 ♘g3 ♗g6 6 h4 h6 7 ♘h3 e6 8 ♘f4 ♗h7 9 ♗c4 ♗d6 10 ♗xe6 fxe6 11 ♘xe6 ♕e7 12 0-0 ♗xg3 13 ♖e1 ♗xf2+ 14 ♔xf2 ♕xh4+ 15 ♔g1 ♔d7 16 d5 ♔c8 17 ♗f4 ♘f6 18 c4 ♘e8 19 ♖c1 ♗f5 20 ♗e5 ♗xe6 21 dxe6 a6 22 c5 ♕e7 23 ♗h2 ♕g5 24 ♕d4 ♕d5 25 ♕f4 ♕xa2 26 ♖cd1 ♕a5 27 ♕f7 ♕xc5+ 28 ♔h1 b5 29 ♖d7 ♕b6 30 ♖ed1 a5 31 ♕e7 ♘d6 32 ♖1xd6 Black resigns.

## (66) Chess Genius 2/486-33 – Bronstein,D

10 minutes each,
Lasne, 1994
*[E68] King's Indian Defence*

1 d4 d6 2 ♘f3 ♘f6 3 c4 g6 4 ♘c3 ♗g7 5 g3
0-0 6 ♗g2 ♘bd7 7 0-0 e5 8 e4 exd4 9 ♘xd4
♖e8 10 h3 a6 11 ♖b1 ♖b8 12 b3 c5 13 ♘c2
b5 14 cxb5 axb5 15 b4 ♗b7 16 ♕xd6 ♖c8
17 ♘xb5 ♗xe4 18 ♗xe4 ♘xe4 19 ♕d3 c4
20 ♕f3 c3 21 ♖d1 ♘e5 22 ♕e2 ♕f6 23 ♗e3
♘d2 24 ♖bc1 ♘ef3+ 25 ♔h1 ♕c6 26 ♘a7
♕a8 27 ♘xc8 ♘d4+ 28 ♔h2 ♘xe2 29 ♘b6
♕c6 30 ♖xd2 cxd2 White resigns.

## (67) Kolbus,D – Bronstein,D

International Tournament,
Hastings, 1994/95
*[E62] King's Indian Defence*

1 c4 ♘f6 2 ♘c3 e5 3 g3 c6 4 ♘f3 d6 5 ♗g2
g6 6 0-0 ♗g7 7 e4 0-0 8 d4 ♕a5 9 d5 cxd5
10 cxd5 b5 11 ♖e1 ♗d7 12 a3 b4 13 ♘a2
bxa3 14 ♘c3 ♕b6 15 ♖xa3 ♘a6 16 ♗f1
♘c5 17 ♘d2 a5 18 ♘c4 ♕c7 19 b3 ♖fb8 20
♗d2 ♘e8 21 ♕c2 f5 22 f3 ♘f6 23 ♖ea1 fxe4
24 fxe4 ♖a7 25 h3 ♖ab7 26 ♘xa5 ♘cxe4 27
♗e1 ♕c5+ 28 ♔h2 ♖c7 29 ♗c4 ♘xc3 30
♕xc3 e4 31 ♕d2 e3 32 ♕g2 ♕d4 33 ♖c1
♘e4 34 ♖a2 ♖f8 35 ♗b4 ♗e5 36 ♗e1 h5 37
♔h1 ♖f2 38 ♗xf2 exf2 39 ♕f3 ♗xh3 40
♘c6 ♘xg3+ 41 ♔h2 ♕h4 42 ♖xf2 ♘e2+
43 ♘xe5 ♗f1+ White resigns.

## (68) Bronstein,D – Roos,L

International Tournament,
Hastings, 1994/95
*[C02] French Defence*

1 e4 e6 2 d4 d5 3 e5 c5 4 c3 ♘c6 5 ♘f3 ♕b6
6 a3 c4 7 ♘bd2 f6 8 b3 fxe5 9 ♘xe5 ♘xe5
10 dxe5 ♗c5 11 ♕h5+ g6 12 ♕h4 ♕c7 13
♘f3 ♘e7 14 b4 ♘f5 15 ♕h3 ♗e7 16 ♗e2
0-0 17 g4 ♘g7 18 ♕g3 a5 19 b5 a4 20 h4
♗d7 21 ♘d4 ♗c5 22 h5 ♗xd4 23 cxd4 gxh5

24 ♖b1 ♔h8 25 ♗g5 ♗e8 26 ♗f6 ♗g6 27 b6
♕d7 28 ♖c1 hxg4 29 ♗xg4 ♔g8 30 ♕h3
♖ae8 31 ♔d2 ♕b5 32 ♕c3 ♕xb6 33 ♖h3
♕b3 34 ♕a1 ♕b6 35 ♕c3 ♖a8 36 ♖g1 ♖a5
37 ♗d1 ♖b5 38 ♖xh7 ♖b2+ 39 ♔e1 ♔xh7
40 ♖xg6 ♔xg6 41 ♕g3+ ♔f5 42 ♕g4 mate.

## (69) Bronstein,D – Chess Genius 3/P 90

10 minutes each,
London, 1995
*[B12] Caro-Kann Defence*

1 e4 c6 2 d4 d5 3 f3 e6 4 ♘c3 ♗b4 5 ♘ge2
dxe4 6 fxe4 e5 7 ♕d3 exd4 8 ♘xd4 ♘f6 9
♗g5 h6 10 ♗h4 0-0 11 ♗e2 ♗xc3+ 12 bxc3
♕d6 13 0-0 ♘bd7 14 ♘f5 ♕e5 15 ♖ae1
♔h8 16 ♗f3 ♕a5 17 ♕d4 c5 18 ♕d6 ♕xc3
19 e5 ♘e8 20 ♕e7 ♕xc2 21 ♗d5 ♘c7 22
♗xf7 b6 23 ♗b3 ♕xf5 24 ♖xf5 ♖xf5 25
♕d8+ ♘f8 26 ♕xc7 ♗a6 27 e6 c4 28 ♗c2
♖c5 29 ♕f7 Black resigns.

## (70) Bronstein,D – Chess Genius 3/P 90

10 minutes each,
London, 1995
*[A28] English Opening*

1 c4 e5 2 ♘c3 ♘f6 3 ♘f3 ♘c6 4 d4 exd4 5
♘xd4 ♗b4 6 ♗g5 ♕e7 7 e3 0-0 8 ♗e2 ♗xc3+
9 bxc3 h6 10 ♗h4 d6 11 0-0 ♘e5 12 ♖b1
♘g6 13 ♗g3 ♘e4 14 ♕c2 ♘xg3 15 hxg3
♘e5 16 f4 ♘g4 17 ♗xg4 ♗xg4 18 e4 b6 19
♖be1 ♕d7 20 f5 c5 21 ♘b3 f6 22 ♘c1 ♗h5
23 ♕d3 ♖fe8 24 ♘e2 ♕a4 25 ♘f4 ♗f7 26
♘d5 ♖e5 27 ♖e2 ♖c8 28 ♖fe1 ♖ce8 29 g4
♔h8 30 ♔f2 ♔h7 31 ♔f3 ♔g8 32 ♖h1 b5 33
♕e3 ♗xd5 34 cxd5 ♖xe4 35 ♕xe4 ♖xe4 36
♖xe4 ♕xa2 37 ♖e8+ ♔h7 38 ♖he1 b4 39
♖d8 ♕xd5+ 40 ♔g3 ♕d3+ 41 ♔h2 h5 42
♖e7 ♕xc3 43 ♖dd7 c4 44 ♖xg7+ ♔h8 45
♖h7+ ♔g8 46 ♖dg7+ ♔f8 47 ♖b7 ♕f4+ 48
♔h1 ♕f1+ 49 ♔h2 ♕f4+ 50 ♔h1 ♕f1+ 51
♔h2 ♕f4+ Drawn by threefold repetition.